BRIDGING NATIONAL BORDERS

in NORTH AMERICA

**AMERICAN ENCOUNTERS/GLOBAL INTERACTIONS**

*A series edited by Gilbert M. Joseph and Emily S. Rosenberg*

This series aims to stimulate critical perspectives and fresh inter-pretive frameworks for scholarship on the history of the impos-ing global presence of the United States. Its primary concerns include the deployment and contestation of power, the construc-tion and deconstruction of cultural and political borders, the fluid meanings of intercultural encounters, and the complex interplay between the global and the local. *American Encounters* seeks to strengthen dialogue and collaboration between historians of U.S. international relations and area studies specialists.

The series encourages scholarship based on multiarchival his-torical research. At the same time, it supports a recognition of the representational character of all stories about the past and pro-motes critical inquiry into issues of subjectivity and narrative. In the process, *American Encounters* strives to understand the con-text in which meanings related to nations, cultures, and political economy are continually produced, challenged, and reshaped.

# BRIDGING NATIONAL BORDERS in NORTH AMERICA

*Transnational and Comparative Histories*

Benjamin H. Johnson and
Andrew R. Graybill, eds.

Duke University Press
Durham and London
2010

*Published in cooperation with the*
*William P. Clements Center*
*for Southwest Studies,*
*Southern Methodist University*

© 2010 Duke University Press

All rights reserved

Printed in the United States of America on
acid-free paper ∞

Designed by Heather Hensley

Typeset in Scala by Keystone Typesetting, Inc.

Library of Congress Cataloging-in-Publication
Data appear on the last printed page of this book.

*To David J. Weber*

*Mentor, friend, and
intrepid border crosser*

# CONTENTS

..........................................

## ACKNOWLEDGMENTS

.........................................

This volume began as a conversation at Southern Methodist University in the spring of 2005. Since that time, we have accrued extensive personal and professional debts, which we would like to acknowledge.

At SMU's Clements Center for Southwest Studies, we thank associate director Sherry Smith, as well as Andrea Boardman and Ruth Ann Elmore, who helped at every step of the way, and never more indispensably than at the "Bridging National Borders" symposium held at SMU in March 2007. Thanks also to the graduate students and university staff who assisted in making that event run so smoothly; and to Johnny Faragher, whose comments in Dallas pushed us to refine (and in some cases to reject) our assumptions and arguments. A generous Canadian Studies Conference Grant from the Canadian Embassy in Washington, D.C., helped offset our meeting expenses.

"Bridging National Borders" marked the first time that the Clements Center had partnered with another institution in hosting its annual symposium, and we could not have been more fortunate than to work with the Department of History at Simon Fraser University in Burnaby, British Columbia. Department chair John Craig was a most gracious host, and Nicholas Guyatt (now at the University of York in England) kept the conference moving (and the audience chuckling) in his role as emcee. Leo Shin, of the University of British Columbia, and SFU's Alec Dawson provided excellent commentary on the papers. Jay Taylor deserves special acknowledgment for his fundraising brilliance, enthusiasm, and unflagging support, without which our September 2006 gathering in Vancouver would not have been possible.

Several scholars in various corners of North America improved the project with their careful readings of the manuscript and suggestions for revision and extension. Thanks to Stephen Aron, Edward Countryman, Sterling Evans, Tom Isern, John Mears, and Sam Truett.

At Duke University Press, we are grateful for the expert assistance of editor Valerie Milholland, who also attended the Vancouver symposium, as well as Miriam Angress and Neal McTighe. Thanks also to Ezra Zeitler for the beautiful maps, and to the two anonymous reviewers for their suggestions and encouragement.

On a more personal note, we thank our excellent contributors for their hard work and good spirits through multiple revisions and seemingly inflexible deadlines. We've both learned so much from the authors, and hope that our work does them justice. And we are grateful to our families for their love and goodwill. Finally, we would like to dedicate this volume to David J. Weber, director of the Clements Center, whose generosity, vision, and perseverance are a source of inspiration to us and to so many others.

# BORDERS AND
# THEIR HISTORIANS
# IN NORTH AMERICA

..........................................

Benjamin H. Johnson
and Andrew R. Graybill

In March 2005 George W. Bush welcomed Mexican president Vicente Fox and Canadian prime minister Paul Martin to his ranch in Crawford, Texas. Their meeting was unusual, if only because the last official U.S. gathering of the three continental heads of state had taken place more than twelve years earlier, for the initialing of the North American Free Trade Agreement. In contrast to the comity of that 1992 visit, this summit revealed significant fissures dividing the nations, including the simmering dispute between Ottawa and Washington over the trade in softwood lumber, and growing vigilantism directed at illegal Mexican immigrants in the American Southwest. But on one thing Bush, Fox, and Martin could readily agree: namely, that the fates of all three countries are knitted together. As Martin put it: "Our safe borders secure our people not only against terrorism, but they make possible a speedy flow of goods, services and people and information among our three nations."[1]

By comparison, historians of North America have been far more hesitant to explore the interconnectedness of Canada, the United States, and Mexico. Doubters need only consult the map section of most books on any one of the three countries; almost invariably, the drawings end abruptly at either the 49th parallel or the Rio Grande, as if weather patterns, topography, or even human beings naturally observe such boundaries. There are several reasons that may explain this persistent habit, but the most significant is the simple fact that the nation-state has come to serve as the basic unit of analysis in the modern practice of historical scholarship. As such, many historians tend to color entirely "within the lines," telling stories, often very good ones, that stop arbitrarily at the boundaries—between North Dakota and Saskatchewan, for example, or between Arizona and Sonora—and that ignore the land and the people just on the other side, as well as the line in between. They also often succumb to the temptation to superimpose these lines on earlier historical periods, when they did not yet exist, thereby assuming the inevitability of the modern map.[2]

Maps of the modern world, in which sharp borders delineate discrete nations marked with different hues, are so deceptively straightforward that it is easy not to interrogate them.[3] National borders represent the territorial embodiment of a bundle of ideas that modern states have propagated and enforced. They tell us that all of humanity is divided up among discrete nation-states; that these nations have sovereign power over particular territory to the exclusion of other nations; and that, collectively, nations exercise this sovereignty over all the earth, save the uninhabitable continent of Antarctica.[4] The existence of national borders implies that those living within the territory demarcated by them are subject to the rule of that nation and owe it their allegiance.[5] The mere fact of living within a nation's borders implies that one is the product of that nation's past, and that one's own fate is inextricably linked to that of one's fellow countrymen above all others. Moreover, should an individual cross a border to live in another country's territory, he or she then becomes subject to the laws of that nation, assuming, in essence, that nation's history.[6]

Indeed, precisely because the nation-state has become the dominant form of political organization in the modern world, we often look at modern maps and the borders that divide nations without questioning or even recognizing these assumptions. By the mid-twentieth century, nation-states had divided up most of the earth's territory, population, and economic life among them, having supplanted, incorporated, or conquered all non-national societies. But rather than unquestioningly accepting the existence of such national borders, we might instead treat them as interesting intellectual problems, and ask some historical questions about them: How did they come to be, and how and why did they take on their current configurations? With what other ways of organizing people and space did they come into conflict, and how were these struggles resolved? What kinds of goods and which sorts of people did national governments want to cross these borders easily, and which ones not at all? And how many of these items and individuals have actually crossed? Did borders mean the same things to local residents of border areas as they did to national policymakers? How have borders and the issues that they raise been represented in film and literature, and how have these depictions changed expectations about border policies and border crossings? And how have the answers to these sorts of questions changed over time, and why?

By posing these sorts of queries, as this volume does in the context of North America, we seek to uncover the meaning and significance of our national borders, rather than taking them for granted. Like other kinds of transnational and comparative history, our approach offers one productive way of telling stories that transcend both the geographic and conceptual limits imposed by national boundaries, a task to which the historical profession is now turning with great vigor. Nations still matter in these stories—indeed, their governments are often the most powerful actors, and they created the very borders under examination. But as Vicente Fox, George Bush, and Paul Martin all recognized, each nation acts in relation to other nations and to political and economic realities that they cannot always control.

The ten original essays in this volume mark the first attempt to integrate the histories of both of the international borders in North America, while demonstrating the intellectual payoffs of such a project. On the most fundamental level, this collection links two areas of parallel but—at least to this point—separate academic inquiry, thus beginning a conversation between scholars of the continent's northern and southern borderlands that seems long overdue. At the very least, such a dialogue will help inform the work of those individuals who specialize in the history of one border region by allowing them to draw on the methodology and findings of studies centered on its northern or southern counterpart. But perhaps more importantly, we hope that *Bridging National Borders in North America* will encourage scholars to investigate larger questions, about statebuilding, national expansion, territoriality, and migration (among others), in a continental context. Such an approach, we think, will allow historians and other scholars to construct a more comprehensive North American history, while also recasting familiar but previously incomplete inquiries.

### A Brief History of the History of North America's Borders

Historians of North America have been posing questions about borders for some time. Recent works on the Canada-U.S. and Mexico-U.S. borders ask similar questions, often feature parallel historical actors, and push accounts of national development to acknowledge wider historical circumstances. Yet scholars of both border regions generally work in personal and intellectual isolation from one another. Indeed, until quite recently, the term "borderlands" served as a sort of shorthand to refer to the present-day U.S. Southwest and the Mexican North, with little thought to the border dividing Canada from the United States. Innovative methodologies and approaches applied to the study of one border have not necessarily been brought to bear on investigations of the other, despite the fact that a range of groups—among them, U.S. government officials, Asian migrants, and smugglers—have adapted the knowledge gained in one borderlands to the challenges posed by its northern or southern counterpart.

A generation ago, "borderlands" referred to the northernmost reaches of the Spanish colonial project, an area that encompasses the present-day U.S. states of California, Arizona, New Mexico, Texas, Louisiana, Alabama, Georgia, and Florida. This borderlands history was originally articulated by Herbert Eugene Bolton in the early 1920s, and continued by his protégé John Francis Bannon as a kind of answer, or at least a Hispanic counterpart, to Frederick Jackson Turner's famous and influential thesis that the frontier experience had shaped a distinctive American character as well as democratic institutions and habits of mind. This field, the original "borderlands" history, challenged U.S. historians to think of national historical origins and influences as having developed beyond the familiar world of the British Empire and the eastern seaboard of North America. Although practitioners of Boltonian borderlands history sought to make a mark on the wider study of U.S. history, for the most part they were unsuccessful. U.S. historians continued to focus on the British roots of American culture and institutions, and historians of Latin America found borderlands scholarship similarly marginal to their enterprise. At the same time, historians of the American Southwest were as uninterested in crossing the 1848 temporal boundary as were Boltonian scholars in pursuing their studies after the Mexican-American War remade their region.[7]

By the 1970s, the Boltonian school of borderlands studies had expanded to include scholars with different agendas and approaches to the study of this region. Students of Mexican American history focused their attention on the marginalization and racialization of people of Mexican descent in the U.S. Southwest after 1848, even as they found the earlier Spanish and Mexican periods relevant to their inquiries. Some scholars in this first wave of Mexican American history had been trained in part as Latin Americanists. They appreciated the continuity between Mexican history and Mexican American history, and recognized the challenge that writing such accounts posed to U.S. historians ignorant of the Latin American past. One of them, Oscar J. Martínez, expanded upon his early work on the twin border towns of El Paso and Juárez to encompass a broader examination of the border itself.[8] At about the same time, scholars of Native American history found much of interest in the areas colonized by New Spain, particularly because the region's Native peoples had endured for nearly four centuries under different forms of colonialism—Spanish, Mexican, and then American—yet had managed to retain their distinct group identity, along with substantial portions of their pre-Columbian territories.[9] In the 1980s, the U.S. Southwest also drew the attention of the "New Western" historians, who found the area—including its colonial past—to be fertile ground for exploration of the themes of conquest, environmental destruction, and myth-making that were so central to their work. Both Patricia Nelson Limerick and Richard White, for example, examined the deep ties between Mexico and the U.S. West in their surveys of the region's history. Limerick even argued for adopting the idea of the *frontera*, a term derived from studies of the U.S.-Mexico borderlands, which she said offered "a realistic view of this nation's position in the hemisphere and in the world," one that the concept of the "frontier" did not, because of the latter term's fostering of an "illusion of vacancy" and "triumphal conclusions." But, for both authors, "border" meant Mexico, and as with the New Western history in general, they almost entirely neglected Canada, its West, and the border that links Canada to the United States.[10]

At about the same time, the Mexican North began attracting greater attention from historians of Mexico. Prompted in part by a broader revitalization of that nation's regional history, these scholars analyzed the relationship of the northern Mexican states with the centers of national power, emphasizing in particular the states' roles in the Mexican Revolution (1911–20). Their work generally treated the North as a set of regions (Baja California and Sonora, Chihuahua, and the Monterrey-dominated

Northeast) rather than a unified border zone. Nevertheless, in their accounts, the border with the United States was seen as a major force in the politics, society, and economy of each of these regions.[11]

Broader developments within the academy gave many of these scholars good reason to call themselves, among other things, "borderlands" historians. As it did for many disciplines, the rise of postmodernism—which seeks to reveal the contradictions, incompleteness, and contingencies of social categories and processes—changed the study of the Spanish or Mexican borderlands. Whereas scholars once viewed "Spaniards," "Indians," and "mestizos" as self-evident and distinct categories, they now began to realize that the boundaries between these groups were in fact quite porous, and changed with circumstance and over time. In nineteenth-century New Mexico, for example, a person who began life as a subject of the Spanish crown might subsequently have claimed membership in a Pueblo Indian community, or assumed an active political role as a Mexican citizen, or become a U.S. citizen—all within the course of three or four decades. The ideas of "borders" and "border-crossing" seemed well suited to grapple with such complexity. The simultaneous connections and distinctions that the term "border" implies—particularly in the case of such seemingly different nations as Mexico and the United States—spoke directly to the core concerns of postmodernism. Indeed, "borders" and "border-crossing" have become leading metaphors for the postmodern condition, and works that study the U.S.-Mexican borderlands are widely cited by scholars of the history and literature of other regions.[12]

The growing interest in transnational history in the 1990s and early 2000s also drew historians to the study of borders in general, including the U.S.-Mexican borderlands. History as a discipline is still structured to a considerable degree around nation-states, whose territoriality and understandings of their antecedents provide historians with the demarcations of their subjects and time frames. Most historians, especially of the modern world, are trained and hired as historians of a particular nation. Recently, however, a rising chorus of historians has questioned the tight focus on nationalist historiographies, arguing that such an orientation minimizes transnational and non-national developments and obscures the extent to which nations themselves are shaped by larger dynamics— such as migration, commerce, technology, and ideas—that may be underestimated or ignored by versions of the past yoked too firmly to nation-based inquiry. These historians continue to find nations and national histories important subjects and frames for their work, but they also write stories centered on regions, like the Atlantic and Pacific worlds, or on processes, like migration or global economic networks, or on intellectual and cultural worlds that cut across national boundaries. Accounts of border areas can similarly illuminate the contingency of national histories and provide opportunities for creating stories about the past that transcend both the geographic and conceptual limits imposed by national boundaries.[13]

Contemporary developments along the U.S.-Mexico border have also heightened scholarly interest in the region's history. Population on both sides of the border has been growing rapidly for two generations, an enormous number of manufacturing and assembly plants have been built on the Mexican side, and Mexican immigration to the United States is transforming the social fabric of both nations even as it generates ongoing controversy. By 2000, the border had become the focus of two Mexican scholarly journals, *Frontera Norte* and *Estudios Fronterizos*, published respectively by the border universities El Colegio de la Frontera Norte and La Universidad Autónoma de Baja California. Although the work of historians from Mexico, the United States, and other countries appears in both journals, the preponderance of the articles they publish are contributed by anthropologists, sociologists, demographers, economists, and policy analysts, with a heavy emphasis on contemporary issues and very recent developments. North of the line, it is estimated that by 2050 one-quarter of the U.S. population may claim Latino—mostly Mexican—ancestry, so the boundary between the United States and Mexico has never seemed so relevant to the U.S. academy as in recent years. And clearly the connections that this border has fostered are as important as the divisions it has ostensibly maintained.[14]

By the first decade of the twenty-first century, then, for an academic to label his or her work as "borderlands" scholarship could mean any number of things: a focus on the northern reaches of New Spain, or on the regional histories of the northern states of Mexico, or on those of the U.S. Southwest; or a concentration on Mexican American history, or Mexican migration, or the region's ethnohistory; or even an interest in cultural hybridity and identity-formation in the area now bisected by the U.S.-Mexico border. Increasingly, however, historians based in the United States who label themselves as "borderlands historians" have emphasized the key role that the border itself has played in shaping this borderlands: its creation as the result of long processes of colonialism and encounter; the way it has reflected the national projects of Mexico and the United States; and its shifting meanings and implications for the diverse groups who cross the border and call the region their home.

Recent studies have demonstrated the productivity of examining border-making and its impacts on both sides of the line. For example, we now know that the international boundary created in 1848, in the wake of the Mexican-American War, altered class relations in much of the Mexican North. Regional economic elites and the central state no longer needed the services of the subaltern class to act as a military check to Apache and Comanche raids, and so felt free to trample on this group's rights to land. At the same time, in the Mexican Northeast, the ease of crossing into Texas for work led to the collapse of debt peonage and to generally milder treatment of peasants by hacienda owners, even as large numbers of slaves in Texas fled south across the Rio Grande to Mexico, where slavery had been abolished decades earlier. The policing of the new border probably had the greatest effect on Native peoples, with the Mexican and U.S. governments cooperating in efforts to end the migration and raiding that had been so essential to continued Native independence. The long-standing efforts of ethnic Mexican borderlands communities to maintain their autonomy vis-à-vis the power of the central government persisted throughout the nineteenth century, often through the continuation of cross-border political and economic ties, and sometimes through armed uprisings. The border also became a site where national notions of race and citizenship were forged; by the twentieth century, U.S. immigration restrictions had led to the active policing of the border against migrants—though not Mexican migrants, as most would assume today, but rather Asians, who had been banned almost entirely from entry into the United States by the 1882 Chinese Exclusion Act and the 1907 Gentleman's Agreement with Japan.[15] By the 1910s, this border also exhibited a certain vitality in the realm of cultural production, as its dividing river, fences, and markers now became symbols of national and racial difference, disseminated across Mexico and the United States in travel accounts, postcards, novels, and films. Often meant to evoke distance, division, and dread, invocations of the border could also provoke yearning, fascination, and desire. Long before the age of NAFTA, then, the U.S.-Mexico border loomed large in the development of both nations.[16]

Much of this new borderlands history is explicitly and proudly transnational, and many of its proponents tout it as part of the effort to transcend what they see as the limiting focus of historians—particularly U.S. scholars—on the nation-state. As Samuel Truett and Elliott Young have argued in an influential historiographic review and critique of the new incarnation of borderlands history, "Studying the U.S.-Mexico borderlands allows one to engage . . . hidden stories [those that escape nation-centered accounts] while reflecting critically on the process of territorialization that coincided with the rise of nation-states." For many borderlands scholars, telling these sorts of stories is also a way to contribute to political projects and movements that are critical of nationalism—particularly U.S. nationalism—in an era of remarkable American power.[17]

Nevertheless, scholars of this new borderlands school remain more rooted in the universities, territory, archives, and historiography of the United States than their transnational rhetoric might lead one to believe. Historians of Mexico, particularly Mexican nationals, have not shown nearly the enthusiasm of U.S. historians (almost all of them American nationals) for embracing a rubric of "borderlands" to frame their work.[18] Despite the strong orientation of Mexican historians to the study of that nation's center of population and political power, there is also a long tradition of writing about the Mexican North. Some of this scholarship consciously uses the border to capture historical subjects and events that do not fit fully within either Mexican or U.S. history. As Bernardo García Martínez observes in his analysis of the different ways of organizing space in the U.S.-Mexico borderlands, writing about this region "is something more complicated than a matter of 'Mexicans and North Americans' . . . for it involves peoples that through various circumstances escape or have escaped from those categories."[19] But most scholars of Mexico's North do not write in this vein; instead, they characterize the border as a zone of conflict between two discrete and highly unequal nation-states, paying scant attention to the cultural hybridity that exists there and overlooking the critique of nation-centered history that characterizes so much of the U.S. literature. When asked by a U.S. historian about Mexican sovereignty, the Mexican historian and diplomat Carlos Rico Ferrat articulated the reasons behind the resistance of some Mexican scholars to the postnational turn. "We have been historically more adamant in asserting our legalistic perspective on legal sovereignty," he explained, "not only because our law is a major defense against a much stronger nation, but also because that nation is on our border."[20]

Compared with the long history and great diversity of scholarship on the U.S.-Mexico borderlands, there has been far less academic attention directed at the Canada-U.S. borderlands. Several factors may help to explain this discrepancy. For one thing, Canada and the United States, as advanced liberal capitalist democracies populated mostly by descendents of European settlers, appear to have more in common with one another than they do with Mexico. Accordingly, for most Americans and some Canadians—at least until the emergence of terrorism as a perceived threat to American national security—the international boundary separating the two countries has seemed largely inconsequential, as suggested by the familiar refrain that Canada and the United States share the longest undefended border in the world. Contrast that with the writer Gloria Anzaldúa's description of the U.S-Mexico border as *"una herida abierta* [an open wound], where the Third World grates against the first and bleeds."[21] Whereas armies and insurrectionists have splashed their way across the Rio Grande on numerous occasions, since the War of 1812 the northern border has experienced much less international conflict. Even the most contentious issue in the history of the northern borderlands—the dispute over the Oregon boundary—was resolved through diplomatic channels (at almost the same moment that the United States invaded Mexico to conquer what later became the American Southwest). Moreover, the border-related issues that usually divide Washington and Ottawa tend to be of a milder nature (concerns about American cattle possibly transmitting mad cow disease to Canadian livestock, for example) than those (like the intractable matter of illegal immigration) that estrange federal officials in the United States from their Mexican counterparts.[22]

Although there is no body of work on the northern borderlands equivalent to that of the Boltonian school, some Canadian historians did probe the significance of their boundary with the United States. Writing in the late 1920s and 1930s, at roughly the apex of Bolton's career, Walter Sage showed that immigrants in the North American West had repeatedly crossed the border in search of available land and economic opportunities, and that Canada's western provinces were more socially and economically integrated with adjacent U.S. states than they were with Canada's economic and population centers farther to the east.[23] John Bartlet Brebner, a Toronto-born scholar who spent his career at Columbia University in New York, took a similarly continental approach.[24] George F. G. Stanley, on the other hand, placed more emphasis on the importance of the border itself; according to Elizabeth Jameson and Jeremy Mouat, for Stanley, "the border separated American violence, lawlessness, and greed from Canadian civility, order, and managed development." Like the much more influential Boltonians, then, these early Canadian scholars formulated historical narratives that placed their nation within a larger, continental framework.[25]

It was not until the period after the Second World War that other writers picked up these lines of inquiry. When they did, their interpretations tended to emphasize the 49th parallel as a clear marker of national difference, confirming the findings of Stanley rather than Sage. In 1955, Wallace Stegner published *Wolf Willow*, a memoir of the six years he spent as a boy on his family's homestead not far from Eastend, Saskatchewan, in the early twentieth century. In his youth, the Iowa-born Stegner had been acutely aware of the existence of the international border with the United States, which passed just south of his parents' farm and whose bifurcating presence saturates the book. Indeed, in one passage from *Wolf Willow*, Stegner noted that the 49th parallel "ran directly through my childhood, dividing me in two."[26] This schism shaped his life in subtle ways: the textbooks he read in school were published in Toronto rather than New York; the signature national holiday he celebrated was Canada Day and not the Fourth of July; his family received mail-order catalogs from Eaton's as opposed to Sears. But even in his childhood, Stegner recognized that the line did more than merely differentiate social norms. As he writes, "the 49th parallel was an agreement, a rule, a limitation, a fiction perhaps but a legal one, acknowledged by both sides."[27]

Surprisingly—considering the relative inattention to the northern borderlands at the time—another book about the region appeared that very same year. Unlike Stegner's volume, however, *Whoop-Up Country* was the work of an academic historian, Paul F. Sharp, and it was concerned less with the fact of the border than with how the boundary had come to be in the first place.[28] Sharp discovered that Canadian and U.S. officials had trained their gaze on the region at roughly the same moment in the late nineteenth century, and for similar reasons: to abolish the area's illicit whiskey trade and to assert control over its indigenous peoples, all in preparation for the arrival of white settlers. Sharp argued that those efforts were so successful that by 1885 the once unified Alberta-Montana borderlands had been divided and then absorbed by their respective nations. It was this reordered landscape that the young Wallace Stegner recalled from his youth. Though Sharp had approached the 49th parallel through archival collections in the United States and Canada, rather than lived experience, like Stegner he saw the border as a fault line, a marker of fundamental national difference.

*Whoop-Up Country* offered a possible model for the trans-border study of the region, and initially seemed to make a wide impact. In the United States, it was broadly and favorably reviewed: the *New Yorker* praised its treatment of "the evolution of two parallel but dissimilar societies," and the *New York Times* and other dailies noted its use of regional history to tell stories of national and global interest. Sharp went on to serve as an officer of the Mississippi Valley Historical Association (which later became the Organization of American Historians), and then as president of several colleges and universities, chief among them the University of Oklahoma. Canadian historians, by contrast, were much less taken with Sharp's account of the border. *Whoop-Up Country* and Sharp's earlier publications remained important works for scholars of the North American West, but Canadian historians roundly criticized him for emphasizing the regional unity of the northern Great Plains. The dominant school of Canadian history at the time, represented by the political economist Harold Innis, stressed the economic links between the eastern core of the nation and its western hinterlands, leaving little room for north-south connections and making it easy for Sharp's more politically oriented account to be treated as a regional, and not national, story. Moreover, the emphasis by Innis and other leading Canadian scholars on Canadian distinctiveness blunted the effect of Sharp's work in Canada. As Thomas Isern and Bruce Shepard have argued, "The reason for Sharp's minimal impact in Canada has been the nationalist orientation of the Canadian historical tradition." Thus, much as in the Mexican academy, Canadian historians resisted integrating their history with that of the United States, and so, again as in Mexico, no cohesive school of border studies emerged in Canada.[29]

In the mid-1970s, however, a fresh generation of historians—mostly from Canada—shifted their attention to the northern borderlands, primarily to the region lying between the Great Lakes and the Pacific Ocean. While these newcomers continued to investigate the area through the prism of real and perceived national divergence, just as Sharp (and Stegner) had, they also infused their work with a heightened sense of Canadian patriotism. Such sentiment was on the rise in Canadian academic circles at that time, fueled by discontent with the ongoing U.S. war in Vietnam, but also by a renewed resistance to the use of American models as explanations for historical development in Canada. Of particular concern to Canadian scholars was Turner's frontier thesis. Though Turner made no particular claims for the relevance of his thesis to Canada, historians north of the border were keen to prove its inapplicability to their nation's past, and to thus assert the significance of the 49th parallel.[30]

Some of these pieces tackled the Turnerian question head on, arguing that while the United States may have acquired and preserved its unique characteristics through constant westward migration, Canada had looked to the east—to the Old World—for its identity, even as the Dominion expanded onto the western prairies and across the Rocky Mountains. How else to explain the rigid Victorian class structure of Alberta's range cattle industry, especially by comparison to its lawless but (supposedly) leveling American counterpart? And what about that most Canadian of all institutions, the North-West Mounted Police, which took its inspiration from the Royal Irish Constabulary and thus developed in precisely the imperial context that Ottawa planned to replicate in its own hinterlands? Such studies identified a distinct Canadian metropolitanism that stood in contrast, even opposition, to Turner's (American) frontier. And the collective message of these contributions was clear enough: the border marked the northward limit of one country, and the beginning of another, presumably better one.[31]

By the late 1970s, however, some scholars had resumed questioning the definitiveness of the 49th parallel as a continental fault line between the United States and Canada, as Walter Sage had done a half century before. Like Sage, most of these scholars adopted a regional rather than a national perspective on the northern borderlands, one that emphasized the social and environmental connections that created trans-border and geographically discrete areas such as the Pacific Northwest or the Great Plains.[32] Their attention was drawn to the western portion of the border, particularly the Plains, perhaps because this region had been the focus of intense Canadian and U.S. efforts to finalize their borders, whereas east of the Great Lakes the boundary had long been taken for granted. In their research, these authors discovered that various groups—from homesteaders to industrial workers—had more in common with their counterparts directly across the international boundary than they did with their respective Canadian and American countrymen in the distant East. Other historians identified ideas and practices, such as anti-black racism or settlement boosterism, that crossed the line and thus came to characterize life and experience on both sides of the 49th parallel. Taken together, such works called for less emphasis on U.S.-Canadian divergence, and more attention to overlap and interplay. The Canada-U.S. border, in these accounts, was important precisely for its failure to create or mark fundamental national difference.[33] A regionalist approach also characterized a cluster of works on the New England–Eastern Canada borderlands that came out of an institute at the University of Maine in the late 1980s and early 1990s.[34]

Until quite recently, scholarly examination of the northern borderlands gravitated toward one of these two poles. Most investigations focused doggedly on the notion of the 49th parallel as a deep fissure dividing U.S. and Canadian society, politics, and culture; a smaller collection of works, meanwhile, identified pockets of regional unity that supersede the boundary line. Both of these approaches have been enormously important in fostering our understanding of the area and its complex development. But the early years of the twenty-first century have seen a surge of renewed interest in the northern borderlands, and historians have begun to examine the significance of the 49th parallel from new perspectives.[35] Like most of the earlier work, this scholarship has a strongly western cast, for reasons that are difficult to parse but may have something to do with the centrality of conquest and colonialism to the history of the western border.[36] Or perhaps such explanations are more deeply rooted—the phrase "the 49th parallel," for example, often serves as a shorthand for the entire border, despite the fact that from Lake of the Woods eastward the line does not run along the geographic parallel.[37] These scholars are prompted, at least in part, by the same developments that have piqued interest in the U.S.-Mexico border—the heightened visibility of international commerce, migration, and the critique of nation-centered history.[38] Their studies move beyond the stark dichotomy of similarity and difference and have pushed the field in promising new directions. Most of the work falls into four broad groups.

The first category includes works that interrogate the implications of border-making for indigenous peoples, who had been largely overlooked by earlier writers. As North America's empires and nations attempted to demarcate and absorb their peripheries, Indian groups witnessed the swift and arbitrary division of their homelands. Such circumstances imposed severe limitations, to be sure, including the rupturing of kinship networks, the reduction of hunting grounds, and a more general loss of geographic mobility. But at times, the drawing of borders opened up new and unforeseen possibilities as well. For instance, Aboriginal inhabitants all along the boundary between the United States and Canada, from the colonial period to the late nineteenth century, used the border to their advantage by pitting rival trading companies against one another in the firms' quest for Indian assistance in the fur trade, or by finding sanctuary from their enemies (white and Native) across the line.[39]

The second group focuses on the cross-border migrations of non-Aboriginal peoples. In general, these volumes emphasize the exceptional permeability of the U.S.-Canadian boundary, noting how—for much of the twentieth century—white movement across the line was effectively unimpeded, especially (though not exclusively) in the West. These scholars have noted the varied reasons that led people to move north or south of the border, but most agree that economic opportunity was of paramount importance. Unlike most of the scholarship focusing on the northern borderlands, migration studies encompass the full length of the border, reflecting the heavy impact of cross-border migration in eastern as well as western portions of the borderlands. And yet, despite their numbers, these newcomers seem to have garnered much less notice from residents and federal officials than did arrivals from Europe and Asia.[40] This trend, no doubt, stemmed from the real and perceived similarities between Anglo-Americans and their Canadian counterparts, a notion recently picked up by a number of historians who have emphasized the social continuities found in trans-border regions such as the Great Lakes and Prairie-Plains.[41]

A third group of works examines the relationship of the border to the natural world that it bisects, a division no less capricious to ecosystems than to human populations. After all, with few topographical features west of the Great Lakes to define it, the boundary between the United States and Canada was marked simply by piles of stones and mounds of dirt for much of the nineteenth century.[42] Given its practical invisibility, it stands to reason that the 49th parallel did little to shape how borderland residents understood their relationship to the land, and indeed some scholars have found that the peculiar and distinct conditions of the region engendered a shared sense of identity rooted firmly in place, one that largely transcended state, provincial, and even national boundaries. Other historians have discovered that the border, in fact, mattered very much, especially for fish and wildlife populations that traversed the line in the course of their migrations. Just as with people, there were animals that states wanted to easily cross borders and those whose mobility it tried to restrict. It took concerted action on the part of government officials in Ottawa and Washington (and beyond) to regulate predation and enforce conservation measures.[43]

A fourth and final collection of studies analyzes the impact of the border on the formation of national identity. In so doing, they revisit some of the observations first made by Paul Sharp in *Whoop-Up Country*, particularly the notion that federal officials in the United States and especially in Canada strove to enforce their shared international boundary beginning in the late nineteenth century. These newer works probe the influence of Washington and Ottawa in amplifying the reality as well as the symbolism of the border, while assessing the long-term success of these efforts. For example, some historians have suggested that the northern borderlands were the object in a continental endgame of national expansion, where federal officials in both capitals projected their newfound or resurgent economic and political power into a region once thought too remote for incorporation. And yet, according to other scholars, these grandiose attempts to divide, conquer, and integrate the hinterlands into their respective nations were, in the main, incomplete, as the 49th parallel seems no more significant in creating or marking national difference today than it did more than a century ago, when it was first enforced.[44]

## Bridging National Borders

As the previous historiographic discussion suggests, there has been a convergence in the kinds of questions asked by historians of North America's two borders. Yet scholars of these places still work in isolation from one another, reading different bodies of literature, working at different institutions, and publishing with different presses. Only a handful of works—among them a monograph on Chinese migrants and U.S. border and port enforcement, a dissertation (and related journal article) about the efforts of undocumented immigrants to circumvent the attempts of American authorities to exclude them, and a cultural studies anthology exploring the U.S.-Mexico border that also contains a few essays on the U.S.-Canadian dividing line—have addressed both boundaries together.[45]

This volume joins emerging scholarship on the borders in order to put these two growing fields in direct conversation with one another. Our goal is explicitly prescriptive—we think that much of the future of these two fields lies in working toward an integrated and comparative history of North American border-making, and that even those scholars interested primarily in the history of one borderland can draw on the findings and approaches of studies centered on the other. Because the fields have been so removed from one another and because so few scholars have addressed both borderlands, a comprehensive account of boundary-making is premature at this point. Accordingly, this volume of ten essays, the first collection devoted to joining the scholarship of both borders, does not aspire to cover the full chronological and geographic scope of North American borders. The essays focus on topics from the mid-nineteenth century through the mid-twentieth century, and collectively tilt toward the western portions of the continent. However, they cover enough ground, and engage such critical themes, that collectively they attempt to set agendas for future research by demonstrating the fruitfulness of an integrated approach to North American borders.

Part I, "Peoples In Between," consists of two chapters that examine the multiple ways that mixed-race groups living on the peripheries of national societies dealt with the new borders of the nineteenth century. In "Conflict and Cooperation in the Making of Texas-Mexico Border Society, 1840–1880," Miguel Ángel González-Quiroga argues that while Hispanic residents on both sides of the Rio Grande experienced enormous dislocation as federal authorities in distant capitals attempted to absorb their nation's respective hinterlands, they managed also to sustain transnational commercial and social networks. And they were not the only peoples to reach across the boundary, as other groups—including Anglo merchants and Protestant evangelicals—crossed borders in the hopes of building and preserving markets for labor, commodities, and even souls. Michel Hogue picks up on similar themes in "Between Race and Nation: The Creation of a Métis Borderland on the Northern Plains," noting the challenges facing the Métis (the offspring of European fathers and Aboriginal women) as they navigated the division of the northern borderlands. On the one hand, the policing of the 49th parallel led the Métis to assume very different identities, either as members of Indian bands, as white settler societies, or as distinct Métis communities. But on the other hand, their continued transnational migrations undermined local and, especially, federal attempts to enforce the international boundary, suggesting that such efforts did not fully overwrite the shared mental geography and history of polyglot borderland populations.

In Part II, "Environmental Control and State-Making," our attention turns to the complicated interactions between environmental dynamics and boundary formation in the late nineteenth and early twentieth centuries. In "Epidemics, Indians, and Border-Making in the Nineteenth-Century Pacific Northwest," Jennifer Seltz shows how outbreaks of communicable diseases and local anxieties about the travels of supposedly sick or contagious Native peoples stimulated some of the first concerted attempts in the Pacific Northwest to make the U.S.-Canadian border an effective barrier to human movement. Prompted by the calls of some border residents, national states began to use medical inspections and public-health knowledge to differentiate among bodies and spaces. On the southern boundary in the same period, as Rachel St. John explains in "Divided Ranges: Trans-border Ranches and the Creation of National Space along the Western Mexican–U.S. Border," the international movement of livestock prompted similar concerns and negotiations between central governments and borderlands communities. The practices established for channeling stock through ports of entry and preventing cattle smuggling became the models for later government efforts at halting the movement of narcotics and illegal immigrants. But, as Lissa Wadewitz demonstrates in "The Scales of Salmon: Diplomacy and Conservation in the Western

Canada–U.S. Borderlands," other state regulatory ambitions foundered when faced with specific border conditions. Efforts to conserve declining fish populations in the waters off Washington State and British Columbia required international diplomacy because the U.S.-Canada border cut through essential salmon spawning routes. Local players on both sides of the border continued to wield significant power, often thwarting progress on a long-sought international treaty out of concern for the adverse impact on their economies.

The increasingly restrictive—if often unsuccessful—efforts of national governments to enforce borders and border crossings are the subject of Part III, "Border Enforcement and Contestation." By the 1920s, border crossings throughout North America numbered in the hundreds of thousands each day and the hundreds of millions each year. At the same time, national governments subjected these border-crossers to new levels of scrutiny. In "Crossing the Line: The INS and the Federal Regulation of the Mexican Border," S. Deborah Kang shows how U.S. immigration authorities dealt with the competing desires of border residents for unimpeded boundary crossings for day laborers, tourists, casual visitors, and businessmen on the one hand, and the mandates imposed by such restrictive measures as the Chinese Exclusion Act of 1882 and the 1924 Immigration Act on the other. But even those at whom border enforcement was most directly targeted were able to find chinks in the armor of national states, as Andrea Geiger discusses in "Caught in the Gap: The Transit Privilege and North America's Ambiguous Borders." As Geiger explains, the first illegal immigrants in North America were Asians barred from entering the United States and Canada in the late nineteenth and early twentieth centuries. But by asserting the "transit privilege," a provision under international law that permitted an individual to cross the United States in order to travel to Canada or Mexico, Japanese labor contractors and immigrants were able to circumvent the law and gain entry ostensibly denied to them.

Part IV, "Border Representation and National Identity," concludes the volume by shifting our attention away from the physical places of borders and toward the worlds of culture and symbolism. In "The Welcoming Voice of the Southland: American Tourism across the U.S.-Mexico Border, 1880–1940," Catherine Cocks analyzes the ways in which Mexican border tourism celebrated the Anglo encounter with tropical abundance, archaeological wonders, and cultural divergence, even as Mexican activists and officials engaged in their own nation-building and anti-imperial campaigns aimed at challenging white supremacy as exemplified by the United States. Meanwhile, in "Projecting the In-Between: Cinematic Representations of Borderlands and Borders in North America, 1908–1940" Dominique Brégent-Heald compares the depictions of the two borders in the Hollywood feature films so influential in Canada, the United States, and Mexico during the cinematic Golden Age of the first half of the twentieth century. She argues that while on-screen depictions of the borders denoted striking differences in climate, geography, and culture, they also shared similar themes of contact and collision, of utopia and dystopia. Bethel Saler and Carolyn Podruchny wrap up the book with "Glass Curtains and Storied Landscapes: The Fur Trade, National Boundaries, and Historians," which considers how the writing of history itself has reinforced our notions of national borders in North America. The two authors show that, despite the fact that the fur trade from the seventeenth to the nineteenth centuries created its own broad notions of territoriality, scholars have too often shuttered their own views of stories emerging from the other side of the subsequent national divide. In this way, the solidification of boundaries in the nineteenth century has circumscribed the work of North American historians, creating discrete, state-centered histories rather than a single, integrated history with continental scope.

## Toward a Richer History of North America's Borders

Although the chapters reflect the individual conclusions, perspectives, and findings of their authors, collectively they offer five forms of intervention into ongoing borderlands scholarship.

First, the essays point to the value of comparative accounts of border-making. On the most general level, comparison can help to destabilize normative or exceptionalist explanations, while casting light on similarities as well as structural and contingent differences.[46] Given the isolated state of the two fields, comparison might also inspire the importation of questions salient in one field but not yet applied to the other. For example, the racialization of those crossing from Mexico into the United States by medical inspections has been the subject of sustained scholarly scrutiny, and similar questions might be asked about migrants moving from Canada into the United States, especially French Canadians. Furthermore, a comparative approach to border formation might well help scholars provide more compelling answers to their shared questions about the ways that boundaries have re-made, and failed to re-make, identities congruent with the claim of modern nation-states to territorial exclusivity. The longer history and greater quantity of literature on the southern border has led many to deploy the U.S.-Mexico border as paradigmatic of borders in general, including the northern border of the United States.[47] The greatly unequal balance of power between Mexico and the United States, and the frequency with which U.S. observers have thought of this in racial terms, however, may make this border more distinctive than diagnostic. Have Canadians and Mexicans and their governments used their borders with the United States in parallel ways, or have the great differences between Canada and Mexico sharply differentiated their border-making projects?

A similar set of questions might be asked with respect to Native peoples and how they dealt with those borders whose creation abrogated some groups' territoriality and sovereignty but offered others the chance to play settler-nations off against one another. For example, the modern national myths of both Canada and Mexico feature celebrations of racial hybridity between European settlers and Indians. To what extent did these racial formations offer political and cultural space for Indian peoples not permitted by the United States' more exclusionist and assimilationist understanding of Indians' place within modernity? More broadly, if some Native peoples were able to navigate a bordered world more successfully than others, was that because of the differing nature of the state-building projects that they faced, or because of their own divisions, heterogeneity, resources, and decisions?[48]

These questions point to more encompassing comparative inquiries. In a more general sense, do the histories of these two borders teach us similar or different lessons about the ability of modern states to enforce their claims to territorial exclusivity on the ground, and about the impact of those claims on the lives of those living on borders?

Second, some questions about borders cry out not just for comparison, but for integrated accounts. Many historical actors in fact engaged both borders, and recapturing their experiences requires historians to follow in their footsteps. Consider the case of Asian migrants to North America. Canada, the United States, and Mexico all share the Pacific Rim with Japan and China, and starting in the mid-nineteenth century Asians migrated to all three nations, forming interconnected diasporic communities, and encountering nativist movements that articulated notions of nationhood in opposition to them and the networks that had brought them to North America. Asian migrants crossed both borders in pursuit of economic, family, and political goals, and, as Andrea Geiger's essay in this volume shows, used the differences in the three nations' immigration laws to secure rights of transit otherwise unavailable to them.[49] Yet we miss these stories if we focus on just one nation, or even two nations and their shared border. Other important stories similarly encompass both borders: U.S. bureaucrats and law enforcement officials moved from one American border to the other, presumably taking their understandings and expectations with them as they implemented immigration, customs, and medical procedures on two sometimes very different frontiers. The cultural production surrounding borders has also often encompassed them both, as suggested by the mid-century Hollywood films described in Dominique Brégent-Heald's essay in this volume, and by the American dime novel series from the early twentieth century titled *The Border Boys*, as well as by the similarities in the lure of border town cantinas and speakeasies during Prohibition.[50]

Third, if borderlands scholars might profit from broadening their frame to continental dimensions, these essays suggest that they would also benefit from narrowing their scope to acknowledge the continued particularities of place. Transnational history can be local history, but some historians writing after the transnational turn emphasize large-scale perspectives that can obscure local and regional distinctiveness. It would be unfortunate if the framing of border histories as transnational studies were to lead scholars to ignore the extent to which border places and border lives have been different from one another, reflective of local and regional histories, geographies, economies, and politics as much as of national and international dynamics. In the essays presented here by Miguel Ángel González-Quiroga and Rachel St. John, for example, both authors write about the same boundary, yet the continuation of long-standing cross-river economic and social ties in the South Texas–Tamaulipas region throughout the nineteenth century made for a very different border region than did the introduction of large-scale, market-oriented cattle ranching in the newly settled border region comprising Baja California, California, Arizona, and Sonora in the same period. Indeed, aspects of the western ranching borderlands of the U.S.-Mexico border may have resembled the Alberta-Montana ranchlands more than other places along the southern boundary. (This is an example of how a consideration of environmental factors can prompt more sophisticated allowance for the difference that place makes, as Part II of this volume demonstrates.) Simply because two places or regions are on the same border, and are marked deeply by that border, does not mean that scholars should ignore the profound differences between them that persist. In this regard, the greater tendency of Mexican scholars to treat border places as parts of specific regions (rather than theorizing and writing about Mexico's northern border as a unitary place) could serve as a reminder to all borderlands scholars of the need to root their studies in place. Borders may be international spaces, but border communities are also local spaces whose distinctiveness should be accounted for rather than obscured by the transnational turn in border studies.[51]

Fourth, the approaches to borders taken in this volume open the way for more-nuanced treatments of the relationship between borderlands communities and national states. Contemporary borderlands scholarship portrays the modern state in almost entirely negative terms, as an outside, coercive force whose arrival ends the autonomy and freedom enjoyed by Natives and other peoples who once lived beyond its control. Indeed, the most influential treatment of the emergence of national borders, Jeremy Adelman and Stephen Aron's "From Borderlands to Borders," depicts the rise of national borders as the end of the more-fluid territoriality and identities allowed for by the earlier borderlands between empires and Native peoples. This is with good reason: North America's borders were far removed from the centers of national power and population at the moment of their creation, and the central state was in fact a distant entity controlled by and serving the interests of people far from the border. The United States in particular projected its power more through violence— forcibly opening its new peripheries to national markets and imposing its more-fixed and hierarchical racial categories—than by capturing the imaginations and loyalties of borderlanders themselves.[52]

But this isn't the full picture of the state. Borderlanders, this volume shows, also used national states and their boundaries for their own purposes and sought to forge nations that reflected their own identities. Various groups in all three countries demanded border policies that served their own interests—to provide or control labor, to protect themselves from human and livestock epidemics, and to defend themselves from enemies, to name a few. Others pressed central states to let goods and people pass unhindered, as when Mexican entrepreneurs lobbied for a duty-free zone on their half of the border with the United States, or when Mexican Americans in South Texas agitated for the rights of their families to move between neighboring border cities without encumbrance, or when Métis refugees who had fled Canada during the 1885 Northwest Rebellion sought to return from their cross-border exile in the United States. These examples reflect the continued importance of non-national imagined communities and territoriality, as well as the ways that these projects could be pursued through the methods of state power as much as in contradiction to them. The state ended up as much an invited guest in the borderlands as it did an armed stranger. The lure of de-centering national histories, an impulse that has given border studies so much of their prominence in the U.S. academy, need not become a brief for anti-nationalist politics or for rejecting historical inquiry centered on the nation-state. As the Canadian literary scholar Bryce Traister has insisted in his trenchant critique of U.S. scholarship on the Mexican border, "We have lost our ability to understand the liberal nation-state as a positive and still intriguing contributor rather than impediment to meaningful and even politically progressive identity."[53]

Fifth, these essays suggest that borders are simultaneously places and ideas, and should be studied through the lenses of cultural and intellectual —as well as social and political—history. Images and accounts of borders circulated by dime novelists, tourism boosters, journalists, filmmakers, and historians made North American borders resonate well beyond the border regions themselves, engaging the same issues of national territoriality, national and racial difference, and state violence that shaped life in the borderlands. The national differences implied by borders could be used to celebrate (and sell) cultural difference, as Catherine Cocks's analysis of the Mexican state and American tourism shows. At other times, as Dominique Brégent-Heald's essay in this volume suggests, depictions of borderlands minimized the starkness of national boundaries, suggesting commonality or solidarity rather than evoking difference or engendering fear. Historians are also producers and consumers of ideas about borders, if often unconsciously. As Bethel Saler and Carolyn Podruchny show in the volume's last essay, much North American historical scholarship has read national boundaries backward into the period before their existence, obscuring non-national forms of territoriality and community that did not simply vanish with the drawing of national boundaries. Exploring the relationship between borders as places and borders as ideas and symbols—tasks that are now split between social and political historians, on the one hand, and cultural historians and literary scholars, on the other—ought to be one of the primary tasks of border scholars.[54]

Taken together, then, these ten essays offer new perspectives on a truly continental approach to the study of North America's past, while pointing the way to future research possibilities. It is our hope that the ideas contained in this volume will help in bridging the intellectual and spatial divides that all too often separate historians engaged with critical questions about a continent (and a planet, for that matter) where border-building and border-crossing have become central features of contemporary life.

## Notes

1. "News Conference with Leaders of U.S., Mexico, and Canada," *New York Times*, 23 March 2005.
2. For a recent critique of this kind of teleology, see Aron, *American Confluence*, xv.
3. Agnew, "The Territorial Trap," 59; Baud and Van Schendel, "Toward a Comparative History of Borderlands," 211.
4. For a sustained argument that the "emergence, ascendancy, and subsequent crisis" of territoriality is one of the "most encompassing or fundamental sociopolitical trends of modern world development," see Maier, "Consigning the Twentieth Century to History," 807; also, Baud and Van Schendel, "Toward a Comparative History of Borderlands," 212–14. For territoriality and national sovereignty, see Kristof, "The Nature of Frontiers and Boundaries," 279; and Agnew, "The Territorial Trap," 60.
5. For the primacy of the national identities attached to state territories, see Agnew, "The Territorial Trap," 60; Maier, "Consigning the Twentieth Century to History," 816; and Kristof, "The Nature of Frontiers and Boundaries," 278.
6. Williams and Smith, "The National Construction of Social Space," 509, 515; Taylor, "The State as Container," 155.
7. Bolton, "The Epic of Greater America"; Weber, "Turner, the Boltonians, and the Borderlands"; Truett and Young, "Making Transnational History."
8. Martínez, *Troublesome Border*; Martínez, *Border People*.

9. See, among others, Spicer, *Cycles of Conquest*; and Gutiérrez, *When Jesus Came, the Corn Mothers Went Away*.

10. Truett and Young, "Making Transnational History," 3–12; Limerick, *The Legacy of Conquest*, especially chap. 7; Limerick, *Something in the Soil*, 88; White, *"It's Your Misfortune and None of My Own."*

11. For a discussion and extensive citations of this literature, see Ochoa, "Investigación reciente en torno al norte de México y la región fronteriza entre Estados Unidos y México a partir del Porfiriato"; and Truett and Young, "Making Transnational History," 8–9.

12. E.g., Kearney, "Borders and Boundaries of State and Self at the End of Empire"; Anzaldúa, *Borderlands / La Frontera*; Saldívar, *Border Matters*; Vila, *Crossing Borders, Reinforcing Borders*; Rouse, "Mexican Migration and the Social Space of Postmodernism"; García Canclini, *Hybrid Cultures*; and Mignolo, *Local Histories / Global Designs*.

13. See, e.g., Bayly et al., "On Transnational History"; Thelen, "Of Audiences, Borderlands, and Comparisons"; Bender, *Rethinking American History in a Global Age*; Migdal, *Boundaries and Belonging*; Tyrrell, *Transnational Nation*; and Bender, *A Nation among Nations*.

14. Thelen, "Rethinking History and the Nation-State"; Gutiérrez, "Migration, Emergent Ethnicity, and the 'Third Space'"; Piñera Ramírez, "La historia de la frontera México-Estados Unidos en el contexto de las fronteras en Iberoamérica."

15. Katz, *The Secret War in Mexico*; Nugent, *Spent Cartridges of Revolution*; Salas, *In the Shadow of the Eagles*; Mora-Torres, *The Making of the Mexican Border*; Hu-DeHart, *Yaqui Resistance and Survival*; Young, *Catarino Garza's Revolution on the Texas-Mexico Border*; Johnson, *Revolution in Texas*; Ngai, *Impossible Subjects*; Lee, *At America's Gates*; Meeks, "Cross-Ethnic Political Mobilization and Yaqui Identity Formation in Guadalupe, Arizona."

16. Spiegelman, "Those Dirty Little Comics"; Fowler and Crawford, *Border Radio*; Los Super Seven, *Heard it on the X*; Fox, *The Fence and the River*; McCrossen, "Disrupting Boundaries."

17. Truett and Young, "Making Transnational History," 2 (quotation); Young, *Catarino Garza's Revolution on the Texas-Mexico Border*; Saldívar, *Border Matters*.

18. This observation would also seem to apply to work on other Latin American borders; see, e.g., Ceballos, *Memoria del Segundo Congreso Internacional sobre fronteras en Iberoamérica*.

19. García Martínez, "El espacio del (des)encuentro," 19 (translation by Benjamin Johnson).

20. Thelen, "Mexico, the Latin North American Nation," 475. For another re-

cent example of how the border is interpreted from an avowedly nationalist perspective—one critical of U.S. imperialism—see Galeana, "Presentación."

21. Anzaldúa, *Borderlands / La Frontera*, 25.

22. It is worth noting that the early history of the eastern Canada-U.S. boundary line looks much more like the bloody nineteenth-century history of the Mexico-U.S. border. At the birth of the United States, in 1776, an American army marched north in a failed effort to conquer Quebec, and as late as the 1830s the United States and Great Britain deployed military forces in the northeastern borderlands, a result of disputes over territory and resources (see Faragher, Commentary; and Taylor, *The Divided Ground*).

23. Sage, "Some Aspects of the Frontier in Canadian History"; Sage, "Geographic and Cultural Aspects of the Five Canadas."

24. Brebner, *North Atlantic Triangle*.

25. Stanley, "Western Canada and the Frontier Thesis"; Jameson and Mouat, "Telling Differences," 197–203.

26. Stegner, *Wolf Willow*, 81. For further discussion of Stegner's depiction of the border, see Williams, "Prairies and Plains."

27. Stegner, *Wolf Willow*, 85.

28. Other notable works by Sharp that address the borderlands of the 49th parallel include *The Agrarian Revolt in Western Canada* and "When Our West Moved North." For additional biographical information on Sharp, see Isern and Shepard, "Paul F. Sharp."

29. Isern and Shepard, "Paul F. Sharp and the Historiography of the North American Plains," 8.

30. For a helpful overview of the contrast in historical literature about the frontiers of Canada and the United States, see Jameson and Mouat, "Telling Differences." It is worth noting that the Canadian historian George F. G. Stanley argued as early as 1940 for the irrelevance of Turner's thesis north of the border; see his "Western Canada and the Frontier Thesis."

31. For a sampling of such works, see Cook, *The Maple Leaf Forever*; Thomas, *Essays on Western History in Honour of Lewis Gwynne Thomas*; Macleod, *The North-West Mounted Police and Law Enforcement*; Dunae, *Gentlemen Emigrants*; Breen, *The Canadian Prairie West and the Ranching Frontier*; and Breen, "The Turner Thesis and the Canadian West." It is worth noting that some American scholars, most notably the political scientist Seymour Martin Lipset, have similarly stressed the differences between Canadian and U.S. society, though without the presumption of Canadian superiority (see Lipset, *Continental Divide*).

32. Konrad, "The Borderlands of the United States and Canada in the Context of North American Development."

33. See, e.g., Schwantes, *Radical Heritage*; Robbins, Frank, and Ross, *Regionalism and the Pacific Northwest*; Edwards and Schwantes, *Experiences in a Promised Land*; Shepard, *Deemed Unsuitable*; and the special issue of *Great Plains Quarterly* titled "Intersections: Studies in the Canadian and American Great Plains," published in 1983.

34. Konrad, "The Borderlands of the United States and Canada in the Context of North American Development"; McGreevy, *The Wall of Mirrors*; and McKinsey and Konrad, *Borderland Reflections*.

35. This trend is suggested by the appearance of a handful of excellent anthologies about the region. See the following: Findlay and Coates, *Parallel Destinies*; Evans, *The Borderlands of the American and Canadian Wests*; Bukowczyk et al., *Permeable Border*; Higham and Thacker, *One West, Two Myths: A Comparative Reader*; and Higham and Thacker, *One West, Two Myths II: Essays on Comparison*.

36. Among the notable recent works that examine the eastern portion of the border are Taylor, *The Divided Ground*; Little, *Borderland Religion*; and Hornsby and Reid, *New England and the Maritime Provinces*.

37. For examples of this shorthand, see the works cited by Jameson and Mouat to document their claim of the importance of the border on the Canadian imagination: Lumsden, *Close to the 49th Parallel Etc.*; and Gwyn, *The 49th Paradox*. They note also the title of the singer k.d. lang's 2004 album, *Hymns of the 49th Parallel* (Jameson and Mouat, "Telling Differences," 189).

38. Ramirez, "Canada in the United States." For recent works that are not focused on borders per se, but that do approach North America as an integrated whole, see García, *Seeking Refuge*; Graybill, *Policing the Great Plains*; and Evans, *Bound in Twine*. For an exploration of the many connections between contemporary Canadian and U.S. societies, see Stuart, *Dispersed Relations*.

39. McCrady, *Living with Strangers*; Taylor, *The Divided Ground*.

40. Friesen, *The Canadian Prairies*, 242–73. Interestingly, in 1900 nearly 20 percent of Canadians were U.S.-born, while for the last third of the nineteenth century, "Canada lost more citizens through emigration to the United States than it gained through immigration" (ibid., 248).

41. See Bennett and Kohl, *Settling the Canadian-American West*; Little, *Borderland Religion*; Bukowczyk et al., *Permeable Border*; Widdis, *With Scarcely a Ripple*; Ramirez, *Crossing the 49th Parallel*; and Ramirez, "Canada in the United States."

42. Reese, *Arc of the Medicine Line*.

43. See Binnema, *Common and Contested Ground*; Dorsey, *The Dawn of Conservation Diplomacy*; Taylor, *Making Salmon*; Evenden, *Fish versus Power*; Rozum, "Grasslands Grown"; Chester, *Conservation across Borders*; and Mortimer-

Sandilands, "The Geology Recognizes No Boundaries." Notable works that address such questions on the U.S.-Mexico border include Truett, "Neighbors by Nature"; and Truett, *Fugitive Landscapes.*

44. See McManus, *The Line Which Separates*; LaDow, *The Medicine Line*; Morris, "Regional Ideas and the Montana-Alberta Borderlands"; and Widdis, "Borders, Borderlands, and Canadian Identity."

45. See Lee, *At America's Gates*; Ettinger, "Imaginary Lines"; Ettinger, "We Sometimes Wonder What They Will Spring on Us Next"; Sadowski-Smith, *Globalization on the Line*; and Sadowski-Smith, *Border Fictions.*

46. Of course, exceptionalism rests on an implicit comparison, and so some forms of historical comparison might in fact reinscribe American and other exceptionalisms. Nonetheless, comparison remains one of the essential tools of those aiming to explode naive or unexamined assumptions of uniqueness.

47. See Álvarez, "The Mexican-U.S. Border," 451; Baud and Van Schendel, "Toward a Comparative History of Borderlands," 235; Kearney, "Borders and Boundaries of State and Self at the End of Empire," 52–53. For a thoughtful comparison of the symbolic importance of national borders in U.S. and Latin American history, see Cueva Perus, "Fronteras y representaciones fronterizas."

48. See Schulze, "Trans-Nations."

49. See also Lee, *At America's Gates*; Ngai, *Impossible Subjects*; Schiavone Camacho, "Crossing Boundaries, Claiming a Homeland."

50. See Deering, *The Border Boys with the Mexican Rangers*; Goldfrap, *The Border Boys with the Texas Rangers*; and Vanderwood, *Juan Soldado.*

51. Contrast García Martínez, "El espacio del (des)encuentro," and St. John, "Line in the Sand," with Martínez, *Border People,* and Lorey, *The U.S.-Mexican Border in the Twentieth Century.*

52. Leading examples of works about this treatment by nation-states include Nugent, *Spent Cartridges of Revolution*; Adelman and Aron, "From Borderlands to Borders"; and Brooks, *Captives and Cousins.*

53. Traister, "Border Shopping," 46. See also Sahlins, *Boundaries*; Reséndez, *Changing National Identities at the Frontier*; Valerio-Jiménez, *Rio Grande Crossings*; Seltz, "Embodying Nature"; and Johnson, *Revolution in Texas.* For trenchant critiques of the enthusiasm of U.S. scholars for de-centering the U.S. state and nation, and affirmations of the continued political and intellectual project of nation-building in the face of U.S. economic power, see Traister, "Risking Nationalism"; and Traister, "Border Shopping." For more theoretical critiques of the widespread notion that globalization means a decline of nation-states as viable or meaningful political projects, see Taylor, "The State as Container"; and Williams and Smith, "The National Construction of Social Space."

54. See McCrossen, *Land of Necessity*; and Fox, *The Fence and the River.*

**PART I**

..........................................

*Peoples In Between*

# CONFLICT AND COOPERATION IN THE MAKING OF TEXAS-MEXICO BORDER SOCIETY, 1840–1880

...........................................

Miguel Ángel González-Quiroga

When contemplating the history of the United States–Mexico border, most people conjure up images of violence and conflict. It is easy to recall the Alamo, or the War of 1846–48, or even Pancho Villa's raid on Columbus, New Mexico, at the time of the Mexican Revolution. Unlike the U.S.-Canadian border, which is generally associated with a placid and benign coexistence, the U.S.-Mexican boundary, even today, evokes images of violence associated with poverty, illegal immigration, and drug trafficking. These historical and contemporary images distort another reality that is less well known but no less compelling: the multiple instances of cooperation, accommodation, and negotiation that have also characterized relations between the border people of the two countries.[1] Conflict and cooperation—between Anglos and Mexicans (living on both sides of the border) and between the governments of both countries—are two sides of a single reality that has typified life in the U.S.-Mexican border region. This study aims to explore that reality by focusing on a particular region along the lower Río Bravo (Rio Grande) during a period when conflict was at its highest level, the years from 1840 to 1880.[2]

The focus on conflict, until quite recently, has also permeated the historiography of the region, and has reinforced the idea that the establishment of the border, in 1848, not unlike the creation of a fork in the road, helped to differentiate the separate and distinct national trajectories of Mexico and the United States. Recent works on North American borderlands, in contrast, demonstrate the parallel connections, continuities, and processes that have affected people on both sides of the border. These studies suggest that the imposition of the boundary between the two nation-states modified, but did not eliminate, the social, economic, and cultural bonds that had been established over a long period.[3] This study supports that view by focusing on instances of cooperation that took place in the Río Bravo region of the Texas-Mexico border before and after the boundary was created in 1848. It demonstrates that an economically, socially, and culturally integrated region existed before the establishment of the border, and that it continued to operate for decades thereafter. Moreover, I show how the border itself, once established, became the source of both cooperation and conflict in succeeding decades.

## The Border as a Zone of Conflict

It is a curious fact that conflict first occurred because there was no border, and later, because there was. The Treaty of Guadalupe Hidalgo, signed in February 1848, established the border between the United States and Mexico as the Río Bravo. Before that date, there was no clear boundary, and this generated conflict, centered mainly on the issues of whether Mexico would accept Texas's independence, and if so, was the border to be the Rio Bravo, as Texas wanted, or the Nueces River, as Mexico insisted. In this hostile climate, both republics launched military incursions and expeditions against one another. After 1848 and until 1880, the sources of conflict were many and varied, but they all shared one underlying factor: the location of the region, far from the centers of power in Washington and Mexico City, and exacerbated by civil wars and a period of reconstruction in both nations, made it impossible for either government to exert its authority along the border and bring peace to the area.

After 1848, the historian Oscar Martínez argues, there existed "an enduring pattern of racial, ethnic, and cultural confrontation," as "armed clashes, raids, thefts, rapes, lynching, murders and other outrages became commonplace in border areas from Texas to California."[4] Another scholar of border history, James Wilkinson, described the worst period of the violence in this way:

> The Border had been accustomed for some years to the violence attendant on Indian warfare, revolution, civil war, and the presence of men who lived outside the law. But in many ways the years that began with

Reconstruction and extended to about 1880 were the most violent the region had ever experienced. On the right bank of the Rio Bravo (Mexico) there was almost continuous revolution. Smuggling engaged a large number of people, absorbed a high percentage of Border trade, and generated a callous disregard of the law and its enforcement. Banditry on both sides of the river attained professional status. Indian depredations were endemic.[5]

Widespread lawbreaking in the absence of effective state control, combined with the existence of a boundary which, upon crossing, afforded refuge, was a sure formula for conflict. The governments of both countries complained that livestock was being stolen and taken across the border, usually cattle to Mexico and horses to Texas. This led to numerous raids and reprisals by armed parties from both sides.[6] The border also permitted Texas slaves to flee to Mexico, Mexican peons to escape their debts by crossing into Texas, and Indian raiders to plunder on one side and seek refuge on the other. The Callahan Expedition of 1855, which ended with the burning of Piedras Negras, is one example: ostensibly a raid into Mexico by armed Texans who were seeking to punish Indian raiders, the participants also sought to retrieve escaped slaves.[7]

But conflict and cooperation often went hand in hand. When Mexicans of the border region, under the leadership of Antonio Canales, rose up against the central government of Mexico in the Federalist Wars of 1839–40, many Texans participated on the side of the Federalists. This is a good example of how the presence of an independent Texas gave the elites of northern Mexico leverage vis-à-vis the central government. The historian Octavio Herrera argues that having defied Mexico's central government, northern elites were nevertheless able to negotiate a return to the public life of the region because they had demonstrated courage and organizational capacity and had carried out "extremely delicate actions such as linking up with Texas." The new Texas Republic thus offered Antonio Canales and other members of the regional elite a sword with which to threaten the central government.[8] Mexicans also participated in warfare alongside the Texans. When the U.S. Civil War enveloped Texas after 1861, many recruits from Mexico's Northeast participated in the Confederate and Union armies.[9]

Border history has registered many instances of "cooperative violence,"

**Table 1**  Incidents, Incursions, and Other Sources of Conflict along the Texas-Mexico Border, 1840–1880

| | |
|---|---|
| 1836–1848 | Dispute over independence of Texas and location of boundary were main sources of conflict |
| 1840 | Federalist wars in Northeast Mexico; Texans participate |
| June–October 1841 | Santa Fe Expedition; Texas invades New Mexico |
| 1842 | Mexican incursions into Texas; Vázquez (March) and Woll (September) attack San Antonio |
| November–December 1842 | Texas attacks Mexico with Somervell and Mier Expeditions |
| 1846–1848 | War between the United States and Mexico |
| 1848–1880 | Indian raids, cattle rustling, trans-border raids, filibustering expeditions, runaway slaves, smuggling, protection of political dissidents, Anglo violations of property rights of Mexicans, and racial hatred were main sources of conflict |
| 1850–1853 | Carvajal Revolt (also known as Merchants' War) in border region with aid of Texas merchants and filibusters |
| October 1855 | Callahan Expedition into Mexico to punish Indian raiders and recapture runaway slaves; Piedras Negras sacked and burned |
| July–November 1857 | Cart War on roads between San Antonio and Gulf Coast; Anglos attack Mexican cartmen, who were principal carriers |
| 1858–1860 | War of the Reform in Mexico |
| July–December 1859 | Cortina War, spurred by Mexican resentment of Anglo despoliation and discrimination in border region |
| 1860s | Skirmishes involving troops of both countries: 1861—Santos Benavides of Laredo defeats Cortina in the second Cortina War 1866—American troops under General Sedwick temporarily occupy Matamoros during War of the French Intervention |
| 1861–1865 | Civil War in the United States; border region becomes a zone of combat |
| 1862–1867 | War of the French Intervention in Mexico |

| | |
|---|---|
| 1870s | Nueces strip, area between Nueces River and Río Bravo, becomes a wild and lawless region disputed by Mexican raiders, Anglo outlaws, and Indian warriors largely beyond the reach of governmental authorities |
| May 1873 | American troops under Colonel Ranald Mackenzie cross border and attack Kickapoo Indian village near Remolino, Coahuila, in attempt to stop Indian raids from Mexico |
| 1875 | McNelly's Rangers cross river to recover stolen cattle and kill several Mexicans (by mistake) near Rancho Las Cuevas |
| May 1875 | Mexican raiders reach outskirts of Corpus Christi; rob, kill, and terrorize farmers and travelers |
| 1876–1878 | Use of border as refuge for political dissidents (Díaz in 1876; Lerdistas in 1877–78) causes friction between the two governments |
| April 1877 | Major William Shafter and his troops occupy Piedras Negras in a dispute over imprisoned scouts |
| June 1, 1877 | General E. O. C. Ord authorized by U.S. government to cross border in pursuit of robbers, with or without permission from Mexico |
| Summer 1877 | Mexican government sends General Gerónimo Treviño to pacify the border region and repel American incursions |
| December 1877 | El Paso Salt War; bloody and destructive conflict in which salt mines were disputed by Mexicans and Anglo merchants |

*Note*: The table includes issues, incidents, and wars (small and large) that confronted Mexicans and Anglos, as well as civil wars within each country that affected the border region.

in which Anglos and Mexicans fought on the same side because it was in their interest to do so. A vivid example is the Carvajal Revolt (1850–53), also known as the Merchants' War because it had the backing of many Anglo merchants of the region. As in the case of the Canales insurrection a decade earlier, many Texas volunteers were included within the ranks of José María Carvajal's insurrection. The central government smashed the revolt, but what is interesting is that the border, in large measure, was the source of the conflict, because of the huge contraband trade that had developed there. Smuggling was a logical response by borderlanders to the Mexican government's policies of prohibiting the importation of many goods and fixing onerous tariffs on others. When Mexico City moved to enforce these policies, merchants, consumers, and freighters on both sides of the border rebelled.[10]

But the border also promoted cooperation, as people of different races and nationalities united around common causes, and it was not unusual for Anglos, Indians, and Mexicans to form alliances for self-defense. In February 1852, for example, Henry Clay Davis, an Anglo merchant from Rio Grande City, led a war party of Indians across the river to rescue Carvajal, who was trapped in Camargo.[11] Thus, the border, with its complicated tariff schedules and abundant incentives for smuggling, could provoke conflict, but practical necessity, or simply the need for survival of the borderlanders, could generate cooperation.

The violence along the Texas-Mexico border in the 1870s was particularly hellish. Raids and claims intensified throughout the decade, culminating in the Ord Order of June 1, 1877. This instruction authorized General E. O. C. Ord to pursue Mexican robbers across the border, with or without consent from Mexican authorities. In the opinion of many Mexicans, the order was tantamount to a declaration of war. Fortunately, war was averted and the border was pacified by the end of the decade, bringing to an end a forty-year period of unremitting border violence.[12]

Pacification was achieved by a process that intimately involved the merchants of the Rio Grande border region. In Texas, Charles Stillman, Richard King, Sabas Cavazos, and others provided men, money, and arms to Porfirio Díaz in his struggle to gain power during the Tuxtepec Revolt of 1876. These merchants wanted the border violence to cease. When Díaz was hiding out in Texas, they offered to help him, with the understanding that he would remove Juan Cortina from the border and pacify the region so as to create more favorable conditions for their commercial enterprises. In his drive to create the conditions for the modernization of Mexico, Díaz eventually did banish Cortina from the Río Bravo and pacified the border region—along with the rest of Mexico. This is an interesting example of a borderland elite injecting itself firmly into the national historical narrative. But in this instance it was the local elite on the U.S. side of the border who assumed an active role in Mexican national politics.[13]

**Map 1.** Northeast Mexico–Texas borderlands. The shaded area is the zone of conflict and cooperation analyzed in this essay. (Map by Ezra Zeitler)

### Coexistince and Cooperation: A Different Border History

Despite the prevalence of violence and conflict along the border, we can discern an alternative history for the region if we put a different set of historical actors under our lens. From 1840 until 1880, when conflict was rife, merchants, teamsters, migrant laborers, and missionaries were creating a diverse history there, one that has been largely obscured by historians' focus on violence.

The loss of Texas and the preoccupation with getting it back was an important concern for political elites in greater Mexico, but this goal was not shared by most people in northeastern Mexico. The majority of the population there was willing to live in peaceful coexistence, or even active cooperation, with the Texans. One of the most important bridges between these two peoples was provided by commerce. From the 1820s, after Matamoros became a port city, a firm connection was established between the province of Texas and the interior of Mexico, extending commerce to points as far south as the states of Zacatecas and San Luis Potosí by way of Monterrey.[14]

As in all human societies, trade was essential to the people of the borderlands, because only through commerce could they obtain a diverse range of goods that they could not produce themselves. When the trade route from Matamoros to Monterrey became too dangerous or was closed due to wars or other disturbances, merchants, teamsters, and cartmen modified their strategies and sought alternative interior routes to bring their goods to market. During the years of the Texas Republic, and with the acquiescence of Mirabeau B. Lamar, who became the Republic's president in December 1838, a flourishing trade developed between the towns along the U.S.-Mexico border and those in the interior of Mexico, as well as with Austin, in central Texas, and Houston, in eastern Texas. The historian Joseph M. Nance wrote about this Texas trade:

> Several thousand dollars in specie (silver coins), a much needed item in Texas, were brought into San Antonio in the course of a week or two, and large quantities of silver were coming in from Chihuahua. One trader arrived with $17,000 in specie, and it was estimated in May 1839 that goods valued between $100,000 and $150,000 could be sold immediately at Béxar for specie or bullion.[15]

The trade in silver, like the fur trade described by Bethel Saler and Carolyn Podruchny in this volume, was a wide-ranging enterprise that extended throughout much of the Atlantic world and defied the confines of national borders or histories.[16]

In spite of the conflict between the two countries, then, cross-border commerce grew stronger because it satisfied an essential need of the borderlanders. Support for this assertion is provided by General P. Hansbrough Bell of the Texas militia, who was sent by Lamar in 1841 to investigate conditions on the frontier. Bell reported that a part of the Anglo population was opposed to the trade, but that the majority supported it because "many of the inhabitants of the West" were its beneficiaries, "from a supply through it of various articles which they need, and which at this time they cannot procure elsewhere." Among these articles, Bell noted, were horses, mules, saddles, blankets, and silver.[17]

The central government of Mexico tried to stop this trade. Its military commander in the north, Mariano Arista, issued a blistering proclamation to citizens of the border to desist in their continued commerce with the Texans because they were providing the enemy with essential resources. He threatened offenders with punishments ranging from forcible service in the militia to long prison terms.[18] These threats did little good. The two governments were at war, but their citizens obeyed a different logic. This was corroborated by a commission sent by Lamar to parley with Arista in Monterrey: "As the Texan commissioners proceeded inland they found the Mexicans east of the mountains and west of the Río Grande anxiously praying for peace and the reopening of a safe and direct trade with Texas."[19]

The breaches which had developed between the residents of the border and the local, regional, and national authorities with respect to commerce are revealed in the official correspondence of the period. Octavio Herrera skillfully utilizes these documents to demonstrate the futility of the government in trying to halt the contraband trade between the people of the Northeast and the Texans during the years of the Texas Republic. The trade was so extensive that in mid-1844 local authorities in Reynosa called a halt to the patrols of the local militia against Indian raiders between the Río Bravo and the Nueces River, because these "lent themselves to the promotion of contraband." They feared that those who were engaged in combating the Indians would also become engaged in the illegal trade![20]

The borderlanders' desire for peaceful trade with Texas underwent a stern test in 1846, when the full force of the American military invaded Mexico's Northeast at the beginning of the U.S.-Mexican War. Despite the profound wounds left by the war, for practical reasons and due to geographic proximity, the diverse ties between the citizens of northeastern Mexico and those of Texas, especially in matters of commerce, were soon restored. Trade, which had been established in an earlier period, resumed with great vigor after 1848. A vast constellation of producers, merchants, and transporters on both sides of the border participated in the ever-growing trade in the three decades that followed the war. The scope of this essay only allows mention of a small number of those who participated, most of whom were concentrated along the border and in Monterrey and San Antonio, the two poles of a growing commercial axis that fused the region into a single economic unit.

The twin cities of Matamoros and Brownsville became the base of operations for merchants like Charles Stillman, a Connecticut Yankee who made a fortune in the Mexican trade, especially during the Civil War, and who would, with his son James, found one of the great financial empires in the United States. Richard King and Mifflin Kenedy ran steamships with Stillman along the Río Bravo and also built fortunes based on commerce with Mexico; they used their fortunes to establish two of the biggest ranches in all of North America. The Spaniard José San Román had a vast network of contacts with producers, merchants, and carriers all over Europe, the eastern United States, Havana, New Orleans, and in most parts of Mexico. All of these merchants are well known to students of border history. But there were others who shone less brightly, but who also contributed to building commercial bridges between the two nations. Joseph Kleiber, a German-born merchant who cursed Mexicans in his private correspondence, had a thousand business cards printed in Spanish in order to attract customers in Mexico's interior regions. Gilbert Kingsbury—merchant, writer, and postmaster of Brownsville—surveyed the commercial scene and declared that, in 1860, about two million dollars a month had passed through the city's customs house, and that in no other town on the continent, in proportion to its size, could there be found as many millionaires as in Brownsville. This was before the Civil War, which would open up an even greater volume of trade in the region.[21]

Further upriver, in Laredo, John Leyendecker, another German immigrant, established a commercial house in the 1850s that specialized in obtaining hides in Mexico and forwarding them to San Antonio and New York by way of Corpus Christi. As a quartermaster's assistant during the Civil War, Leyendecker had obtained huge quantities of goods in Mexico for the Confederate cause. Still farther up the Río Bravo, William L. Cazneau, one of the founders of Eagle Pass and prominent in Texas politics, had "gone North for the purpose of selecting a large stock of goods for the Chihuahua market."[22] Also prominent in Eagle Pass were the Groos brothers, Friedrich, Karl, and Gustav, who established an extensive trade network connecting Texas with the northern region of Mexico. Before moving to San Antonio, Friedrich visited Evaristo Madero, one of the principal merchants of Monterrey, and established a friendship that would last for the remainder of his life.[23]

The merchants of San Antonio who had ties with Mexico are too numerous to mention, but a few examples are revealing. George T. Howard had participated in the Santa Fe and Somervel expeditions, as well as in

**Figure 1.** Charles Stillman, Brownsville businessman. (Center for American History, University of Texas, Austin, di_04491. Ferguson [Henry Noel] Photographic Collection)

the war against Mexico. In the 1850s, he established, with D. C. Ogden, the largest freighting company in San Antonio, mainly contracting Mexican freighters. His contacts with Mexican suppliers during the Civil War served to procure goods for the Confederacy. Jean Baptiste Lacoste, a Frenchman, and John Twohig, an Irishman, both established commercial establishments in the 1850s and quickly looked to Mexico for trading and investment opportunities. Both became enormously rich with the Civil War trade, and both continued to trade and make investments in northern Mexico during the 1870s. They established business and personal relations with the principal merchants and political figures of Nuevo León and Coahuila.[24]

Henry L. Kinney, the founder of Corpus Christi, was an emblematic figure among the Texas merchants who traded with Mexico. His experience best illustrates the persistence of commercial activities there, even in the face of ferocious conflict. Kinney was a hard-driving man who established a trading post on the fringes of the Nueces Strip during the 1840s and 1850s, when the region was ablaze with violence. In the early 1850s, he was a principal backer of the Carvajal Revolt. His philosophy for survival involved getting along with everyone, including his enemies. He said of himself: "When Mr. Mexican came, I treated him with a great deal of politeness, particularly if he had me in his power; when Mr. American came, I did the same with him; and when Mr. Indian came, I was also very frequently disposed to make a compromise with him."[25]

The merchants in northern Mexico had several things in common with their Texan counterparts. They shared a pragmatic and acquisitive spirit, and most had a European background. Moreover, they were not deterred by wars; indeed, they profited from them. Two examples from the merchant class of Monterrey who had extensive Texas contacts will illustrate this. Mariano Hernández, a Spaniard, established a commercial enterprise in the mid-1850s with far-reaching connections in the United States and Europe. With two of his brothers, Hernández established branches of the business in Matamoros, Brownsville, and in Durango, Mexico. He became one of John Leyendecker's principal clients and suppliers. With other merchants, he established the first textile plant in the region, in 1854, relying heavily on Texas cotton supplied by John Twohig and other San Antonio merchants. One of the partners in this enterprise, Valentín Rivero, was another Spaniard who had important ties with Texas and U.S. merchants through the commercial house of Samuel Belden, in Brownsville. Rivero was also a vice-consul of Spain in Monterrey during various periods.[26]

The two most recognizable Monterrey merchants of the period, and the greatest beneficiaries of the trade with Texas, were Patricio Milmo and Evaristo Madero. Milmo was an Irish immigrant who married the daughter of Santiago Vidaurri, the Nuevo León strongman who established political hegemony over most of Northeast Mexico during the decade from 1855 to 1864. He established branches of his commercial empire in Matamoros and Laredo, and also managed to obtain vast land holdings in various states within Mexico and in Texas. Evaristo Madero, the patriarch of a dynasty that included Francisco I. Madero, who initiated the Mexican Revolution, was from Coahuila, but during a brief period he established his commercial business in Monterrey. Madero traded in all kinds of goods, but especially in mules and horses. Like Milmo, he became vastly rich as a result of the Civil War trade, and he developed ties with Lacoste, Twohig, and other Texas merchants that would last for the remainder of his life. Twohig would call on Madero when the latter became the gover-

**Figure 2.** Evaristo Madero, grandfather of the revolutionary hero Francisco I. Madero, made a fortune in the trans-border trade. (Courtesy of the Fototeca, Municipal Archive of Saltillo)

nor of Coahuila in order to facilitate the construction of the International Railroad through the region in the early 1880s.[27]

Alongside the big merchants who helped shape the economic life of the region and part of its politics, a phalanx of lesser traders and transporters made their living in the commerce between Texas and Mexico. There was August Santleben, who transported goods and people between San Antonio and the mining regions of Chihuahua and Zacatecas, and who established a stagecoach line between that Texas city and Monterrey in 1867. There was Santiago Lincoln, a merchant and freighter who plied the dangerous roads between San Antonio and Monterrey taking hides north and cotton south. There was Joseph Ulrich, an abolitionist who was forced to find refuge in Monterrey during the Civil War, and who established a store in that city and served as the American consul from 1867 to 1875. Ulrich, who had a very low opinion of Mexicans, sent the State Department reams of information on the Americans who, for a wide variety of reasons, had chosen to live or invest in Mexico.[28]

Trade served to unite the people of Texas and Northeast Mexico before and after the establishment of the border. The market dynamics of producers, merchants, freighters, and consumers created an economically integrated region that encompassed a large part of Texas and most of northeastern Mexico and that could not be signed or wished away by nationalist or racist politicians of either country. The variegated racial and ethnic composition of the border region, including San Antonio and Monterrey, cities with a large number of Europeans of various nationalities, may have served to soften some of the rougher edges of the habitual racism and mistrust between Anglos and Mexicans. In any case, the economic cooperation among the people of the borderlands should not be confused with altruism or goodwill. It was often based on selfish motives, and commonly energized by ambition or greed, traits that are all too human.

Continuity characterized the development of the commercial networks before and after the establishment of the boundary between the two nations, and commerce was the grand bridge that connected people on both sides of the border, regardless of the differences, the obstacles, and the conflict. New networks of interdependence also began to emerge after 1848, even as greater levels of violence were being reached. Many of these new connections were of a social and cultural nature. One involved the migration of thousands of Mexicans from Mexico's Northeast, who were needed to work in Texas's expanding economy. Another had its roots in a religious movement that had originated deep from within America's Second Great Awakening in the nineteenth century and which spawned a missionary movement that swept westward and southward until it reached the border with Mexico and crossed beyond.

The pattern for Mexican labor migration to the United States did not begin during the Mexican Revolution in 1910, as many believe. It was firmly established by the middle of the nineteenth century and has continued unabated to this day.[29] Paradoxically, and for diverse reasons, the war between the United States and Mexico was an early impulse in driving Mexicans to the border. Mexican laborers from the interior began to gravitate toward the border region in search of work. Some had been displaced from their haciendas, which had been razed by the invading army. Others went simply because there was work available, even if it was at the service of the Americans. In its march toward the interior, Zachary Taylor's army contracted hundreds of *arrieros* (mule drivers) to haul military supplies. Others found employment in the army camps and on the steamships that navigated the Río Bravo and which supplied the American troops. There was employment for dock workers, stokers, and cowboys, with salaries considerably higher than those available before the war. Those who participated transmitted this information to relatives and friends in their home region and, in this way, a south-to-north pattern of labor migration was established.[30]

After the war and throughout the 1850s the flow of Mexicans to Texas in search of work was discreet but steady and growing, in spite of the racism and hatred left over from the conflict.[31] Mexican workers were needed in the ranching and agricultural economy as cowboys, sheep-herders, and farm laborers. Higher salaries were a principal attraction for these workers. They were paid from four pesos to six pesos a month in the farms of the Montemorelos region of Nuevo León, which was a typical salary in most of Northeast Mexico. But in Texas, they could obtain up to fifty cents a day.[32]

Another reason that explains the labor migration is that many of the migrant laborers were *sirvientes*, or peons, who sought to escape the cruel system of debt peonage that they suffered in the haciendas. The proximity of Texas and the refuge that it offered to escaping servants began to affect agricultural production in Mexico's Northeast. This was the conclusion that was reached by a group of Montemorelos planters, who complained of "the lack of a solution to the constant and terrible flight of servant labor to the neighboring republic."[33] In Coahuila, the situation was similar. According to Moisés González Navarro, in 1848 the governor of that state "ordered the municipalities to report on the flight of servants in order to recover them because agriculture was being paralyzed because of that situation." The planters demanded an extradition treaty with the United States in order to get their peons back.[34]

As can be seen, the ink was barely dry on the Treaty of Guadalupe Hidalgo and Mexican citizens were marching north, into the country of the enemy, in search of work. Furthermore, the flight of the sirvien-tes poses an interesting juxtaposition. While black slaves were escaping south to gain freedom from slavery, sirvientes were heading north to find freedom from a similar system in Mexico. The presence of the border made this possible, even inevitable.

Labor migration from Mexico to Texas assumed vigorous proportions during the brief period of the American Civil War in the 1860s. The reason has its origin in the prodigious commerce that developed between Texas and Northeast Mexico. This commerce surged in response to two basic needs of the Confederacy: to get its cotton to European markets through the free port of Matamoros and to obtain vital articles from Europe and Mexico in order to wage war.[35] Much of this commerce was carried out through the long interior routes that connected San Antonio to Monterrey and Matamoros through such inland ports as Laredo and Eagle Pass. For that reason, and because of the enormous volume, a veritable army of men was required to move the needed goods. Union and Confederate agents swept down on Monterrey in search of men and wagons. José A. Quintero, the Confederate representative in the city, reported that most of the freighters in the region had gone to Texas to participate in the war traffic because of the high wages being paid.[36] Merchants like Milmo, Madero, Twohig, Lacoste, Leyendecker, and San Román had hundreds of freighters on their payroll. Both merchants and freighters, working in cooperation, forged another link in a chain that further bound together the region on both sides of the border.

The need for migrant labor in Texas slackened after the war, but continued apace with the reconstruction of the region. The spread of cotton cultivation, the end of slavery, and the extension of the railroad into the state would open up new areas of opportunity for Mexican laborers, but this was a process that began to occur toward the end of the 1870s. Earlier in the decade, the surge of stock-raising, both cattle and sheep, especially in the southern region of the state, created most of the jobs for the Mexicans who were coming across the border. The cattle industry had its greatest expansion during this period, and it is estimated that between 1866 and 1880 about four million head of cattle trod the dusty roads of Texas on their way to northern markets. It is also estimated that one-third of the 35,000 cowboys who participated in these drives were black or Mexican. William Waugh, one of the big cattle ranchers of South Texas, crossed the border into Mexico to recruit cowboys for his annual drives.[37]

Sheep grazing also experienced phenomenal growth during the period. By 1886, Texas, with its 4,750,000 sheep, was second only to California in production of wool in the United States. Most of the shearers were from Mexico and they traveled north during the cycles of May–June and August–September to do the shearing. In Nueces County alone, there were 650,000 sheep in 1876. A great number of shearers were required to handle the volume. One observer reported that four hundred shearers had crossed through Piedras Negras in a single week, headed for ranches in the interior of Texas.[38]

**Figure 3.** Mexican *vaqueros* (cowboys) working in South Texas, ca. 1870s. (University of Texas, San Antonio, Institute of Texan Cultures, #075–0138)

The dependence of certain sectors of the Texas economy on Mexican labor during this period raises interesting issues on the role of borders. The racism directed against Mexicans in Texas was still present in the 1870s, if not at the same level as during the height of the Know-Nothings in the 1850s. But racism and exclusion had to be tempered so as not to destabilize the labor needs of the Texas economy. Anglos could—and did—discriminate against Mexicans in Texas and oppressed them in many ways, but the border served as a leveling instrument, where Anglo racism had to be suppressed or subordinated in order to gain access to Mexican labor.[39]

Mexicans continued to travel to Texas in the 1870s for the same reasons that had made them go there earlier: they were escaping oppressive conditions in Mexico and seeking better wages in the growing Texas economy. The law of supply and demand was plainly at work, extending across the border region. But these Mexicans were taking more than their labor power to Texas; they were taking their culture as well, injecting a permanent dose of *mexicanidad* into the developing Mexican American society and culture of Texas. Simultaneously, a different kind of cultural transmission was taking place along the border and in Mexico's interior, but this process mainly flowed north to south and involved the Protestant missionaries who moved into the region in the 1860s and 1870s. They offer another glimpse, from a cultural perspective, of the alternative history that was being written in the border region.

The advance of Protestantism into Mexico was enabled by two earlier developments. One was the advent of religious freedom in the country as a result of the Reform Laws of 1860 that allowed the introduction of other religions. It cannot be said that this created a huge demand for Protestantism, but it is plain that some sectors of the population felt alienated from the Catholic Church, which had unleashed a ferocious conflict in order to protect its wealth and privileges. These sectors, including many of the triumphant Liberals in the Wars of the Reform and the French Intervention, clearly felt a need for an alternative religion. The other precondition was the presence of Protestant missionaries in Texas waiting for a religious opening below the border. Texas became an important platform for the introduction of Protestantism in Mexico. A central figure in this process was Melinda Rankin, a Presbyterian missionary who established a school for Mexican girls in Brownsville in 1852 and bided her time until she could set up operations in Mexico. In the meantime, she sent hundreds of Bibles across the Río Bravo, and ten years later she was able to send a representative to begin mission work in Monterrey. He was James Hickey, a Spanish-speaking Baptist preacher who had worked with Mexicans in Texas and who felt increasingly uncomfortable in the hostile Confederate environment that dominated Texas in the early 1860s.[40]

The Civil War had just ended in the United States but the War of French Intervention was still raging in Mexico when Rankin decided to travel to Monterrey in May 1865. In the face of many obstacles, including the implacable hostility of the Catholic Church and incessant political turmoil, Rankin established her mission, which consisted of a temple, a school, and various congregations in Monterrey and other towns of Nuevo León. Soon she had prepared enough native missionaries to branch out to Coahuila, in the state of Tamaulipas, and even as far as the states of Zacatecas, Durango, and San Luis Potosí. In the meantime, Hickey had worked closely since his arrival in Monterrey in 1862 with Tomás Westrup, an English immigrant, who helped the American missionary found various churches in Nuevo León.[41]

These first missionaries opened the doors and others soon followed. Henry C. Thompson was a very capable minister who established schools and seminaries in the cities of Monterrey, Saltillo, and San Luis Potosí.[42]

The creation of schools was one of the vital components of the mission movement because these were valuable tools in the transmission of values. Protestants made few converts in Mexico (just over 1 percent of the population by the time of the Revolution in 1910), but they promoted a change in thinking, attitudes, and values disproportionate to their number. Jean Pierre Bastian, the foremost scholar of Protestantism in Mexico, has stated that the Protestant missionaries worked for a change in values in order to build a new society based on individualism, not corporativism. This society would be "centered not on the natural order pre-established by divine right, but on the individual as a subject of religious and political life." For this reason, concludes Bastian, the methods of the missionaries "were genuine laboratories for inculcating democratic traditions." What is most important is that this vision was embraced by people who would assume leadership roles in Mexican society at the end of the Porfiriato and during the Revolution.[43]

One interesting dimension of the mission movement is the reciprocity that developed among Protestant churches in Texas and northeastern Mexico. Converts to Protestantism in Mexico were recruited to do mission work among the population of Mexican descent in Texas. Such was the case of Alejo Hernández, a native of Aguascalientes, who became a Methodist minister and preached to congregations in South Texas between Corpus Christi and Laredo in the early 1870s. In 1874, the Methodist Church of Texas sent a representative to Monterrey to recruit persons with the appropriate profile to do mission work north of the Río Bravo. Three men, Doroteo García, Fermín Vidaurri, and Felipe N. Córdova, were invited to Texas for that purpose. They eventually headed missionary districts in Corpus Christi, Laredo, and San Diego, Texas.[44]

Another important aspect of this missionary work is that it occurred during the most acute period of conflict. The violence was not restricted to the border region. In 1871, just four years after the war with the French, a major uprising occurred in Nuevo León headed by Gerónimo Treviño as part of a larger national movement led by Porfirio Díaz to take power with his "Plan de la Noria." Five years later, Treviño, the man later sent to pacify the border, again joined Díaz in his "Plan de Tuxtepec," which succeeded in overthrowing the national government. On both occasions, Nuevo León was under attack, and the missionaries suffered the same risks as the rest of the population. On more than one occasion, Rankin had to negotiate the survival of her mission with military leaders.[45] After the armies left, life returned to normal, although one could argue that normality, at least during this period, was often reflected by armies on the march.

## Conclusion

All borders tend to generate conflict. This is what is most visible; it is what captures the attention both of contemporary observers and of many historians. Less seen and less studied is the cooperation that borders also generate among people who are very different but who share similar needs and problems. This essay, which covers a particularly violent period in the history of the Texas-Mexico border, argues that conflict was not the only, or even the predominant, reality, and that even within the violence there were cooperative processes.

The presence of the boundary line generated both conflict and cooperation. Despite the complexity of the relations between Anglos and Mexicans in the border region, and notwithstanding the conflict generated by racial, ethnic, and national differences, there was always ample room for pragmatism and cooperation between different groups. The sight of Texans fighting on the side of Mexican Federalists, or of Mexican workers migrating to the country of the enemy, among many other examples, bears this out. Moreover, the propensity to trade, the will to trade, was always present, in spite of the racial animosity and the conflict.[46] The reason is simple: on either side of the border were things that people on the other side needed or wanted. Jobs were offered on the northern side; silver was obtainable on the southern side; diverse opportunities were available on both sides. This created a relationship of interdependence that often transcended the differences and the conflict.[47]

This study also helps to shed light on some of the processes that occurred after the imposition of the boundary, when national identities were being solidified. This is an important issue in the debate over the ways by which "borderlands" became "borders." Jeremy Adelman and Stephen Aron stress the increasing imposition of the nation-states in solidifying the boundary and limiting the movement and autonomy of the inhabitants of their borderlands. Samuel Truett and Elliott Young question this emphasis by revealing the multiple transnational linkages that characterize borderlands long after a formal boundary is established.[48]

Elements to fit both interpretations are present in this study. The border was solidified: the Indians were subjugated; Carvajal was defeated; Cortina was removed; and the border was pacified by 1880. But that, like the conflict, is only part of the story. As this study also shows, the commercial bridge established in an earlier period withstood the imposition of the boundary. The ebb and flow of human migration continued in obedience to the demands of the Texas labor market. Religious people also went back and forth in a work of evangelization that respected no boundaries. These movements and linkages observed market forces—less studied by historians than they once were—more than the dictates of nation-states. There was a market for goods, a market for labor, and, if we enter the realm of the supernatural, a market for souls to save.

**Notes**

1. This essays draws its inspiration from an article by David Weber ("Conflictos y acuerdos: Las fronteras hispanomexicanas y angloamericanas"), in which he argues that "Anglos, Hispanos, and Mexicanos found common ground through mutual accommodation and developed a sense of regional identity, even in times of conflict" (89). The topic of conflict and accommodation is also explored by Marcela Terrazas in "Colaboración y conflicto: Relaciones tranfronterizas," and by Manuel Ceballos-Ramírez and Oscar J. Martínez in "Conflict and Accommodation on the U.S.-Mexican Border." The term "cooperation," as used here, does not necessarily imply harmony or friendship, but rather refers to mutually beneficial relations or interactions among diverse groups.

2. Michiel Baud and Willem Van Schendel argue that a regional focus that encompasses both sides of the border makes it "easier to understand the social, cultural, and economic dynamics of borderlands and the particular historical transformations that they have experienced" (see "Toward a Comparative History," 241). Given the scope of this essay, it is impossible to deal with the many important issues raised by these authors, but one of their recommendations is reflected in the text: that borderlands studies can be realized in such a way as to correct the "distortions inherent in state-centered national histories" (ibid.).

3. Some works by U.S. historians that have explored conflict along the Texas-Mexico border in the nineteenth century are Rippy, *The United States and Mexico*; Martínez, *Troublesome Border*; Metz, *Border*; Wilkinson, *Laredo and the Rio Grande Frontier*; McWilliams, *North from Mexico*; and Taylor, *An American-Mexican Frontier*. From a Mexican perspective, see Bosch García, *Historia de las*

*relaciones entre México y los Estados Unidos*; García Cantú, *Las invasiones norte-americanas en México*; and Zorrilla, *Historia de las relaciones entre México y Estados Unidos de América*. For recent works that stress the cooperation and linkages among peoples of the borderlands, see Cerutti and González Quiroga, *El norte de Mexico y Texas (1848–1880)*; Truett and Young, *Continental Crossroads*; Young, *Catarino Garza's Revolution on the Texas-Mexico Border*; and McManus, *The Line Which Separates*. Most laypeople do not read scholarly works; they are more likely to see films. In her essay in this volume, "Projecting the In-Between: Cinematic Representations of National Borders in North America, 1908–1940," Dominique Brégent-Heald demonstrates that, in many films, borders are areas generally associated with violence.

4. Martínez, *Troublesome Border*, 80–81.

5. Wilkinson, *Laredo and the Rio Grande Frontier*, 331.

6. Convenient summaries of the findings of two separate commissions, sent by the United States and Mexico to study the border violence, may be found in Rippy, *The United States and Mexico*, 286–87; and Metz, *Border*, 159–64.

7. Tyler, "The Callahan Expedition of 1855," 574–85. In a recent article, Sean Kelley shows that many slaves associated Mexico with freedom, investing the border with "a set of meanings that formed the core of an oppositional culture, shaping numerous acts of resistance" (Kelley, "Mexico in His Head," 709).

8. Herrera, *El norte de Tamaulipas y la conformación de la frontera México–Estados Unidos*, 42. For a variant of this relationship between borderland elites and the state, see note 13 below.

9. Many of the approximately four thousand Mexicans who participated in the two armies came from the states of northeastern Mexico (see Thompson, *Mexican Texans in the Union Army*; and Thompson, *Vaqueros in Blue and Gray*). For the participation of Texas volunteers in the Federalist Wars, see Nance, *After San Jacinto*, 142, 152, 248.

10. Rippy, "Border Troubles along the Rio Grande," 94–96. The Carvajal Revolt illustrates the collision in the borderlands of two competing forces; in *Changing National Identities at the Frontier*, Andrés Reséndez has observed that the "Mexican state and American markets collided at the frontier, often pulling in opposite directions, and thus forced the frontier population to confront a remarkably consistent set of identity choices and tensions" (3–4).

11. Chance, *Jose Maria de Jesus Carvajal*, 142.

12. A good discussion of the Ord Order and the process of pacification of the border is found in Cosío Villegas, *Historia moderna de Mexico*, 5–6:64, 76–77, 190, 229–31.

13. Baud and Van Schendel provide a somewhat hazy schema for the interaction of borderland elites with their respective national states, but they do not take

into account the fact that, in helping Porfirio Díaz gain power, it was non-national borderland elites who played a prominent role (see Baud and Van Schendel, "Toward a Comparative History of Borderlands," 217–19, 235). For the role of the Brownsville merchants in supporting Porfirio Díaz, see Hart, *Revolutionary Mexico*, 122–23, 127.

14. For a history of this commerce, see the masterful doctoral dissertation by Graf, "The Economic History of the Lower Rio Grande Valley."

15. Nance, *After San Jacinto*, 155–56.

16. According to Weber, the Mexican silver peso, which was roughly equivalent to the American dollar, became the principal medium of exchange in Missouri and helped to stabilize the monetary situation of the western territories of the United States (see Weber, *La frontera norte de México*, 185).

17. Nance, *After San Jacinto*, 490.

18. "Proclama," 13 April 1841, Matamoros Archives, vol. 38, box 2Q275, p. 196, Center for American History, University of Texas at Austin [hereafter cited as CAH].

19. Nance, *After San Jacinto*, 438.

20. Herrera, *El norte de Tamaulipas y la conformación de la frontera México–Estados Unidos*, 49–52. Ample evidence of the contraband trade and the defiance of national policies by border residents is provided in Green, "The Texas Revolution and the Rio Grande Border."

21. Kingsbury to Warren, June 1860, Gilbert Kingsbury Papers and Memoirs, box 2R72, CAH. For information on Stillman, King, and Kennedy, see Hart, *Revolutionary Mexico*, 105–28; for data on Kleiber, see Joseph Kleiber Papers, CAH.

22. *Corpus Christi Star*, 19 September 1848. Leyendecker left a vast trove of documents that detail his commercial and other activities and his ties to Mexico and Mexicans. They are found in the John Z. Leyendecker Papers, CAH.

23. Mayer, "San Antonio, Frontier Entrepôt," 492; Chabot, *With the Makers of San Antonio*, 380–81.

24. Lackman, "George T. Howard." Both Lacoste and Twohig left collections of documents that are housed in the CAH.

25. Quoted in Nance, *After San Jacinto*, 464. It is believed that Kinney was killed in Matamoros during a gunfight between two factions in which he had no part. For a man who had survived and prospered by not taking sides, this must surely rank as one of the supreme ironies in border history. Kinney's reference to accommodation with Indians, Anglos, and Mexicans raises important issues of identity among the people of the border region. Reséndez argues that the choices that borderlanders made with respect to their identity commonly followed a "situational logic"; a person was "not a mission Indian *or* a Mexican, a black slave in Mexico *or* an American, a foreign-born colonist

*or* a Texan, but could be either depending on who was asking" (Reséndez, *Changing National Identities at the Frontier*, 3; emphasis in original).

26. Cerutti, *Burguesía, capitales & industria en el norte de México*, 54–57.

27. Twohig to Madero, 13 January 1881, Twohig Papers, box 3N3, CAH. See also Cerutti, *Burguesía, capitales & industria en el norte de México*, 57–58.

28. Santleben, *A Texas Pioneer*. For Santiago Lincoln, see the James Lincoln Papers, Daughters of the Republic of Texas Library, San Antonio, Texas; for Ulrich, see reel 1, Microfilm M165: Consular Despatches, Monterrey, 1849–1906 [hereafter cited as M165], Record Group 59: Records of the U.S. Department of State [hereafter cited as RG 59], National Archives and Records Administration, Washington, D.C. [hereafter cited as NARA 1].

29. For more on nineteenth-century labor migration, see Cerutti and González Quiroga, *El norte de Mexico y Texas (1848–1880)*.

30. See the *Telegraph and Texas Register* for 7 October 1846 (p. 5) and 1 June 1846, both in the Matamoros Archive, vol. 55, box 2Q 279, p. 165, CAH. Rip Ford, a legendary Indian fighter and Texas public figure, wrote that many peons from Mexican haciendas "were hired by our quartermaster at thirty dollars a month" (see *Rip Ford's Texas*, 214).

31. It should be recalled that these were years in which the Know-Nothing Party was making inroads in Texas and calling for the expulsion of Mexicans, many of whom were driven from various Texas counties (see Montejano, *Anglos and Mexicans in the Making of Texas*, 28; and Crews, "The Know-Nothing Party in Texas," 48). The evidence for Mexican migration throughout the 1850s is to be found in eyewitness reports; see the *Corpus Christi Star* for 19 September 1848. It can also be deduced by analyzing the census figures. Although there is no reliable data for 1850, the statistics for 1860 reveal that about two-thirds of the Mexican population had been born outside of Texas (see Zamora, *The World of the Mexican Worker in Texas*, 211).

32. For wages for farm work in Montemorelos, see Estadísticas, Montemorelos (23 February 1843), box 2, Archivo General del Estado de Nuevo León; for wages in Texas, see, Montejano, *Anglos and Mexicans in the Making of Texas*, 78.

33. "Informe Anual de 1850," Estadísticas, Montemorelos, box 2, Archivo General del Estado de Nuevo León.

34. Gonzaléz Navarro, *Anatomía del poder en México*, 150–51.

35. The historiography of the Civil War trade through the Río Bravo is vast. A synthesis is provided in Cerutti and González Quiroga, *Frontera e historia económica*. Lead is an example of one of the items Mexico could provide that were essential to the Confederacy. The U.S. consul in Monterrey, understandably, wanted this traffic stopped. He wrote to Washington: "The only lead the rebels west of the Mississippi get comes from Mexico. The blockade of the

frontier of Texas would do more good to our cause in Texas than an army of ten thousand men sent into the state" (Kimmey to State Department, 21 May 1864, reel 1, M165, RG 49, NARA 1).

36. Irby, "Line of the Rio Grande," 76–77, 100. Irby writes that freighters were making five or six times more than before the Civil War. This is an early use of *enganchadores*, or labor recruiters, who would be prominent during the Porfiriato. Pressure from business interests to maintain a free flow of labor across American borders are also described in the studies of Jennifer Seltz and Andrea Geiger, in this volume.

37. Ramírez, "The Vaquero and Ranching," 105–7; Montejano, *Anglos and Mexicans*, 54–55, 60.

38. De Leon, *La comunidad tejana*, 82; Calvert and De Leon, *The History of Texas*, 163; Taylor, *An American-Mexican Frontier*, 71, 100.

39. During times of crisis, like the U.S. Civil War, the tolerance toward Mexicans was greater. This is illustrated by the case of Vicente Hernández, who, as a resident of San Antonio, was hauled into court for refusing conscription into the Confederate Army. Hernández argued that he was a citizen of Mexico and his loyalty was to his native country. The court sided with him because, according to the judge, it was necessary to "cultivate friendly relations" with Mexico, "which government had afforded us every facility for obtaining munitions of war, which we so much needed, whilst other nations had shown an unfriendly disposition" (*San Antonio News*, 14 May 1864).

40. Rankin, *Twenty Years among the Mexicans*, 106–9. A biography of Rankin is provided in the introduction to the 2008 edition of this book, originally published in 1875.

41. Ibid., 130–49; Westrup, *Principios*, 45.

42. Thompson's vital role in the mission movement in Mexico can be traced through his correspondence with the Presbyterian Church of the United States; see Correspondence and Reports, 1833–1911, reels 162–66, Board of Foreign Missions, Presbyterian Church in the United States of America, Benson Latin American Collection, University of Texas at Austin.

43. Bastian, *Los disidentes*, 311, 313; Bastian, "Las sociedades protestantes y la oposición a Porfirio Díaz en México," 143.

44. Nañez, *History of the Rio Grande Conference of the Methodist Church*, 42–45, 47–48.

45. Several harrowing experiences are described in Rankin, *Twenty Years among the Mexicans*, 150–60.

46. Historian James Crisp has written that "interethnic alliances along class lines based on mutual economic interests at times proved stronger than the pride and prejudice of race" (Crisp, "Race, Revolution, and the Texas Republic," 41).

47. See Baud and Van Schendel for a discussion of a framework created by Oscar

Martínez that outlines four models of borderland interaction. The models reflect borderlands that are alienated, coexistent, interdependent, and integrated, with levels of animosity and conflict being greater in the first model and gradually diminishing as the borderlands become integrated. The lower Río Bravo seems to defy this scheme, because there conflict and interdependence were concurrent (Baud and Van Schendel, "Toward a Comparative History of Borderlands," 220).

48. Adelman and Aron, "From Borderlands to Borders"; Truett and Young, *Continental Crossroads*. It should be noted that Adelman and Aron argue that "borders formalized but did not foreclose the flow of people, capital, and goods. . . . International boundaries remained dotted lines that took a generation to solidify" (840).

## BETWEEN RACE
## AND NATION

The Creation of a
Métis Borderland on
the Northern Plains

..........................................

Michel Hogue

I am now 56 years of age," Joseph Laverdure told Roger Goulet in 1895.
"I have lived at Wood Mountain on the 15th July 1870, I was there with
many other people, we had left St. Joe North Dakota in May 1870." As
Laverdure began his schematic account of his family history and their
migration from North Dakota across the border into Canada, Goulet wrote
it down. An official with the Canadian Dominion Lands Commission,
Roger Goulet had been sent to record the stories of people like Joseph
Laverdure, mixed-race Métis residents of Belcourt, North Dakota, whose
families had roots in Canada and who had outstanding claims against the
Canadian government. This was not Goulet's first such encounter. He had
been a member of the traveling commissions that had held hearings
between 1885 and 1887 weighing Métis claims. In the 1880s, many Métis
residents of Canada's North-West Territories had applied for scrip, negotiable certificates redeemable in land or cash, which purported to extinguish their Aboriginal title to the lands of the Canadian West formerly
held by the Hudson's Bay Company (HBC). Goulet understood the complications involved in such claims as well as anyone. He had made several
trips in the preceding few years to North Dakota to investigate a series of
applications for half-breed scrip on which the Scrip Commission had
withheld judgment. At issue: whether applicants like Laverdure were in
Canada or the United States on July 15, 1870, the date Canada assumed
control of HBC lands. Canadian government policy dictated that anyone
who had resided outside HBC lands on that date was not eligible for scrip.[1]

The stories Goulet recorded revealed a complicated trans-border network of Métis families whose lives straddled the 49th parallel in the 1870s. For example, Joseph Laverdure was a plains hunter who had lived and hunted buffalo on both sides of the border. Born in the Red River settlement in Canada, he had eventually relocated to St. Joseph, Dakota Territory, in the 1850s. From there, Laverdure and his family ventured forth as part of the large, organized Métis buffalo-hunting camps. It was the continued search for buffalo, which were becoming increasingly rare on the northeastern Plains, that led them west. Laverdure and about one hundred other Métis families packed all of their possessions, oxen, horses, and carts and left in May 1870 for Wood Mountain, located some 270 miles west and just north of the 49th parallel. Goulet worked to trace these movements. In addition to recording Métis memories, he also searched the parish registers and interviewed the Roman Catholic clergy for any clues about the timing of the departure of the "St. Joe people" for Canada. Even so, Goulet was unable to establish with any great certainty whether the St. Joseph Métis had lived north of the border in July 1870 and whether they might properly be termed "Canadian" or "American."[2]

Goulet's search underscored the difficulty of determining the nationality of the itinerant Plains Métis. Laverdure and his fellow travelers were part of the clusters of Métis settlements that formed and dissolved across the northern Plains in the 1860s and 1870s as transitory communities of mixed-race buffalo hunters spread westward from their homes in Manitoba and Dakota Territory. They did so at a moment when nation-states consolidated their hold on the northern Great Plains and supplanted the fur trade economies and societies in which Métis people were involved. Their ambiguous nationality, mixed racial heritage, and close relations with Plains Indians challenged the more restrictive notions of territory and discrete, state-sponsored ethnic identities new states sought to enforce. Métis attempts to reestablish themselves in the Plains borderlands ran headlong into the more determined efforts by national governments to mark and enforce the boundary between Canada and the United States as well as racial/ethnic boundaries among their respective citizens.[3]

Goulet's investigations into the life histories of Métis borderlanders attempted to sort out who, on the basis of both their indigenous ancestry and their nationality, had outstanding claims against the Canadian government. Instead, they revealed how preexisting territorial arrangements based in kin relations and fur trade economies—like those described by Saler and Podruchny in this volume—confounded the precise national and racial classifications government officials sought to apply. The presence of trans-border Plains Métis communities destabilized the criteria officials used to assign racial and national markers. As a result, federal efforts to make racial or ethnic boundaries correspond with the crisp territorial divisions etched on maps foundered on the unruly realities of the borderlands.[4]

This essay focuses on the cross-border Plains Métis trade networks and wintering settlements that so muddied the results of Goulet's investigations. These networks, I argue, also complicated federal efforts to secure the territorial sovereignty of the nation, as well as federal Indian policies aimed at administering newly incorporated Indian peoples. Specifically, the Métis presence undermined the race-based criteria that underpinned the creation of Indian reservations/reserves in both the United States and Canada.[5] As important, the continued power of local Indian peoples, such as the Assiniboines and Gros Ventres of Montana's Fort Belknap Agency, to assert their own criteria for belonging to the reservation exposed the limits of federal efforts. Kin ties between the Métis and indigenous peoples in the borderlands, and older exchange patterns rooted in fur trade economies, continued to vex the attempts to mark the lines between races and between nations.

### Creating a Métis Borderland

The history of the Métis and their migration in growing numbers onto the Plains is intimately linked with that the fur trade, and especially the trade in buffalo robes and provisions. Fur trade unions between European men and indigenous women (usually Cree or Ojibwa) in the Great Lakes and Canadian Northwest solidified trade and diplomatic relations between Natives and newcomers. The women and men who formed them became cultural brokers, and facilitated the flow of furs from indigenous trappers and goods from European posts. Their mixed-race children, the Métis, continued these roles. The Métis were central to the expansion of the fur trade across the Northwest, especially as the Montreal-based North West Company (NWC) tried to undercut the trading monopoly over Rupert's Land (encompassing the Hudson Bay watershed) that had been guaranteed to the HBC under its 1670 royal charter. The far-flung network of NWC posts increased the demand for Métis labor and for the furs and subsistence goods needed to keep the posts supplied. By the end of the eighteenth century, the Métis had become the central provisioners of many of the fur trade posts in the Canadian interior.[6]

The merger of the rival HBC and NWC trade empires in 1821 and the subsequent retrenchment by the HBC sharply reduced the opportunities for the Métis within the trade. In response, large numbers of the Métis migrated to the Red River settlement, a colony originally established in 1811 at the confluence of the Red and Assiniboine Rivers. The settlement became a new Métis homeland, providing families with the chance to practice small-scale agriculture, as well as continued opportunities to hunt buffalo and to sell the meat and other products to the HBC. The establishment of a separate geographic, economic, and cultural space at Red River, historian Heather Devine argues, allowed a distinct Plains Métis consciousness to flourish.[7]

From their inception, the Métis settlements at Red River were entangled with the 49th parallel. The Convention of 1818 had set the international boundary from Lake of the Woods to the summit of the Rocky Mountains at the 49th parallel. In the early 1820s, the HBC shut its post at Pembina, one of the first Plains Métis communities, when surveys determined that the settlement was located just south of that boundary. The company feared that the Métis living there would take advantage of their residence in the United States to undermine its trade monopoly, and thus pressured the Pembina Métis to resettle north of the border. While most did relocate, growing numbers found their way south again in the 1840s. Their return coincided with the opening of a trading post at Pembina by Norman Kittson, a U.S.-based trader. Kittson's post provided an alternative market to that of the HBC and became a magnet for young Métis men who smuggled furs across the border. Plains Métis involvement in this cross-border trade effectively toppled the HBC's trade monopoly.[8]

In the middle decades of the nineteenth century, ever greater numbers of Métis responded to the economic opportunities that accompanied the expansion of U.S. markets south of the 49th parallel. For many, a successful summer or autumn hunt—that is, one that had satisfied their material wants—had long meant that hunting families could avoid making a winter hunting trip. A new demand for bison robes at American posts, however, transformed economic equations for hunting families

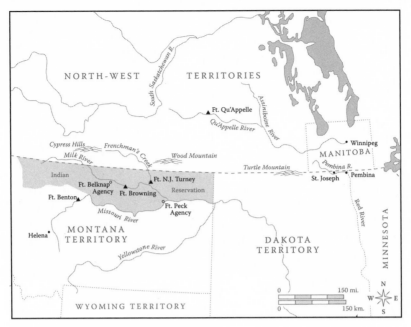

**Map 1.** The Northern Plains. (Map by Ezra Zeitler)

and their annual cycles. Since bison robes could only be taken in the winter, when the animal's coat was at its thickest, and when the bison herds scattered in search of forage, the would-be bison hunters began to establish small, scattered, wintering sites, or *hivernements*, across the northeastern Plains.[9]

The region bound on the south by the Milk and Missouri Rivers and on the north by the Cypress Hills and Wood Mountain, and bisected by the 49th parallel, became a favored destination for Métis traders, hunters, and winterers. Métis traders first began to visit it and the Plains Indian bands who congregated there in the 1830s. In the winter of 1868–69, Métis hunters from settlements in both the United States and Canada became the first Métis winterers to establish wintering sites in the Wood Mountain area.[10] Two years later, in 1870, the Métis population surged when Joseph Laverdure and about one hundred other Métis families, or approximately a thousand people, left their homes in Dakota Territory and Red River in the spring for Wood Mountain.[11]

Métis migrations were both a response to the contraction of the bison herds that were the center of their economic world and to the shifting

**Figure 1.** Half-breed traders. (Archives of Manitoba, Boundary Commission [1872–1874] 165 [N11932])

social and political climates in their homes. The influx of land-seekers into Red River and eastern Dakota Territory destabilized older fur trade economies and societies. In 1869, rumors that the HBC had sold its lands to Canada caused a group of Métis nationalists led by Louis Riel to prevent the newly appointed governor of the colony from taking power and to form their own provisional government. The armed Métis resistance to the transfer eventually secured, among other things, guarantees of Métis religious and linguistic rights and a 1.4 million acre land grant. The Manitoba Act, passed by the Canadian Parliament in 1870, enshrined these protections in legislation. But many of the Métis successes were short-lived. Harassment at the hands of Anglo-Canadian troops sent to occupy the province and long delays in implementing the land grants promised under the act led many Métis to leave their Red River homelands for settlements in the West.[12]

As older fur trade empires frayed at the edges, the familial and economic arrangements that had underpinned them continued and simultaneously exposed the limits of nation-states and the difficulties they faced in overwriting preexisting local political and cultural maps.[13] The pursuit of the buffalo and trade opportunities in the Plains borderlands created a dense, trans-border network of ties that bound Métis families across the

49th parallel. Large extended families often migrated together, or followed in later chain migrations. Joseph Laverdure, for example, traveled with his family and that of his father and brother in a pattern that typified the kin-based nature of Métis migration. They settled in small, flexible units where kinship continued to determine membership. Such flexibility allowed for their subsequent division or reconstitution as environmental or other conditions allowed.[14] In the following years, the region's Métis families formed a shifting network of communities in the trans-border region. Kin, community, and environment offered their own organizing logic that frequently did not coincide with the more exclusive notions of territory and belonging that nation-states sought to impose.

Indeed, the genealogies of the people within these communities blurred the lines that federal officials would later use in their effort to distinguish members of different "races." By the 1860s, intermarriage between the Plains Métis and indigenous peoples occurred much less frequently than it had decades earlier. These ties, however, remained important. Their shared ancestry with the Crees, Assiniboines, and Ojibwas helped some Métis families gain access to their distant relatives' camps and to their hunting territories more generally.[15] Such relations did not guarantee harmony. Cooperation could just as easily give way to conflict as indigenous Plains peoples began to resent the intrusions of all outsiders on their lands. The fur trader Isaac Cowie noted, in 1868, that the Crees, Assiniboines, and Ojibwas who congregated in present-day southern Saskatchewan admitted small numbers of Métis within their camps but kept a watchful eye on their movements. According to Cowie, the Indians objected to the growing Métis presence and their assault on the buffalo herds.[16] These complaints multiplied as the Plains Métis population exploded and competition for access to the buffalo herds intensified.

That Métis migrations hinged on constant negotiations with other Plains peoples underscores the extent to which U.S. and Canadian control of the Plains borderlands in the 1860s remained elusive. Even as these two states evinced a growing determination to regulate Métis cross-border movement and the terms of their belonging within those states, these efforts were profoundly uneven. Canadian claims to the northwestern Plains were particularly tenuous. Having only acquired Rupert's Land from the HBC in 1870, there was no official Canadian presence on the southwestern Canadian Prairies until the North-West Mounted Police arrived in

1874. The Canadian government was also slow to extinguish Aboriginal title to HBC land. It was only in 1874 and 1876 that the Crees, Assiniboines, and Ojibwas of present-day Alberta and Saskatchewan concluded treaties with the Canadian government. Even so, several years elapsed before the government began to set aside reserves and to make provisions for their support. Thus, the Métis who left the postage-stamp province of Manitoba in the early 1870s inhabited a territory in which Canadian claims of sovereignty were weak and indigenous claims paramount.

In the United States, by contrast, the Métis became enmeshed in federal measures designed to administer the newly organized Montana Territory and to secure its boundaries as well as the boundaries of the Indian lands within it. The 1860s witnessed dramatic transformations in Montana. Settlers streamed into the territory following the discovery of gold in the Yellowstone country. The rush to the Montana goldfields sparked conflict with Plains peoples such as the western Sioux (Lakota) and Cheyenne, who responded to the rush of migrants across their lands by waging a successful campaign against the construction of army posts along the Bozeman Trail. Even though the federal government had set aside the lands between the Missouri and the international boundary as an Indian reservation, the designation provided little guarantee against white encroachments. Indeed, the entry of newcomers into the profitable (but illegal) liquor trade with indigenous peoples heightened the potential for conflict. The threat of continued clashes between Natives and newcomers brought federal Indian policy in the territory into sharp focus.[17]

### Confounding the Boundary Line: The Métis in Montana

The first Métis traders who arrived in Montana in the late 1860s experienced the early efforts by officials in the United States to regulate trade and access between indigenous peoples on Montana reservations and outsiders. Federal officials in Montana evinced a growing determination to enforce the provisions of the 1834 Intercourse Law that governed trade between Indians and non-Indians in the United States. Specifically, the act restricted trade with Indians to federally licensed and bonded traders, levied stiff fines for trading liquor with Indians, and prohibited the entry of foreigners into "Indian Country." These prohibitions dated back to the earliest days of the republic, when the intertwined problems of unregulated trade with Indians (especially the trade in alcohol) and encroachments by foreign fur traders upon U.S. territory, prompted a series of trade and intercourse laws that attempted to delineate the boundary between Indians and whites, as well as to shore up the nation's boundaries.[18] U.S. officials took aim at the Métis trade networks they believed undermined national territorial sovereignty and the government's assimilationist policies, which aimed to segregate Indian peoples on Indian reservations.

Reports in the late 1860s from U.S. Indian Affairs officials that itinerant Métis traders were crossing the border to trade liquor on the Montana Indian reservation were among a growing chorus of complaints from federal officials stationed in Montana about the widespread trade in liquor with the region's Indians and the demoralizing effects of the trade.[19] Here, as in the Río Bravo region along the Texas-Mexico border, contraband helped stitch borderland populations together across the international boundary. But Métis traders who ventured onto the reservation to do business with the burgeoning Métis and Indian populations were increasingly subject to fines, imprisonment, and the seizure of their goods, on the basis that they had "smuggled" goods across the border and were trading with Indians on an Indian reservation without a license. On several occasions during the late 1860s, U.S. deputy marshals raided Métis camps in search of traders violating U.S. laws. For example, in the fall of 1867, Deputy Marshal John X. Beidler confiscated goods worth $15,000 from traders Antoine Gladue and James Francis, set fire to their cabins, and expelled them from the country. Beidler returned the following year and arrested another Métis trader, who had crossed the border from Canada hoping to trade for buffalo robes. Beidler's actions underscored the overriding concern among officials with the (illegal) trade Métis traders conducted with local Indians on the northern Montana Indian reservation and their determination to bar all foreigners from trading with Indians. At the same time, however, Beidler also enabled the more permanent presence of Métis settlements on the Indian reservation. In what would become a pattern for most of the following decade, Beidler expelled the traders but allowed their Métis clients to remain on the reservation.[20]

U.S. officials were equally concerned about another aspect of Métis trade: the trade in ammunition between Métis and Sioux. Since the Dakota Uprising in Minnesota in 1862, the Métis had been important trading partners with the Sioux. In the aftermath of the conflict, U.S. officials routinely accused the Métis and British traders with supplying arms and ammunition to the Sioux, and even fomenting further hostilities with U.S. troops. During the remainder of the decade, Santees, Yanktons, Yanktonais, and even some western Sioux, migrated in increasing numbers into the Milk River country of northern Montana. In so doing, they maintained close ties with the Métis whose westward migration occurred in tandem with that of these groups. The unwillingness of chiefs like Crazy Horse and Sitting Bull to cede claims to their lands added to U.S. concerns about the growing numbers of Sioux in northern Montana. The Montana press, in turn, seized upon the issue, publicizing the growing threat of hostilities between the Sioux and the Northern Pacific Railroad surveyors who first arrived in the Yellowstone Valley in the autumn of 1871 to plot its route. Trade between Métis and the Sioux, the *Helena Weekly Herald* claimed, threatened the completion of the Northern Pacific Railroad and the security of "the exposed frontiers of the Territory."[21] Army and territorial officials contended that the contraband, especially the arms and ammunition Métis traders brought from north of the border, aggravated a volatile situation.[22]

The charge that the liquor and ammunition the Métis traded with the Hunkpapa and Teton Sioux encouraged them to wage war and undermined the Indian Department's peace efforts prompted Indian Department officials to call for army assistance to stop the trade. In October 1871, Jaspar Viall, Montana's superintendent of Indians, called for the expulsion of sixty to seventy families of Métis and Santee Sioux who had settled along Frenchman's Creek just south of the 49th parallel in order to conduct their winter buffalo hunts. Army officials obliged, sending Captain H. B. Freeman and troops from the U.S. 7th Infantry to take possession of the camp, spill all liquor found there, destroy any houses or valuable goods, and drive the traders out of the country with a warning not to return.[23] Early on the morning of November 2, 1871, Freeman and his troops laid siege to the Métis camp. The soldiers then set fire to the storehouses and dwellings belonging to the traders in the settlement. In all, the soldiers burned eight buildings, turning the goods they did not destroy over to U.S. Deputy Marshal Charles Hard, who also accompanied the party.[24]

The raid on the Frenchman's Creek settlement in 1871 was a rude reminder of the growing federal presence in the region and of their efforts to consolidate their hold over the territory. As Captain Freeman had explained to the Métis, selling liquor and ammunition to Indians and purchasing stolen goods from them violated U.S. trade laws and would no longer be tolerated. The Métis insisted that they had no intention of violating U.S. laws, and instead fingered the traders who had settled among them for trading with Indians. The Métis residents of the Frenchman's Creek settlement insisted, in a letter to the lieutenant-governor for Manitoba and the North-West Territories, Adams Archibald, that their camp had been located some thirty-five miles north of the border, in Canadian territory. Their claims became the basis for an investigation into whether the U.S. Army had conducted its operations on Canadian soil.[25] In the meantime, the Métis secured permission from Milk River Indian agent Andrew Simmons to remain on the reservation, in exchange for the promise not to allow any traders into their camps in the future and to keep their distance from agency Indians.[26]

The persistence of cross-border trade networks and the persistent Métis presence on the reservation led to renewed federal efforts to restrict both. Three years later, Métis and Santee Sioux families continued to camp together along the banks of Frenchman's Creek, and U.S. officials continued to blame the Métis for smuggling arms, ammunition, and liquor from Canada into the hands of related Sioux groups. By 1874, relations between the Sioux and the U.S. government had deteriorated further still. Conflicts had erupted over the continued advancement of the railroad survey in 1872 and 1873. Then, in 1874, Lt. Colonel George Armstrong Custer led a military expedition into the Black Hills, sparking a rush of gold prospectors into territory guaranteed to the Sioux under the terms of the 1868 Fort Laramie Treaty, an area the Sioux considered the center of their land. These actions and the continued Sioux refusal to cede their lands or report to agencies established under the treaty set the stage for the outbreak of the Great Sioux War two years later.[27]

Sworn statements by the Indian Department interpreter at Fort Peck that Métis traders at Frenchman's Creek were using Santee Sioux intermediaries to supply arms and ammunition to the Teton and Yanktonai Sioux in and around the agency led U.S. Marshal Charles Hard back to Frenchman's Creek in early May, 1874.[28] U.S. Deputy Marshal Hard again arrived in the middle of the night and surprised two traders who were living in the mixed Métis, Sioux, and Assiniboine settlement there. He seized goods belonging to Métis traders François and Antoine Ouellette, and to Jean Louis Legaré, a French Canadian trader who had formerly worked for Antoine Ouellette. The personal losses for those involved were again staggering. Legaré and Ouellette claimed to have lost over $9,000 worth of furs, buffalo robes, and dry goods. Other traders were more fortunate and once again eluded Hard's capture by slipping across the border to Wood Mountain.[29]

The traders whose goods Hard confiscated responded as they had in 1871: they insisted that they had been in Canadian, not U.S. territory, and protested to officials in Canada that Hard had exceeded his jurisdiction by crossing the border and confiscating their goods. Claims by François Ouellette and Jean Louis Legaré to Lieutenant Governor Alexander Morris (Archibald's successor) spawned another set of diplomatic exchanges but failed to bring about any restitution of their losses. In the end, Morris accepted that the Métis settlement was located well within the United States and that Métis claims otherwise were merely calculated to avoid prosecution.[30] The diplomatic correspondence surrounding these conflicting claims underscored the continued ambiguity about the precise location of the international boundary. As in 1871, when the Métis appealed to officials on both sides of the border following the first raid on Frenchman's Creek, the precise location of the boundary remained largely a matter of conjecture in spring 1874, since boundary surveyors only reached the region later that summer. The encounters on Frenchman's Creek both underscored how national claims to the region were contested and exposed the limits of official knowledge about the Plains borderlands.

The persistent Métis presence, meanwhile, suggested that Métis communities in northern Montana were an important part of the region's human landscape. After all, the raids in 1871 and 1874 had targeted traders and left the Métis families who traded with them alone. Those who remained could continue to trade at federally licensed trading posts such as Fort N. J. Turney, on Frenchman's Creek, a trading post run by Francis Janeaux in the early 1870s. The Indian Bureau sanctioned and regulated the trade by Janeaux and others who worked for established U.S.-based trading firms like Leighton and Brothers through a system of permits meant to monitor the sales of arms, ammunition, and other supplies to Indians on the reservation. The post offered a ready market for their furs and robes and tied them to the vast U.S. market for such items. Although they operated outside this system and therefore faced periodic crackdowns

**Figure 2.** Sappers building Boundary Mound. (Archives of Manitoba, Boundary Commission [1872–1874] 148 [N11937])

by U.S. officials, independent Métis and Canadian traders continued to ply their goods on the margins of both the Indian reservation and the law.[31]

The presence of large numbers of Métis hunters looking to sell their robes, and traders who would both purchase them and supply the hunters with the goods they needed, created a mutually reinforcing set of conditions that underpinned Métis borderland communities. Estimates in 1874 put the number of Métis families living between Frenchman's Creek and Wood Mountain at 150. The combined Indian and Métis population totaled 400 families.[32] Even as Indian agent William Alderson ordered Charles Hard to break up the camps of Métis traders in the spring of 1874, his diary entries for the remainder of the year document continued visits by "half-breeds" to Fort Peck. Likewise, Thomas Bogy, an affiliate of Fort Benton-based T. C. Power and Company, recorded even more frequent interactions with Métis visitors to his Fort Belknap trading post beginning in the autumn of 1874. Indeed, the Métis remained important clientele at trading posts across northern Montana and often filled important positions as guides, laborers, and interpreters.[33]

Notwithstanding the complicated national allegiances that might have arisen from the personal and family histories of Métis borderlanders, officials in Canada and the United States both maintained that the Métis properly belonged north of the 49th parallel. For this reason, individual reprieves Indian agents issued did little to settle long-term questions about their status in the United States. Indeed, the persistent identification of the Métis as "Canadian" continued to have important ramifications for those who remained or returned to Montana as the decade wore on, especially as the federal presence on both sides of the border increased and the competition for resources among Plains peoples intensified.

### Contesting Boundaries on the Fort Belknap Reservation

As the Métis population in the trans-border region continued to increase, the calls for Métis exclusion came increasingly from the Indians assigned to northern Montana Indian agencies. For the Upper Assiniboines and Gros Ventres of the Milk River Valley, the contraction of the buffalo herds onto lands they considered their own, the subsequent influx of buffalo hunters, and the obvious dwindling of those herds, dramatically undermined their ability to provide for themselves. It also added urgency to their calls for government assistance in guaranteeing access to the buffalo herds and expelling those hunters they deemed foreign. By cultivating relationships with U.S. agents, and emphasizing their value as allies, the Assiniboines and Gros Ventres sought to leverage their relations with American officials in order to safeguard their position on the reservation and their access to vital resources.[34] In their calls for Métis expulsion, local and federal agendas coincided in their desire to define the boundaries of the Fort Belknap Indian Reservation and to decide who belonged within it.

Allegations that Métis settlers prevented agency Indians from hunting buffalo became a common refrain among agency Indians and one of the central arguments for Métis exclusion. Assiniboine chief Little Chief told U.S. Army Captain Constant Williams in February 1878 that approximately one hundred Métis families had settled on the Milk River during the previous summer and had kept the buffalo away by setting fire to the prairie. With no buffalo to be found near their camps, Little Chief explained to Williams that they did not dare hunt downriver for fear of the Sioux. Impressed by the dire circumstances the Assiniboines faced, Williams agreed that the Métis "trespassers" had reduced the Indians to the verge of starvation and ought to be removed.[35]

By securing U.S. assistance, the Assiniboines looked to secure an advantage over their rivals in their struggle for security on the reservation. To seal his case, Little Chief provided an ultimatum of sorts. Unless the army sent soldiers "so that they could feel strong and have help against the Sioux," Little Chief warned, the Assiniboines would have little choice but to join forces with their enemies or to migrate north to Canada, where they claimed they would be assured asylum, regular annuities, and the ability to hunt in peace. Williams reminded his superiors that the Assiniboines were a bulwark of sorts against Sioux attacks and that their departure would only leave the Territory more exposed. He urged the army and the Indian Bureau to take immediate action to secure Assiniboine goodwill.[36]

Certainly, the burgeoning Métis population on the reservation, their prolific hunting, and their close relations with different branches of the Sioux meant that U.S. officials shared many of the concerns of agency Indians and were receptive to the calls for their expulsion. The arrival of thousands of Sioux who took refuge near Wood Mountain, just north of the 49th parallel, in the aftermath of the battle at Little Big Horn in June 1876, was particularly critical in heightening American resolve. With the buffalo almost entirely gone from Canadian soil, observers predicted that "refugee" Sioux incursions into the United States would only increase, and with them the chance for repeated clashes with U.S. forces.[37] As a result, the continued complaints from agency Indians about the "roving bands of hostile Indians" and "swarms of French and Canadian Half Breeds" who traded ammunition and liquor to the "hostile" Sioux prompted increasingly determined American responses. In April 1878, General Alfred Terry ordered that the officers visit the Métis camps in the Milk River Valley and notify them of the need "to remove to their own country" and never again to return to the reservation.[38]

The existence of the border helped mark the Métis as "foreign" and lent weight to arguments for exclusion. In the hands of Indian agents and army officials, Assiniboine and Gros Ventre complaints that the Métis interfered with their hunting or supported their enemies became calls for the removal of "foreign half-breeds."[39] Their alien status also underpinned the army's rationale for removing the Métis. General Terry contended that the Métis were British subjects and, as such, were subject to the penalties imposed on "foreigners" who entered Indian country without the required written permission from Interior Department or Indian Affairs officials.[40]

Determining who belonged on the reservation was a delicate business.

After all, the border also bisected the Assiniboines, leaving some bands in Canadian territory and others in the United States. Binationality created opportunities for playing one state against another. In this case, Little Chief attempted to use the promises from Canadian government officials to secure better terms from those in the United States.[41] But the Assiniboines were also subject to state efforts to determine belonging. Through the late 1870s Indian agents at the Fort Peck and Belknap agencies refused to count "British" Assiniboines as agency Indians, and in Canada, Assiniboine men and women who sought entry into Canadian treaties had to prove that they were not already included on U.S. tribal rolls.[42] Officials in both countries were content to read the border back into history, as if it had always divided the Assiniboines.

With personal genealogies and family histories that were entwined around the border, distinctions between "U.S." and "Canadian" Métis were equally arbitrary. Indeed, the Assiniboines and Gros Ventres argued that a group of forty "American half-breeds" living along the Milk River with their families should be allowed to remain on the reservation.[43] Included among them were families like the Azures, Laverdures, Klines, Fayants, and others whose genealogies linked them to Métis communities in Pembina, North Dakota, and even the Great Lakes region. More importantly, many were bound to the neighboring Assiniboine, Gros Ventre, and Piegan tribes through marriage.[44] One of the leaders of this group, Gabriel Azure, was the son of a French Canadian fur trader and an Assiniboine woman. Azure, along with members of his extended family, was among the Métis groups who had previously lived at Pembina and who had arrived in northern Montana to hunt and, in the late 1860s and early 1870s, to set up more permanent settlements.[45]

In this way, local understandings about belonging shaped decisions about who could remain. Because of their demonstrable ties to the local Assiniboine, Gros Ventres, or Yanktonai Indians, Gabriel Azure, Pierre Berger, and the members of their camps were allowed to remain on parts of the reservation. Indian agent Lincoln, too, sanctioned their presence there. Lincoln instructed the group that they could remain so long as they did not interfere with the Indians' hunting, did not trade with or allow any smugglers into their camps, and did not communicate with "hostile Indians," but rather, inform the authorities when any hostile parties crossed the line. Azure and his family were eventually incorporated onto the rolls of the Assiniboine band at the Fort Belknap Agency. Their inclusion reflected the U.S. government practice of only recognizing the Métis as members of "full-blood" Indian groups, so long as those groups consented to their inclusion.[46]

The distinctions the Assiniboines and Gros Ventres drew between the Métis guided army practices. In October 1878, agency Indians renewed their complaints that increasing numbers of Métis had returned and were once again driving away the buffalo and trading with the Sioux. Accordingly, army officials in Montana instructed Major Guido Ilges to remove the Métis from the Milk River Valley by force, leaving only the "American half-breeds" undisturbed.[47] In the first settlement he visited, Ilges found four "British" Métis living among the group of "American" Métis. Despite their claims that they were simply visiting relatives, Ilges ordered them away.[48] The army's efforts depended on the sharp distinction between "American" and "British" Métis, between those who were on the Assiniboines and Gros Ventres list and those who were not. The recurring presence of Canadian-born relatives on the reservation, however, suggests that Métis kin networks continued to transcend the boundary.

In fact, the warnings that "American" Métis gave to their "British" relatives nearly helped them elude capture. At the first encampment Ilges encountered as he swept the Milk River country for Métis settlements, he found only the deserted houses of Métis winterers who had fled in advance of the troops' arrival. Two days later, however, Ilges and his troops captured forty-six Métis with their carts and horses and marched them back to Fort Belknap. In order to underscore the U.S. government's resolve to keep foreigners off the Indian reservation, Ilges confiscated their horses and property and then escorted them to the border. At the same time, Ilges extracted from them a promise that they would not return to the Milk River country.[49]

If Ilges's actions rested on tenuous distinctions between "American" and "British," they nonetheless had important material consequences for the Métis he captured. The Métis returned to communities north of the border with the news that American soldiers would imprison anyone caught hunting on the reservation, as well as confiscate their goods and carts. During the winter of 1878–79, few animals were found north of the 49th parallel, and the absence of buffalo and other game became more acute during the following winters.[50] Despite the risks, many Métis hunters re-crossed the border in order to hunt the buffalo that were vital both to their commercial interests and the ways of life they had developed on the Plains. The Métis presence in Montana laid bare the difficulties in marking clear distinctions between Indians and non-Indians, as well as the enduring power local Indian people had in determining who belonged on the Indian reservation.

### The Métis and Canadian Treaties

The more determined attempts by U.S. officials to enforce the boundaries between Canada and the United States, Indians and non-Indians, convinced many Métis to negotiate with the Canadian government as a means to secure their future. Whereas the U.S. government never recognized the Métis as a distinct people, the Canadian government had extended such recognition through the Manitoba Act. But Canadian officials later equivocated in their guarantees of Métis rights and the designation of the Métis as a separate Aboriginal group. As in the United States, Métis populations in Canada complicated efforts to implement federal Indian policies that were premised on clear distinctions between Indian and non-Indian and the process of allocating land and regulating access to resources on the basis of racial identification.[51] But, as government policy took shape through the 1870s, those distinctions became more sharply drawn. Canadian officials weighed the claims to Aboriginality by the region's inhabitants, effectively drawing lines between Indians and Métis and determining the rights that would accrue to each. As in the United States, such boundary-setting sharply restricted opportunities for Plains Métis.

The effects of government efforts to distinguish between Indians and Métis became clear when the North-West Council, the appointed body the Canadian government had charged with the administration of local matters in the North-West Territories, enacted a series of restrictions on bison hunting on the Canadian Prairies that distinguished between Indian and non-Indian hunting rights. The council's 1877 "Ordinance for the Protection of the Buffalo" established a closed season between November 15 and August 15 when only Indians could hunt bison cows.[52] The ordinance thus prevented the Métis from engaging in their winter hunts when the bison robes were at their thickest, and thus threatened to shut them out of the lucrative buffalo robe trade. Such regulations not only cut to the heart of Plains Métis cultural practices, they also represented a significant economic threat, since the profits derived from the robe trade were critical to their subsistence.[53]

The Plains Métis vigorously protested the government's new law. Rumors of the proposed game laws had circulated across the Prairies for years, and the suggestion that Métis hunters might face seasonal or other restrictions had convinced many to cross the border into Montana, where no such restrictions were in place (and where the bison herds were much larger than in Canada).[54] With the legislation came more direct protests. The following year, 272 Métis men assembled in the Cypress Hills to ask the government for assistance and protested their exclusion from the bison hunt in terms that stressed their dependence on the hunt and their distinctiveness as Métis. Despite the differences between themselves and Indians, they argued, "the greater part of us have no more than the Indians the ability to amass sufficient provisions for five or six months in advance," and thus they asked the lieutenant-governor of the North-West Territories, David Laird, to accord to them "at least the same privileges that are granted the Indians regarding the chase."[55]

The Cypress Hills petitioners asked for many of the same rights guaranteed to Indians under the treaties concluded between Plains Indians and the Canadian government in the early 1870s. Chief among these was the request that the government set aside lands where Métis families could establish themselves permanently, free from the intrusions of white settlers. Specifically, the Métis asked the Canadian government to set aside a 150-x-50-mile tract of land lying immediately north of the 49th parallel and west of the Pembina River for their exclusive use and occupation. They also requested that the government exempt them from taxes and underwrite the cost of the schools, churches, instruction in trades, and agricultural assistance they needed in order to adopt "a life more conformable to a true civilization."[56] The urgency behind the Métis demands arose from both the bison's rapid demise north of the 49th parallel and the fact that Plains Métis communities were seemingly being left out of the treaties with the government. The Métis petitions reflected the need for the material benefits that treaties offered, especially in what must have seemed like a very uncertain future. They also represented a challenge of sorts to the emerging definitions of "Indians" and the boundaries of belonging they represented.

The relationship of Métis to Indians had long complicated treaty nego-

**Figure 3.** Buffalo. (Montana Historical Society, 981-115)

**Figure 4.** Buffalo skinning. (Montana Historical Society, 981-013)

tiations between Canadian First Nations and the government. Beginning with the negotiation of the Robinson Treaties in 1850 along the shores of Lakes Superior and Huron, Canadian policy dictated that people of mixed Indian-white descent could join treaties as members of Indian bands, but the Canadian government refused to grant treaty rights to separate Métis groups.[57] In 1869, however, the actions of the Louis Riel and the Red River Métis secured Canadian government recognition of Métis corporate rights as a distinct people whose Aboriginal ancestry gave them rights to land. But the benefits that were to flow from that recognition—namely, access to the 1.4 million acres allocated to them under the Manitoba Act to "extinguish" those rights—came in the form of individual land grants to be distributed to "half-breed" children and heads of family. To acknowledge the Métis as "special bands," J. A. N. Provencher, the Indian commissioner for Manitoba and the North-West argued, would be to create "a new class of inhabitants, placed between the Whites and the Indians—having, in a political and legal point of view, special and separate rights."[58] To avoid this, Alexander Morris asserted that half-breeds "must be either white or Indian. If Indians, they get treaty money; if the Half-breeds call themselves white, they get land."[59] For government officials, the choice was an either / or proposition: individuals had to select a single racial marker.

Yet, slotting peoples into neat organizational schemas often proved difficult in practice. For the Métis in the North-West Territories, there was no offer comparable to the land grants made to the Manitoba Métis in 1870. The problems that had attended the distribution of Métis lands in Manitoba, meanwhile, did little to allay Métis' anxieties and made treaties seem like a desirable option. The uncertainty and delay that surrounded the government's response to Métis claims in the Northwest encouraged many mixed-race peoples who may or may not have considered themselves culturally "Indian," to enter into the treaty as individual members of Indian bands for the economic benefits it offered.[60]

Canadian officials were decidedly cool to the Métis proposals for a reserve or other forms of assistance. By 1877, all Indian department officers in the field had apparently received instructions to prohibit the growing numbers of Métis from entering into treaties as separate bands.[61] The government's directive seemingly left little chance that the demands of the Cypress Hills petitioners for a reserve would receive a favorable hearing. Colonel J. S. Dennis, deputy minister of the Department of the Interior, argued that it was neither in the interest of Métis people nor in the country's interest to establish reserves for them.[62]

Not keen to see valuable lands "tied up" in additional reserves or to increase the number of federal wards, Canadian officials based their refusal to establish a separate Métis reserve on the border on the presumed racial differences separating Métis and Indians. Although the Métis petitioners carefully distinguished themselves from Indians, Colonel Dennis claimed that the Plains Métis who inhabited the Cypress Hills–Wood Mountain region "differ[ed] but little, excepting in name, from the Indians." To treat them as the government had treated Plains Indians, he reasoned, would only cause them to remain "in their present semi-barbarous state." Instead, he recommended that the government offer the Métis some inducements to learn to farm or raise cattle.[63] Similarly, Lieutenant-Governor David Laird told a group of Métis from northern Alberta who had petitioned him for assistance that the government's refusal to admit them into treaties was based on its wish to see them "enjoying the full franchises and property rights of British subjects, and not labouring under the Indian state of pupilage."[64]

The very in-between-ness of the Métis, particularly of the buffalo-hunting Plains Métis, befuddled Canadian policymakers. Despite the different history of the Métis north of the border and the guarantees they had secured in the aftermath of the 1869–70 North-West Resistance, they continued to occupy a legal and conceptual borderland. Federal officials allowed *individuals* of mixed indigenous and white descent who lived with and otherwise acted as Indians to be included in the treaties between the Canadian government and indigenous peoples in the Prairie West. But the government was unwilling to do the same for the Métis who formed culturally distinct Métis communities. In this way, Canadian policy echoed that of the U.S. Indian Bureau and of U.S. Army officials in Montana. Officials looked for kin or cultural ties to Indian bands in order to determine whether people of mixed descent were "Indian" or not. In the absence of such ties, the Plains Métis faced a narrowing set of options on both sides of the border.

By the summer of 1879, the choices the Métis borderlanders faced were increasingly stark. Whereas the Métis in Canada could secure no assurances from the Canadian government about their future, those who ventured into the United States faced continued army harassment. That summer, the Métis who continued to venture into Montana to hunt buffalo became embroiled in the army's efforts to stop the continued Sioux incursions into the United States and end the trade in ammunition, food, and other goods between them and the Métis. The stepped-up patrols ensnared hundreds of Métis families, and the expulsions from the reservation that followed attempted to accomplish by force what government policies had previously been unable to do: to separate "Canadian" and "American" Métis and banish "foreigners" from the Indian reservation altogether.

Brute force could not prevent the continued cross-border movement of the Métis and other indigenous peoples. So long as U.S. authorities continued to view the Métis as foreigners, regardless of their place of birth or the amount of time they had resided in the United States, Métis families were left to negotiate with both Indian bands and government representatives for a space on the northern Montana Indian reservation. The experience of the Métis in Montana demonstrates that the categories of belonging which indigenous peoples like the Assiniboines and Gros Ventres applied mattered a great deal in determining who would be allowed to remain in the United States. Their objections to Métis trade relations with the Sioux and Métis encroachment on hunting territories led the Indians at the Fort Belknap Agency to mark the Métis as foreigners and to call for army action to expel them. Only Métis families with recognized ties to the Assiniboines and Gros Ventres were permitted to remain. In Canada, officials concurred with American designations of the Métis as "Canadian" or "British," but wavered on the question of how to deal with their presence in the borderlands. In the absence of close ties to local indigenous peoples, officials denied Métis requests for admission into treaties or for rights guaranteed to indigenous peoples.

But, as Roger Goulet discovered decades later, race and nationality were not easily mapped onto Métis life histories. The density of ties across the border and ubiquitous Métis mobility meant that distinctions between "American" or "British" Métis were tenuous at best. The tactical use of the border by the Métis and the continued presence of large seasonal Métis encampments in U.S. territory, moreover, helped undermine those national designations and made the bureaucratic task of untangling these ties nearly impossible. At a moment when U.S. and Canadian efforts to organize and control the northwestern Plains were still in their infancy, Métis borderlanders exposed the limits of U.S. and Canadian policies that were meant to organize and administer newly incorporated Indian peoples. Their mixed ancestry and ongoing connections with Indian peoples compromised the policies that were premised on the existence of sharp (and self-evident) racial distinctions. Nowhere was this more true, perhaps, than along the international boundary, where conflicting claims regarding nationality complicated the already difficult task of sorting people according to their presumed "races." For the Métis, the lines between races and between nations were anything but clear-cut.

## Notes

1. Affidavit of Joseph Laverdure, 19 January 1895, file 367406, vol. 713, reel T-12442, Dominion Land Branch Files, Record Group 15: Records of the Department of Interior [hereafter cited as RG 15], Library and Archives Canada, Ottawa [hereafter cited as LAC]; R. Goulet to Unknown, 26 February 1895, ibid.; N. O. Coté to A. M. Burgess, 13 March 1895, ibid. Cf. R. Goulet to [unknown], 31 March 1890, file 138656, vol. 493, reel T-13172, ibid. Scholars continue to debate whether the Canadian government did in fact extinguish Métis title by issuing scrip (see Tough, *As Their Natural Resources Fail*, 140–41).

2. R. Goulet to Unknown, 26 February 1895, file 367406, vol. 713, reel T-12442, Dominion Lands Branch Files, RG 15, LAC.

3. Following the definitions used by the Métis National Council, I use the term "Métis" (with a capital "M") as "a socio-cultural or political term for those originally of mixed [Indian and European] ancestry who evolved into a distinct indigenous people." I recognize, however, that this risks imposing arbitrary ethnic labels on those individuals discussed in this essay, at a moment when those ethnic labels were very much in question. For a discussion of the complexities of Métis naming, see Peterson and Brown, Introduction to *The New Peoples*, 5–7.

4. Stoler, *Carnal Knowledge and Imperial Power*, 79; Cronon, Miles, and Gitlin, "Becoming West," 11–22. Cf. Harris, *Making Native Space*, xvii–xviii.

5. Perry, *On the Edge of Empire*, 71.

6. Peterson, "Many Roads to Red River," 37–73; Foster, "The Plains Métis," 420–21.

7. Devine, *The People Who Own Themselves*, 202–4.

8. Macleod and Morton, *Cuthbert Grant of Grantown*, 78; Spry, "The 'Private Adventurers' of Rupert's Land," 52–55; Ens, *Homeland to Hinterland*, 20–21, 38–40, 72–78.

9. Beal, Foster, and Zuk, *The Métis Hivernement Settlement at Buffalo Lake, 1872–1877*, 4, 82–83.

10. Ens, "The Border, The Buffalo, and the Métis of Montana," 143–44; Giraud, *The Métis in the Canadian West*, 2:403–5; Dobak, "Killing the Canadian Buffalo," 40–47; Loveridge and Potyondi, *From Wood Mountain to the Whitemud*, 58–61.

11. These population estimates are based on the lists of families who accompanied Joseph Laverdure in 1870 and the reports of Father Joseph-Jean-Marie Lestanc, which placed the size of Wood Mountain area communities at between 112 and 120 families in December 1870. See the affidavits of Isabelle Fagnant and Joseph Laverdure, in file 367406, vol. 713, RG 15, LAC; and Fr. Lestanc to Archbishop Taché, 1 December 1870, T8196–99, Alexandre-Antonin Taché Papers, Roman Catholic Archdiocese of Saint-Boniface, Saint-Boniface Historical Society, Saint Boniface, Man., Canada [hereafter cited as SBHS]. Scholars who have studied other Métis wintering communities during this era have placed the average family size at ten people (see Beal, Foster, and Zuk, *The Métis Hivernement Settlement at Buffalo Lake*).

12. For an overview of the 1869–70 Métis resistance at Red River, see Carter, *Aboriginal Peoples and Colonizers of Western Canada*, 105–11. For a description of Métis migrations, see Rivard and Littlejohn, *The History of the Métis of Willow Bunch*, 106–7; Rondeau Manuscript, 2–3, Musée de Willow Bunch Papers, file 2a, R-1145.1, Saskatchewan Archives Board, Regina.

13. McManus, *The Line Which Separates*, xi–xiii.

14. Foster, *We Know Who We Are*, 71; Hourie and Carrière-Acco, "Metis Families," 56.

15. Albers, "Changing Patterns of Ethnicity in the Northeastern Plains," 108–9.

16. Cowie, *The Company of Adventurers*, 302–3.

17. Burlingame, *The Montana Frontier*, 179–80; Dempsey, *Firewater*, 17–22. The 1855 treaty between the U.S. government and the Blackfeet, Bloods, Piegans, and Gros Ventres confirmed these lands as "Indian Country." In 1873, an executive order by President Ulysses S. Grant formally created the Indian reservation. Subsequent executive orders gradually whittled away at the reservation. Cf. Merrill Burlingame, "Political Divisions in Montana," 3–5, Merrill G. Burlingame Writings, Small Collection [hereafter cited as SC] 1244, Montana Historical Society Research Center, Helena [hereafter cited as MHS].

18. Prucha, *American Indian Policy in the Formative Years*, 77–78.

19. Geo. M. Penney to Nathan Sargeant, 1 September 1867, frames 833–36, reel 488, Microfilm M234: Letters Received by the Office of Indian Affairs [hereafter cited as M234], Record Group 75: Records of the Bureau of Indian Affairs [hereafter cited as RG 75], National Archives and Records Administration,

Washington, D.C. [hereafter cited as NARA I]; Secretary, Treasury Department to D. H. Browning, Secretary of the Interior, 30 October 1867, frames 827–29, reel 488, ibid.; W. J. Cullen to N. G. Taylor, 2 February 1869, frames 172–75, reel 489, ibid.; Dempsey, *Firewater*, 23–25.

20. Father Van den Broeck, "Sketch of Ben Kline's Life," Ben Kline Reminiscence, SC 942, MHS.

21. J. A. Viall to Lt. John Gibbons, 18 October 1871, file 1330 (1872), vol. 228, reel T-12177, Dominion Lands Branch Files, RG 15, LAC; *Helena Weekly Herald*, 16 November 1871 (reprinted in ibid.).

22. Geo. M. Penney to Nathan Sargeant, 1 September 1867, frames 833–36, reel 488, M234, RG 75, NARA I; McCrady, *Living with Strangers*, 27–28, chap. 4 passim.

23. The creek is known as Frenchman's or Whitemud Creek in Montana but appears as Rivière Blanche in the Canadian documents. J. A. Viall to Lt. John Gibbons, 18 October 1871, file 1330 (1872), vol. 228, reel T-12177, Dominion Lands Branch Files, RG 15, LAC; Captain H. B. Freeman to Acting Asst. Adjutant General, 27 November 1871, file 3996 AGO 1878, reel 37, Microfilm M666: Letters Received by the Adjutant General's Office (Main Series), 1871–1880 [hereafter cited as M666], Record Group 94: Records of the Adjutant General's Office [hereafter cited as RG 94], NARA I; Adams Archibald to Secretary of State for the Provinces, 22 May 1872, despatch 68, reel 3, MG 12 AI, Adams George Archibald Papers, Provincial Archives of Manitoba [hereafter cited as PAM]. Cf. Ens, "The Border, The Buffalo, and the Métis of Montana."

24. Affidavit of Gabriel Beauchemin, 22 May 1872, file 1330 (1872), vol. 228, reel T-12177, Dominion Lands Branch Files, RG 15, LAC; J. A. Simmons to J. A Viall, 6 November 1871, ibid.; Captain H. B. Freeman to Acting Asst. Adjutant General, 27 November 1871, file 3996 AGO 1878, reel 37, M666, RG 94, NARA I.

25. Jno. Kerler to [Adams Archibald], 10 November 1871, reel M3, MG 12 AI, Adams George Archibald Papers, PAM. See also claims in Affidavit of Gabriel Beauchemin, 22 May 1872, and Freeman to [Benson], undated, file 1330 (1872), vol. 228, reel T-12177, Dominion Lands Branch Files, RG 15, LAC.

26. Sanno to Freeman, 19 October 1871, file 1330 (1872), vol. 228, reel T-12177, Dominion Lands Branch Files, RG 15, LAC; Simmons to Viall, 6 November 1871, ibid.; Captain H. B. Freeman to Acting Asst. Adjutant General, 27 November 1871, file 3996 AGO 1878, reel 37, M666, RG 94, NARA I.

27. Ostler, *The Plains Sioux and U.S. Colonialism from Lewis and Clark to Wounded Knee*, 52–53, 58–62.

28. Statement of William Benoit, ca. May 1874, frames 150–51, reel 498, M234, RG 75, NARA I.

29. Chas. D. Hard to W. Alderson, 16 May 1874, frames 148–49, reel 498, M234, RG 75, NARA I; Jean Louis Legaré to Commissioner of Indian Affairs, 15 July

1874, frames 438–41, reel 500, ibid.; [Alexander Morris] to Unknown, ca. 6 June 1874, doc. 760, reel M135, MG 12 B1, Alexander Morris Papers, PAM.

30. Affidavit by Jean Louis Legaré, 16 June 1874, doc. 772, reel M135, MG 12 B1, Alexander Morris Papers, PAM; J. Wheeler to Jas. W. Taylor, 3 July 1874, doc. 824, ibid.; N. P. Langford to [Taylor], 16 July 1874, doc. 824, ibid.

31. Foster, *We Know Who We Are*, 67; Samuel O'Connell, "Reminiscence," Samuel O'Connell Papers, SC 597, MHS.

32. "Substance of the information given by Michael Klyne, Junr to the Lieut. Governor," 6 June 1874, file 3529-2, vol. 3610, reel C-10106, Black (Western) Series, Record Group 10: Department of Indian Affairs [hereafter cited as RG 10], LAC. The seasonal Métis population of the region may even have been larger still; see Turner, "Surveying the International Boundary," 19n40.

33. Diary entries for 25 August, 3 September, 4 September, and 15 November 1874, William W. Alderson Papers, SC 356, MHS; Thomas J. Bogy Diary, SC 150, ibid.

34. Hoxie, *Parading through History*, 115–16. Cf. Baud and Van Schendel, "Toward a Comparative History of Borderlands," 214–15.

35. Constant Williams to Acting Asst. Adjutant General, 6 February 1878, file 1652 AGO 1878 (f/w 1056 AGO 1878), reel 394, M666, RG 94, NARA I.

36. Ibid.

37. Guido Ilges to W. Bird, 16 August 1877, frames 409–10, reel 507, M234, RG 75, NARA I.

38. W. Bird to Commissioner of Indian Affairs, 3 October 1878, frames 487–90, reel 509, M234, RG 75, NARA I; Guido Ilges to Joseph Hale, 11 October 1878, file 8215 AGO 1878 (f/w 4976 AGO 1877), reel 362, M666, RG 94, NARA I; Guido Ilges to A/Asst. Adjutant General, 4 November 1878, ibid.; Terry to Lieutenant Colonel Brooke, 1 April 1878, frames 119–24, reel 512, M234, RG 75, NARA I.

39. W. Bird to Commissioner of Indian Affairs, 3 October 1878, frames 487–90, reel 509, M234, RG 75, NARA I; W. L. Lincoln to Col. H. W. Black, 12 October 1880, frames 1023–25, reel 516, ibid.; W. L. Lincoln to Commissioner of Indian Affairs, 8 May 1881, Letterbook 1880–, 48–49, box 1, Letters Sent to the Commissioner of Indian Affairs, Records of the Fort Belknap Indian Agency, RG 75, National Archives and Records Administration, Rocky Mountain Region, Denver, Colo.

40. Guido Ilges to Acting Asst. Adjutant Genl., 8 February 1878, frames 55–57, reel 512, M234, RG 75, NARA I; Terry to Lieutenant Colonel Brooke, 1 April 1878, frames 119–24, ibid.; *Revised Statutes of the United States*, section 2134 (p. 372).

41. See Constant Williams to Acting Asst. Adjutant General, 6 February 1878, file 1652 AGO 1878 (formerly, 1056 AGO 1878), reel 394, M666, RG 94, NARA I.

42. W. L. Lincoln to Guido Ilges, 15 October 1878, frame 236, reel 511, M234, RG

75, NARA I; J. M. Walsh to Minister of the Interior, 12 September 1876, file 7088, vol. 3637, reel C-10112, Black (Western) Series, RG 10, LAC; David Laird to Minister of Interior, 19 April 1877, ibid.; [D. M. Meredith] to J. M. Walsh, 22 June 1877, file 8280, vol. 3649, reel C-10190, ibid.

43. Constant Williams to Acting Asst. Adjutant General, 27 February 1878, frames 98–111, reel 512, M234, RG 75, NARA I.

44. Foster, *We Know Who We Are*, 49–50; H. M. Black to Captain C. H. Potter, 26 November 1879, frames 52–83, reel 518, M234, RG 75, NARA I.

45. Morin, *Métis Families*, 1:65–66; Foster, *We Know Who We Are*, 64, 69–72.

46. Brown and Schenk, "Métis, Mestizo, and Mixed-Blood," 332.

47. Guido Ilges to 1st Lieut. Joseph Hale, 11 October 1878, file 8215 AGO 1878 (f/w 4976 AGO 1877), reel 362, M666, RG 94, NARA I. Indian agent Bird placed the number of Métis families hunting between the Milk and Poplar Rivers at three hundred. W. Bird to Commissioner of Indian Affairs, 3 October 1878, frames 487–90, reel 509, M234, RG 75, NARA I.

48. Guido Ilges to Lieut. Joseph Hale, 11 October 1878, file 4976 AGO 1877, reel 362, M666, RG 94, NARA I.

49. Guido Ilges to Acting Asst. Adjutant General, 22 October 1878 and 4 November 1878, file 4976 AGO 1877, reel 362, M666, RG 94, NARA I.

50. Patrice Breland to "Doctor," November 1878, file 13607, vol. 3687, reel C-10120, Black (Western) Series, RG 10, LAC; Fr. Hugonnard to [Archbishop Taché], 7 February [1879], T21441–8, and 9 December 1879, T22935–40, Alexandre-Antonin Taché Papers, Roman Catholic Archdiocese of Saint-Boniface, SBHS.

51. Perry, *On the Edge of Empire*, 71.

52. Northwest Territories Council, *Journals*, 8 March 1877, 6; "An Ordinance for the Protection of the Buffalo," 22 March 1877, in Northwest Territories, *Ordinances*, 39–40.

53. Giraud, *The Métis in the Canadian West*, 2:417–18.

54. Ibid., 2:413.

55. David Laverdure et al. to President and Honourable Members of the Privy Council, ca. July 1878, file 89435, vol. 341, reel T-13062, Black (Western) Series, RG 15, LAC. Cf. [Métis petitioners] to David Laird, 19 September 1877, file 89436, vol. 341, reel T-13062, Dominion Lands Branch Files, RG 15, LAC.

56. David Laverdure et al. to President and Honourable Members of the Privy Council, ca. July 1878, file 89435, vol. 341, reel T-13062, Dominion Lands Branch Files, RG 15, LAC.

57. McNab, "Metis Participation in the Treaty-Making Process in Ontario," 60–62.

58. Canada, Parliament, House of Commons, *Sessional Papers 1876*, Paper no. 9: "Report of the Department of the Interior," 33–34.

59. McNab, "Metis Participation in the Treaty-Making Process in Ontario," 69; St. Germain, *Indian Treaty-Making Policy in the United States and Canada*, 76–77.

60. Devine, *The People Who Own Themselves*, 144–45, 278–79n8.

61. M. G. Dickieson, "Memorandum," ca. September 1877, file 9092, vol. 3656, reel c-10115, Black (Western) Series, RG 10, LAC; A. M. McDonald to Lt. Governor, 20 October 1877, ibid.

62. Resolution passed by the Council of the North-West Territories in Legislative Session, 2 August 1878, file 89435, vol. 341, reel T-13062, Dominion Lands Branch Files, RG 15, LAC; Canada, Parliament, House of Commons, *Sessional Papers, 1885*, Paper no. 116, "J. S. Dennis to John A. Macdonald, 20 December 1878," 93–96.

63. Canada, Parliament, House of Commons, *Sessional Papers, 1885*, Paper no. 116, "J. S. Dennis to John A. Macdonald, 20 December 1878," 93–96.

64. David Laird to [Métis petitioners], 22 September 1877, file 89436, vol. 341, reel T-13062, Dominion Lands Branch Files, RG 15, LAC.

**PART II**

....................................................

*Environmental Control*

*and State-Making*

# EPIDEMICS, INDIANS, AND BORDER-MAKING IN THE NINETEENTH-CENTURY PACIFIC NORTHWEST

..........................................

Jennifer Seltz

Late in September 1876, residents of Port Townsend, at the northeastern corner of Washington Territory's Olympic Peninsula, a few watery miles from the boundary between British and American possessions, held an "indignation meeting." The people at Port Townsend gathered to protest the recent arrival of "smallpox afflicted Indians" from the town of Victoria, just across the Strait of Juan de Fuca, on the American steamer *Dakota*.[1] Both the *Dakota* and Native people traveling between Victoria and Washington Territory were ordinary sights in local waters by the fall of 1876. The steamer, along with many other, similar ships, regularly sailed between San Francisco, Victoria, and towns along Puget Sound.[2] By the mid-1870s, Haida, Kwakwaka'wakw, Tsimshian, Tlingit, and other Aboriginal people from Vancouver Island, northern British Columbia, and southeastern Alaska crossed and re-crossed the international border for a myriad of reasons—to pick hops, to sell baskets, to see family, to gather for annual ceremonies, to buy goods.[3] These trips both retraced earlier kinds of regional travel and elaborated new social and commercial networks.

Smallpox, too, was a relatively ordinary, if still feared, visitor for both Indians and non-Indians in northwestern Washington. By the late 1870s, many Indians on both sides of the border, like their non-Indian neighbors, had either survived earlier epidemics and acquired immunity against the disease, or had been vaccinated within the ten-year window of the vaccine's effectiveness, albeit with occasionally unreliable virus.[4] Smallpox was still a serious concern, and it still augured catastrophe for some Aboriginal communities.[5] But overall, it was no longer the great killer it had been on the Northwest Coast earlier in the century. And for non-Aboriginal communities, smallpox was scary, but it was a less frequent killer than other, more mundane illnesses.

Epidemics and local anxieties about the travels of sick or contagious Indians stimulated some of the first attempts since the decline of inter-tribal raiding a few years earlier to make the far western U.S.-Canada border a barrier to movement. Like cattle grazing in Arizona and Sonora and salmon returning to Pacific waterways between Washington and British Columbia, microbes and their travels showed the border region to be one common environment.[6] Smallpox, measles, influenza, and other ill-nesses moved easily between the two countries. During the rainy winters the same respiratory ailments flourished on both sides of the line. Unlike fish and cows, however, border-crossing pathogens were not desirable resources. And while the fates of both salmon and cattle were intimately linked to human action, the movement of disease was even more insepa-rable from the movement of people. Drawing the border, in fact, had created new paths for diseases to travel and new concentrations of human carriers. The division of the Northwest Coast into British (then Canadian) and American territory redirected flows of people and goods and stimu-lated the growth of towns both close to the border, like Victoria and Port Townsend, and further from the line, like Seattle and Vancouver. Disputes over jurisdiction and federal authority slowed salmon conservation in border waters. Competing visions of the proper relationship between the state and capitalist power made managing cross-border ranches difficult. But cultural confusion, rather than political gridlock, hampered efforts to control the movement of disease and the movement of Indian people in the late nineteenth century across the far western Canada–U.S. border. Uncertainty over how diseases started and spread, and over non-Native responsibility for Native health, combined with the weakness of both national states and the desire of American employers for Indian labor, kept the border largely permeable to disease and to potentially sick and vulnerable Indian people.

The people gathered at Port Townsend, however, chose to see both smallpox and the people they called "northern Indians" as threats, rather than as accepted parts of daily life, and to link the travels of the two.[7] And although smallpox hit the Pacific Coast from southern California to Vancouver Island in 1876, other Washingtonians also blamed the disease's presence in the territory specifically on infected Indians from across the border.[8] In British Columbia and in western Washington, discussion of that year's smallpox focused on northern Indians' travels and on Indian responsibility for the disease's spread in both Native and non-Native communities. Seattle newspapers waged a campaign against the danger posed by Native prostitutes, supposedly from Victoria, in that city.[9] American Indian agents, as they had for the previous decade, traced the outbreaks of smallpox and other serious illnesses at reservations and agencies scattered throughout northwestern Washington partly to the untrammeled movement of Native peoples around Puget Sound and the Gulf of Georgia.[10] At the same time, Canadian Indian agents also blamed the outbreak of smallpox around Victoria on "northern Indians" from the west coast of Vancouver Island and from the Queen Charlotte Islands.[11] Canadians also looked south for the sources of Aboriginal people's illnesses, reversing Washingtonians' accusations and attributing epidemics of measles and other illnesses to the time British Columbia Indians spent around Puget Sound.[12]

Blaming Aboriginal people for the spread of disease was ironic, of course. For over a century, it was Native peoples in the region, not American or British settlers, who had been most at risk from infectious disease spread by strangers. Indians along the Northwest Coast had endured at least three catastrophic smallpox epidemics since the late eighteenth century. Syphilis and tuberculosis had become endemic. The arrival of dysentery, influenza, and other respiratory and gastrointestinal illnesses along with new settlers had come to mark the local calendar.[13] But by the early 1870s the devastation of virgin-soil epidemics had slowed. While measles, smallpox, and, especially, endemic respiratory illness and sexually transmitted diseases continued to take a serious toll, according to many observers, parts of the Indian population around Puget Sound and the southern Gulf of Georgia were beginning to recover from the huge losses of the previous hundred years.[14]

This tentative recovery was obscured by a dramatic rise in the non-Native population of the region, especially in Washington Territory, as farming, logging, mining, shipping, canning, and other industries on both sides of the border expanded with the completion of new transcontinental railroads and the development of new trade and immigration links with China and Japan. The industrializing Northwest and West Coast still needed both Indian labor and Indian spending power, though, and Native people, many of whom were steadily losing access to productive land, fisheries, and other resources, needed the work.

These failed panics over the travels of disease and Indian peoples across the northern border provide a sharp contrast to a better-known story in recent U.S. historiography: the later, apparently top-down and national implementation of stringent medical tests for immigrants and travelers. Alexandra Minna Stern, Nayan Shah, Amy Fairchild, and Adam McKeown have traced the expansion of public health at different locations along the nation's borders where medical inspections worked at both abstract and intimate scales to differentiate American from non-American space, and healthy white bodies from diseased Mexican, Chinese, Southern European, or Eastern European bodies.[15] In the first decades of the twentieth century, American public health officials from Angel Island to Brownsville to Ellis Island interviewed, poked, prodded, vaccinated, sprayed, and even branded potential entrants to the United States. These inspections humiliated and alarmed the people subject to them, but neither diplomatic nor popular protest did much to slow the development of intrusive routines of sorting and surveillance.[16]

In the late nineteenth century, on the other hand, Washingtonians and British Columbians did not enlist the power of the state to slow or stop the movement of Aboriginal people across the far western border; they never developed a coherent or convincing rationale for medical inspections and for other kinds of border enforcement on the bodies of individual Indians. This failure suggests that strengthening national borders in the name of health and racial and ethnic purity was hardly easy or automatic, even as racial definitions and hierarchies hardened in both nations and state power over the border expanded in general. The group gathered at Port Townsend in September 1876 had, after all, surprisingly limited aims: they voted to "censure" the officers of the *Dakota*, which had supposedly brought the smallpox-infected British Columbia Indians to their town.[17] They did not, and could not, force the Indians' return to Victoria, or elsewhere in British Columbia. They might have demanded that the *Dakota* be quarantined, but they did not, perhaps recognizing the rarity of effective quarantine in northern Washington ports. Their attempt to medicalize the border and to draw lines between healthy American and un-healthy British Columbia Indians remained improvisational and local, a matter of scolding frequent visitors.

Episodes like the Port Townsend indignation meeting, however, were not just preludes to efficient and coercive modernization. They had less to do with widely shared ideas about contagion and race than with the idiosyncrasies of the border's history in western Washington and British Columbia. Both Americans' calls to exclude Native peoples from the other side of the border, and the resistance to such measures, drew on older preoccupations: first with Native peoples' health and its connection to non-Native ailments, and second with the threat posed to American settlements and to urban development in British Columbia by the travels of the so-called northern Indians. Race, disease, and mobility were linked and debated between Vancouver Island and the Olympic Peninsula, in the passages between the San Juan Islands, and in the forests, foothills, and prairies west of the Cascades, well before the consolidation of federal power and the passage of more restrictive federal immigration legislation —and in terms that owed as much to local experience and the local history of negotiations between Native and non-Native people, as they did to broader national or transnational arguments.

## Linking Disease and Region

When Washingtonians tried to slow and limit the travel of the diverse peoples they lumped together as "northern Indians," and when British Columbian Indian agents blamed the Indians' travels to Washington's hop fields and cities for winter sickness nearby in Victoria and far away in the Queen Charlotte Islands and northern Vancouver Island, both the Canadians and Americans were relating their own stories about both the international border and the region's recent disease history. In these stories, dividing the mixed world of the Salish Sea at the 49th parallel had also produced a new division, between healthy places and healthy Indians on one side of the border, and unhealthy places and unhealthy Indians on the other. Americans and Canadians disagreed over which side of the border was sicker, but they agreed about what constituted sickly places and sickly bodies. Indian bodies, they assumed, were and would continue to be inherently weaker and more vulnerable to disease. This biological judgment was matched by a cultural assumption. Both Americans and

Canadians also assumed that Indian health practices and medical epistemologies over the past seventy years had been, simultaneously, inflexible, persistent in the form of superstition, and entirely disrupted by new illnesses. Whites on both sides of the border convinced themselves that Native demographic decline and Euro-American increase were equally inevitable. At the same time, however, sick Indians could still pose threats to individual settler communities and households. By the end of the nineteenth century, this story of the vanishing and sickly Indian was as powerful and conventional along the far western border as it was elsewhere in North America. In the 1870s, however, as cross-border travel by northern Indians for work increased and as smallpox outbreaks worried residents of both British Columbia and Washington, this perceived wisdom was contested by Indians peoples, and contradicted by a persistent, if reduced, mixed world of environmental and medical knowledge around the region.

Europeans, Americans, and local indigenous people had argued about the meaning of epidemic disease in Coast Salish territory since the 1830s. The first generations of newcomers in the Pacific Northwest noted and discussed Native ill health in large part because they were concerned about their own well-being in a new environment, not because they feared specific contagions. Both American and British physicians, military officials, colonial administrators, and traders evaluated Native and settler health and western environments simultaneously, building on and reshaping well-established colonial habits of medical geography.[18] By the time significant numbers of Europeans and Americans began to arrive in Puget Sound and in the territory that would become British Columbia, they had already learned to see tight links between settler and Native health on the one hand, and between weather and local geography and the body's ability to acclimatize on the other. They thought that newcomers might get sick at first, and that Native bodies' ongoing disease history would predict how sick those newcomers could expect to become after they had spent some time in the region.

Euro-Americans who spent any time at all in the Northwest in the first half of the nineteenth century were also well aware of the recent and ongoing epidemics and endemic illnesses with which most Indian groups were struggling. Both English and American visitors and settlers tried to explain, in largely similar terms, how the Northwest Coast could contain such beautiful (and potentially valuable) scenery and such sickly people at one and the same time. They worried that Indians' bad health might be evidence of unproductive land, and therefore of poor prospects for non-Indian inhabitants on both sides of the changing international border. Early visitors quickly concluded, however, that there was no simple equation between place, disease, and race at work in the region. Even to newcomers, it was obvious that, like non-Native sickness, Indian ill health was neither uniform across space nor constant through time. For more judgmental observers, like the military surgeons who reported on local health and topography, it was Native people's bad habits and immoral behavior, combined with their smoky houses and the damp climate, that produced their poor health.[19] Visitors who were less committed to clichés noticed that smallpox might devastate one tribe, and allow another to expand its territory. War or a poor salmon run could bring on seasonal sickness and poverty at one village, while a neighboring group thrived.[20]

Like ethnographers and army physicians, Native people themselves had learned to associate mobility with the emergence of sickness, but unlike emigrants, sensitive to their own bodies' responses to travel, Indians around Puget Sound and the Strait of Georgia initially worried mostly about the problems caused by other people's movements.[21] And while Indian peoples in the region, like Europeans and Americans, saw connections between some kinds of sickness and place, they rooted these judgments less in generalizations about what kinds of landscapes and weathers might produce fevers or coughs, and more in grounded and geographically specific histories of different families, spirits, and events.[22] Illnesses, like other important moments, defined particular places—a hill, a stretch of river, a beach.

These grounded histories of illness helped create a mixed world of medical and environmental knowledge. Settlers sometimes learned to take Native stories seriously as explanations of why some groups appeared to thrive under evolving colonial regimes and others struggled to survive. Both British and American newcomers owed their understanding of the complicated new landscape of disease around the Salish Sea in part to what Native people chose to tell them. By the middle of the nineteenth century, settler concerns about the health of new places and questions about the racial changes worked by relocation mingled with Indian peoples' efforts to make sense of and respond to colonial diseases. And Indian people throughout the region articulated their own clear views of the connections among disease, identity, and environment in a variety of contexts.[23]

At the same time, Native people also clearly blamed European and American carelessness or malice for both new diseases and more frequent waves of illness. Many Native people who worked closely with Hudson's Bay Company posts on both sides of the border let the fur trade company's employees and tenants know that they held more recent settlers responsible for new sicknesses.[24] Newcomers who visited HBC posts also heard often about how American and British ship captains were to blame for the devastating malaria epidemics of the 1830s.[25] These early disease histories partly framed American and British responses to sickness among Indians later in the nineteenth century.[26] Even as they described Aboriginal bodies as inherently more vulnerable to smallpox and other diseases, colonial and territorial governors and other officials acknowledged a responsibility to improve Native health and prevent further epidemics.[27]

Over the course of nearly thirty years in the middle of the nineteenth century, as the far western border was partly established and surveyed, Indians on both sides of the border resisted attempts to define them as intrinsically unhealthy and to limit their movements in the name of either Native or non-Native health. Especially in Washington, where the existence of treaties gave Indians a legal voice they did not have in British Columbia, Native people continued to tell a story insisting on American responsibility for ensuring the health of mobile Indians. The 1855 treaties negotiated by Isaac Stevens with groups around Puget Sound all included a slightly unusual stipulation: that the federal government hire one physician for each central Indian agency, "to furnish medicine and advice to their sick" as well as to provide smallpox vaccinations.[28] When superintendents and agents failed to hire doctors—the pay, as many agency physicians complained for years, was terrible—Indians throughout western Washington made it clear that they took this treaty clause seriously.[29] By 1869, tribes near the border were irritated enough by the continuing absence of American doctors and medicine to take their concerns directly to Ely Parker, the newly appointed commissioner of Indian Affairs. Four representatives of the Lummi and Nooksack Indians sent him a letter pointing out the United States' failure to uphold its treaty obligations. Their first concern was the disappearance of annuities for land concessions, but their second was lack of medical attention.[30]

These protests only went so far. Indian agents, as well as Native people, sometimes saw the limits of the evolving arrangements around the Sound, as specific places became less healthy and less accessible than they had been for Native people, and as new kinds of movement became necessary for subsistence. But American officials also began to see Native illness as a result of exposure, poor diet, and inadequate shelter, as habitual problems, not as the product of new or rare circumstances. Chronic diseases replaced epidemics in officials' accounts of the kinds of illnesses that separated Indian bodies from non-Indian bodies. Indians seemed particularly vulnerable to respiratory illnesses, including but not limited to consumption, and they seemed particularly unable to accommodate themselves to the problems with the local climate. Earlier observers had marked out a calendar of illness, dependent as much on the movements of sailors, traders, soldiers, and families as on seasonal changes in the weather. Reservation physicians continued to focus on sickness that emerged from and that accompanied both Native and non-Native mobility and mixing, but they saw that movement itself as more dangerous to debilitated people. They also emphasized "those kinds of disease connected most especially with the respiratory organs, such as Asthma, Bronchitis, Catarrh, and Croup, which are scarsely seen in the pleasant part of the year."[31] In these accounts, settlers and Indians switched places: Indians were the ones who failed to acclimate to the quirks of the local climate—the long, rainy winters—and Americans were the ones who adapted to a seasonal round.

Even this argument simply reversed, and did not eliminate, older ideas of where disease came from, of how local environments shaped epidemics, and of who was most vulnerable to illness. When Americans, Canadians, and Indians argued about the connections between Native mobility—including border crossings—and illness among both Natives and non-Natives, they all continued to see and talk about a mixed world, albeit an increasingly unequal one. In tourist and emigrant guides, and in other narratives of Indian demographic decline and Euro-American growth written for faraway audiences, residents of both Washington and British Columbia increasingly evoked the familiar image of the sickly and intrinsically different vanishing Indian.[32] Closer to home, however, Canadian and American Indian agents continued to find a variety of causes for outbreaks of smallpox and other illnesses around the border: poor sanitary conditions, as well as the inherent weakness of Aboriginal bodies; contaminated vaccine, as well as the persistence of smallpox among local tribes even in years without epidemics. And Aboriginal people living near the border continued to tell both geographically and historically specific narratives of disease causation, and continued to argue for American and Canadian responsibility for Indian health. But new variations on old patterns of travel increasingly subsumed these stories and arguments. The health and movements of northern Indians in particular now came to define the larger question of the health and movements of all Indians around the border.

## From War to Disease

American and British settlers and officials had been especially concerned about and fascinated by the people they called northern Indians, since before the western border was surveyed and ratified, either on land or on water, and since before the rise of the hops industry, lumber mills, canneries, and other industries drawing workers across that border. They had learned this concern, like so much else about the region, from local Indian people.[33] Worrying about war canoes from the north was an old habit for people around Puget Sound and the Gulf of Georgia. From at least the beginning of the nineteenth century, Kwakwaka'wakw raiders had periodically came south, returning to northeastern Vancouver Island and Queen Charlotte Strait with slaves. Stikine Tlingit and Tsimshian people, from southeastern Alaska, raided less often, but were also feared. By the early 1860s, northerners' raids, while mostly still targeted at Aboriginal settlements, occasionally threatened white property, and, more generally, exposed the weakness of both American and British authority over regional waters.

Northern Indians' less violent activities also intermittently annoyed American and British officials. On both sides of the border, Northern women, like other indigenous women in the region, lived with Euro-American men, creating households which became less acceptable as white settlement increased and Victorian respectability and racial norms gained traction in the region.[34] Trade with northerners kept some groups, notably the Makahs at the western edge of the Olympic Peninsula, economically independent and beyond the civilizing mission of Indian agents, and not incidentally, hurt American traders' profits.[35] Northern

Indians' role in the socially disruptive trans-border whiskey trade concerned both Americans and Canadians; each blamed lax laws or enforcement in the other jurisdiction for making alcohol easily available.[36]

Americans, often already confused by the intricacies of shifting social ties and overlapping identities around Puget Sound, could not figure out how they should view the northerners—as raiders, trading partners, or companions. They sought to understand these diverse groups, with divergent histories of travel to and from Puget Sound, through the new binational lens of the border: were all northerners controlled by the British? Were these Indians enemies or friends of people theoretically owed protection by the American government? Until at least the 1870s, American officials and politicians, responding to public pressure and wanting to increase their own importance, vacillated among several options: they alternately tried to treat the northern Indians as a constant, collective threat; they confused northerners with the Coast Salish people, who had long-standing family ties across the border; they acknowledged the northerners' importance in Puget Sound labor markets; or they tried to lump northerners together with all other Indians in American territory as non-citizens.[37]

British and American observers did agree on one characteristic dividing all northerners from Coast Salish people. Northerners, they claimed, were healthier and stronger. At least until a well-publicized smallpox epidemic struck Vancouver Island and parts of mainland southwest British Columbia in 1862, both Americans and British settlers and visitors had consistently praised the Northern physique and northerners' vigor.[38] In the 1850s and 1860s, Americans—particularly those who had knowledge or memory of the malaria that had ravaged the southern part of the Oregon country in the 1830s and 1840s—consistently claimed that Indian health and strength increased steadily as one moved north.[39] In part—but only in part—this conventional wisdom reflected the actual history of epidemics on the Northwest Coast in the first half of the nineteenth century. Neither malaria-bearing mosquitoes nor the virus itself thrived north of the Columbia River. But residents of what would become coastal British Columbia and the border region did suffer from some of the same measles and smallpox outbreaks that afflicted many of their neighbors to the south. However, non-Natives' approval of northern bodies went beyond the northerners' apparent ability to withstand epidemic disease. Newcomers looked at people from Nanaimo in central British Columbia to southeastern Alaska, and saw bodies they judged to be altogether healthier and more appealing than those Native people from the border region—taller, sturdier, fairer-skinned, sexually attractive people.[40] This admiration for northerners' health stemmed mostly from their military reputation, but also sometimes justified northerners' increasing importance in the labor markets of Victoria and Puget Sound, in terms of their bodily fitness for the necessary work of settlement and improvement.[41]

When border residents and Indian agents began singling out northern Indians as "unhealthy" in the 1870s, this judgment marked an abrupt, if incomplete switch in public discussion. In part, seeing northerners as scarily diseased simply reframed older settler fears of scarily energetic raiders. This reframing—which apparently drew on emerging ideas of Indian bodily difference, but which actually just reversed earlier ways of looking at Haida, Tsimshian, Tlingit, and Kwakwaka'wakw people as distinctive—was only partially successful. Washingtonian and Canadian observers, particularly those outside of Victoria or Seattle, or those writing for a tourist audience, continued to praise northerners' military skill and to contrast their vigor with the weakness of Indians from Puget Sound, the area around Victoria, and the Lower Mainland.[42] And so long as Native people continued to remind Americans in particular of their responsibility for Indian health, the bodily marks left behind by diseases like smallpox and measles were still signs as much of the world Native people and newcomers shared, if on an increasingly unequal basis, as of the divisions between them. Within that world, though, both British and American settlers and officials began to work harder by the early 1870s to separate and sanitize Indian and non-Indian spaces, and to control Indian mobility in the name of health and order. These efforts mostly failed. What they showed, however, was that Indian mobility continued to connect and define the border region, and that apparently modern arguments about Indians' health and the spread of disease remained rooted in earlier experience.

### Unhealthy Crossings

The far western border itself was part of a world long defined by regional movement across long distances. Native trade and kin networks predated, and then enabled and shaped, Euro-American settlement. Drawing the northern boundary of the Oregon country at the 49th parallel in 1846 had not much disrupted long-standing patterns of movement in the region. Native people, from Cape Flattery and Vancouver Island on the west to the foothills of the Cascades on the east, commonly traveled long distances through a complicated and cosmopolitan landscape of towns, fishing sites, fur trading posts, and cultivated prairies. Both British and American new-comers recognized and alternately exploited and condemned this travel from the 1830s on.[43] American and Canadian laments about Indian trade, socializing, and consumption were only acknowledgments of an estab-lished fact in the region from 1846 forward. For their part, Aboriginal people in the region did not just ignore the border: they first turned the final division of the Oregon country into American and British space, and then the drawing of the actual border, to their own advantage.

Both the land boundary and the contested water boundary were shaped by movement—movement largely made possible by Native people's labor and knowledge. Common routes of travel and exchange, as much as car-tographers' parallels, initially defined the border. The American boundary surveyors, struggling in 1857 just west of Mount Baker through "the dense forests everywhere encountered" and through the "frequent 'burnt districts' where the huge trunks as they lie piled one upon another form an almost impassable barrier," depended on the experience and family ties of the local Nooksack and Lummi peoples to travel safely to the north and east and to find accessible places from which to fix the astronomical and geodetic points they needed.[44] Farther west, at their camp on Bound-ary Bay, surveyors provided a new market for Indian hunters, and a new reason for canoes to stop at Semiahmoo.[45] The discovery of gold north along the Fraser River made travel along the still largely hypothetical boundary line easier, but surveying became prohibitively expensive. The surveying team reported in the fall of 1858 that a trail had been "opened up through the Cascade Mountains to the Thompson's River country, crossing the boundary line, and for many miles, it is believed, passing in its immediate vicinity"; not coincidentally, locals had raised their rates to be guides and porters.[46] As the gold rush waned, the British surveying team used the labor of "broken miners" to mark the boundary itself, "a line 30 feet broad" through "thick forests of cedar trees all the way."[47] Still, one member of the British commission admitted, "No one could travel *along* the Boundary Line. The 2 Commissions in the course of their work have cut a trail parallel to the Boundary Line and as near to it as possible, but in many places the trail is 20 or 30 miles north or south of the Line, and the intervening portion of ground has often to be left unexplored."[48] The surveyors' frustration, the temporary nature of the gold rush, and the thick forests all obscured a pattern that would become familiar. The border itself was useful to those who knew the region well, but only so long as it could be crossed and re-crossed freely.

The Native people who facilitated the construction of the land border, as well as those who lived well north of the new line, did not necessarily recognize the authority of either state over their movements, as both British and American commissioners knew.[49] The 1855 treaties negotiated by Isaac Stevens with a number of Indian groups around Puget Sound all included clauses prohibiting trade outside the United States and forbidding "foreign Indians" to live on American reservations, but these restrictions usually had little effect.[50] Over at least the next two decades, even if it had been physically possible to enforce strict separation between Indians north and south of the line, territorial, state, federal, colonial, and provincial governments would rarely have the power—on paper or on the ground—to do so, despite their sporadic (and often illegal) attempts.[51] Beginning in the late 1850s, American naval steamers and "revenue cutters" occasionally patrolled the northwestern waters, but they were mostly unable to stop the smuggling and raiding.[52]

As Superintendent of Indian Affairs R. H. Milroy explained to his superiors in Washington in 1873, "Indians of this superintendency, and of British Columbia, near the border, are more or less intermarried, visit each other, and have much intercourse."[53] The border, Milroy went on to say, had in fact stimulated new kinds of movement in the three decades since its inception: "British Columbia Indians, from Vancouver and other islands, and the mainland, come in their canoes in swarms around our logging camps and towns around the sound, get all the whiskey they want, and their women engage in prostitution."[54] Milroy's unremittingly negative view of cross-border Indian travel was not the majority view on the U.S. side of the border after the 1850s. Too many farmers and traders in Washington Territory depended on the labor and cash provided by the people they called northern Indians. Furthermore, Milroy, like his predecessors, possessed little real power to stop Native people from traveling back and forth across the border, just as he and his agents had little real power to keep Indians on the Washington reservations. By the early 1880s, Milroy's British Columbia counterparts echoed his complaints in reverse, bemoaning the presence of Indians from Washington and objecting to Native people from British Columbia traveling south.[55]

At the mouth of the Fraser River west to Vancouver Island and south along the rivers and coastal waterways that most people in the region used for travel, the difference between American and British, later Canadian, territory was made concrete only at border towns like Victoria and Port Townsend, and at the few sites—customs houses, marine inspection stations—where either state asserted its power to at least track who and what entered its territory. Even then, attempts to enforce the boundary in a region where settlers depended on Native mobility for communications as well as goods were informal at best, and absurd at worst. When, in 1856, the governor of Washington Territory wanted to stop "northern Indians" from entering Puget Sound waters, the note he sent asking for the British governor's help was itself carried by some of the same "northern Indians," on their way back from Port Townsend.[56]

Even after the water boundary had finally been determined and national ships and officials could freely navigate in border waters, they were as much conduits for the flow of information, goods, and people back and forth across the border as they were symbols and enforcers of national authority. In the summer of 1875, the sometime customs collector, Indian agent, and ethnographer James Swan, looking for Indian artifacts to send back to Spencer Baird at the Smithsonian, came along for a cruise on the American revenue steamer the *U.S.S. Wolcott*. The *Wolcott* sailed from Port Townsend in American territory to Victoria in British Columbia, then up the Gulf of Georgia, back into American territory in Alaska, then back into Canadian waters with a stop at Fort Simpson on the mouth of the Skeena River in northern British Columbia. Along the way, Swan encountered a Tshimshian woman he had last seen ten years earlier on the Olympic Peninsula, where she had survived an attack by Clallam raiders and Swan had helped her return, first to Victoria, and eventually to Fort Simpson. The next day, Swan ran into a Tshimshian man whose sister was married to a Mr. Appleton in Port Townsend. This man asked Swan to pass along a message for another sister, who had "gone to Victoria on the last trip of the Otter." He wanted Swan to tell Mr. Appleton to "send to Victoria and get the sister and send her home as his mother is old and feeble and poor."[57] Two weeks later, Swan met yet another Native man whose economic ties extended even farther south on both land and sea; a resident of Edinso, the man had worked as a coalman on a steamer for three years and in Port Townsend for two years.[58] Swan's cruise on the government ship, his time taken up with collecting and delivering messages to be taken back to Victoria and Port Townsend, only partly demonstrated his success as a colonial scavenger.[59] The trip also serves as a reminder of how existing intimate connections across the international border, and of how the differentiation of the Northwest Coast between Canadian and American territory mostly facilitated rather than restricted movement.

### From "Damp, Dark Huts" to the Border

Those connections also included epidemic disease, and the state was limited in its power to control their spread. In the years leading up to the smallpox epidemic of the mid-1870s, Indian agents and superintendents on both sides of the border, as well as local leaders and officials, had become increasingly concerned about the perceived connection between Native mobility, Native neighborhoods, and the spread of disease, but that concern had rarely translated into control. In the summer of 1875, I. W. Powell, the superintendent of Indian affairs in Victoria, had spoken approvingly of James Swan's collecting trip, but he and other officials in British Columbia also spoke of another kind of movement—the spread of smallpox, carried by members of "Northern tribes" from Puget Sound to Victoria and to "distant camps."[60] Powell and his counterpart on the mainland established temporary quarantines and pest houses within city limits and tried to persuade more Indians to disinfect their houses and be vaccinated. As they readily admitted, these measures could not contain smallpox entirely. All around Puget Sound, beginning with the 1875 smallpox epidemic, agents and local officials from Olympia to Vancouver Island also tried to impose quarantine measures in an attempt to temporarily keep out potentially infected Indians and other travelers. But local quarantine capacities were limited, and national officials were not much interested in maintaining a strong medical presence at the far western border.[61]

Around the border, however, both Canadian and American officials began to focus their long-standing concerns about Indian mobility, and especially northerners' movements, on the question of how that mobility itself produced unhealthy spaces. Concern about border crossings by sick or infected Indians was partly an outgrowth of this anxiety. The new language of sanitation actually drew heavily on old complaints about Native houses and Native bodies, and extended those charges to include new judgments about northerners' health. Limiting Indian mobility, especially but not exclusively northerners' mobility, increasingly came to be seen as the key, not only to social order around the international boundary, but also to both Native and non-Native health.

By the mid-1870s, British Columbian Indian officials had targeted Aboriginal travel to and from Puget Sound as one potential source of the spread of smallpox to remote parts of the province, to the growing settlements on the Lower Mainland, and to Victoria. Agents and other government officials tacitly conceded, however, that they could not stop Native peoples from moving to Victoria or from traveling across the border for work. Instead, they focused on controlling northerners' movements within and around Canadian towns, and on trying to separate Indian and non-Indian spaces, or local and northern Indian spaces. They confined sick Indians to "pest houses," quarantined Native neighborhoods, and recommended whitewashing and disinfecting all houses where northern Indians had lived.[62] At the same time, they tried to harden Aboriginal bodies, newly defined as particularly vulnerable, against smallpox, embarking on sometimes successful vaccination campaigns across the province.[63] On western Vancouver Island at least, some Native people contested some of these measures, as well as strictures against international travel, in the same terms they had earlier used to argue for European responsibility for new illnesses, countering warnings "not to travel to the American side" with claims that the local "white man had given them the sickness."[64]

At the same time, agents across the border in Washington had also become more interested in restricting and controlling Indian movement, including movement back and forth across the border, as a therapeutic tool. Since the wars that had followed the hasty treaty negotiations of the mid-1850s, American officials had struggled to establish some kind of authority over the territory's newly created reservations and agencies. Authorities unfamiliar with the intricate coastline and hilly forests of Puget Sound often found it difficult simply to figure out which Indians they were responsible for.[65] During the 1860s and 1870s, as reservation and agency boundaries and resources fluctuated (usually to no one's satisfaction), American officials had a hard time making sense of the linked pattern of Indian mobility and Indian disease.

If American officials could not control Indian mobility, they could still organize their knowledge of Indian bodies into familiar categories. These categories, inherited from the older colonial project of medical geography, both explained physicians' interest in Indian mobility and highlighted their inability to control it. In the three decades following the Stevens treaties, the Americans who were responsible for explaining and taking care of Indian bodies around Puget Sound continued to focus simultaneously on lists of diseases, assessments of climate, and narratives of Indian habits, but these categories now came to operate differently. Rather than focusing on whether or not the climate of Puget Sound was benevolent overall, especially for immigrant bodies prone to fevers, Indian agents and other employees of the Indian Bureau shifted the focus of discussion to the question of how Puget Sound's rainy winters might harm Indian bodies weakened by poor shelter and inadequate food. The agents' reports show the everyday construction of a new way of linking environment to illness and bodily identity. In this interpretation, Indian improvidence mixed with governmental fecklessness had made Native people around the region more vulnerable, both to the climate itself and to the diseases that arrived with winter, than they had been just a few years earlier. Excessive mobility exacerbated this vulnerability, and sedentary agricultural labor lessened it. In 1870 the farmer at the Puyallup reservation wrote to the Washington superintendent: "I think that the great reason why there has been so little sickness this season is that the adults have been encouraged to labor regularly in the fields and to stay at home. This compensated employment has made them contented and kept them free from those dissatisfactions that in former years have told seriously on their health."[66] Farm work compensated for frivolous "exposure to the cold and dampness" over the winter, when too many people at Puyallup were "in the habit . . . of squatting on the damp ground and passing the time in amusing themselves at cards and other games."[67] These moments of praise for local Indians who stayed home and did not mix with others, including sometimes troublesome or competitive northerners, only highlighted American agents' standing discontent with most other Native people's movements, housing, and health practices, and their powerlessness to do much about these perceived problems.

Newly minted "old settlers" also worried about the travels of sickly bodies, both Indian and non-Indian. They focused on the creation of sickly spaces where apparently transient, unsettled, or unsanitary workers and immigrants lived and gathered. And because many of the people who congregated in these spaces had crossed the international border to get to Puget Sound, border crossings drew attention and alarm too. Such worries took shape in newspaper articles, in government reports, and, most destructively, in concrete efforts to get rid of infected spaces and infected people. To Americans trying to define themselves as the true natives of the Northwest and the people most suited to improve the region, Native towns and villages, both old and new, now looked not only temporary but also potentially unhealthy and dangerous. Indian houses were like urban slums—"smoky huts," "Damp, Dark, and poorly ventilated"—sources of illness in themselves.[68] Local newspapers identified specific neighborhoods and institutions, especially those spaces where Indians and other undesirable immigrants and travelers mixed, as sick with smallpox, measles, and diphtheria: the Seattle madhouse, a seasonal workers' camp near the mills of Port Ludlow on the Olympic Peninsula, the waterfront redlight districts of Seattle and Victoria.[69] During the 1860s and 1870s, smallpox scares even prompted settlers and Indian agents to burn down Indian houses from Birch Bay, very near the border, to Port Madison, further south on Bainbridge Island.[70]

It was in this climate of a rapidly changing economy and ambivalence over the presence of new immigrants, continued discontent in some quarters over Indians' refusal to stay on reservations or to disappear altogether from the region, and official redefinition of both Indians and Indian spaces as often infected and dangerous to larger groups, that Americans initiated their efforts to monitor and deter the travel of Indians from British Columbia into Washington Territory. In this case, efforts to make the border stronger apparently served only to point out its weakness and the strength of economic and social, not to mention epidemiological, connections along the Northwest Coast. Yet these indignation meetings, editorials, reports, and attempted dispossessions in the name of sanitation also suggest a complicated and local history for two kinds of medical modernization that would arrive in the region by the early twentieth century—medical policing at the border and the introduction of more effectively coercive colonial medicine on both sides of the line.

## Notes

1. "Citizens of Port Townsend," *Washington Standard*, 30 September 1876, 2.
2. For the *Dakota* in Port Townsend in August and September 1876, see diary entries for 24 August and 14 September 1876, folder 1, box 2, James Gilchrist Swan Papers, Special Collections, University of Washington Libraries, Seattle [hereafter cited as Swan Papers].
3. For cross-border travel by Native people in this period and later, see Lutz, "Work, Sex, and Death on the Great Thoroughfare," 80–103; Raibmon, *Authentic Indians*, 102–19; Thrush, *Native Seattle*, 105–13.
4. For earlier epidemics, see Boyd, *The Coming of the Spirit of Pestilence*, esp. 21–60, 145–201. For vaccination in the region, see Seltz, "Embodying Nature," 170–222.
5. Boyd, *The Coming of the Spirit of Pestilence*, 301–4.
6. See St. John, "Divided Ranges: Trans-border Ranches and the Creation of National Space along the Western Mexico–U.S. Border," and Wadewitz, "The Scales of Salmon: Diplomacy and Conservation in the Western Canada–U.S. Borderlands," in this volume.
7. Washingtonians and British Columbians often did not distinguish among the diverse groups of people they called "northern Indians," and when they did label these visitors, they often did so inaccurately (calling all northerners "Haidas," for example), which makes it very difficult to determine exactly when people from places as different as central and northern Vancouver Island, southeastern Alaska, or the Queen Charlotte Islands were at particular places along the border at particular times.
8. "Hydah Indians Living near Port Ludlow Afflicted with Smallpox," *Washington Standard*, 27 November 1875, 2.
9. Thrush, *Native Seattle*, 61.
10. U.S. Office of Indian Affairs, *Annual Report of the Commissioner of Indian Affairs* 1863, 446, 448 [hereafter cited as FARCIA followed by the year of the report]; FARCIA 1873, 304; "Report of Tulalip Physician for August 1873," reel 26, Microfilm A171: U.S. Bureau of Indian Affairs, Records of Washington Territory Superintendent of Indian Affairs [hereafter cited as A171], University of Washington Libraries, Seattle [hereafter cited as UW Libraries].
11. Canada Department of Indian Affairs, *Annual Report of the Department of Indian Affairs* [hereafter cited as ARDIA followed by the year of the report] 1876, 35; ARDIA 1877, 48.

12. *ARDIA* 1883, 44; *ARDIA* 1885, 83; *ARDIA* 1888, 100, 103.

13. For a chronology of Northwest Coast epidemics, see Boyd, *The Coming of the Spirit of Pestilence*; see also Harris, *The Resettlement of British Columbia*, 3–30. For examples of Indians anticipating and explaining the simultaneous arrival of new illnesses and travelers and immigrants in Oregon Territory in the 1840s, see Wilkes, *Narrative of the United States Exploring Expedition*, 5:140. For one later explanation of the epidemiology of smallpox in the region, see Collins, "John Fornsby," 306–7.

14. See, e.g., L. Chalmers to Henry Webster, 31 December 1862, reel 31; Byron Barlow to Ross, 31 August 1870, reel 24; W. E. Bryant to R. H. Milroy, 1 September 1872, reel 33; and C. M. Sawtelle to R. H. Milroy, 31 March 1874, reel 33; all in A171, UW Libraries. For mixed to optimistic assessments of Indian health by Canadian agents, see *ARDIA* 1881, 139–40; *ARDIA* 1885, 78, 83, 85; *ARDIA* 1886, lxvii.

15. Fairchild, *Science at the Borders*; McKeown, "Ritualization of Regulation," 377–403; Shah, *Contagious Divides*, 179–203; Stern, "Buildings, Boundaries, and Blood"; Stern, *Eugenic Nation*, 57–81. See also Geiger, "Caught in the Gap: The Transit Privilege and North America's Ambiguous Borders," in this volume; and Kraut, *Silent Travelers*, 31–135.

16. See Stern, *Eugenic Nation*, 57–58, 61–62; Fairchild, *Science at the Borders*, 2–4; and Shah, *Contagious Divides*, 181–82, 195–96, 198–203. For colonial medicine in British Columbia and Canada as a whole, see Kelm, *Colonizing Bodies*; and Waldram, Herring, and Young, *Aboriginal Health in Canada*.

17. "Citizens of Port Townsend," *Washington Standard*, 30 September 1876, 2.

18. For arguments dating back to the sixteenth century on how resettlement and colonization in North America might affect European and American health, see Chaplin, *Subject Matter*, 116–80; Nash, *Inescapable Ecologies*, 16–49; and Valencius, *The Health of the Country*.

19. Haden, "Medical Topography and Diseases of Fort Steilacoom," 480–81.

20. See entries for 20 August 1857 and 20 July 1858, George Gibbs Notebooks of Scientific Observations of the Pacific Northwest, Western Americana Collection, Beinecke Rare Book and Manuscript Library. For the diversity of Northwest Coast subsistence regimes and the importance of local variations to regional demography, see Ames and Maschner, *Peoples of the Northwest Coast*, 43, 113–14.

21. For example: "Every fall the indians were excited as to what new ill was to come—Whooping cough—measles—Typhoid fever &c, & they used to be very anxious to hear from Tolmie at Nesqually the news in my letters" (George B. Roberts to Frances Fuller Victor, 28 November 1878, "Letters to Mrs. F. F. Victor," 193–94; see also Bowsfield, *Fort Victoria Letters*, 21–23).

22. Eells, *The Indians of Puget Sound*, 411–13; Smith, *The Puyallup-Nisqually*, 75–79; Swan, *Almost Out of the World*, 91; Thrush, *Native Seattle*, 223, 247, 254.

23. The ill will of shamans sometimes explained otherwise mysterious deaths or sickness, as settlers noted when shamans were killed. See Asher, *Beyond the Reservation*, 175–77, 184–88.

24. Gibbs, *Tribes of Western Washington and Northwestern Oregon*, 208–9.

25. Boyd, *The Coming of the Spirit of Pestilence*, 110–15; Harmon, *Indians in the Making*, 39, 53; Heath, *Memoirs of Nisqually*, 39; Tolmie, *The Journals of William Fraser Tolmie, Physician and Fur Trader*, 238.

26. For a discussion of how stories shape definitions of and reactions to illness, see Kleinman, *The Illness Narratives*, 55; and Rosenberg and Golden, "Framing Disease," xiii–xxvi.

27. See, e.g., Isaac Stevens to Commissioner of Indian Affairs, 6 December 1853, reel 1, A171, UW Libraries; *Reports of Explorations and Surveys*, vol. 1, 179, 408, 429; FARCIA 1872, 333; Dr. Smith to E. C. Chirouse, 1 September 1873, reel 26, A171, UW Libraries.

28. United States, *Indian Affairs*, vol. 2, *Treaties*, 664, 672, 676.

29. Reel 23, 31 December 1857, A171, UW Libraries. See also Nathan D. Hill to M. T. Simmons, 30 July 1856, quoted in Garretson, "A History of the Washington Superintendency of Indian Affairs," 59.

30. Whe-land-hur, Ge-le-whomist, Quima, Hump-Klalm, Slow-el, E. C. Finkboner, and Richard Romy to Commissioner of Indian Affairs, 26 June 1869, in reel 14, A171, UW Libraries.

31. Paget to Gosnell, 30 July 1861, reel 19, A171, UW Libraries.

32. See, e.g., [Author unknown], *Guidebook to British Columbia*, 4–5. See also Thrush, *Native Seattle*, 138–50.

33. FARCIA 1857, 11–12, 327, 331–32; FARCIA 1858, 8–9, 219; FARCIA 1859, 25, 396. See also Bancroft, *History of Washington, Idaho, and Montana*, 211–13. Both John Lutz and Lissa Wadewitz point out that American officials in particular, angling for greater federal investment in the region, sometimes exaggerated the military threat posed by northerners. See Lutz, "Inventing an Indian War"; and Wadewitz, "After 1846: Native vs. Newcomer Cartographies in the Western Canada–U.S. Borderlands" (unpublished manuscript in author's possession), 4–5.

34. Lutz, "Making 'Indians' in British Columbia," 67–68; Perry, *On the Edge of Empire*, 48–78, 97–123.

35. FARCIA 1857, 331; FARCIA 1858, 232; FARCIA 1867, 44; FARCIA 1871, 271; Swan, *Almost Out of the World*, 68, 76–78.

36. ARDIA 1875, 48; ARDIA 1876, 36; ARDIA 1877, 47; ARDIA 1878, 71; ARDIA 1881, 169; FARCIA 1857, 331; FARCIA 1873, 304.

37. *FARCIA* 1873, 304. See also Lutz, "Work, Sex, and Death on the Great Thoroughfare," 92; and Lutz, "Inventing an Indian War," 7–13.

38. "Smallpox Epidemic in Victoria," *Washington Standard*, 29 March 1862; "Severe Epidemic of Smallpox among Northern Indians," *Washington Standard*, 14 June 1862; "Epidemic of Smallpox at Victoria," *Washington Standard*, 31 January 1863. See also Boyd, *The Coming of the Spirit of Pestilence*, 172–201.

39. See, e.g., Wilkes, *Narrative of the United States Exploring Expedition*, 4:355; Swan, *The Northwest Coast; or, Three Years' Residence in Washington Territory*, 154.

40. Stanley, *Mapping the Frontier*, 36, 46.

41. Swan, *Almost Out of the World*, 98.

42. Ibid., 96–98; Wright, "Indians of British Columbia," 263.

43. In 1828, e.g., the Hudson's Bay Company employee at Fort Langley, east of present-day Vancouver, recorded one woman's travel to Puget Sound: "The widow of the Okinukun . . . that was drowned a few days ago, left this [day] to go to her own lands. She goes up the river and Crosses over near the foot of Mount Baker, to the Scadget and Sinihooms Country, from thence to the Sinuwames . . . where she considers her home" (McLachlan, *The Fort Langley Journals*, 55).

44. John G. Parke to Archibald Campbell, 4 December 1857, reel 1, Microfilm A1265: Records Relating to the Northwest Boundary, 1853–1901 [hereafter cited as A1265], UW Libraries; Archibald Campbell to Lewis Cass, 25 September 1858, ibid.; Boundary Survey Report vol. 1, G. Clinton Gardner Papers, Western Americana Collection, Beinecke Rare Book and Manuscript Library [hereafter cited as Gardner Papers].

45. Joseph Smith Harris to mother, 28 January 1858, folder 29, box 2, Joseph Smith Harris Papers, Western Americana Collection, Beinecke Rare Book and Manuscript Library [hereafter cited as Harris Papers].

46. Archibald Campbell to Lewis Cass, 25 September 1858, reel 1, A1265, UW Libraries; John G. Parke to Archibald Campbell, 20 September 1858, ibid.; "Report to [George Clinton] Gardner, work Aug–Dec," 10 December 1858, Northwest Boundary Survey Reports, folder 60, box 3, Harris Papers. See also Ficken, *Unsettled Boundaries*, 27–119.

47. Samuel Anderson to Janet, 6 January 1860, folder 17, box 1, Samuel Anderson Papers, Western Americana Collection, Beinecke Rare Book and Manuscript Library [hereafter cited as Anderson Papers].

48. Samuel Anderson to Janet, 1 September 1861, folder 19, box 1, Anderson Papers.

49. As one American astronomer explained about the Lummi and Nooksack: "In our intercourse with them I found them well disposed but curious to know

our business in their country, which I found it difficult to explain, and finally thought it best simply to let them know that we were making a map of the country; for they never could have understood how we were running a boundary line between nations over their lands, of which they were very pertinacious in explaining to us the limits" (see Boundary Survey Report, vol. 1, Gardner Papers).

50. United States, *Indian Affairs*, vol. 2, *Treaties*, 664, 672, 676, 684, 721.

51. Bancroft, *History of Washington, Idaho, and Montana*, 211–13. Jay's Treaty also guaranteed the free movement of Indians across the U.S.-Canadian border, a point the Washington territorial legislature in particular often tried to ignore.

52. FARCIA 1857, 332.

53. FARCIA 1873, 304.

54. Ibid.

55. ARDIA 1883, 43–45; ARDIA 1884, 82–83; ARDIA 1885, 80, 92.

56. John J. H. Van Bokkelen to the Honorable James Douglas, 17 January 1856, Western Americana Collection, Beinecke Rare Books and Manuscript Library.

57. James Gilchrist Swan, entries for 14 and 15 July 1875, "Journal of a Cruise," folder 3, box 6, Swan Papers.

58. James Gilchrist Swan, entry for 30 June 1875, "Journal of a Cruise," folder 3, box 6, Swan Papers.

59. Swan was sharply rebuffed at least once in his efforts to get artifacts, when a woman in the Queen Charlotte Islands who had "been in Victoria and understands the ways of the whites" refused to sell him totem poles he admired, telling him "'these posts are monuments for the dead and we will not sell them any more than white people will sell the gravestones or monuments in cemeteries but you can have one made for you'" (James Gilchrist Swan, entry for 30 July 1875, "Journal of a Cruise," folder 3, box 6, Swan Papers).

60. ARDIA 1875, 47–48, 54.

61. See Marine Hospital Annual Reports, 1874–1912, CIS US Exec Branch, Microfiche T2701–27, UW Libraries, and finding aid: "Records of the U.S. Customs Service."

62. ARDIA 1875, 48; ARDIA 1876, 35; ARDIA 1877, 48; ARDIA 1879, 132–33; "Report of Sanitary Commission," Mifflin Wistar Gibbs Papers concerning Victoria, British Columbia, James Weldon Johnson Collection in the Yale Collection of American Literature, Beinecke Rare Book and Manuscript Library. See also Perry, *On the Edge of Empire*, 114–23, for segregation efforts in Victoria during and after the 1862–63 epidemic.

63. ARDIA 1875, 55; ARDIA 1876, 35; ARDIA 1879, 137.

64. ARDIA 1883, 44.

65. E. C. Fitzhugh to Isaac Stevens, 7 February 1857, reel 20, A171, UW Libraries.

66. Byron Barlow to Ross, 31 August 1870, reel 24, ibid.

67. Byron Barlow to Ross, 31 August 1870, reel 24, ibid.

68. Dr. Paget to W. B. Gosnell, 30 July 1861, reel 19, ibid.; G. W. Weston to Byron Barlow, 1 October 1873, reel 24, ibid.

69. *ARDIA* 1876, 35; "Hydah Indians Living near Port Ludlow Afflicted with Smallpox," *Washington Standard*, 27 November 1875, 2; Klingle, *Emerald City*, 38–39.

70. U.S. Court of Claims, *Duwamish et al. v. United States*, 1:487; *FARCIA* 1877, 199. See also Thrush, "City of the Changers," 99–100, for other examples of Indian dispossession through arson, apparently unrelated to fears of disease.

## DIVIDED RANGES

*Trans-border Ranches and
the Creation of National
Space along the Western
Mexico–U.S. Border*

................................................

Rachel St. John

In 1909 the U.S. government began construction of the first border fence between the United States and Mexico, along the California–Baja California boundary line. After years of relying on customs checkpoints, roving patrolmen, and respect for the law, U.S. officials finally resorted to fencing in response to concerns that unrestricted trans-border movement was spreading infectious disease and threatening the U.S. economy.

In the context of current debates about border control, the call for fencing is probably familiar. What is surprising is not the fence, but the interests and actors involved. This first fence was not a product of immigration reform or homeland defense, but the work of the Bureau of Animal Industry. And rather than immigrants or smugglers, the illegal crossers evoking concern were cattle and the Texas fever-ticks which infested them.

In contrast to the present-day emphasis on immigration, in the late nineteenth century cattle ranching was at the center of debates about border control. By the turn of the century, ranchers, scientists, and government officials had eradicated Texas fever in most of California, but had little success along the border in the southern part of the state. Ranchers in the counties nearest the border complained that dipping and quarantining their animals would accomplish nothing as long as their stock continued to come into contact with tick-infested Mexican herds. The only solution, the Bureau of Animal Industry concluded in 1909, was to build a fence along the border. The completion of the fence in 1911 marked the final stage in the eradication of Texas fever in California.[1]

It also marked the beginning of the end of the open-range era of trans-border ranching and the further division of national space along the international boundary line. As with other fences throughout the West, the Bureau of Animal Industry's border fence restricted the movement of cattle and reinforced property divisions that had previously existed only on paper.[2] However, the border fence marked not only the divide between ranches, but also that between nation-states. As such, it was at the center of the transition of the borderlands from a peripheral, pastoral landscape to one of capitalism and state control.

The processes which brought state sovereignty and capitalism to the border are difficult to disentangle. The establishment of a basic level of sovereignty by the U.S. and Mexican militaries enabled the initiation of market-oriented ranching in the borderlands. Once ranching got underway, the states had new reasons to assert their dominion through the regulation of property ownership and trans-border movement. State concerns about trans-border ranching extended beyond controlling disease to land ownership requirements, cattle rustling, and customs collection. Along the border, each of these areas involved not just practices of animal husbandry, but sovereign principles. For the United States and Mexico, national sovereignty was made real in the division of binational ranches and the regulation of the trans-border movement of cattle.

While ranchers and government officials shared a commitment both to sovereignty and the cultivation of capitalism in the borderlands, they often had different ideas about the place of the international boundary within the context of an integrated binational ranching economy. In the eyes of state agents, the boundary line divided property regimes and created a customs and quarantine barrier. They expected that ranchers would respect this boundary by crossing their stock at official ports of entry, paying customs duties, and submitting to health inspections. In contrast, despite their own efforts to divide the ranges into exchangeable pieces of private property, ranchers resisted the government-imposed limitations on land ownership and restrictions on crossings as unnatural and inconvenient divisions of an integrated landscape.

Ranchers and state officials gradually worked out these conflicts through a series of compromises. Although not without hardship and complaints, ranchers learned to navigate two property regimes and a series of laws restricting trans-border movement. At the same time, in response to ranchers' objections and with a growing awareness that it was often inefficient and difficult, if not impossible, to separate sovereign space along the border, state agents backed away from their aspirations of absolute control. In place of a tightly controlled border, the U.S. and Mexican governments established a conditional set of crossing laws and spatial restraints, including the Bureau of Animal Industry's border fence, which regulated trans-border ranching without disrupting it. As a result of these compromises, borderlands ranching flourished within the context of negotiated, if not necessarily compromised, sovereignty.

### The Template for Trans-border Ranching

The struggles over the division of border ranges emerged in part because of the strength of the environmental, historical, and economic ties that unified the borderlands. Like the epidemic diseases and salmon that circulated across the U.S.-Canadian border, as described by Jennifer Seltz and Lissa Wadewitz elsewhere in this volume, the cattle that crossed the U.S.-Mexico border were part of a transnational environment. But while pathogens were inadvertent imports to the northern borderlands and salmon were indigenous to the region, cattle were intentionally introduced into the U.S.-Mexican borderlands, as part of an effort to transform the desert grasslands into a landscape of profits. The history of this process, from initial Spanish settlement and Mexican land distribution to the arrival of railroads and the turn to U.S. markets, further contributed to the creation of a transnational ranching landscape which resisted any clear division of national space.

Water, grass, and geography created the initial limits of cattle-raising in the U.S.-Mexican borderlands. The availability of water and grass determined where cattle could survive and reproduce. The San Pedro, Santa Cruz, and Colorado River valleys, with their rare year-round above-ground flows, were particularly well suited to stock-raising. In the arid desert grasslands, streams, springs, and seasonal washes were also critical sources of water. Along with the grasslands they supported, these water sources created a natural landscape that did not correspond to later political divisions. The Santa Cruz River, for instance, would be crossed twice by the international boundary line as it flowed from its headwaters in the San Rafael Valley just north of the border, dipped down into Sonora, and then crossed back into Arizona near Nogales. Both before the creation of

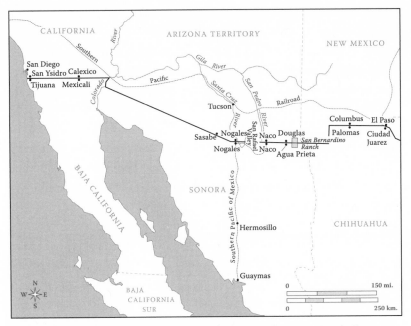

**Map 1.** Western U.S.–Mexican borderlands in the late nineteenth century. (Map by Ezra Zeitler)

the boundary line and long after it was drawn, the borderlands environment, not the position of the border, would define the boundaries of cattle-raising in the borderlands.[3]

The first cattle to feed on borderlands grasses arrived with Spanish explorers, missionaries, and settlers in the sixteenth and seventeenth centuries. With the introduction of cattle, Spanish colonizers began the process of physically and conceptually transforming the natural environment into a productive pastoral landscape.[4] Over the two hundred fifty years that elapsed between their introduction by Spaniards and U.S. conquest of the region, cattle became integrated into the borderlands environment as first Spanish and later Mexican settlers attempted to establish ranches on the northern frontier. While their herds reproduced and expanded, the settlers' ability to protect and profit from them waxed and waned with the balance of power between colonial military forces and Indian raiders. In the vicinity of what would become the Arizona-Sonora and New Mexico–Chihuahua borders, Apache bands were a particular threat due to their raids on Spanish and Mexican settlements. Settlers moved stock onto the ranges during times of peace, only to abandon them with the resumption of raiding. The creation of a borderlands pastoral economy was a long, bloody process.[5]

Despite the persistent violence, the introduction of cattle, followed by the establishment of property divisions, formed the basis of a pastoral landscape in the borderlands. In the early nineteenth century, Spanish officials began carving borderlands ranges into productive space by awarding immense land grants to loyal subjects. Spanning the site of the future boundary line, these grants were oriented around range and water resources. In 1821, First Lieutenant Ignacio Pérez received title to a land grant encompassing the San Bernardino Valley (near present-day Douglas/Agua Prieta) and its abundant groundwater. Other grants, including the San Rafael de la Zanja Grant, in the vicinity of the Santa Cruz's headwaters, and the Arivaca Grant, in the Altar Valley near Sasabe, also claimed areas known for their grasslands, groundwater, and creeks and rivers.[6]

Claims, however, were all these grants were. The settlers who brought their herds into the borderlands soon abandoned them in the face of a resurgence in Apache raiding in the 1830s. By the time the boundary line had been established by the 1848 Treaty of Guadalupe Hidalgo, followed by the 1853 Gadsden Treaty, Indian raids had effectively depopulated the border region. Of the rich pastoral landscape only wild cattle and ruins remained. Passing through southern Arizona in 1864, an America traveler observed: "Ruined houses, broken fences, and deserted pastures are the prominent marks of [the Apaches'] ravages. Where vast herds of cattle once grazed is now a rank growth of mesquite, grass, and weeds, inhabited only by deer, rabbits, and wild turkey."[7]

Yet where this man saw failure, more optimistic observers imagined the rebirth of ranching in the borderlands. U.S. Boundary Commissioner Major William H. Emory was one of these optimists. Following his 1856 survey of the boundary line, he submitted a report that translated ruined ranches into signs of future progress. Of the San Pedro Valley on the eastern Arizona-Sonora border, he wrote, "There are also to be found here, in the remains of spacious corrals, and in the numerous wild cattle and horses which still are seen in this country, the evidence of its immense capacity as a grazing country." For Emory, the San Bernardino Ranch, which straddled the boundary line to the east of the San Pedro River, exemplified the combination of prior evidence of pastoralism and natural advantages that he found so promising. Although its stock had "been killed or run off by the Indians, and the spacious buildings of adobe which accommodated the employés of this vast grazing farm are now washed nearly level with the earth," Emory nevertheless found the reports of its once vast herds and the presence of perpetual springs encouraging. "Wherever water is sufficient," he concluded, "this whole region presents marvelous advantages for the raising of stock, owing to the character and quantity of the grass, the mildness of the winters, and its almost perfect exemption from flies and mosquitos."[8] Emory was convinced that under U.S. control ranching could rise from the ashes.

And to some extent he was right. While the establishment of the border did not immediately revive border ranching, it did initiate a concerted binational effort to wrest control of the borderlands from the Apaches and to link the region to markets in the United States. In the years following the boundary survey, the U.S. and Mexican militaries undertook campaigns to confine the Apaches to reservations in the United States and to put an end to border raiding. At the same time, the construction of American railroads first up to and then across the border brought the borderlands within reach of U.S. markets. In 1880, the Southern Pacific Railroad arrived in Tucson, making it possible for borderlands ranchers to transport their cattle to points throughout the United States. Two years later, subsidiaries of the Atchison, Topeka, and Santa Fe Railroad completed the first trans-border railroad, running from Benson, Arizona, to the Sonoran port city of Guaymas.[9] By the end of the nineteenth century, the once isolated and dangerous borderlands had become accessible and secure.

The suppression of raiding and the arrival of railroads provided the prerequisites for the borderlands to become part of the cattle boom that swept across western North America in the late nineteenth century, integrating rangelands across the continent into a market-oriented ranching economy. Beginning in the 1870s new ranchers arrived in the borderlands who increased herd sizes with an eye to shipping their stock outside the region. By the end of the nineteenth century, borderlands ranges carried hundreds of thousands of cattle that would end their lives far from the border on butchers' tables all across the United States.[10]

The potential for market production drew both longtime Mexican and Native American residents of the borderlands and newcomers from the United States and Europe into the ranching economy. While dominated by Anglo names, the Arizona registries of brands for the 1880s included a handful of Spanish-surnamed individuals. Their numbers were particularly high in the border counties of Yuma and Pima, comprising two-thirds of the registrants in Yuma County. Native people also participated in the ranching economy. For Native Americans and ethnic Mexicans on both sides of the new boundary line, ranching represented both an opening and a narrowing of economic opportunity. The increased interest in developing borderlands ranges resulted in growing competition for land and water, but it also offered opportunities to engage in the market and profit from selling both land and cattle.[11]

Pedro Aguirre was one of the success stories. Born in Chihuahua in 1835, Aguirre and his brothers operated a freighting and stage business in Arizona and New Mexico in the mid-nineteenth century. When the arrival of the Southern Pacific Railroad threatened to cut into their business, the brothers shifted to ranching. Aguirre founded the Buenos Aires Ranch along the border near Sasabe in the 1870s. Despite struggles caused by droughts and market fluctuations, he managed to stay afloat until his death in 1907, after which his family sold the Buenos Aires to the Anglo-American-owned La Osa Cattle Company.[12]

The transfer of property from ethnic Mexicans (of both U.S. and Mexican citizenship) to Anglo-Americans was typical of the transition from pastoralism to market-oriented ranching along the border. In fact, the sale of the Buenos Aires came relatively late in that process. With the cattle boom of the 1870s and 1880s, many Mexicans who had inherited or bought land on both sides of the border took advantage of the increased interest in borderlands ranges by selling off large tracts of property to incoming Americans. One of these new arrivals was a Texas cattleman named John Slaughter, who purchased the San Bernardino Ranch from Mexican land speculator Guillermo Andrade in 1884. The San Bernardino Ranch, which Ignacio Pérez had received in exchange for his military service in 1821, and which Boundary Commissioner William Emory had singled out for praise, was, by the 1880s, divided by the international boundary line. Slaughter gained control of 65,000 acres, one-third of which lay within the United States, with the remaining two-thirds in Mexico.[13]

Throughout the borderlands, American ranchers followed Slaughter's model, acquiring title to land grants and replicating the landholding and

**Figure 1.** Boundary Monument No. 115, located on a high ridge in the Patagonia Mountains, to the west of the San Rafael Valley and to the east of Nogales. (From United States Senate, "Survey and Remarking of the Boundary between the United States and Mexico west of the Rio Grande, 1891–1896")

grazing patterns of the pastoralists who had preceded them. Partners Frederick Maish and Thomas Driscoll bought up a number of properties in Arizona and Sonora, including the trans-border Rancho Santa Maria Santísima del Carmen, or Buenavista Land Grant, from José María Quiroga and Susana Urea de Quiroga. Brothers Colin and Brewster Cameron acquired the San Rafael de la Zanja Land Grant in 1882. By 1885, the governor of Arizona claimed that Arizona ranges contained 652,500 cattle. In 1887, the Cameron brothers' San Rafael Ranch alone ran a herd of more than 17,000 cattle.[14]

As ranchers arrived in the borderlands, they followed the same property lines and patterns of movement as their predecessors, buying property and running cattle on both sides of the line. In a landscape of limited water, ranchers valued rivers, springs, and the grasslands they supported, regardless of which side of the boundary they were on. Given that the preexisting property divisions corresponded to the areas best suited to stock-raising, ranchers were eager to invest in land grants, once again indifferent to their orientation on the boundary line. The U.S. and Mexican states, however, were far from indifferent in these matters. Not long after the ranchers arrived, both nations began to assert their sovereignty by regulating property ownership and controlling the movement of cattle across the border.

### Negotiating Nationalized Property Regimes

While rangelands, property lines, and market forces transcended the boundary line, property regimes did not. The border did not prevent Americans from owning land in Mexico, or Mexicans from owning land in the United States, but it did create subtle shifts in the legal requirements of ownership and require ranchers to negotiate different legal systems on each side of the line. Challenges to land grant claims forced ranchers who derived their property titles from those grants to petition the Mexican government for redress or to enter into lengthy proceedings in U.S. land courts. South of the boundary line, the Mexican government imposed citizenship requirements on the ownership of land along the border, so as to limit American encroachment and maintain Mexican sovereignty. These measures did not put a stop to trans-border ranching— something neither government wanted, given their desire for economic development in the borderlands—but rather resulted in an arrangement in which ranchers had to adopt different methods to secure land on each side of the border so that they could continue to operate across it. The end result was a transnational ranching landscape that conformed to, but was not confined by, the new international boundary.

Challenges to property titles that derived from land grants were a particular problem on the U.S. side of the border. Despite the provisions of the Treaty of Guadalupe Hidalgo that obligated the U.S. government to respect Spanish and Mexican land grants, American surveyors and settlers challenged the validity of a number of the land grant titles along the boundary line. In response, ranchers, like John Slaughter, who believed they had paid for outright title to their land, went to court to defend their claims. By 1891, the conflict over land grants had become such a problem that the U.S. Congress established a special Court of Private Land Claims to adjudicate contested claims. In this court, which pitted ranchers who derived their title from Mexican and Spanish grants against U.S. attorneys who sought to enlarge the public domain, the claimants were clearly at a disadvantage. Government attorneys and surveyors researched title documents, surveyed the land, and evaluated claims. The claimants had no choice but to enter into expensive court proceedings or lose their land. "The land grant fight and costs were terrible," recalled Viola Slaughter, John's wife. "We had all our papers clear back to the grant itself, but the U.S. government sent out surveyors and lawyers and all sorts of people to take it away from us. It went on for years and we had to send lawyers twice to Mexico City and you know that costs, and we sent them repeatedly to Santa Fe—everywhere. There were court and suit costs. It was terrible."[15]

The Slaughters' case, like those of other claimants, required them not only to demonstrate their chain of title, but more difficult still, to explain the unfamiliar provisions of Spanish and Mexican land law to a skeptical U.S. court.[16] While Slaughter provided an authentic chain of title, the court questioned the authority of the *intendente* of Sonora and Sinaloa to make land grants after Mexican Independence in 1821 and ultimately rejected Slaughter's claim because the grant was not recorded in the Toma de Razón (Book of Land Titles) in Hermosillo. Unfortunately for Slaughter, his counter-argument, that the Toma de Razón had only existed for three years and that the San Bernardino Grant was duly recorded in the previous record of titles, the Grand Libro de Registros, failed to convince the court. While Slaughter's surveyors determined that the grant contained 13,746 acres north of the boundary line in the United States, the government only approved his title to 2,383 acres.[17]

The rejection or reduction of land grant claims by the court was consistent all along the border. Partners Maish and Driscoll lost 11,621 of the 17,354 acres of the Yerba Buena, or Buenavista Ranch, that they claimed lay north of the boundary line in Arizona. Two prominent Sonoran families, the Camous and the Elíases, had two claims denied completely.[18] The court's largest blow, however, was to the Cameron brothers, who saw their holdings in the San Rafael de la Zanja Grant reduced from 152,890 acres to only 17,352 acres after the court rejected their claim that the grant included surplus lands.[19]

When it came to the portions of their land grants that lay in Mexico, some of these ranchers had a better record of retaining control of their property. The ranches' trans-border locations sometimes meant that grants rejected by the U.S. courts were still accepted in Mexico. For instance, the Slaughters, despite their losses on the American side of the line, managed to hold on to the 38,000 acres of the San Bernardino Grant which lay within Mexico.[20] Other landholders, however, were not so lucky. In the 1880s and 1890s, private land surveyors contracted by the Mexican government rejected the broad claims of grant holders like the Elías family, who saw large swaths of their Sonoran ranchlands redefined as public domain. Despite protests from members of the Elías clan, these lands, like those lost by land grant claimants to the north of the line, were soon on the market, where a growing number of American investors were willing to pay top dollar for surveyed lands with secure titles.[21]

American ownership of Mexican lands, however, was not easy. Regardless of whether a title stemmed from a Spanish land grant or from a more recent sale of surveyed land, all prospective American buyers faced Mexican laws that restricted foreign ownership of land near the border. In 1856, the Mexican federal government had enacted a law forbidding foreigners from owning land within a twenty-league "prohibited zone" along the boundary line. This restriction created an obstacle, although by no means an insurmountable one, to American economic incursions across the border. Under President Porfirio Díaz, the Mexican state embraced foreign investment as a source of national economic strength. For this reason, despite the legacy of American territorial encroachment and official restrictions on foreign ownership within the prohibited zone, Mexican officials worked with American ranchers to facilitate their acquisition of rangeland along the border.[22]

American ranchers, with the help of their allies in the Mexican government, were able to acquire land in the prohibited zone by adopting a variety of methods, including long-term leases, government permits, partnerships with Mexican citizens, naturalization, and, eventually, the formation of Mexican corporations. John Slaughter gained control of the majority of the San Bernardino Ranch on the Mexican side of the boundary line through a ninety-nine-year lease. The Cameron brothers secured an even longer lease, for 999 years, which, as Brewster Cameron noted was, "about the same [as owning land]."[23] Ranchers also paid the Mexican government for special permits that allowed them to own land within the prohibited zone. In 1890, the Cameron brothers secured such a permit for one of their properties for $500. However, as their failure to attain another permit for the Mexican portion of the San Rafael Ranch attested, this kind of concession depended on the whims of Mexican officials.[24]

Other ranchers used Mexican citizenship to get around the prohibited zone laws. Guillermo Andrade, the same Mexican entrepreneur from whom John Slaughter acquired the San Bernardino Ranch, worked with a series of American investors to develop land in the Colorado River Delta in Baja California.[25] One of his competitors, William Denton, managed to evade the restriction on foreign ownership by becoming a Mexican citizen himself. Originally from England, Denton had arrived in California during the Gold Rush. He had subsequently married Elena Cano de los Rios, of Mulege, Baja California, in 1860, and had settled with his family in San Diego in 1874. It was not until the 1880s, however, after he had begun investing in Baja California borderlands, that he became a naturalized Mexican citizen. By the time of his death in 1907, Denton's estate included interest in two ranches near the border in northern Baja California.[26]

Faced with Mexican citizenship restrictions and assaults on land grant titles in American courts, ranchers learned to engage two legal systems in order to hold together the transnational ranching landscape to which they had been drawn. As a result of their efforts, and despite periodic downturns caused by drought and depression, by the beginning of the twentieth century, ranchers had accumulated virtually all of the range land along the Western U.S.–Mexico border. Some ranching pioneers, like John Slaughter, continued to operate across the border. Others, including the Cameron brothers, sold out to new and even bigger ranchers who soon dominated borderlands ranching. In 1903, the mining entrepreneur William Cornell Greene bought the Camerons' San Rafael de la Zanja ranch, incorporating it into a vast trans-border ranching realm that extended from the San Pedro Valley seven miles north of the border to the mining camp of Cananea in Sonora.[27] Along the border between California and Baja California, a group of Los Angeles investors, organized as the Colorado River Land Company, purchased over 800,000 acres in the Colorado River Delta and began leasing land to ranchers.[28] An even larger ranch emerged to the east, where the American-owned Palomas Land and Cattle Company operated on 2,000,000 acres of ranchland in Chihuahua and controlled the entire 140-mile border with New Mexico.[29] These vast trans-border ranches became the symbolic centerpieces of a trans-border ranching economy that reached for hundreds of miles into Mexico and the United States, linked together by the steady flow of cattle south to Mexican pastures and north to American markets.

## Navigating the Divided Range

To ranchers' chagrin, the negotiation of property titles was only the first hurdle in trans-border ranching. Borderlands ranching, like ranching elsewhere in western North America, operated on an open-range model in which cattle roamed widely to access sufficient grass and water. In the borderlands, this meant that cattle not only moved across the range, but also across the international boundary line. By the end of the nineteenth century, borderlands ranchers regularly moved their stock between pastures in the United States and Mexico before driving them north to the railroads that carried them to markets throughout the United States.[30]

All of this movement was, at least in theory, subject to both U.S. and Mexican customs and quarantine laws. Whether part of an organized cattle drive or a wandering stray, every cow that crossed the border penetrated the sovereign boundary between the United States and Mexico. As ranching emerged in the borderlands, it became increasingly profitable and important for the U.S. and Mexican states to enforce their authority along the boundary line through the collection of customs duties and the enforcement of crossing regulations. However, as they worked to collect customs and control the movement of cattle, customs agents, health inspectors, and consular officials quickly discovered how difficult and inefficient it was to stake out sovereignty on the border. Enforcing seemingly simple requirements that ranchers pay customs duties and cross their cattle at official ports of entry was virtually impossible given the small force of customs officers and the frequency of trans-border movement along the long and unfenced border. Furthermore, the two states' commitment to economic development in the borderlands meant that officials had to be careful not to impose taxes or other bureaucratic requirements that would derail trans-border business. Instead, through a process of establishing laws and listening to ranchers' protests, local representatives of both states gradually constructed a system of border controls that balanced sovereign principles with the demands of binational ranching and an awareness of governmental limits. The border they built included such innovative spatial controls as ports of entry, border patrols, and, finally, fences, but it also established a pattern of compromise and accommodation in which border control was flexible and conditional.

Most of the laws that regulated borderlands ranching originated far from the border. Based in Washington, D.C., and Mexico City, policy-makers negotiated tariffs and crossing regulations within the context of national debates about trade and economic development.[31] Yet while they thought on a national scale, their decisions had a profound effect on the local economy of borderlands ranching. Quarantines, tariffs, and customs regulations remade trans-border ranching.

Quarantines and tariffs could be particularly disruptive. At their worst, quarantines bifurcated the borderlands, leaving ranchers in Mexico without access to U.S. markets. In 1887, Sonoran officials resorted to diplomatic channels to prevent the governor of Arizona from including Mexican cattle in a ninety-day quarantine which threatened to decimate the Sonoran ranching economy.[32] High tariffs could have a similar effect by making the movement of cattle across the border prohibitively expensive. This was most apparent in 1890, when the highly protectionist McKinley Tariff Act raised American import duties to $10 per head for cattle over a year old and $2 per head on those under a year, sending the Sonoran cattle industry into a steep decline from which it would take almost twenty years to recover.[33]

While government policies had the potential to devastate the trans-border ranching industry, they more often had a more subtle effect. Rather than stopping all trans-border movement, the goal of customs officers and health inspectors was primarily to channel cattle crossings into designated ports of entry where Customs and Bureau of Animal Industry officials could monitor, tax, and restrict them. As early as 1880, the Mexican government established four new customs stations on the line at Quitoba-quito, Sasabe, Palominas, and Nogales. By 1892, there were numerous customs houses located both immediately on the boundary line and a few miles to the north or south. As ranching and other forms of trans-border commerce continued to flourish, both governments created new customs houses to accommodate them.[34]

The creation of official ports of entry altered the spatial dynamics of trans-border ranching. While convenient for government agents and nearby ranchers, crossing through a designated port of entry meant an unwelcome detour for many ranchers who preferred to simply drive their stock across the line at the nearest point. "To compel them to drive [their cattle] to Nogales for inspection, adds greatly to the cost, besides working a great loss in shrinkage of the animals," protested the Nogales Oasis in

1895. "And it works a hardship on the cattlemen here, for the cattle from afar eat up the feed on the hills about Nogales, which is needed to sustain the animals who find their natural crossing place at this point."[35] This cost and inconvenience frustrated ranchers like Brewster Cameron, who complained that crossing through designated ports of entry "would accomplish no good whatever to the government but would result in the destruction of the cattle business on the border."[36] On the other hand, one can only suppose that the Elíases, who hosted an annual roundup at their ranch near the San Pedro customhouse, would have seen this reorientation of border spaces as more advantageous. From the perspective of the states, ports of entry were simply a rational way to divide and manage national space, but for borderlands ranchers they represented a reorganization of the landscape that had consequences for the way they did business and the profitability of their operations.[37]

For ranchers whose property straddled or abutted the boundary line, many of these regulations were both particularly inconvenient but also easy to avoid. Before the gradual government fencing began in 1909, nothing prevented cattle from moving across the border. It was common practice for cattle to graze across the line, either on their own or driven by cowboys to better pasture. "In the absence of any natural or other barrier at the international boundary line, and during stormy and cooler portions of the year, when all stock move southward," wrote a group of Arizona ranchers, "it is practically impossible to prevent our cattle and horses from straying into the State of Sonora."[38] As the cattle were bound at roundup to be returned to U.S. soil, ranchers thought little of this practice.

Some of the new customs agents appointed to control the line, however, saw the situation differently. The deputy collector at Lochiel, Arizona, explained to the Cameron brothers that if cattle that strayed into Mexico "are not reported for inspection they in my opinion are seizable as it is impossible for me to tell the length of their stay in Mex. or whether the same are contraband."[39] Another group of American ranchers complained that the Mexican collector of customs at Nogales would not even allow them to cross the line to retrieve their strays.[40]

In response to these policies, some ranchers turned to smuggling. Taking the form of both trade in stolen cattle and the crossing of herds at unofficial points without paying duties or submitting them to inspections, smuggling grew alongside legitimate trans-border ranching. While most ranchers were unwilling to think of themselves as smugglers, many participated in petty smuggling, refusing to drive their herds to out-of-the-way ports of entry for inspection, or neglecting to pay duties on imported cattle. Cattle which strayed across the boundary line could even be said to smuggle themselves. Smuggling then was not just a matter of money, but of convenience, since customs and quarantine regulations that required detours to official ports of entry could easily be evaded by smuggling stock across the open border.[41]

In addition to these more innocent acts of smuggling for convenience, a thriving trade in stolen stock also developed along the border. Cross-border cattle rustling fell particularly hard on Mexican ranchers, who were hard-pressed to track their stolen stock across the border before it disappeared into the American market. In 1900, the Mexican consul in Nogales wrote to his superiors in Hermosillo calling for stricter laws to curtail the prevalent horse and cattle theft that was hamstringing ranching operations along the border.[42]

By the 1880s, the pervasive and persistent smuggling led both states to establish forces of roaming customs agents to patrol the border. On the U.S. side of the line, the Treasury Department augmented the customs officers stationed at ports of entry with a handful of mounted inspectors. In 1887, just eleven line riders were responsible for patrolling the border. After their establishment in 1901, the Arizona Rangers would also aid in the pursuit of cattle rustlers, but their forces never numbered more than twenty-five.[43] South of the border, customs enforcement was in the hands of a larger and more martial force—the Gendarmería Fiscal. Established by Porfirio Díaz in 1885, the Gendarmería Fiscal operated under the authority of the Ministry of Finance but became synonymous with not just customs enforcement, but law and order in general along Mexico's northern border. Its officers, most notably the well-known Indian fighter Emilio Kosterlitzky, came from the ranks of the border military elite. Well armed and quick to dispense justice, the Gendarmería Fiscal gained a reputation in local lore for its members' ruthless patrol of the border. C. E. Wiswall, the longtime manager of the Cananea Cattle Company, remembered that a particular cottonwood tree on the company's property gained notoriety as the place where Kosterlitzky hung cattle thieves. Kosterlitzky himself was reported to entertain other guests at the Slaughters' dinner table with "stories too gory to believe. Each course brought half a dozen more oral killings."[44]

Of course, violently suppressing every violation of customs and quarantine regulations was neither possible nor practical. Instead, local officials and customs inspectors responded to the pressure of ranchers who were inconvenienced by customs regulations by making some exceptions to accommodate local crossing practices. In the late 1880s, Arizona Territorial judges found in favor of border ranchers who argued that they should not have to pay duties on cattle that had simply strayed across the line. Praising one of these decisions, the editors of the *Arizona Daily Star* noted, "It is not possible to drive every animal that steps over an imaginary line past the custom house, nor is that necessary to protect the revenues."[45] According to Brewster Cameron, this opinion was shared by the customs collector in charge of the district as well: "The absurdity of requesting a man whose cattle merely graze across an imaginary line to drive them twenty-five miles or more away from their own range to be inspected by an officer of customs was so apparent to Collector Magoffin that he said it would be an outrage upon citizens which he would not countenance."[46]

Despite the presumptions of authority of officials in Washington, D.C., and Mexico City, it was individual officials like Magoffin who were responsible for much of the day-to-day business of adjudicating crossing regulations and negotiating sovereignty along the border. Customs agents and consuls not only enforced national laws, but helped their countrymen navigate and occasionally evade them. This occurred on both formal and informal levels, as government officials both petitioned their superiors to change the laws and worked out off-the-record agreements with local ranchers. Consuls, who were officially charged with facilitating international relations, were particularly active in lobbying for measures that would ease trans-border movement. Prior to the passage of the McKinley Tariff, the U.S. consul in Nogales, Delos H. Smith, had sent a steady stream of dispatches to his superiors warning that the high tariffs would strike a blow to U.S.-Mexican relations. "We are now as a nation making every effort to cultivate friendly commercial relations with our Sister Republics of the two continents," he wrote, "and consequently the propriety of taxing these ores and cattle to the extent proposed by this bill is a matter of grave doubt with many."[47] When the McKinley Tariff went into effect despite his pleas, Smith took up its burden by negotiating with both U.S. and Mexican customs officials on behalf of ranchers who sought to enter Mexico to round up their stray cattle and return them to the United States without paying the new duties.[48]

While Smith's efforts were ultimately helpful, they were not always efficient. Rather than pursuing compromises through these formal channels, some ranchers instead negotiated informal crossing agreements on their own. Citing a report printed in the *Tombstone Daily Epitaph*, historian Samuel Truett has described how John Slaughter worked out an agreement with Colonel Juan Fenochio of the Gendarmería Fiscal to allow Arizona ranchers to cross the border in pursuit of strays: " 'There was no Brussels carpet on the floor, champagn [*sic*] on ice, private secretaries and red tape, but a good old frontier 'Hello Cap,' and 'Howdy do John' and an adios.' "[49]

It was only through the interaction of men like John Slaughter and Juan Fenochio that both ranching and sovereignty took shape along the border. Operating a transnational ranch, Slaughter depended on the ability to move stock across the line without the inconvenience of having them inspected at an official port of entry or the expense of paying customs duties. Charged with policing the border, Fenochio would undoubtedly have had a much easier job if Slaughter's ranch and the animals on it conformed to national boundaries. Instead, the men were forced to negotiate with each other in an attempt to create a border that could be crossed without being transgressed.

**Conclusion**

The border was not, and is not, a space of absolutes. While the clear lines on a map depict a neat division between U.S. and Mexican space, in reality, movement—of water, air, people, goods, cash, and, of course, cattle—has blurred these lines. Sovereignty, then, has never been clear cut, but always contingent.

The history of trans-border ranching in the Western U.S.–Mexico borderlands provides a window into how government agents and private citizens reconciled the theory and the practice of national sovereignty, and the effect it had on the development of one industry in the late nineteenth century. Shaped by the flow of water, the distribution of land grants, and

**Figure 2.** Present-day view of the Slaughter Ranch looking south into Mexico, 2001. (Author's collection)

the pull of American markets, the borderlands ranching landscape initially seemed to defy the national boundaries imposed by the state. This insubordination continued through the persistent wandering of strays and the deliberate transgressions of smugglers. Yet, despite these acts of defiance, neither state sought to halt trans-border ranching. Rather than stamping out trans-border movement and demolishing transnational spaces, both states, by choice and necessity, focused their energies on limiting land ownership to state-regulated property regimes and on channeling trans-border movement into ports of entry where government officials could monitor, tax, and control it. At the same time, ranchers reacted to government efforts with responses that ranged from complete acquiescence to outright resistance, but that were most often characterized by accommodation and compromise.

While ranching continues along the border today, it no longer provides the prominent paradigm for understanding border control. The political and economic importance of drug smuggling, undocumented immigration, and post-NAFTA trade now dwarf the movement of cattle. A century ago, border control was primarily a local matter, the purview of a handful of ranchers and the agents charged with regulating their movement, but today it is often in the national spotlight in both the United States and Mexico. Unaware of or ignoring the local and historical context in which border controls and national sovereignty developed, politicians and the public frequently talk in absolutes about controlling the border or breaking down national barriers. But, rather than one or the other, the border has always been a compromise between these two extremes—a border that contains, but never completely controls; a border that divides, but does not sever.

## Notes

1. McKellar and Hart, "Eradicating Cattle Ticks in California," 283–300; Pulling, "California's Range Cattle Industry," 28.

2. For a discussion of fencing in western ranching, see Frink, Jackson, and Spring, *When Grass Was King*, 57–58, 86–88, 246–47; Jordan, *North American Cattle-Ranching Frontiers*, 265–67, 286, 305–7.

3. Bahre, *A Legacy of Change*; McClaran and Van Devender, *The Desert Grassland*; Gehlback, *Mountain Islands and Desert Seas*, 109–241; Hadley and Sheridan, "Land Use History of the San Rafael Valley, Arizona."

4. Pastoralism was a precapitalist form of stock-raising that relied on grass and water to create wealth in the form of large, loosely controlled herds of cattle. Drawing on Tim Ingold's analysis of the shift from pastoralism to ranching in Finland, Nathan Sayre has distinguished between the natural surpluses on which pastoral economies rely and the emphasis on monetary value and markets in ranching economies (see Sayre, *Ranching, Endangered Species, and Urbanization in the Southwest*, 51).

5. Sheridan, *Landscapes of Fraud*, 78–93; Gehlback, *Mountain Islands and Desert Seas*, 109; Weber, *The Mexican Frontier*, 82–87, 183–84; Weber, *The Spanish Frontier in North America*, 235; Spicer, *Cycles of Conquest*, 547–48; Goodwin and Basso, *Western Apache Raiding and Warfare*; Camou Healy, *De rancheros, poquiteros, orejanos y criollos*, 61–74.

6. "In the Court of Private Land Claims, District of Arizona, Involving the property claimed under the San Bernardino Land Grant, Transcript of oral evidence and proceedings," 18–19 March 1895, folder 4, box 1; Copy of "Testimonio of four sitios of land for Cattle in the Hacienda of San Bernardino," folder 2, box 1, Slaughter Financial Papers, Arizona Historical Society–Southern Arizona Division [hereafter cited as AHS–SAD]; Earman et al., "Hydrologic Framework and Groundwater Characteristics, San Bernardino Valley, Arizona and Sonora"; Hadley and Sheridan, "Land Use History of the San Rafael Valley, Arizona"; Sayre, *Ranching, Endangered Species, and Urbanization in the Southwest*, xxxvi–xlii, 29.

7. Browne, *Adventures in the Apache Country*, 161. See also Weber, *The Mexican Frontier*, 82–87, 183–84; Weber, *The Spanish Frontier in North America*, 235; Spicer, *Cycles of Conquest*, 547–48.

8. U.S. Department of the Interior, *Report on the United States and Mexican Boundary Survey*, 1:94.

9. St. John, "Line in the Sand," chap. 2; Hatfield, *Chasing Shadows*; Haskett, "Early History of the Cattle Industry in Arizona," 25–26; Boyd, "Twenty Years to Nogales"; Trennert, "The Southern Pacific Railroad of Mexico," 265–66; Ready, *Open Range and Hidden Silver*, 26–27; Lewis, *Iron Horse Imperialism*, 43–44; Sheridan, *Arizona*, 122–23.

10. Ford to Fulford, 12 May 1892, folder 3, box 2, San Rafael Cattle Company Papers [hereafter cited as SRCC], University of Arizona Special Collections [hereafter cited as UASC]; Colin Cameron to Fulford, 16 November 1899, folder 4, box 2, ibid.; "Statement for the Months of April and May, 1903," prepared by Colin Cameron, 31 May 1903, folder 1, box 3, ibid. See also Haskett, "Early History of the Cattle Industry in Arizona"; Camou Healy, *De rancheros, poquiteros, orejanos y criollos*; Sheridan, *Landscapes of Fraud*, 83; Sayre, *Ranching, Endangered Species, and Urbanization in the Southwest*, 30–32, 53–54. For more general discussions of cattle ranching in the West, see Frink, Jackson, and Spring, *When Grass Was King*; Jordan, *North American Cattle-Ranching Frontiers*; Cronon, *Nature's Metropolis*, 207–61.

11. Lists from Arizona Brand Books, reprinted in Haskett, "Early History of the Cattle Industry in Arizona," 31–35; Tinker Salas, *In the Shadow of the Eagles*, 109; Coolidge, *Old California Cowboys*, 59; Haskett, "Early History of the Cattle Industry in Arizona," 13.

12. Aguirre, "The Last of the Dons," 243–48; Sayre, *Ranching, Endangered Species, and Urbanization in the Southwest*, 27–51.

13. Agreement between Camou brothers and G. H. Howard and associates, 9 May 1873, box 2, Francis Henry Hereford Papers, UASC; Jose Maria Elias & Maria P de Elias to Thaddeus D. Bryant & Juan N. Acuna, 11 May 1881, ibid.; Jose Maria Elias, Manuel Elias, Santiago Ainsa, Esteban Ochoa, P. R. Tully, to James M. Hall, 2 April 1883, ibid.; other, miscellaneous documents, ibid.; Tinker Salas, *In the Shadow of the Eagles*, 62; "In the Court of Private Land Claims, District of Arizona, Involving the property claimed under the San Bernardino Land Grant, Transcript of oral evidence and proceedings," 18–19 March 1895, folder 4, box 1, Slaughter Financial Papers, AHS–SAD; copy of "Testimonio of four sitios of land for Cattle in the Hacienda of San Bernardino," folder 2, box 1, ibid.

14. "Brief Summary of Title History of the Rancho Santa Maria Santisima del Carmen" and "Santa Cruz County Ranches," Ephemera Files, Pimeria Alta Historical Society [hereafter cited as PAHS]; Hadley and Sheridan, "Land Use History of the San Rafael Valley, Arizona," 99–102; Sheridan, *Arizona*, 131–34.

15. Cora Viola Slaughter, "Reminiscences," ca. 1937, folders 93–98, box 5, Ber-

nice Cosulich Papers, AHS–SAD. See also Bradfute, *The Court of Private Land Claims*, 14–16. For discussions of land grant claims in other parts of the West, see Montoya, *Translating Property*; Pitt, *The Decline of the Californios*, 86–119; Almaguer, *Racial Fault Lines*, 47, 75–90; Montejano, *Anglos and Mexicans in the Making of Texas*, 38, 43.

16. María Montoya has aptly described these processes in New Mexico as "translation." See Montoya, *Translating Property*.

17. Judgment of Joseph R. Reed, Chief Justice, in *John H. Slaughter v. The United States*, 27 March 1896, folder 4, box 1, Slaughter Financial Papers, AHS–SAD; Statement of Allen R. English, Attorney for the Petitioner in *John H. Slaughter v. The United States*, 25 March 1896, ibid.; "Testimony of H. G. Howe in the Court of Private Land Claims," 18–19 March 1895, ibid.; Bradfute, *The Court of Private Land Claims*, 151–52; Walker and Bufkin, *Historical Atlas of Arizona*, 14–15.

18. Walker and Bufkin, *Historical Atlas of Arizona*, 14–15; "Brief Summary of Title History of the Rancho Santa Maria Santisima del Carmen" and "Santa Cruz County Ranches," Ephemera Files, PAHS; *Ainsa v. U.S.*, 161 U.S. 208 (1896); *Ainsa v. U.S.*, 184 U.S. 639 (1902); Bradfute, *The Court of Private Land Claims*, 163–66, 168–70.

19. For more regarding the Camerons, see St. John, "Line in the Sand," 86–87; Hadley and Sheridan, "Land Use History of the San Rafael Valley," 97–103.

20. Cora Viola Slaughter, "Reminiscences," folders 93–98, box 5, Bernice Cosulich Papers, AHS–SAD.

21. Holden, *Mexico and the Survey of Public Lands*, 105, 154, 187–88; Truett, *Fugitive Landscapes*, 95.

22. Law of February 1st, 1856, translated in Mexico, Hamilton, *Hamilton's Mexican Law*, 11. For further discussion of the Prohibited Zone, see St. John, "Line in the Sand." For discussion of foreign investment in Mexico during the Porfiriato see Hart, *Empire and Revolution*; Katz, *The Secret War in Mexico*; Ruiz, *The People of Sonora and Yankee Capitalists*.

23. Brewster Cameron to Fulford, 24 January 1887, folder 5, box 1, SRCC Papers, UASC. See also "In the Court of Private Land Claims, District of Arizona, Involving the property claimed under the San Bernardino Land Grant, Transcript of oral evidence and proceedings," 18–19 March 1895, folder 4, box 1, Slaughter Financial Papers, AHS–SAD. Some historians have written that Slaughter purchased the San Bernardino Ranch. This may be because they considered the ninety-nine-year lease as de facto ownership, or because they only considered his ownership of the American portion of the ranch. See Erwin, *The Southwest of John Horton Slaughter*, 139. For a discussion of the role of Mexican corporations, see St. John, "Line in the Sand."

24. Brewster Cameron to Fulford, 19 May 1890, folder 1, box 2, SRCC Papers, UASC.

25. Hendricks, "Guillermo Andrade and Land Development on the Mexican Colorado River Delta"; Hendricks, "Developing San Diego's Desert Empire."

26. The exact sequence of Denton's naturalization and purchase of the Rancho Jacume is not entirely clear. Denton was naturalized in May 1886, but there are discrepancies as to when he took possession of the Rancho Jacume. It appears that Denton gradually gained control of Rancho Jacume between 1877 and 1887 through his negotiation of power of attorney for its previous owner. See "Historical Background," Denton Ranch Collection, Mandeville Special Collections Library, University of California, San Diego; copy of deed of sale of Jacume, stamped 7 March 1877 and 21 March 1872, folder 1, box 1, ibid.; William Denton's Mexican Naturalization Certificate, 28 May 1886, file 3, oversized box FB-082, ibid.; Certificación, 5 May 1887, file 5, oversized box FB-082, ibid.; Secretario de Estado y del despacho de Fomento, 25 December 1885, file 2, oversized box FB-082, ibid.; Denton to Co. Juez de Distrito, 3 August 1886, folder 21, box 1, ibid.

27. Hadley, "Ranch Life, The Border Country, 1880–1940"; Sonnichsen, *Colonel Greene and the Copper Skyrocket*, 24, 102, 237; Miscellaneous files related to the Claims of the Cananea Cattle Company, S.A., entry 125, box 188, Records of the United States–Mexico Claims Commission, Record Group 76 [hereafter cited as RG 76], National Archives and Records Administration, College Park, Md. [hereafter cited as NARA II]; Brewster Cameron to Ely, 26 May 1903, folder 5, box 2, SRCC Papers, UASC; Fulford to Stockholders, 7 July 1903, ibid.

28. For archival material on the Colorado River Land Company, see Anderson Portfolios, Colorado River Land Company Papers [hereafter cited as CRLC Papers], Sherman Library, Corona del Mar [hereafter cited as SL]. For overviews of the history of the Colorado River Land Company, see St. John, "Line in the Sand," chaps. 3–5; Kerig, "Yankee Enclave"; Herrera Carrillo, *Reconquista y colonización del valle de Mexicali*.

29. Deposition of Charles W. Newman, 9 June 1936, claim file for Palomas Land and Cattle Company, agency file no. 1850, entry 125, box 349a, RG 76, NARA II; Statement of Claimant in the Claim of The United States of America on behalf of *Palomas Land and Cattle Company v. United Mexican States*, ibid.

30. Ford to Fulford, 12 May 1892, folder 3, box 2, SRCC Papers, UASC; Colin Cameron to Fulford, 16 November 1899, folder 4, box 2, ibid.; "Statement for the Months of April and May, 1903," folder 1, box 3, ibid.; Sheridan, *Arizona*, 133–34. For discussions of open-range ranching in the West, see Frink, Jackson, and Spring, *When Grass Was King*, 247–48; Jordan, *North American Cattle-Ranching Frontiers*, 7–11.

31. Northrup and Turney, *Encyclopedia of Tariffs and Trade in U.S. History*, vols. 1 and 2; Terrill, *The Tariff, Politics, and American Foreign Policy*; Taussig, *The*

*Tariff History of the United States*. For examples of U.S. congressional debates over the tariff, see the *Congressional Record* for the 51st Cong., 1st sess. (vol. 21, pt. 5, 4838–59); and "William McKinley's 1888 Speech on Tariff Benefits for Labor," in Northrup and Turney, *Encyclopedia of Tariffs and Trade in U.S. History*, 2:257–60.

32. Governor of Sonora to the Secretary of Exterior Relations, 28 September 1887, tomo 592, año 1888, Ramo Exportación de Ganado, expediente 7, Archivo General del Estado de Sonora.

33. Taussig, *The Tariff History of the United States*, 251–83; "Tariff of 1890 (McKinley Tariff)," reprinted in Northrup and Turney, *Encyclopedia of Tariffs and Trade in U.S. History*, 3:214; Ruíz, *The People of Sonora and Yankee Capitalists*, 140–41.

34. Tinker Salas, *In the Shadow of the Eagles*, 118; "Survey and Remarking of the Boundary Between the United States and Mexico West of the Rio Grande, 1891–1896: Part I," 55th Cong., 2nd sess., S. Doc. 247, 1898, 19–23; Tout, *The First Thirty Years*, 273; *Calexico Chronicle*, 4 May 1905; "Custom House Is Open," *Calexico Chronicle*, 18 April 1910, 2; Lawler to the President, 31 December 1910, Anderson Portfolios, folder 18, CRLC Papers, SL; Creel to Otis, 3 January 1911, ibid.

35. "Burdensome and Useless," *Nogales Oasis*, 26 October 1895, 4.

36. Brewster Cameron to Chalmers, labeled exhibit "B," ca. 1887, folder 6, box 1, SRCC Papers, UASC.

37. Truett, *Fugitive Landscapes*, 85. In thinking about state agendas, I am influenced here and elsewhere by Scott, *Seeing Like a State*.

38. Town, Altschul, and Breen to Blaine, 9 December 1890, reel 1, Microfilm M283: Despatches from United States Consul in Nogales, 1889–1906 [hereafter cited as M283], Record Group 59: Records of the Department of State [hereafter cited as RG 59], NARA II.

39. Chalmers to Cameron Brothers, labeled exhibit "E," 20 November 1887, folder 6, box 1, SRCC Papers, UASC.

40. Town, Altschul, and Breen to Blaine, 9 December 1890, reel 1, M283, RG 59, NARA II. See also Aspe to Smith, 12 July 1890, reel 1, M283, RG 59, NARA II; Aspe to Smith, 25 September 1890, ibid.

41. Brewster Cameron to Fulford, 26 January 1885, folder 2, box 1, SRCC Papers, UASC; Smith to Wharton, 25 April 1890, reel 1, M283, RG 59, NARA II. For more on smuggling, see Andreas, *Border Games*, 15–17; Sahlins, *Boundaries*, 89–93, 240–43; Nugent, *Smugglers, Secessionists, and Loyal Citizens on the Ghana-Togo Frontier*.

42. Secretary of State to Governor of Sonora, 1 March 1900, tomo 1567, expediente 5, Archivo General del Estado de Sonora; Hadley, "Ranch Life," 10.

43. Haley, *Jeff Milton*, 148–50; Miller, *The Arizona Rangers*.

44. Smith, *Emilio Kosterlitzky*, 96–111; Erwin, *The Southwest of John Horton Slaughter*, 319; Truett, *Fugitive Landscapes*, 139–42.

45. Clipping from the *Daily Star*, 22 January 1888, folder 2, box 1, SRCC Papers, UASC.

46. Brewster Cameron to Chalmers, labeled exhibit "B," ca. 1887, folder 6, box 1, SRCC Papers, UASC.

47. Delos H. Smith to William Wharton, 17 July 1890, reel 1, M283, RG 59, NARA II.

48. Delos H. Smith to Alonso Aspe, 23 September 1890, reel 1, M283, RG 59, NARA II; Alonso Aspe to Delos H. Smith, 25 September 1890, ibid.; Delos H. Smith to Thomas Ryan, 1 October 1890, ibid.; Juan Fenochio to U.S. Consul, 31 December 1890, ibid.

49. "Cattlemen Can Cross the Line without Papers from the Custom House," *Tombstone Epitaph*, 4 January 1891, cited in Truett, *Fugitive Landscapes*, 86.

# THE SCALES OF SALMON

*Diplomacy and Conservation in the Western Canada–U.S. Borderlands*

..........................................

Lissa Wadewitz

S ome Canadian fishermen longed for barriers in the Western Canada–U.S. borderlands at the turn of the last century. Unlike the epidemics discussed by Jennifer Seltz, or the cattle fence described by Rachel St. John, the obstructions envisioned by these Canadian fishermen were not to control the spread of disease or to simplify customs processes. Instead, a few Canadians toyed with ambitious, and sometimes outrageous, projects that would have diverted Pacific salmon runs toward waiting Canadian nets north of the 49th parallel and away from the more numerous, more efficient, American fish traps located south of the border. One proposal would have constructed a wall of sorts in the waters through which the salmon passed on their way to their natal streams. According to one Canadian canner, "The idea of this scheme was all right, for it was to keep the fish out of the way of the Americans entirely." There was just one problem: "It was, of course, absolutely impracticable." Still, that these plans were put forth at all suggests the intensity of the competition for salmon and the lengths to which both Canadians and Americans might go to limit their neighbor's catch. Managing and working such a messy, transborder salmon fishery was obviously fraught with complications.[1]

The drawing of the Western Canada–U.S. boundary in 1846 transformed the Pacific salmon (*Oncorhynchus* spp.) into a borderland fish. Salmon from the Fraser River, in British Columbia, now became available to fishermen from both the United States and Canada, since these salmon return from the ocean primarily via the Strait of Juan de Fuca—the same body of water that divides British Columbia from Washington State.

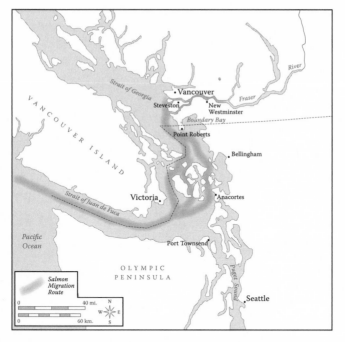

**Map 1.** Settlements and salmon migration routes of the Pacific Northwest. (Map by Ezra Zeitler)

Relying heavily on Fraser River salmon stocks, particularly the sockeye species (*O. nerka*), Americans and Canadians developed lucrative salmon canneries on both sides of the 49th parallel in the late nineteenth and early twentieth centuries. Since this fishery straddled the border, local authorities soon realized that effective fishing restrictions had to be either uniform or complementary in nature, but neither side could compel the other to voluntarily enact the laws that were subsequently proposed. Given earlier successes in negotiating treaties on seals and migratory birds, an international treaty seemed the logical solution to the stalemate in enacting transnational measures for salmon conservation.[2] But, although both countries initiated talks on the matter in the 1890s, a treaty was not approved for more than forty years. Although clear signs of decline in the sockeye runs of the 1910s spurred stronger interest in an international salmon conservation treaty, conditions at the local level consistently thwarted progress on such an agreement.

The international border bisected this valuable transnational fishery and created competing economies and jurisdictions that fostered infighting and mistrust and created difficulties for authorities. Recognizing the

opportunities offered by the proximity of the border, fishermen and cannery workers learned to traverse the line in order to elude arrest and to
smuggle salmon. This border fishery also translated into a regulatory
nightmare for government officials because its management involved
several departments with mismatched jurisdictional authority.[3] States and
provinces have very different powers relative to their respective federal
governments, especially when it comes to fish. Due to the nature of U.S.
federalism, the states had total control over their fisheries within the
three-mile coastal limit but were legally unable to make agreements with
foreign countries. In Canada, the Department of Marine and Fisheries
(DMF), a federal agency based in Ottawa with agents placed locally, was
charged with recommending and enforcing fishing laws in British Columbia, sometimes with the assistance of the Provincial Fisheries Department.[4] These distinctions brought a plethora of agencies to the negotiating table and meant that legally binding salmon conservation laws could
only come in the form of an international treaty approved by both federal
governments. Because it would necessarily transfer Washington State's
authority over its sockeye salmon fishery to agents in the nation's capital,
the possibility of a negotiated treaty raised questions about states' rights as
well.[5] All of these issues led to suspicions on both sides of the border,
delays in treaty talks at the federal level, and, ultimately, to less stringent
conservation efforts.

While a few historians have traced the evolution of the 1937 Sockeye
Salmon Treaty between the United States and Canada, they have tended to
emphasize the diplomatic discussions and events that took place at the
federal and international levels.[6] These conversations were certainly important, but the history of this landmark agreement owes as much, if not
more, to how the Canada-U.S. border mitigated and shaped events and
relationships in western boundary waters. The spatiality of salmon migration routes and the presence of the border worked in tandem to direct the
diplomatic push-and-pull between local industry players and federal officials in Washington, D.C., and Ottawa. This case study thus illustrates
how the interplay of local, national, and international interests influenced
the binational conservation policies that emerged. Unfortunately, this attempt to better match the scale of salmon management to the trans-
border reality of this fishery came too late to save the regional salmon
population.[7]

## On the Water

When the Fraser River and Puget Sound canned salmon industries boomed in the late nineteenth and early twentieth centuries, the 49th parallel presented new and shifting challenges for the governments of Canada and the United States. The industry expanded so rapidly that by 1900 there were forty-six canneries in operation on the Fraser and twenty-one in northwestern Washington State.[8] As will be discussed in more detail in the next section, the governments of Canada, the United States, and the state of Washington gradually developed fishery and customs patrols to police boundary waters. Despite the confusion on questions of legality, both American and Canadian authorities deemed fishing by the other on their side of the 49th parallel to be an act of trespass, and both governments reacted to such infringements accordingly. Both sides would periodically impose duties on fresh and, later, frozen salmon, essentially making border fishing, fish sales, or the failure to pay these duties to the customs agents in charge potentially arrestable offenses. Fishing across the border was also a way to evade differing American and Canadian laws on allowable net mesh sizes and legal fishing hours. Due to the international tensions created by the ongoing competition for fish, regional authorities increasingly worried about illegal trans-border activities and strove to restrict the physical movement of people, goods, and salmon across the line. Ultimately, however, the local workers' border manipulations, the official boat seizures, and the related retaliatory campaigns aggravated the existing animosities between Canadian and American fishery interests and diminished local support for an international salmon treaty.

Both cannery owners and fishery workers quickly learned how to use the jurisdictional and economic advantages offered by living in the Western Canada–U.S. borderlands. As I outline in detail elsewhere, some cannery owners hired fish buyers to cross the border to buy salmon at cut rates; they also began to invest in establishments on both sides of the line. Laborers likewise crossed the border to steal fish, to fish for salmon illegally, or to search for the best prices. As boats and nets grew more expensive over time, thieves found a ready transnational market in fishing gear as well. Those individuals who engaged in these illicit activities purposefully crossed the border to avoid detection or to solicit higher returns for their merchandise and, in the process, heightened tensions between classes (fishermen vs. canners/trap owners), between ethnic groups affiliated with specific gear types (traps, gillnets, and purse seines), and between competing American and Canadian fishing interests.[9]

International boat seizures for fishing over the border or within the three-mile offshore limit occurred from the 1890s onward and occasionally escalated into international incidents that strained Canadian-U.S. relations. For example, after the sockeye salmon run of 1899 ran almost entirely on the American side of the line, the U.S. customs patrol arrested twenty-one Canadian fishing vessels for illegal trans-border fishing.[10] To avoid trouble, authorities on both sides of the border agreed that the U.S. patrols should be more lenient in their application of the law for the remainder of the season.[11] Canadian forces arrested one American vessel in 1904 and another "Yankee Poacher" fishing too close to shore the following year. In 1911, British Columbia patrols made several attempts to seize dozens of American salmon boats that were "preying" on the inward-bound salmon off of Vancouver Island, but they only managed to take one into custody.[12]

The events of 1912 illustrate how officials in both countries sometimes used boat seizures to lay claim to their nation's portion of this shared fishery, and of how they intensified international hostilities in the process. The Canadian arrest of two American seine boats, the *Thelma* and the *Bonita*, sparked a flurry of letters to Washington, D.C., and Ottawa. According to the Puget Sound Canners' Association, the Canadian patrol was "entirely too anxious to make seizures" that summer and took advantage of fishers who accidentally drifted too close to shore.[13] Soon after, U.S. forces captured six Canadian salmon boats for fishing in American waters. The Canadians deemed this last arrest strictly retaliatory. One Canadian newspaper observed, "It is a well known fact that the American fishermen are 'sore' against the Canadian authorities in seizing American vessels recently engaged in fishing off the British Columbia coast."[14] U.S. sources are silent on these accusations, but Washington State officials did unnecessarily retain custody of the boats for several weeks after the case was dismissed in court and, as they performed no maintenance on the nets, effectively ruined them for future fishing.[15]

Although pinpointing the precise number of international arrests on either side of the border is impossible, given the lack of uniformity among

**Figure 1.** Fishing fleet on the lower Fraser River, British Columbia, Canada (1901). (Courtesy of University of Washington Libraries, Special Collections, UW5714)

**Figure 2.** Salmon catch on the floor of cannery, with Chinese worker in background (ca. 1900). Photo by Anders Beer Wilse. (Courtesy of University of Washington Libraries, Special Collections, WILSE-U-1)

the records that have survived, boat seizures persisted through the 1930s even as negotiations for an international sockeye salmon treaty at the federal level ebbed and flowed. For example, American customs patrols seized at least twelve B.C. fishing boats and arrested eighteen people engaged in illegal fishing across the line in the 1917 season.[16] The American consul general found that Canada had captured thirty boats for illegal fishing between 1912 and 1932 (twenty-five were fishing for salmon, and five for halibut). Interestingly, Canadian patrols arrested fourteen of these vessels in the 1929 season—a year marked by failed treaty talks.[17] The 1930 season was no better. Despite an agreement between Canadian and American authorities and canners that they would cease fishing that fall season, three canners broke ranks; illicit border fishing quickly escalated. Officials on both sides of the border seized several boats, chased countless more across the international line, and warned others not to fish. According to one patrol boat captain, the boundary waters were "a mad house," due to the large number of boats and the thick fog.[18] While the record is admittedly incomplete, it is at least possible that the high number of seizures in the 1929–30 fishing season was linked to the collapse of the 1929 treaty negotiations.[19]

Other events in these western boundary waters encouraged international arrests and fueled anti-American and anti-Canadian sentiments among borderlanders. Importantly, salmon was not the only fish attracting fishermen from both nations. Halibut fishers also competed off the west coast of Vancouver Island, and sometimes found themselves arrested and their boats confiscated.[20] As the salmon industry migrated northward to fresher waters, a number of seizures along the B.C. border with Alaska further added to the tension.[21] That these confrontations sometimes grew violent likewise generated hostility. In 1923, a halibut boat fishing illegally within the three-mile coastal limit tried to outrun Canadian authorities. Accounts of what happened next differ according to the nationality of the witnesses, but when the American vessel refused to stop as requested, shots were exchanged and crewman Jacob York ended up dead on the deck.[22]

Boat seizures and illegal fishing practices along the border thus created significant discord between Americans and Canadians. Citizens of both nations hurled nationalistic slurs at one another with alarming frequency, complaining about the prospect of an international treaty.[23] Each side blamed the other for illicit border fishing, the Canadians complained about American fish traps and lax enforcement of fishing regulations in Washington, and the Americans wanted Canada to devote more resources to hatchery efforts on the Upper Fraser.[24] Because Fraser River salmon spawn in B.C., the Canadians were also upset because, they believed, American fishermen were taking what were essentially "Canadian fish." According to one B.C. resident, it was "exceedingly annoying to see millions of fish put upon the American side that are Fraser River fish attempting to make their way up the River to reproduce sockeyes at this season of the year."[25]

### The Limits of Local Diplomacy

Even as economic competition spurred illegal border fishing and international boat seizures, agencies in both countries struggled to regulate their respective portions of this fishery. The number of entities involved, the spatial limits of their authority, and how they were structured all had important implications for the treaty negotiation processes that occurred at the federal level. A major point of contention for Washington State was that a treaty would require it to relinquish control of its salmon fishery to the federal government. This in turn raised the broader question of states' rights in the U.S. federal system. How officials chose to deal with many of these issues tended to add to the hostilities between different agencies. Representatives from both the DMF and Washington State repeatedly met to discuss salmon conservation and border policing strategies, but while their agents sometimes were able to work together in patrolling the border, their general inability to cooperate often impeded talks between D.C. and Ottawa.[26]

Because of the political clout of those individuals who profited most from the salmon industry, Washington State fishery managers initially found it difficult to enact more stringent conservation measures. Until 1921, such fishing regulations had to be passed by the state legislature, and powerful constituents with investments in both canneries and fishing gear regularly stymied the fishery department's attempts to implement stricter regulations. For example, some government officials and canners spent years negotiating a trans-border fishery closure for the 1906 and 1908 seasons, but fishermen protests killed the bill in the state legislature.[27] The fishery department's inability to guarantee passage of specific regulations interfered with international negotiations again in 1918. "They could only agree to *recommend* legislation," one Canadian attendee complained about the Americans after a meeting that year. "They could not insure it."[28] According to the fish commissioner, "Under the present system, any attempt to have the legislature pass fishery conservation measures only serve to bring to the state capitol those who oppose the measures through selfish interest."[29] The commissioner knew this from firsthand experience. When the Washington State Department of Fisheries proposed a new fishing code in 1919 that would have prohibited purse seiners from taking sockeye salmon, a huge purse seine contingent appeared in Olympia and successfully defeated the bill.[30]

Given the importance of the salmon fishery to the state's economy, Washington officials consistently refused to cede control of the state's fisheries to the federal government, and most Washingtonians wholeheartedly supported this stance. In fact, arguments on this point tended to bring federal treaty negotiations to a standstill. In response to the first draft treaty of 1909, for example, some local American fishermen argued that the proposed agreement was a breach of states' rights and/or unconstitutional; these complaints helped defeat the bill in Congress in October 1914.[31] Washington State authorities used this same reasoning to forestall the next version of a treaty, in 1921, insisting that the fisheries should be managed through a new state fish board. According to then Washington Governor Louis Hart, an international salmon treaty would have been too costly a sacrifice. "Our people are not all children whose playthings should be taken away and given to older people," he wrote to state Senator Wesley Jones in 1921. "Neither are they citizens of a weakling nation to have their heritage taken from them and given to another power."[32]

While the motivations behind the formation of the state fisheries board in 1921 may initially have been sincere, the board's record is eyebrow-raising, to say the least. In an audacious move, Washington State purposefully used the board to circumvent federal authority in negotiating an agreement with a foreign government.[33] Seemingly not grasping that Ottawa was in charge, board members mistakenly believed for a time that the province of British Columbia could simply take over management of its fisheries.[34] Instead of supporting the version of the treaty then pending in the U.S. Senate, state officials clung to the issue of states' rights, assured politicians in D.C. that they would work things out with British

Columbia, and ultimately derailed the talks taking place at the federal level.[35] In addition, all of the state fisheries board members expressed hostility toward an international treaty and found the DMF's unwillingness to abandon the document frustrating.[36] Moreover, while the Canadians waited for a final treaty decision in Congress that same year, the state board arranged to pay Henry Doyle, a B.C. canner, $1,000 to secretly explore the feasibility of building a fish hatchery on the Upper Fraser River.[37] Although Canadian authorities were not interested in new hatchery efforts, some B.C. canners and industry players in Washington State were fixated on the prospect. The state board was fully aware of the implications of its actions. "Being a creature of the State," the board chairman wrote Doyle in the summer of 1921, "you can very readily see that in an official way, we could not take the initiative in matters of this kind, particularly within the confines of another State."[38]

That the very first meeting between the DMF and the fledgling Washington fisheries board was a complete failure further undermined the board's pro-conservation claims. When the protests of Washington State successfully defeated the 1921 treaty in the nation's capital, the DMF agreed to meet the state board and discuss a total closure of the fishery as well as other gear restrictions. However, while both sides believed that the sockeye fishery had to be shut down, the Washington contingent refused to enact regulations extending more than five years into the future. The creation of the state board was supposedly an attempt to free the regulatory process from the control of the state legislature, but its chairman then reminded his Canadian colleagues that any action taken by the board was ultimately subject to the approval of that same legislature, as was the ongoing existence of the board itself. The meeting ended in a stalemate when both sides admitted that even if they passed the agreed-upon laws, unlike a treaty, the laws would not be binding to either side.[39] "It was made very manifest," one B.C. official said of the 1921 meeting, "that this matter could only be handled satisfactorily by the terms of a treaty which cannot be amended by legislative action for the period for which the treaty is drawn."[40]

Given their track record, the true intentions of the Washington State fisheries board members are certainly questionable, but the agency was more flexible than the state legislature and it did admittedly usher in more comprehensive fishing regulations until its demise in 1929.[41] For example, the board created a number of new salmon preserves within which one could fish only with a hook and line. The board also applied additional time and space restrictions on fishing and dictated specific gear size limits. Overall, the board passed more regulations than its predecessor, but its work with Canada on a transnational solution to the fishery issue remained patchy at best.[42]

Despite Washington's foot-dragging, official records demonstrate that each country gradually devoted additional resources to law enforcement and developed increasingly effective fishery and border patrols. In the mid-1890s, Canada employed just five fishery guardians to cooperate with both local police and customs agents. By 1910, there were at least nine employees working as fishery guardians and inspectors in four boats.[43] Although they were still not very effective overall, fishing authorities did prosecute 120 people that year in the two districts closest to the border.[44] The DMF also experimented with the use of seaplanes in the early 1920s and found them to be extremely effective.[45] By then, the B.C. patrol consisted of three large steamers with over seventy employees, one smaller steamer for northern waters with a crew of seven, crews of from two to seven people running nineteen gasoline boats, and approximately twenty to thirty-five other boats that were hired for specific periods throughout the year.[46] A decade later, the patrol had matured further. The DMF used a total of 145 boats during the 1930 fishing season (although only two of them appear to have been sizable steamers) and reported 150 arrests for violations of the fishery statutes in the border area.[47] According to a patrol officer on the American side, once the Canadians assigned one of their larger steamers to boundary waters that season, their patrol was "quite effective."[48]

Policing efforts in Washington State also yielded better results over time, but the efficacy of their patrols consistently lagged behind that of their northern neighbors. Boasting just six vessels between them, the state fishery patrol and the U.S. Customs Service were both in bad shape up through the 1910s.[49] Statistics on the number of employees and boats employed each year are unavailable, but expenditures for patrol services in Washington State rose from $7,580 in fiscal year 1919 to $36,312 in 1930. Arrests by fishery patrols in the counties nearest boundary waters mirrored this funding increase. The state reported 62 arrests in 1919, and 174 in 1930, for all infractions of the state fish and game laws in those counties.[50] The agency's arrest record for illegal fishing did not compare well to that of the Canadian forces, but it did appear to improve over time.

Despite these efforts by both states to rein in illegal and excessive fishing, many American and Canadian officials remained wary of one another, and occasionally sent spies across the border to investigate the quality of their neighbors' patrols. The B.C. Provincial Fisheries Department hired a yacht to clandestinely check that American fish traps and seiners were abiding by the weekly closed-time laws in 1909; the "tourists" aboard witnessed and documented a number of violations.[51] In 1911, Washington trap owners denied Canadian patrols the right to tie up or land at their trap structures. The Americans claimed this move was to prevent damage to their traps, but it was more likely a way to limit Canadian awareness of American illegal fishing practices.[52] In 1912, a Canadian fisheries department employee met with the Pinkerton's National Detective Agency in Seattle to inquire about hiring someone to spy on several canneries, presumably on the U.S. side of the line.[53] The perceived ongoing impact of a major rock slide at Hell's Gate on the Upper Fraser in 1913 likewise led to years of bickering.[54] By the 1920s, ongoing skepticism prompted the Washington State supervisor of fisheries to assign an agent to regularly visit the spot in question and report back on conditions there.[55]

Washington State officials' unwillingness to match the more stringent Canadian regulations and their inability to halt illegal fishing prompted Canadian officials to repeatedly relax their own conservation laws. Due to complaints received from B.C. canners in the 1890s, the Canadian fishery department decided to allow some fish traps in boundary waters, although only gill nets were legal in B.C. at that time. This measure was designed to "place Canadian canners on a more even footing with their neighbours across the line."[56] The DMF responded favorably to similar arguments about permitting traps and shortening the traps' weekly closed period throughout the early 1900s.[57] In 1904, the Canadian commissioner suggested lifting the weekly closed time entirely due to American competition, and though the practice was outlawed or severely restricted in every other province, he allowed purse seines and additional fish traps in B.C. waters that same year.[58] Similarly, when the Washington State legislature failed to agree to the proposed 1906 and 1908 sockeye closures, the DMF let their traps fish longer, and for species other than sockeye. In fact, the fisheries commissioner specifically encouraged the traps to catch "American cohoes" as retribution. Wrote the DMF's E. E. Prince in 1906, "It is *advantageous* to capture *all we can* of these inferior kinds [of fish] *belonging to U.S. waters*, in view of the toll taken of *B.C. Sockeyes* by the U.S. traps."[59]

The practice of rescinding or watering down Canadian fishing regulations persisted into the next decade. Canadian officials initially adhered to the laws outlined in the first draft of the 1909 international sockeye salmon treaty, but when the U.S. Senate continued to sit on the bill, the DMF gave up and granted to British Columbia a fishing season extension in the 1913 season. This move by Canadian authorities was clearly a response to "the non-adoption of the regulations by the United States recommended by the International Fisheries Commission."[60] Similar events occurred up through the 1930s, when the DMF allowed purse seines to fish the Gulf of Georgia, because "Seines will be used very extensively in the Gulf of Georgia south of the International line by American interests."[61] Fault for the failed treaty process and the weakening of conservation regulations clearly lay on both sides of the border.

As each successive effort to pass an international sockeye salmon treaty stalled, Canadian authorities and B.C. fishing interests considered other possible strategies for limiting Washington fishers' access to "Canadian salmon." A recurring proposition was to dig a ditch from the Fraser River to the coast at Boundary Bay, in the hopes that sockeye salmon would swim up this canal to the Fraser and bypass American traps. As mentioned earlier, some Canadians suggested building a barrier in the Strait of Juan de Fuca that would direct the salmon northward into Canadian waters.[62] Canadian officials also repeatedly tried to purchase Point Roberts outright from their neighbors south of the line, but since this small peninsula had become so critical to the success of the Washington fishery, U.S. authorities politely declined these offers.[63] By the 1930s, the B.C. government had scientists investigating the feasibility of taking Fraser River sockeye eggs and moving them to northern B.C. rivers, so as to further limit American access to Canadian fish.[64]

Many involved in the B.C. canning industry believed that if they lifted their regulations completely and/or allowed more seines and traps, their American neighbors would be frightened into enacting more comprehensive laws or supporting the international treaty. "Let us then commence to use traps and fight them with their own weapons," one industry player wrote to a B.C. member of Parliament as early as 1902, "and if the fish begin to diminish they will be only too glad to diminish the traps or abolish the traps altogether."[65] Similar calls were repeated over the next thirty years. In 1932, one newspaper wrote that lifting all restrictions would mean "that British Columbia fishermen will have several glorious years of fishing on the river, and then, to all intents and purposes, the sockeye will be a thing of the past." Believing they could develop their fisheries in northern B.C. to compensate for the loss of the Fraser, Canadian industry players appear to have seriously contemplated this course of action on several occasions.[66] In turn, such talk north of the 49th parallel fed rumors in Washington State about Canadian schemes that would leave the American industry to die a slow death.[67]

## A Question of Scale

The continued decline of the Fraser River / Puget Sound salmon fishery in the late 1920s and early 1930s finally pushed regional fishermen, canners, scientists, and authorities to come to terms on a sockeye treaty. Numerous developments precipitated this change of heart. In the mid-1920s, several government officials and scientists established an organization dedicated to studying salmon and sharing their knowledge across the border. As a result, by the late 1920s, local and federal agents from both nations had built up a measure of trust along with a scientific consensus on the status of the fishery.[68] Border patrols grew more effective over time, and other officials cooperated across the border to arrest illegal fishers or retrieve stolen gear.[69] The 1935 election of a new Washington State governor who was amenable to the treaty also signified a critical shift in local politics.[70] The proven success of the 1923 halibut treaty was an additional, noteworthy precedent that industry players likewise took to heart.[71] A treaty proposal that advocated a 50–50 split of the sockeye catch by Americans and Canadians and the passage of a 1934 initiative sponsored by Washington sports fishers came at a critical juncture. When Initiative 77 garnered voter approval, fish traps became illegal in the state of Washington. The eradication of traps made purse seining the predominant fishing method for Washington fishermen and removed the sensitive issue of fish traps from the ongoing, increasingly productive, treaty talks. Due to its heavy reliance on traps, the industry in Washington had consistently taken greater numbers of fish than their Canadian neighbors. With no traps fishing, the American portion of the catch plummeted and the 50 percent split began to look quite reasonable to American interests. Recognition that the sockeye fishery was in serious trouble forced the hands of all sides between 1930 and 1936, but the abolition of fish traps was the crucial turning point; a treaty was finally passed in August 1937.[72]

Because the imaginary line at the 49th parallel divided distinct national jurisdictions and economies, it encouraged competition, generated international hostilities, and complicated efforts to draft an international salmon conservation treaty between the United States and Canada. Canadian and American fishermen followed salmon throughout boundary waters, and found that their border crossings and illicit fishing reverberated at the federal level. Both nations worked to police the international border and restrict the ability of their neighbors to catch salmon, but, in so doing, contributed to infighting and tensions that hampered international treaty negotiations and limited the effectiveness of the few fishing regulations already in place. While diplomatic discussions between U.S. and Canadian representatives at the federal level were indeed critical to the final text of the 1937 salmon treaty, so too were these evolving, contentious borderland ties and events that—just like salmon migration routes themselves—firmly linked the local to the international. Salmon mobility through boundary waters and the presence of the border itself thus created a series of dialectical relationships among local, national, and international interests that greatly influenced the diplomatic discussions taking place in D.C. and Ottawa.

Despite this achievement, problems of scale continued to plague the management of this fishery. As the historian Joseph Taylor has noted, the convention waters identified in the final 1937 agreement did not match shifting fishing patterns. By the 1930s, purse seiners and trollers had increasingly taken advantage of new technology to fish further from shore, far away from treaty waters and thus from any oversight or binding regulation. The initial agreement also ignored the fact that Canadian and American coastal fishermen shared species other than sockeye. Later disputes thus circulated around the allocation of other Pacific salmon species between the citizens of both nations. Indeed, salmon managers still struggle with similar problems today as they search for ways to match the scale of management to the vast distances crossed by these anadromous fish and the fishers who pursue them.[73]

As I write this in 2008, on the cusp of the meetings for the renegotiation of the 1985 Pacific Salmon Treaty, the need for an accurate understanding of the meaning of scale as it relates to salmon conservation seems particularly acute. In such a complex set of fisheries, scale matters. As this example so clearly suggests, the scope of regulation must match that of the fishery itself. If it does not—and it currently does not—we have little hope of restoration. Perhaps a stronger grasp of this fishery's history—warts and all—may begin to pave the way for a new treaty agreement and more accurate scales of oversight.

**Notes**

1. "Point Roberts Canal Scheme," *Vancouver Province*, 3 September 1903, box 53, International Pacific Salmon Fisheries Commission Collection [hereafter cited as IPSFC], University of British Columbia Special Collections, Vancouver [hereafter cited as UBC]. All of the articles in this collection are clippings removed from their original publications and preserved in scrapbooks; most are labeled, but some include no indication of the original source.

2. On the seal and bird treaties, see Dorsey, *The Dawn of Conservation Diplomacy*. An international treaty on halibut also became another important precedent in the 1920s. See Thistle, "As Free of Fish as a Billiard Ball Is of Hair."

3. Joseph Taylor also makes this important point in his analysis of the treaty's history. See Taylor, "The Historical Roots of the Canadian-American Salmon Wars," 163, 172.

4. British Columbia's processors pressed the local government to create its own, provincial fisheries department in 1901. A Privy Council ruling in 1898 made this new agency legally viable, granting the Dominion the right to regulate the provincial fisheries and the province the right to grant licenses and leases. This arrangement caused confusion and led to disputes for industry players. See "Fishermen May Fight over Fish," *Tacoma Ledger*, 2 May 1901, Newspapers and Clippings, January 1901–July 1901, Alaska Packers' Association Collection, Center for Pacific Northwest Studies, Western Washington University; and "Provincial Control of Salmon Canneries," *San Francisco Chronicle*, 23 April 1901, ibid. On the Provincial Fisheries Act, see F. Gourdeau to R. H. Coats, 23 July 1907, file 6, pt. 4, vol. 79, reel T-2663, Record Group 23: Records of the Department of Fisheries and Oceans [hereafter cited as RG 23], Library and Archives Canada, Ottawa [hereafter cited as LAC]; and C. B. Sword

to Minister, 2 May 1908, ibid. On the Privy Council decision, see F. J. Fulton to A. Bryan Williams, 8 May 1906, file 100–1, box 2, GR-0446: Provincial Game Warden Records [hereafter cited as GR-0446], British Columbia Provincial Archives, Victoria [hereafter cited as BC Archives].

5. For Canadians, some of the objections to an international treaty were based on concerns about the future of hydroelectric power development on the Fraser River. See J. C. MacDonald to Commissioner of Fisheries, 27 May 1929, box 1, GR-1378: Commercial Fisheries Branch Records [hereafter cited as GR-1378], BC Archives.

6. Taylor, "The Historical Roots of the Canadian-American Salmon Wars," 155–80; Dorsey, *The Dawn of Conservation Diplomacy*, 19–104.

7. Here I am building on the writings of both Richard White and Joseph Taylor with regard to the problem of pinpointing scale when studying and managing Pacific salmon. See White, "The Nationalization of Nature"; and Taylor, "The Historical Roots of the Canadian-American Salmon Wars," 169–75.

8. Canada Department of Marine and Fisheries, *Annual Report*, 1900, 159; Washington (State) Department of Fisheries, *Biennial Report*, 1902, 79. The number for Washington State includes only those canneries operated that season; there were an additional five canneries that were not operated.

9. For a more detailed analysis of such illegal fishing, see Wadewitz, "Pirates of the Salish Sea"; and Wadewitz, "The Nature of Borders." On canners' use of the border, see Wadewitz, "The Nature of Borders," 217–19, 252.

10. F. D. Huestis to Secretary of the Treasury, 4 August 1899, 377–79, box 43, vol. 2, Letters to the Secretary of the Treasury, 1898–99, Puget Sound Collection District, Record Group 36: Records of the United States Customs Service, National Archives and Records Administration, Pacific Alaska Region, Seattle [hereafter RG 36, NAS]; A. G. Collier to F. D. Huestis, 20 July 1899, file 5, box 64, RG 36, NAS; Meriden Hill to F. D. Huestis, 18 July 1899, ibid.; A. G. Collier to F. D. Huestis, 16 July 1899, ibid.

11. A. G. Collier to F. D. Huestis, 27 July 1899, file 5, box 64, RG 36, NAS; A. G. Collier to F. D. Huestis, 8 August 1899, ibid.

12. On the 1904 seizure, see "Ottawa Sustains Seizure," *Vancouver Province*, 22 December 1904, box 53, IPSFC, UBC; "Seized Steamer Sold," *Vancouver Province*, 2 February 1905, ibid.; and "Yankee Poacher Captured," unidentified newspaper clipping, ca. 12 July 1905, ibid. For the 1911 arrest, see "Pirating Sloop Is Seized," *Vancouver Province*, 28 August 1911, box 54, ibid.

13. For the quote, see W. I. Crawford, Puget Sound Canners' Association, to Senator Wesley Jones, 3 August 1912, file 4119, vol. 401, reel T-3390, RG 23, LAC. On the seizures, see "Fishery Cruiser Finds No Trouble Seizing Poacher," *Vancouver Sun*, 26 July 1912, box 54, IPSFC, UBC; and "Exciting Chase after Poachers," *[New Westminster?] News-Advertiser*, 18 July 1912, box 54, ibid. For

more on this conflict, see "American Story of Capture of Thelma," unidentified newspaper clipping, 9 September 1912, ibid.; Seattle Chamber of Commerce Secretary to Capt. B. P. Bertholf, 5 June 1912, file 4119, vol. 401, reel T-3390, RG 23, LAC; and A. Johnston to Under Secretary of State, 26 September 1912, ibid. The *Thelma* case was ultimately reversed. See Memorandum, William Found, 16 February 1914, ibid.; and G. J. Desbarats to Macneill Bird, MacDonald and Darling Barristers, 17 August 1914, ibid. The *Bonita* was finally sold at auction in 1914; see "Fisheries Department Sells Poaching Ships Seized Inside Limits," 27 March 1914, box 55, IPSFC, UBC.

14. "Fraser River Fishing Boats Are Seized," *Vancouver Province*, 1 August 1912, box 54, IPSFC, UBC. See also "Seized Fishing Boat Released," *Vancouver Province*, 2 August 1912, ibid. Despite the title of this last article, the evidence indicates that while the arrested fishermen were let go the day following their arrest, Washington State officials held onto the boats and gear for several weeks (see note 15).

15. W. D. Burdis to D. N. McIntyre, 13 August 1912, file 1912 #4, box 183, GR-0435: Department of Fisheries Records [hereafter cited as GR-0435], BC Archives; "Still Hold Fishing Boats," *Vancouver Province*, 29 August 1912, box 54, IPSFC, UBC. The boats were finally released in October. See "Four B.C. Fishing Schooners Released," *Vancouver Province*, 1 October 1912, ibid.

16. Washington (State) Department of Fisheries, *Biennial Report*, 1919–20, 32.

17. Ely E. Palmer to State Supervisor of Fisheries, 11 July 1932, box 4, vol. L-42, Department of Fisheries, Administration [hereafter cited as DFA], Washington State Archives, Olympia [hereafter cited as WSA]. Canadian patrols captured additional Washington vessels in Boundary Bay in 1932. See Found to W. S. Edwards, 7 September 1932, file no. 1932-1399, series A-2, vol. 373, Department of Fisheries—Boundary Bay Egress, RG 13: Records of the Department of Justice, LAC; Memorandum for the Deputy Minister of Justice, 14 September 1932, file no. 1399–32, ibid.; and Edwards to Found, 14 September 1932, ibid.

18. Arthur S. Einarsen to Charles R. Pollock, 3 October 1930, box 6, vol. L-35, Fish and Game Director Correspondence, DFA, WSA; J. W. Mack to Charles Pollock, 6 October 1930, ibid.

19. On the failure of the 1929 treaty negotiations, see Taylor, "The Historical Roots of the Canadian-American Salmon Wars," 168–69. According to regional newspapers and trade journals, many more such seizures occurred during this period.

20. See, e.g., John McNab to William Smith, 30 April 1894, file 1075, pt. 1, vol. 207, reel T-3122, RG 23, LAC; E. E. Prince Memorandum, 3 September 1902, file 1075, pt. 21, vol. 207, reel T-3123, RG 23, LAC; "Seizure of Fishing Schooner," *News-Advertiser*, 16 November 1911, box 54, IPSFC, UBC; "Schooner Val-

iant Confiscated" and "Schooner Prince Olaf Seized," *Pacific Fisherman*, May 1914, 31, in box 53, IPSFC, UBC; and "American Halibut Pirates Are Busy," unidentified newspaper clipping, ca. 22 December 1904, ibid.

21. On Alaska patrols and arrests, see U.S. Bureau of Fisheries, *Report of the United States Commissioner of Fisheries for the Fiscal Year 1920*, 53; "Trap Robber Convicted," *Pacific Fisherman*, March 1920, 29; "Trap Robbers Still Active," *Pacific Fisherman*, August 1920, 23; and "Resume of Annual Convention for Association of Pacific Fisheries," 2 October 1926, bulletin no. 267 (1926), in file 941, box 95, GR-0435, BC Archives. On British Columbia's concerns about American border crossings in the North, see William Sloan to P. J. A. Cardin, 29 April 1926, file 1926 #2, box 161, GR-0435, BC Archives.

22. "Canadian Guard Kill Seattle Fisherman," *Pacific Fisherman*, May 1923, 11; "Sockeye Treaty Drafted by Canadians Not Equitable or Efficacious," report in box 4, vol. L-42, p. 83, DFA, WSA.

23. See, e.g., "Sockeye Treaty Drafted by Canadians Not Equitable or Efficacious," report in box 4, vol. L-42, p. 83, DFA, WSA.

24. Everett Packing Co. to the British Columbia Canners Association, 22 October 1919, enclosed in H. Bell-Irving to J. P. Babcock, 3 November 1919, file 1919 #1, box 193, GR-0435, BC Archives.

25. W.W. Stumbles to Louis Davis, 12 July 1899, file 6, pt. 2, vol. 79, reel T-2663, RG 23, LAC.

26. For an overview of some of the early talks, see Roos, *Restoring Fraser River Salmon*, 42–44. For more detailed coverage of the negotiations between the DMF and Washington State that occurred prior to the First World War, see Wadewitz, "The Nature of Borders," chap. 6.

27. J. D. Hazen to W. J. Bowser, 18 April 1912, file 1912 #3, box 183, GR-0435, BC Archives; "Statement Made by Mr. Roth in Support of House Bill No. 183," enclosed in W. D. Burdis to M. McDonald, 15 February 1917, file 1917 #1, box 193, ibid. Note that Canada's DMF initiated the first 1905 meeting with Washington State regarding the need for complementary legislation and then Governor Albert Meade complied. While the group drafted new regulations for both sides of the border, local opposition stymied these efforts. On the 1905 meetings, see Washington (State), Department of Fisheries, *Biennial Report*, 1905–6, 46–48; and "Interim Report of the B.C. Fishery Commission," E. E. Prince, Chairman, to L. P. Brodeur, 2 October 1906, file 2918, vol. 336, reel T-4022, RG 23, LAC.

28. For the quotation, see Memorandum for the Honourable Commissioner of Fisheries, 15 April 1918, file 1918 #1, box 193, GR-0435, BC Archives (emphasis mine). See also J. O. Morris to B. C. Salmon Canner's Association, 22 October 1919, file 1919 #1, box 193, ibid.

29. Washington (State) Department of Fisheries, *Biennial Report*, 1917–19, 38.

30. The code was to match that proposed in the treaty of 1919. See ibid., 14–15.

31. J. D. Hazen to W. J. Bowser, 18 April 1912, file 1912 #3, box 183, GR-0435, BC Archives; W. J. Bowser to J. D. Hazen, 30 April 1912, U.S. Bureau of Fisheries, *Report of the United States Commissioner of Fisheries for the Fiscal Year 1914*, 80.

32. For the Hart quote, see Louis Hart to Wesley Jones, 26 July 1921, box 7, vol. L-3, DFA, WSA. See also Conference of the Sub-Committee of the Washington Fisheries Association and the Fraser River Canners Association, Vancouver, B.C., 10 April 1918, p. 147, in IPSFC, UBC; and Minutes of Meetings, Fraser River Canners' Association, 23 March 1914–9 October 1920, ibid. Successive governors of Washington State used these same arguments through the early 1930s. See "Radio Address by Governor Hartley and Miller Freeman," 4 December 1930, copy in box 6, vol. L-38, DFA, WSA.

33. On the rationale behind forming the state board, see Washington (State), Department of Fisheries, *Biennial Report*, 1919–21, 8–10; and John Cobb to J. P. Babcock, 21 February 1921, file 1921 #1, box 160, GR-0435, BC Archives. On the limited negotiating powers of Washington State, see Henry O'Malley to J. W. Titcomb, 5 April 1924, enclosed in Edwin Sanborn to Babcock, 20 September 1924, file 1924 #1, box 160, GR-0435, BC Archives; John Cobb to J. P. Babcock, 28 February 1921, file 1921 #1, box 160, ibid.; and Secretary of Governor to E. A. Sims, 12 April 1921, Fisheries file, box 19, Subject Files, Governor Louis Hart Papers, WSA.

34. The state board once denied they had such misunderstandings about which level of government had charge of fishery management in Canada, but it continued to make mistakes on the issue. See L. H. Darwin to Louis Hart, 5 August 1921, Fisheries file, box 19, Subject Files, Governor Louis Hart Papers, WSA. The provincial fisheries department also at least once added to this confusion by contacting the Washington board on its own, without authority to do so from Ottawa. See State Fisheries Board to Wesley Jones, 30 August 1922, box 7, vol. L-2, DFA, WSA; and Washington State Fisheries Board to Louis Hart, 12 August 1921, box 7, vol. L-3, ibid. There is some evidence that these misconceptions continued through the 1930s; see Washington State Fisheries Board to J. P. Babcock, 29 April 1931, box 7, vol. L-2, ibid.

35. J. P. Babcock, Memorandum for the Honorable Commissioner of Fisheries, 28 February 1921, 3, file 1921 #1, box 160, GR-0435, BC Archives.

36. E. P. Blake to Wesley Jones, 11 August 1921, box 3, vol. L-14, DFA, WSA. On Canadian officials' refusal to negotiate, see A. Johnston to Washington State Fisheries Board, 15 April 1921, box 7, vol. L-2, ibid.; and J. P. Babcock to Manning Cox, 10 October 1921, file 1921 #3, box 160, GR-0435, BC Archives.

37. State Fisheries Board to Henry Doyle, 11 June 1921, box 7, vol. L-2, DFA, WSA.

38. Washington State Fisheries Board to Henry Doyle, 18 June 1921, box 7, vol. L-2, DFA, WSA; and Henry Doyle to E. P. Blake, 29 August 1921, ibid. On

Canada not supporting a new hatchery, see W. A. Found to Henry Doyle, 25 November 1921, ibid.

39. On the failure of the 1921 treaty negotiations, see J. A. Motherwell to J. P. Babcock, 21 November 1921, file 1921 #2, box 160, GR-0435, BC Archives. On the 1921 meeting, see "Copy for News Agreed Upon," copy in box 3, vol. L-14, DFA, WSA; J. P. Babcock to H. Bell-Irving, 31 December 1921, file 1921 #2, box 160, GR-0435, BC Archives; J. P. Babcock to Henry O'Malley, 13 June 1922, file 1922 #3, box 160, ibid.; E. A. Sims to W. A. Found, 20 January 1922, box 7, vol. L-3, DFA, WSA; and W. A. Found to Washington State Fisheries Board, 1 February 1922, box 7, vol. L-2, ibid.

40. For the quote, see J. P. Babcock to H. Bell-Irving, 15 December 1921, file 1921 #2, box 160, GR-0435, BC Archives.

41. The state fisheries board was unceremoniously abolished in 1929 and its powers transferred to the Director of Fish and Game. In 1933, food and game fish were classified separately and managed by two separate agencies. See Washington (State) Department of Fisheries, *Fortieth and Forty-First Annual Reports of State Department of Fish and Game*, 3; Washington (State), Department of Fisheries, Management and Research Division, *State of Washington Legislative Laws Pertaining to Puget Sound Salmon Fisheries, 1921 through 1928*, 7.

42. On regulations after 1921, see Washington (State), Department of Fisheries, Management and Research Division, *State of Washington Legislative Laws Pertaining to Puget Sound Salmon Fisheries, 1921 through 1928*, 5–8.

43. Canada Department of Marine and Fisheries, *Annual Report*, 1909–10, 238–46.

44. Ibid., 366–67.

45. "Airplane Patrol Successful," *Pacific Fisherman*, September 1923, 16; "Aerial Patrol for British Columbia Fisheries," *Pacific Fisherman*, June 1924, 14; Canada Fisheries Branch, *Annual Report*, 1927–28, 75; Canada Fisheries Branch, *Annual Report*, 1929–30, 99–100.

46. J. A. Motherwell to E. P. Blake, 2 June 1922, box 7, vol. L-10, DFA, WSA.

47. Canada, Department of Fisheries, *Annual Report*, 1930–31; for the number of boats, see p. 100; for arrests, see pp. 286–89, 291–93.

48. Arthur Einarsen to Charles Pollock, 10 October 1930, box 6, vol. L-35, DFA, WSA.

49. The U.S. Revenue Cutter Service worked with the U.S. Customs Service to control smuggling and collect duties. The federal government combined several earlier agencies concerned with customs and marine safety to form the U.S. Coast Guard in 1915, but the number of patrol boats remained low for many years. See Report by H. M. White, Ralph D. Nichols, Josiah Collins to M. E. Hay, Governor of the State of Washington, enclosed in M. E. Hay to Richard McBride, 26 December 1912, file 1913 #912, box 93, GR-0435, BC

Archives. On patrol boats available by 1912, see "Ordered to Anacortes," *Anacortes American*, 3 October 1901. See also O. H. Culver to F. C. Harper, 17 October 1912, file 621, box 1401, Records of the Revenue Cutter Service and its Predecessors, Record Group 26: Records of the United States Coast Guard [hereafter cited as RG 26], RG 36 NAS; F. M. Dunwoody to F. C. Harper, 14 November 1912, ibid.; F. M. Dunwoody to Commanding Officer, Coast Guard Cutter Arcata, 11 October 1915, ibid.; and Washington (State) Department of Fisheries, *Twenty-fourth and Twenty-fifth Annual Report*, 15–16.

50. For the 1919 numbers, see Washington (State), Department of Fisheries, *Biennial Report*, 1919–21, 152, 201–5. For the 1930 statistics, see Washington (State), Department of Fisheries, *Biennial Report*, 1929–31, 69, 146. These figures refer only to the following counties: Whatcom, Skagit, Snohomish, King, Pierce, Kitsap, Jefferson, Clallam, Island, and San Juan.

51. Log of the *Homespun*, enclosed in Frank S. DeGrey to W. J. Bowser, 26 August 1909, file 1909 #718, box 76, GR-0435, BC Archives.

52. S. North to D. McIntyre, 22 September 1911, file 1911 #723, box 76, GR-0435, BC Archives.

53. P. K. Ahern to W. J. Bowser, 31 May 1912, file 1912 #4, box 183, GR-0435, BC Archives.

54. Report of W. H. Pugsley, enclosed in E. P. Blake to J. P. Babcock, 23 October 1922, file 1922 #2, box 160, GR-0435, BC Archives; Arthur Einarsen Report, 3 September 1929, box 5, vol. L-39, DFA, WSA; Washington (State), Department of Fisheries, *Biennial Report*, 1921–23, 14–15. The Hell's Gate slide did remain an obstacle for salmon up through the 1940s. See Roos, *Restoring Fraser River Salmon*, 63–75; and Evenden, *Fish versus Power*.

55. R. A. Spence, Report of Conditions on the Fraser, September 1925, box 7, vol. L-8, DFA, WSA.

56. For the quote, see unknown correspondent to James Gaudin, 18 September 1894, file 222, vol. 131, reel T-2819, RG 23, LAC.

57. H. Bell-Irving to L. H. Davies, 20 March 1897, file 222, vol. 131, reel T-2819, RG 23, LAC; E. E. Prince to John McNab, 26 March 1897, ibid.; L. H. Davies to Aulay Morrison, 14 April 1900, ibid.; L. H. Davies to Aulay Morrison, 9 May 1900, ibid. On relaxing regulations in British Columbia, see E. E. Prince to C. B. Sword, 20 July 1900, ibid.; C. B. Sword to E. E. Prince, 25 July 1900, ibid.; H. Bell-Irving to C. B. Sword, 10 July 1900, ibid.; and C. B. Sword to E. E. Prince, 12 July 1900, ibid. Similar concerns also influenced the passage of import duties on fish. See, e.g., unsigned to G. E. Courbould, 20 June 1895, file 2265, vol. 293, reel T-3218, RG 23, LAC.

58. On the 1904 suggestion, see R. Prefontaine to W. Templeman, 2 February 1904, file 6, pt. 3, vol. 79, reel T-2663, RG 23, LAC; Memorandum, E. E. Prince, 3 February 1904, ibid.; and W. Templeman to R. Prefontaine, 4 April 1904,

ibid. On purse seines and trap nets being allowed in British Columbia, see Memorandum of William Found, 13 April 1909, file 6, pt. 5, vol. 80, reel T-2664, RG 23, LAC; "Conference on British Columbia Fishery Matters," 26 June 1903, file 6, pt. 2, vol. 79, reel T-2663, ibid.; and Order in Council, 2 May 1904, file 6, pt. 3, vol. 79, reel T-2663, ibid. Federal officials limited traps to the west coast of Vancouver Island and to Boundary Bay. See "Fisheries Report for Last Season," *Victoria Times*, n.d. (ca. 1903), copy in scrapbook, accession no. 860-1, John Pease Babcock Papers, UW Libraries. British Columbia canners apparently continued to push for more traps. See A. E. White to R. Prefontaine, 18 March 1904, file 6, pt. 3, vol. 79, reel T-2663, RG 23, LAC; and Howard J. Duncan to R. Prefontaine, 27 February 1904, ibid.

59. The cohoes referred to fish spawned in rivers on the U.S. side of the border. On extending the open season in 1906 and 1907, see E. E. Prince to Deputy Minister of Marine and Fisheries, 16 August 1906, file 6, pt. 4, vol. 79, reel T-2663, RG 23, LAC; Memorandum by E. E. Prince, 30 August 1906, ibid.; Governor General in Council, 4 September 1906, ibid.; and, for the quotation, Memorandum by E. E. Prince, n.d. (ca. August 1907), ibid. (emphasis in original).

60. The International Fisheries Commission was the small committee appointed to draft the text of the first treaty. On relaxing the regulations, see W. J. Bowser to L. H. Darwin, 25 August 1913, file 1913 #912, box 93, GR-0435, BC Archives. On sticking to the 1909 treaty regulations, see R. N. Venning, Memorandum, 19 May 1909, file 6, pt. 5, vol. 80, reel T-2664, RG 23, LAC; Memorandum by R. N. Venning, 11 September 1909, ibid.; and unsigned Memorandum, 17 September 1909, ibid.

61. This decision was also influenced by some problems with spoilage experienced by the British Columbia industry. Officials thought that if seiners took fish outside the mouth of the river, they would stay fresh longer. See Memorandum for the Honourable Commissioner of Fisheries, 21 February 1935, file 1934–35, box 156, GR-0435, BC Archives.

62. "Point Roberts Canal Scheme," *Vancouver Province*, 3 September 1903, box 53, IPSFC, UBC; Thomas Connor to Minister of Fisheries, 27 May 1932, box 1, GR-1378, BC Archives.

63. "Point Roberts Is Gage of Peace," *News-Advertiser*, 12 November 1913, box 55, IPSFC, UBC; "Why Not Buy Point Roberts? Asks Maiden," *Vancouver Sun*, 25 September 1925, enclosed in R. A. Spence, Report of Conditions on the Fraser, September 1925, box 7, vol. L-8, DFA, WSA.

64. R. E. Foerster to Einarsen, 21 January 1931, box 6, vol. L-38, box 6, DFA, WSA.

65. For the quote, see H. Helgeson to George Riley, 26 February 1902, file 6, pt. 2, vol. 79, reel T-2663, RG 23, LAC.

66. "Action of U.S. May End Fraser Salmon Fishing for Ever," *Victoria Colonist*,

10 March 1932, newspaper clipping from Pacific Press Clipping Bureau, Seattle, Wash., in box 4, vol. L-42, DFA, WSA (quotation); W. D. Burdis to L. P. Brodeur, 14 September 1909, file 6, pt. 5, vol. 80, reel T-2664, RG 23, LAC.

67. Washington (State), Department of Fisheries, *Biennial Report*, 1917–19, 13. Washington State also had some far-fetched schemes in mind for increasing sockeye on their side of the line. See, e.g., Washington (State), Department of Fisheries, *Biennial Report*, 1915–17, 18–19.

68. Taylor, "The Historical Roots of the Canadian-American Salmon Wars," 165–68. On trans-border communications, see W. A. Found to Miller Freeman, 15 January 1925, box 1, accession #1038, pt. 1, Correspondence Incoming, Canada Department of Marine and Fisheries, Miller Freeman Papers, UW Libraries; J. P. Babcock to Henry O'Malley, 28 May 1929, box 1, GR-1378, BC Archives; Miller Freeman to J. P. Babcock, 3 June 1935, ibid.; and Miller Freeman to J. P. Babcock, 4 June 1925, ibid.

69. For example, American and Canadian authorities banded together with unprecedented cooperation to halt rampant illegal fishing in the 1934 season. See B. M. Brennan to Richard Hamilton, 21 September 1934, Fisheries Department 1934, box 44, Subject Files, Governor Clarence Martin Papers [hereafter Martin Papers], WSA.

70. Clarence Martin to Lewis Schwellenbach, 4 May 1935, Fisheries Department 1935, box 44, Subject files, Martin Papers, WSA; Clarence Martin to the Fishery Industry of Washington, n.d. (ca. spring 1935), Fisheries Department 1935, box 44, ibid.

71. Clarence Martin to Edward Allen, 10 May 1933, Fisheries Department 1933, box 43, Martin Papers, WSA; S. H. Calvert to Miller Freeman, Fisheries Department 1934, box 44, ibid.

72. For a more complete discussion of this turn of events, see Taylor, "The Historical Roots of the Canadian-American Salmon Wars," 155–75.

73. Ibid., 169–75.

# PART III

.........................................

*Border Enforcement*

*and Contestation*

# CROSSING THE LINE

*The INS and the
Federal Regulation of
the Mexican Border*

...........................................

S. Deborah Kang

No regulatory measures could possibly be devised on this border in any
way affecting the freedom of movement of the people living on the
border or touching their financial interests which would not be the
object of attack and criticism. Every innovation of such a character, of
which the Public Health Quarantine measures, head tax and illiteracy
provisions are notable examples, have evoked similar protest.

GEORGE J. HARRIS, ACTING SUPERVISING INSPECTOR OF THE
EL PASO DISTRICT, BUREAU OF IMMIGRATION

The exasperated declaration of George J. Harris expressed what many
Bureau of Immigration officials in the Southwest accepted as a fact of
life along the U.S.-Mexico border.[1] Prior to 1917, geography, institutional
weaknesses, and local custom all contributed to the lax enforcement of
immigration laws on the international line. Few appeared troubled by the
unfettered crossing and re-crossing of thousands of Mexicans at points all
along the border each day. Indeed, the opposite attitude seemed to prevail,
as recounted by an El Paso community leader and lifetime resident in the
early 1900s: "There were no restrictions as to crossing the bridge, or
passports or anything like that. Everyone was happy, coming and going without any customs restrictions, any immigration restrictions, any
health department restrictions."[2]

The First World War transformed this orientation toward the border,
raising concerns about a foreign invasion along the southern line and
compelling southwestern Bureau of Immigration officials to take their

jobs more seriously. In response to this wartime threat, Congress passed a set of laws, specifically, the Immigration Act of 1917 and the Entry and Departures Control Act of 1918 (also known as the Passport Act), which created a new tapestry of regulations along the boundary with Mexico.[3] Long accustomed to crossing the border without restriction, local residents vehemently protested the enforcement of these laws by the Immigration Service. Lacking the money, manpower, and, many times, the will to adequately enforce the new laws, southwestern immigration officials often waived the rules or created new ones that made their lives, and the lives of border residents, much easier. To the chagrin of anti-immigration advocates in Washington, the southern border remained porous and open.

Through an examination of Bureau of Immigration operations during the First World War, this study reveals the contingencies of immigration law enforcement on the U.S.-Mexico border. In so doing, I present a more complex account of immigration law enforcement than that offered by the current historical literature. While immigration historians have demonstrated how American immigration law and policy "hardened" or closed the nation's ports of entry and the northern and southern borders to unwanted immigrants, in this essay I show how Bureau of Immigration officials in the Southwest deployed the very same laws in ways that opened the border and, in turn, sustained the transnational character of the borderlands.[4]

All of this is not to deny the agency's vigorous efforts to bar Mexican, Asian, and European nationals from admission for permanent residence, or to expel unwanted illegal aliens in this period. It is, however, to say that in the Southwest, as well as in the nation as a whole, the substance and scale of the Bureau's enforcement efforts were variable, dependent on factors that included social status (race, class, and gender), legal, political, and institutional considerations (both international and domestic), and even time and place.[5] Erika Lee's study of Bureau of Immigration operations on Angel Island offers one example of the regional variation in the administration of the immigration laws.[6] This and other studies also reveal the disparate approaches adopted by the Immigration Service toward Asian, European, and Mexican immigrants.[7] Other works explore the ways in which the Bureau made intragroup distinctions, particularly on the basis of class and gender, within these nationality groups.[8] And, in this volume, Andrea Geiger deftly recounts how Japanese immigrants themselves resisted exclusion by taking strategic advantage of the transit privilege on the Canadian and Mexican borders.

This essay also adds to our understanding of immigration law enforcement by arguing that the Bureau of Immigration applied a spectrum of policies vis-à-vis disparate populations who were attempting to cross the line. Based on the agency's archival records, this study demonstrates that, during the First World War and well into the 1920s, the Bureau was concerned not only with restricting the number of immigrants but also with regulating the local border population. While immigration historians have provided extensive accounts of those migrants who sought entry for permanent residence (formally referred to as "immigrants" by the Bureau of Immigration), in this essay I shift the focus of attention from immigrants to border-crossers (categorized as "non-immigrants"). This population typically included laborers, tourists, local residents, dignitaries, and businessmen who crossed and re-crossed the border on a regular basis for short periods of time. In a stunning departure from the exclusionary intent underlying the Immigration Act of 1917 and the Passport Act of 1918, Bureau of Immigration officials effectively nullified provisions of these laws in order to craft a migration, or border-crossing, policy for these border residents and businesses.

By offering a history of this border-crossing policy, the essay also addresses the ways in which *local* conditions influenced the formation and administration of federal immigration law and policy. In so doing, it contributes not only to our understanding of immigration history, but also of borderlands history. More specifically, just as the essays in this volume of Jennifer Seltz, Rachel St. John, and Lissa Wadewitz show how *border* interests played a profound role in the shaping of federal policies pertaining to public health, the management of ranch lands, and salmon fishing, respectively, my own essay describes this same process for immigration. I find that both American and Mexican residents, businesses, and state officials, by protesting or defying federal immigration mandates, often played a policymaking role, just as was the case for Washington State officials in Wadewitz's study, and for local ranchers in St. John's work. As a result, in the Southwest, immigration law and policy proved highly responsive to local needs and concerns.[9] More broadly, all of these essays reveal the ways in which federal agencies, transnational industries, and local communities expressed competing visions of the border, and complicated the processes of border-making and nation-building.

The first section of this essay offers a snapshot of the U.S.-Mexico borderlands. It describes the major demographic, economic, and social trends which created an intricate network of binational relationships along the U.S.-Mexico border from approximately 1900 until 1920. Yet, as I show in the second section, during the First World War these very links became a cause for concern among federal, state, and local officials. Fearing the possibility of enemy invasion through Mexico, Congress and the Bureau of Immigration adopted a more restrictive approach to border control. Through the passage of the Immigration Act of 1917 and the Passport Act of 1918, the Bureau of Immigration sought to bar the entry of unwanted immigrants and enemy aliens. The passage of legislation in Congress, however, did not guarantee its seamless or effective implementation on the ground. As the final section reveals, the realities of the borderlands—the sheer volume of migrants crossing the line, the ceaseless demand for migrant labor, and the vehement protests of border residents—eroded the restrictive intent underlying Progressive Era immigration legislation. As a result, Bureau of Immigration officials in the Southwest exercised their administrative discretion, waived provisions of the Immigration Act of 1917 and the Passport Act of 1918, and fashioned a policy which opened the line to the border-crossers.

### Migration and the Transformation of the U.S.-Mexico Borderlands

At the turn of the twentieth century, the northward migration of Mexican nationals constituted one of the most important events along the southern border of the United States. Historians estimate that approximately 1.5 million Mexican nationals entered the country between 1910 and 1920.[10] Many of them ultimately settled permanently in the United States, resulting in a dramatic increase in the Mexican-born population, from 110,393 in 1900 to 700,541 in 1920.[11] Hundreds of thousands more immigrants entered on a temporary basis, crossing and re-crossing the border as laborers, merchants, or casual visitors. This category of migrants, referred to by the Bureau of Immigration as "non-immigrants," or "non-statistical entrants," outnumbered "immigrants" (those entering for permanent residence) by a factor of three to one.[12] In addition, thousands more entered as refugees fleeing Revolutionary violence and economic displacement in Mexico. This massive demographic shift not only attested to the openness of the border in this period, it also played a pivotal role in the formation of transnational communities all along the international line.

Until the First World War, the economic and social needs of the borderlands, rather than the precepts of immigration law, served as the driving forces underlying migration between Mexico and the United States. As historian Mario T. García explains, Mexican immigration was "inextricably linked with the growth of American industrial capitalism."[13] The primary southwestern industries—railroads, mining, ranching, and agriculture—met their labor needs with migrant workers.[14] After passage of the Chinese Exclusion Acts (which barred the entry of Chinese laborers), and given the proximity of Mexico, it was Mexican nationals who comprised the bulk of this immigrant workforce.[15] While southwestern developmental imperatives served as pull factors, political upheavals in Mexico, especially the redistributive land policies of the Díaz regime and the Mexican Revolution, functioned as push factors, leading to the massive migration of Mexican nationals well into the 1920s.[16]

Recognizing the importance of immigration to the border economy, federal officials adopted a laissez-faire stance toward Mexican migration across the line.[17] Indeed, at the urging of corporations like the Southern Pacific Railroad, Congress exempted Mexican immigrants from the head taxes that were stipulated under the Immigration Acts of 1903 and 1907.[18] While southwestern officials possessed other statutory means to restrict Mexican immigration, they chose not to exercise this authority on a regular basis.[19] Instead, they allowed most Mexican immigrants to cross the international line without inspection.[20] According to historian George Sánchez, some immigration inspectors played a more active role in facilitating the labor needs of southwestern agribusiness, accepting bribes from representatives of the farm and rail industries who sought a steady supply of Mexican workers.[21]

Mexican migration not only fueled the growth of border industries, it also contributed to the growth and development of binational communities from Texas to California.[22] At the turn of the century, the rise of El Paso was completely dependent upon the labor provided by Mexican nationals.[23] This reliance extended from the primary economic sectors (including the rail, mining, and ranching industries) to the secondary economic sectors (including manufacturing, wholesale and retail trade, and construction).[24] As a result, the city's Mexican population grew from 736 in 1880 to 100,000 in 1920.[25] These demographic and economic processes transformed El Paso into a major urban center and an entrepôt of southwestern economic activity within the span of forty years.[26]

Economic and demographic expansion also propelled the social transformation of the city. Mexican immigrants formed their own communities, living in segregated barrios, as well as founding their own business establishments (such as shops, restaurants, and newspapers), cultural and educational institutions, entertainment venues, and political organizations.[27] Many of these institutions maintained ties to Mexico. The Spanish-language press, for example, featured news stories about Mexican politics, offered a forum for Mexican Revolutionaries, and accepted advertising from Mexican business establishments on both sides of the line.[28] These transnational social and cultural links also complicated notions of identity. As historian Monica Perales has written of El Paso's Smeltertown, "Far more than being the meeting place of two nation states, the borderlands is a cultural crossroads where what is Mexican and what is American cannot be neatly separated."[29]

Border towns in Arizona experienced a similar pattern of binational economic development. Along the Arizona-Sonora border, the major industries—mining, ranching, and agriculture—grew in tandem. American capital funded the construction of mining facilities on both sides of the line, irrigation projects in Mexico which supported farms in the United States, and ranching ventures which participated in transnational grazing arrangements.[30] As in El Paso, these industries relied heavily upon Mexican immigrant labor. Yet, given the racial segmentation of the workforce, these industries placed Mexican nationals in unskilled occupations, while hiring Anglos to fill skilled and managerial posts on both sides of the line.[31] Thus, they depended not only on the unfettered crossing and re-crossing of Mexican migrants, but also on the labor of U.S. citizens. Given these long-standing crossing patterns, the border between Arizona and Sonora was "just as permeable" as elsewhere along the international boundary.[32]

In Tijuana, border-crossing was also bidirectional and multinational. Both Americans and Mexicans often traveled south of the border to patronize entertainment and nightlife venues, particularly with the start of Prohibition in 1920. The border at El Paso/Ciudad Juárez was often swamped with American tourists headed south to imbibe. As historian David Romo has written: "It was no longer arms smugglers, spies, soldiers of fortune, journalists and revolutionaries crossing the lines. Suddenly the ludic zone across the border became packed with American tourists. Between 1918 and 1919, about 14,000 tourists crossed the border into Mexico; a year later the official U.S. Customs tally was 418,700."[33] Ciudad Juárez may have drawn thousands of casual visitors, but it was Tijuana that surpassed all other border towns, north or south of the line, as one of the most popular tourist destinations in the Southwest.[34] Indeed, given the volume of traffic flowing from north to south, Tijuana identified itself less with Mexico than with California.[35] Tijuana boosters, including both Mexican and American investors, actively encouraged this traffic by constructing gambling halls, race tracks, theaters, and spas.[36] According to historian Paul J. Vanderwood, even the State Department facilitated economic development in the region: "United States consuls . . . were placed there to promote and protect American business interests, and as a distant second task to assist their countrymen and women in need."[37]

While Mexicans and Anglos formed the two largest migratory streams, Japanese, Chinese, and other foreign nationals also joined the flow of migrants crossing and re-crossing the border each day. In El Paso, after the railroad had been completed in 1881, many of the Chinese immigrant laborers remained. After the passage of the Chinese Exclusion Act in 1882, others used El Paso as a surreptitious gateway into the United States. Sometimes they slipped past immigration inspectors by posing as Mexicans. Setting up laundries, restaurants, and grocery stores, according to Romo, they became "a dominant component of the petit bourgeois class" in El Paso. Similar Chinese communities emerged in Arizona and in border towns in Mexico (an 1893 diplomatic agreement permitted Chinese to immigrate to Mexico).[38] Like the Chinese, the Japanese in Ciudad Juárez operated small businesses. In El Paso, a small Japanese community lived just outside the city limits, where they owned and operated their own truck farms.[39] In Tijuana, along with Americans and Mexicans, Armenians, Syrians, Japanese, Spaniards, Italians, and Chinese all launched successful businesses.[40] One Tijuana school even opened its doors to the children of these various nationality groups.[41]

Together, these cross-border demographic, economic, and social ties led local residents to construe the border as an "imaginary line."[42] Yet, on the eve of the First World War, these very ties generated concerns about border security among federal officials in the Southwest and Washington, D.C. In particular, the cross-border raids of Mexican Revolutionaries exposed the weaknesses of federal authority and the strength of transnational loyalties to the rebellion. In American border towns, Revolutionary forces found a safe haven from advancing Mexican federal troops, moral support for their political cause, and even a supply of arms and basic necessities.[43] While cross-border raids had been a feature of the Revolution from its inception, by 1913 a violent regime change had intensified political rivalries and military hostilities within Mexico and along its northern frontier.[44] By 1916, the increase in border raiding drew the focused attention of Washington officials as they sought to bring order to the region.[45] In pursuit of Revolutionary leader Pancho Villa and his forces, President Wilson sent General John Pershing and ten thousand troops into Mexico in retaliation for Villa's attacks on American citizens.[46] But Pershing's punitive expedition failed to establish peace along the border, instead bringing the United States to the brink of war with Mexico.

At the same time, national anxieties about border security were only exacerbated by the First World War. Under pressure from German submarine warfare in the Atlantic, federal officials expressed concerns about the possibility of the nation's seaports and land borders being breached.[47] The Zimmerman Telegram lent credence to fears about a possible German invasion from Mexico.[48] In addition, federal officials worried that Mexican Revolutionaries, acting to avenge Villa's defeat, would assist Germany in this effort. Finally, the persistence of the geographical, social, and economic networks between border towns rendered them "logical haven[s]" for enemy aliens as well as Revolutionary forces.[49] According to Romo, the Emporium Bar in El Paso served as a meeting place for Pancho Villa and a German spy who allegedly sought leasing rights to submarine bases in Baja California.[50]

At the local level, the anxieties surrounding Villa's raids and the war increased public antagonism toward Mexican immigrants, which in turn led to a tightening of border inspection procedures. In an atmosphere of paranoia, El Paso city officials alleged that the massive influx of migrants fleeing the Revolution would create a public health crisis, specifically, a typhus epidemic. As a solution, they initially proposed a quarantine of all new arrivals.[51] In lieu of the quarantine, city officials conducted health inspections of all the homes in Chihuahuita (the largest Mexican neighborhood in El Paso), while El Paso Mayor Tom Lea proposed to destroy them altogether.[52] By 1917, local representatives of the U.S. Public Health Service had adopted more severe measures, subjecting 127,173 Mexican immigrants to a delousing and bathing procedure, followed by a rigorous physical and mental examination.[53]

### The View from the Center: The Immigration Act of 1917 and the Passport Act of 1918

Federal, as well as local, officials evinced a more enforcement-minded orientation toward the border during the First World War, launching cavalry patrols and air surveillance teams in search of Revolutionaries and German spies.[54] Congress also enacted statutory measures, specifically the Immigration Act of 1917 and the Passport Act of 1918, to secure the line against alien enemies and unwanted immigrants.[55] In this wartime context, southwestern Bureau of Immigration officials changed their lax orientation toward immigration law enforcement and, for the first time, took seriously their responsibility to enforce the new laws vis-à-vis Mexican nationals. In so doing, they attempted to impose a new tapestry of regulations upon a population long accustomed to crossing the border without any restrictions.

In passing the Immigration Act of 1917, Congress created an omnibus bill which consolidated immigration legislation from the prior three decades.[56] Its passage marked an apex in Progressive Era efforts to restrict immigration from Southern and Eastern Europe and from Asia. In the latter category, it excluded immigrants from a geographic area labeled the "Asiatic Barred Zone," which included all of Asia except for Japan and the Philippines. In order to limit admission from Europe, the Act created a literacy test for all individuals seeking admission into the United States.[57] Despite President Woodrow Wilson's veto of the legislation (Wilson was unwilling to reverse a campaign promise not to restrict European immigration[58]), Congress overrode his veto and passed the bill on February 5, 1917.

While the Immigration Act of 1917 was not conceived as a wartime measure, policymakers later relied on its provisions to implement a domestic defense policy within the nation and at the borders. Indeed, once the country entered the war (one month after the bill's passage), Wilson's concerns about the entry of radicals "dominate[d] the politics of immigration policy."[59] As a result, federal officials began to use the looser deportation standards created by the new Act to expel suspected alien enemies and subversives throughout the country.[60] In the Southwest, the Bureau of Immigration began to reverse its long-standing practice of allowing Mexican nationals to freely cross the border; it now attempted to control and restrict their movement under the authority of the new immigration law. For the first time in its history, the Bureau began to enforce the head tax, as well as instituting the Act's new literacy test provisions with respect to Mexican immigrants.[61]

Initially, the Immigration Act of 1917 had a significant impact on migration across the U.S.-Mexico border. The literacy test plus the head tax created serious restrictions against the admission of Mexican immigrants, particularly agricultural workers who, for the most part, were poor and illiterate.[62] For the first few months that the new law was in operation, Mexican immigration declined sharply from the same period the previous year. Cardoso reports that only 31,000 Mexicans emigrated to the United States in 1917, whereas 56,000 had entered in the prior year.[63] By 1918, Cardoso notes, 1,771 Mexicans had decided against emigrating to the Untied States because of the literacy test, and the Immigration Service had rejected the applications of 5,745 others for failure to pay the head tax.[64]

These new restrictions also exacerbated the problem of Mexican illegal entry across the border. Prior to the passage of the Act, southwestern immigration officials had concerned themselves primarily with the illegal entry of Chinese and European immigrants. In his annual report for fiscal year 1917, the supervising inspector for the Mexican Border District highlighted continuing concerns about the smuggling of Chinese and Japanese nationals. In the same report, he also discussed the problem of entry without inspection from Mexico, but characterized it as a mere technical violation, meriting a lesser punishment than the smuggling of Asian laborers or the illegal entry of immigrants who were unable to meet the moral turpitude provisions of the 1917 Act.[65] By the following year, the Bureau's attitude toward Mexican immigration had changed, as reflected in the observations of the supervising inspector: "The suppression of attempted illegal entry of countless aliens of the Mexican race, excluded or excludable, under what they deem to be the harsh provisions of the immigration act of 1917, has constituted one of the most difficult problems with which this district has had to contend in the past year."[66] The head tax and literacy test created a new population of illegal immigrants—Mexican nationals—that the Bureau had long ignored.

In order to restrict the entry and departure of suspected alien enemies, federal officials initially relied on the immigration statutes. They found, however, that the immigration laws failed to provide the regulatory authority necessary to restrict and supervise this category of foreign nationals. An assistant to the attorney general observed:

> When we got into the war we were met, of course, immediately with the necessity of supervising exit from the country and entrance into the country of undesirable persons, and the only law on the subject that came anywhere near reaching them was the immigration law, which was not designed to fit a situation in which spies were moving to and from the country, because the tests prescribed by the immigration statutes for admittance to the country were, of course, simple and designed to meet certain requirements of intelligence, character, previous history, etc.[67]

In response to this lack of authority to prevent the entry of alien enemies, Congress passed the Passport Act, which specifically required aliens and U.S. citizens to present passports for inspection at the nation's ports of entry for the duration of the war.[68] Implementation of the Act would constitute another new layer of restrictions that would have a serious impact on the movement of populations across the U.S.-Mexico border.[69]

The administration of the Passport Act was divided among several federal agencies, including Justice, Labor, Commerce, and State. While the State Department was responsible for the issuance of passports and visas, the Bureau of Immigration was responsible for actual enforcement. Thus, prior to conducting their usual immigration inspection, immigration officers would act as passport agents, inspecting passports and visas, collecting visa fees, and taking the declarations of aliens and U.S. citizens as they entered or departed the country. The new responsibilities increased the workload of an agency that already lacked the resources it needed to successfully fulfill its own mandate to enforce the nation's immigration laws.[70] And this, in turn, would compound the problems faced by the Bureau of Immigration in expanding the presence of the federal government in a community long accustomed to its absence.

### The View from the Border: Local Perspectives on National Mandates

While immigration restrictionists celebrated the passage of the Immigration Act of 1917, Bureau of Immigration officials in the Southwest recognized the logistical difficulties of closing a two-thousand-mile stretch of rugged terrain to unwanted immigration, as well as the incongruity of foisting a restrictionist immigration regime upon a community long accustomed to a virtually open border. This is not to say, however, that southwestern Bureau officials were unconcerned about the threat of wartime invasion or Revolutionary incursion along the border. They were worried, but they also understood the ways in which the new federal regulations would impinge upon everyday life in the borderlands. Their perspective on immigration restriction was not only informed by the view from the top (Washington politicians and policymakers), but also by the view from the bottom—by the outlook and experiences of border residents, businesses, and politicians. This section recounts that view, describing the ways in which the Immigration Act of 1917 and the Passport Act of 1918 threatened to disrupt the lives of border-crossers and the society of the borderlands.

In 1918 El Paso General Consul Ralph J. Totten conducted a tour of immigration stations and consulates along the U.S.-Mexico border. Focused on the issue of border security during wartime, Totten's report evaluated Department of State and Bureau of Immigration joint enforcement of the Passport Law. Its overview of conditions along the international line conveys a sense of the openness and freedom of movement that existed from west Texas to the California coast. The unceasing border traffic, ranging from 100,000 to 200,000 crossings per day, reflected the transnational character of border communities.[71] Totten was able to observe the symbiotic relationship between adjacent Mexican and American communities all along the border. In Brownsville, he noted, "the population on the Mexican side of the river is entirely dependent on Brownsville for a great part of the necessities of life, especially sugar, lard and a number of other food products. There are from 500 to 1,500 daily crossings."[72]

Moving west to Laredo, Totten estimated that approximately 80,000 individuals crossed the border each year, but that after the passage of the Passport Law, the number of officially recorded crossings in Laredo had fallen to 36,000. Totten concluded that, at points all along the border, the new passport requirements had led migrants to evade the formal inspections process by entering the country clandestinely between the official ports of entry.[73]

Illegal entry, Totten blithely noted, was "a condition for which no one is to blame."[74] Rather, Totten attributed the increase in surreptitious entry to the geography of the borderlands. It was the vast, two-thousand-mile expanse of the border region that posed the major challenge to the enforcement of the immigration laws:

> By far the greatest weakness in the border situation, however, is the fact that it is comparatively easy for anyone to illegally cross the line at almost any point away from the cities. The frequency of raids from the Mexican side into the United States, the fact that a certain amount of smuggling is going on all of the time, and hundreds of known instances where individuals and parties have crossed the line from both sides, prove the possibility of illegal entry into the United States.[75]

Even at the populated towns and cities along the border, the size of the territory and the lack of available manpower to patrol such a large area made illegal entry quite easy. For example, in Brownsville, Totten observed, "cavalry patrols do their best to prevent illegal crossings but it must be remembered that there are 500 miles of the river in the Brownsville district alone and a limited number of soldiers for this work."[76]

At the border ports of entry, Totten found that few natural or man-made barriers existed to prevent migrants from simply walking, or even swimming, across the international boundary. In El Paso, Totten noted that "the Rio Grande is little more than a brook and can be forded at almost any point."[77] And in Nogales it was a public street, rather than a river, that marked the international boundary:

> Conditions in Nogales are entirely different from any of the above mentioned cities. There is here no river or other natural boundary. The line runs through the town along a street some forty yards wide. One side of the street is in the United States and the other side is in Mexico.

Formerly people crossed the street at any point. There are now only two points where legal crossing is permitted, at the principal business street which runs through both the American and the Mexican town, and along the railroad track in front of the stations.[78]

In 1920 Immigration Service officials estimated that sixty thousand aliens had entered without inspection at a single border port of entry.[79] The geography of the border would prove to be one of the greatest obstacles to immigration law enforcement.

Concerns about U.S. relations with Mexico also served to check, if not undermine, the rigorous implementation of the immigration laws.[80] In the 1920s, the State Department expected border officials to facilitate cross-border ties with Mexican officials. As part of his inspection, Totten reviewed the performance of consular officials in this regard, praising the consular officer at Eagle Pass for his fluent Spanish and for being "on the best of terms with the local officials, both Mexican and American."[81] State Department officials also encouraged consular and immigration officers to treat the Mexican immigrants courteously. Such close relationships, however, often vitiated the enforcement goals of the Bureau, as Totten observed in Calexico, California:

> The inspectors seeing the same people crossing day after day soon come to know the habitual crossers of the frontier and can generally pick out a stranger at a glance. The danger of this system is that they become careless and it soon gets so that anyone can cross, also if people get to know that their papers will not be asked for they could easily sell them or lend them to others for use at a different port of entry.[82]

For the remainder of the twentieth century, these informal diplomatic arrangements, as well as more formal diplomatic agreements, between the United States and Mexico would inform the shaping of American immigration policy.[83] Moreover, these binational accords, on occasion, would ease the restrictive impact of immigration laws, leaving the border open to locals long accustomed to free ingress and egress across the line.[84]

Southwestern border officials also realized that restrictive immigration policies threatened the economy and society of the borderlands. The correspondence files of the Immigration and Naturalization Service are replete with protests—letters, telegraphs, official accounts of exchanges

**Figure 1.** The international boundary between Nogales, Arizona, and Nogales, Sonora, in the early twentieth century. (Courtesy of the National Archives, Washington, D.C.)

at inspection counters—from local residents. Indeed, throughout the agency's history, border residents have been some of the most vehement and persistent opponents of any regulation that threatened to encroach upon their freedom of movement across the international line. These protests were not only prolific on the U.S.-Mexican border; they were also usual along the U.S.-Canadian border. Like their counterparts to the south, border residents along the northern line saw the passage of the Passport Law as a substantial threat to the transnational economy and society of the Canadian borderlands. In response, both Canadian and American businessmen, tourists, property owners (particularly U.S. citizens with vacation homes in Canada), and entertainers expressed their concerns that the Passport Law would hinder their ability to cross the border.[85]

In the Southwest, those industries reliant on Mexican labor were the most vocal and politically powerful opponents of the new restrictions imposed by the Immigration and Passport Acts.[86] Knowing that Mexican laborers would be unable to meet the provisions of the Acts, southwestern employers argued for exemptions to these laws.[87] Mexican workers were in particular demand, since agribusiness anticipated a debilitating decline in the number of farm workers as a result of the military draft, the lure of higher-paying jobs in wartime industries, and the new restrictions on European migration under the literacy test. Southwestern businesses further claimed that without access to a steady supply of labor, their ability to provide essential supplies to the war effort would be severely impaired.[88]

It is important to note that it was not only southwestern agribusiness—with the greater means and incentives to protest—who opposed the new federal laws. Ordinary individuals from all walks of life, of all ethnicities, and of all nationalities also protested. In short, the new regulations affected everyone who had any reason to cross the U.S.-Mexico border. The INS correspondence files contain hundreds of complaints from persons traveling from Mexico to shop, work, patronize entertainment venues, or socialize with friends and family.[89] Historian Vicki Ruiz has documented the strategies employed by women to procure exemptions to the passport requirements that would allow them to cross and re-cross the border for work and to visit family members.[90] Bureau of Immigration records also contain letters of protest written on behalf of Chinese and Japanese nationals, many of whom were merchants who crossed the line in order to trade.[91]

Federal regulations threatened not only Mexican interests in the United States, but also American interests in Mexico. Representatives from the Imperial Irrigation District protested that the Passport Law would halt construction of a canal project in Mexico (by delaying the entry of skilled American laborers) and thereby hurt American farmers who relied on the water from the canal to irrigate their crops.[92] In San Diego, American backers of a Tijuana race track became vehement opponents of the Passport Law, arguing that the regulations would deter patrons from traveling south of the border, instead drawing them north to competing entertainment venues in Los Angeles.[93] An Arizona mining company requested exemptions for its Mexican workers, who hauled ore mined north of the border to a processing facility south of the border.[94] In Texas, passport regulations threatened the business of American ranchers who grazed their stock in Mexico.[95] Passport regulations affected not only large businesses, but also small, individually owned ventures as well. An American dentist requested exemptions for his patients who lived south of the border; and an American doctor asked for special permission to cross the border to visit patients in Mexico.[96]

Finally, the new regulations affected American citizens living on both sides of the border. American citizens living on the Mexican side of the border requested more-lenient border-crossing privileges into the country.[97] Some sought these privileges in order to work. Noting the demand for skilled American laborers, the inspector in charge at Calexico, California, wrote, "These undertakings necessitate many skilled laborers of various kinds as cannot be had among the common laboring people of Mexico."[98] Conversely, American citizens living on the U.S. side of the border demanded border-crossing privileges into Mexico. Many sought to evade Prohibition—by either imbibing south of the border or by making liquor purchases there and smuggling the liquor back into the United States.[99] Others crossed into Mexico for other kinds of entertainment—to attend festivals, conventions, horse and dog races, dance venues, or to gamble. In short, the passport regulations, in Totten's words, caused "a considerable amount of irritation on both sides of the Border. The Mexicans, in ignorance, feel that it is a measure directed especially against them, to cause them annoyance and prevent them from purchasing the food and supplies they greatly need. The American merchants are dissatisfied because of the loss of trade. Of course this loss is due much more to the regulations of the War Trade Board than to the passport regulations, but it is all coupled together in their minds."[100]

### The Exception to the Rule: Creating an Immigration Policy for the U.S.-Mexico Border

In 1918 Commissioner General Anthony Caminetti asked how the United States could maintain an immigration policy that closed the border to subversives and unwanted immigrants but, at the same time, kept it open to local residents who had legitimate reasons for crossing and re-crossing the border each day.[101] Southwestern immigration officials addressed this problem by waiving or amending the rules set forth in the Immigration Act of 1917 and the Passport Act of 1918. In the face of tremendous public opposition to the new federal regulations, Bureau of Immigration officials chose to respond to local needs rather than national mandates in their administration of immigration laws. In the process, they contravened the exclusionary objectives underlying the new laws.

Specifically, Service officials created a wartime labor-importation program to overcome the objections of southwestern agribusiness and industry to the head tax and the literacy test provisions of the Immigration Act.[102] Addressing opposition to the Passport Act, the Service created a temporary exemption to the passport requirement, referred to as the Section 13 certificate, which facilitated border crossing. These administrative devices were significant, not only because they modified immigration regulations, but also because they effectively *nullified* the restrictions imposed on the U.S.-Mexico border by the two Acts. The wartime agricultural labor program rendered inoperative the head tax, contract labor laws, and the literacy test on the U.S.-Mexico border.[103] Meanwhile, the Section 13 certificate (and the subsequent exemptions to the Section 13 certificate itself) removed any incentive for individuals to procure passports. The remainder of this essay will focus on the Section 13 certificate program, since it is less well known than the wartime labor-importation program, and since it reflects the role of border residents and local businesses, as opposed to that of powerful agribusiness organizations, in the formation of immigration policy.

In response to demands for more lenient border-crossing regulations, the State Department turned to the Bureau of immigration for a solution. Relying on a provision of the Immigration Rules of 1917, State Department officials authorized the issuance of border-crossing cards in lieu of passports.[104] More specifically, Rule 13 (titled "Inspection on the Mexican Border") provided that aliens who lived in close proximity to either side of the border and who frequently crossed the border for "legitimate pursuits" could receive a pass (a border-crossing card), enabling them to cross the line without embarrassment or delay. The card was also available to U.S. citizens desirous of a quick form of identification. In order to facilitate inspections at the ports of entry, the card included a photograph and the signature of the bearer. These cards were also put into use along the U.S.-Canadian border.

By 1918, State Department officials had incorporated Immigration Rule 13 into their own regulations regarding the administration of the Passport Act.[105] Referred to as Section 13 certificates, they were to be issued to both U.S. citizens and aliens who frequently crossed the border for legitimate business purposes.[106] The 1918 Act further stipulated that Immigration Service officials could exercise their administrative discretion when deciding whether to issue cards good for a single crossing or for unlimited crossings.[107] Those presenting Section 13 certificates were also exempted from paying the head tax.[108] These cards were not intended to replace passports. Rather, they were issued due to wartime exigencies, intended primarily for Europeans who were unable to obtain passports from their home countries. Alien identification cards, then, would only be valid for "a sufficient period for them to procure passports of the country to which they owe allegiance."[109]

Given wartime concerns about border security, border-crossing cards were issued with circumspection.[110] At the same time, the State Department adopted the border-crossing card procedure as the only viable means of regulating cross-border traffic essential to local border communities. In the issuance of these cards, the State Department and the Bureau of Immigration tried to balance the nation's security needs with the borderlands' economic and social interests. Thus, alien and citizen recipients of the Section 13 certificates were required to be residents of the border region, which meant residence "at no greater distance than ten miles from border."[111] In addition, these border-crossing cards limited the radius of travel allowed: U.S. citizens and aliens were restricted to travel within a ten-mile radius north and south of the border.[112] Border-crossing cards were not issued to American citizens who made more frequent trips to areas in the interior of Mexico (which is to say, non-border regions). Those individuals were required to obtain passports.

Despite the existence of such wartime safeguards, the Immigration Service eventually relaxed the regulations and began issuing cards to those for whom they were not intended. As a Prohibition measure, the agency had originally denied identification cards to "pleasure seekers[,] tourists[,] idlers[,] gamblers[,] race horse followers and the like."[113] Yet, in 1919, after much protest from border residents and from proprietors of entertainment establishments, the Immigration Service instituted a tourist pass system for those wishing to travel south of the border.[114] Tourist passes, initially good for a single day, but later extended for ten-day use, allowed visits "in the border zone on either side of the Mexican border, whether such persons reside within or without the zone [the ten-mile limit], provided their identity, nationality and bona fides are established to the satisfaction of permit agents [immigration officials]." The permits were limited to American citizens, but immigration officials could, at their discretion, issue them to aliens.[115]

The Bureau and the Department of State also made exemptions on an ad hoc basis, again to cater to the needs of local communities.[116] In Nogales, Sonora, the local American consul issued four thousand provisional passports to Mexican citizens so that they could cross the line into Nogales, Arizona, in order to shop. Under pressure from local businessmen who complained that passport regulations had caused a downturn in the local economy, local Immigration and State Department officials agreed to repeated extensions of these provisional passports.[117] The State Department permitted residents south of the California border who possessed passports with visas unlimited trips north in order to purchase subsistence items.[118] And in 1920 (when passport regulations had loosened somewhat, but still required non-border residents from Mexico to present visaed passports), the State Department authorized the issuance of identification cards to aliens from non-border (interior) regions of Mexico who wished to attend fairs in El Paso and Dallas.[119] Despite his doubts, Supervising Inspector Berkshire permitted the Calexico office to continue its practice of issuing identification cards to the owners and employees of gambling houses and bars in Mexicali.[120]

While the Immigration Service relaxed border-crossing regulations for the benefit of border residents, the same border residents continued to complain about the impositions of the law. Furthermore, despite wartime concerns about border security, local residents demanded fewer restrictions, with some even advocating an open border. Writing on behalf of San Diego's business community, William Kettner, the congressman for the Eleventh District, called for "discontinuing war time restrictions against American citizens going into Mexico," since San Diego businessmen were "at peace with the people of Lower California."[121] According to Kettner, "full ingress and egress" was essential to the San Diego tourist industry, especially since the town was losing business to Los Angeles under the wartime passport and immigration restrictions. Even San Diego labor unions encouraged a relaxation of passport restrictions, as a stimulus to the local economy.[122] Similarly, one B. Rojo, the ad interim chargé d'affaires for the Mexican embassy, requested a loosening of border-crossing conditions between Presidio, Texas, and Ojinaga, Mexico, for the benefit of Mexican business.[123]

A few immigration officials even proposed a more lenient interpretation of border-crossing regulations. In Laredo, for example, the inspector in charge recommended the temporary admission of local aliens who could not meet the literacy test and health requirements of the Immigration Act.[124] He argued that, as property owners and established members of the local community, these aliens would not risk losing their livelihoods and reputations by violating the terms of a temporary admission. His recommendations were not approved by the central office. A. A. Musgrave, the inspector in charge at Calexico, admitted to a more liberal issuance of identification cards than that permitted by Rule 13, for the sake of sustaining American business interests south of the border. Adopting the perspective of border residents, he argued that proprietors and employees of saloons and gambling halls would lose their primary, if not their only, means of subsistence if they couldn't easily cross the line.[125]

The Bureau's experiences with the enforcement of the Immigration Act of 1917 and the Passport Act of 1918 revealed the limits of the national immigration policy network. On the U.S.-Mexico border, local administrative practices contravened national legislative mandates. Southwestern immigration officials ignored or changed the rules on behalf of those populations—including Asian nationals, contract laborers, pleasure-seeking tourists, and illiterate aliens—whom nativists sought to bar by means of the immigration laws. While border residents may have shared the nativist views of anti-immigration advocates, they were not necessarily part of the national consensus on immigration restriction. Indeed, many local residents would have preferred an open border.

In the immediate aftermath of the war, southwestern Bureau of Immigration officials, frustrated with haggling with border residents, considered the elimination of the border-crossing card system altogether. Yet they ultimately retained the system, realizing that it afforded one of the only identification systems along the southern line.[126] By 1924, what had originally been conceived as an ad hoc solution was accepted as standard policy and procedure. For the next forty years, Congress, the courts, and the INS would demonstrate a tacit unwillingness to disturb this border-crossing policy.[127] In so doing, federal policymakers also implicitly acknowledged that the free movement of populations across the line was essential to the society and economy of the border region, if not to the nation as a whole.

### Conclusion

While the Immigration Act of 1917 sharply curbed the numbers of Mexican immigrants—that is, those aliens seeking admission for permanent residence—it did not diminish the number of border-crossers, those border residents who entered the United States for temporary and limited stays. By the mid-1920s, it was the regulation of this non-immigrant border-crossing population—not the restriction of the immigrant population—that had become the central concern of the Bureau of Immigration. By 1928, the commissioner general of immigration underscored this point when he observed that the nation's borderlands had surpassed Ellis Island as the country's major ports of entry. On the Mexican and Canadian borders, the commissioner continued, "a great change has been taking place. . . . Steadily are they approaching a place of first importance in the scheme of things from an immigration standpoint. The fiscal year just closed witnessed a movement back and forth across these frontiers made up of citizens and aliens aggregating 53,000,000 entrants. Many of these, of course, were commuters, visitors, excursionists, etc."[128]

Historian George Sánchez has argued that "the new immigration laws were rarely conceived with the realities of the border in mind."[129] It was for this very reason that Bureau of Immigration officials in the Southwest ultimately waived provisions of the Immigration Act of 1917 and the Passport Act of 1918 for border residents. On the U.S.-Mexico border, the realities of the borderlands, more than the rhetoric of immigration restrictionists, played a pivotal role in the shaping of American immigration policy. While nativists imagined a border closed to unwanted immigrants, southwestern immigration officials understood that this aspiration could not be achieved in a community that not only welcomed immigration but also demanded it. The developmental imperatives of the region necessitated a constant flow of cheap migrant workers. And, over time, the binational communities which emerged out of the economic boom defended the free and open access across the border as if it were a natural right. As a result, Bureau of Immigration officials fashioned an immigration policy which sustained the transnational economy and society of the borderlands.

**Notes**

1. Johnson, *Revolution in Texas*, 72.
2. Dr. Cleofas Calleros, interview by Oscar J. Martínez, 14 September 1952, interview 157, transcript, Institute of Oral History, University of Texas, El Paso.
3. See *Immigration Act of February 5, 1917*, Public Law 64-301, *U.S. Statutes at*

*Large* 874 (1917): 39; and *Entry and Departures Control Act*, Public Law 65, *U.S. Statutes at Large* 559 (1918): 40.

4. Ngai, *Impossible Subjects*, 131; Sánchez, *Becoming Mexican American*, chap. 2; Stern, "Buildings, Boundaries, and Blood," 52, 80; Lytle Hernandez, "Entangling Bodies and Borders."

5. Kang, "The Legal Construction of the Borderlands."

6. Lee, *At America's Gates*.

7. See Ngai, *Impossible Subjects*; Lytle Hernandez, "Entangling Bodies and Borders"; Tichenor, *Dividing Lines*; Chan, "European and Asian Immigration into the United States in Comparative Perspective."

8. See Ruiz, *From Out of the Shadows*; Romo, *Ringside Seat to a Revolution*; Lee, *At America's Gates*; Calavita, "Collisions at the Intersection of Gender, Race, and Class."

9. St. John finds the same dynamic at work for customs policies in her essay in this volume, "Divided Ranges." This, however, is not to say that the Bureau of Immigration was completely beholden to these factions; throughout its history, the Bureau also pursued its own institutional and political goals in the administration of the law. Yet, due to space limitations, this chapter will focus exclusively on the connections between borderlands history and immigration history. For a more in-depth account of the institutional and political factors informing border immigration policy, see, Kang, "The Legal Construction of the Borderlands."

10. Hall and Coerver, *Revolution on the Border*, 126. Lorey estimates that, between 1910 and 1930, "almost 10 percent of Mexico's population migrated north to the United States" (Lorey, *The U.S.-Mexico Border*, 69). On the causes of the migration, see García, *Desert Immigrants*, 33; Acuña, *Occupied America*, 145; and Barrera, *Race and Class in the Southwest*, 68–69.

11. Cardoso, *Mexican Emigration to the United States*, 35; García, *Desert Immigrants*, 35. Historians, however, agree that the census figures, like the immigration statistics, grossly underestimate the number of Mexicans in the United States. They fail to account for illegal entrants, for those who entered as refugees, and for those Mexicans who were counted as "white."

12. Indeed, Hall and Coerver assert that those entering for permanent residence "formed by far the smallest category of migrants" (Hall and Coerver, *Revolution on the Border*, 130; see also García, *Desert Immigrants*, 35). Lorey estimates that, from 1910 to 1920, 206,000 Mexican nationals entered as legal immigrants, while 628,000 arrived as temporary workers (Lorey, *The U.S.-Mexico Border*, 70).

13. García, *Desert Immigrants*, 1.

14. The completion of the railroads in the late nineteenth century fueled the expansion of the regional economy, particularly the agricultural, mining, ranch-

ing, and commercial sectors (see García, *Desert Immigrants*, 3). García observes that the growth of these four sectors stimulated, in turn, the manufacturing, tourist, and construction industries. On the role of the railroad in the economic and environmental transformation of the West, see, e.g., Orsi, *Sunset Limited*; and St. John, "Line in the Sand."

15. The Chinese Exclusion Act of 1882 suspended the immigration of Chinese laborers for ten years. An 1884 amendment required all Chinese non-laborers to present certificates from the Chinese government and endorsed by the American consul in order to reenter the country. The Scott Act of 1888 prohibited the return of a laborer once he had left the United States. The Geary Act of 1892 extended the original exclusion act for another ten years, required Chinese immigrants to apply for a certificate of residence, and created the first internal passport system. See Salyer, *Laws Harsh as Tigers*; McClain, *In Search of Equality*; Wunder, "The Chinese and the Courts in the Pacific Northwest"; Saxton, *The Indispensable Enemy*. On the turn to Mexican immigrant labor after the passage of the Chinese Exclusion Acts, see García, *Desert Immigrants*, 2, 33.

16. García, *Desert Immigrants*, 33.

17. In Mexico, government officials also made little effort to clip the emigration of its nationals, believing that this migration would relieve some its own economic and political pressures. González, *Mexican Consuls and Labor Organizing*, 28.

18. The Immigration Acts of 1903 and 1907 charged a head tax of $2 and $4, respectively. Cardoso, *Mexican Emigration to the United States*, 34; Lorey, *The U.S.-Mexican Border in the Twentieth Century*, 69–71.

19. Cardoso, *Mexican Emigration to the United States*, 34. This relaxed orientation toward Mexican migration, however, did not apply to Chinese immigration. Prior to 1917, the Bureau of Immigration focused much of its enforcement efforts on the Chinese. For an account of Immigration Service operations on the U.S.-Mexico border in the early twentieth century, see Smith, "Early Immigrant Inspection along the U.S.-Mexican Border," 2.

20. Johnson, *Revolution in Texas*, 72.

21. Sánchez, *Becoming Mexican American*, 51–53. See also Barrera, *Race and Class in the Southwest*, 71–72.

22. Hall and Coerver, *Revolution on the Border*, 126.

23. García, *Desert Immigrants*, 4.

24. Ibid., 3.

25. Ibid., 31. By 1930, the city's population grew to 68,476 (Ruiz, *From Out of the Shadows*, 35).

26. García, *Desert Immigrants*, 31.

27. Ibid., 4; Romo, *Ringside Seat to a Revolution*, 136.

28. Romo notes that over forty Spanish-language newspapers were published in El Paso between 1890 and 1924. See Romo, *Ringside Seat to a Revolution*, 18–20.

29. Perales, "Smeltertown," 168.

30. Hall and Coerver, *Revolution on the Border*, 29, 41; St. John, "Line in the Sand," 89–90, 158; Truett, "Transnational Warrior," 249.

31. Hall and Coerver, *Revolution on the Border*, 93–101; García, *Desert Immigrants*, 5; Sheridan, *Los Tucsonenses*, 6.

32. Hall and Coerver, *Revolution on the Border*, 29.

33. Romo, *Ringside Seat to a Revolution*, 145.

34. The growth of the tourist industry in Tijuana was due, in part, to the dry and mountainous landscape which rendered it inhospitable to the development of the mining and agriculture industries. See Álvarez, *Familia*, 32.

35. Vanderwood, *Juan Soldado*, 76–81.

36. Ibid., 83, 87.

37. Ibid., 55.

38. Romo, *Ringside Seat to a Revolution*, 198–202.

39. Ibid.

40. Vanderwood, *Juan Soldado*, 105.

41. Ibid., 113.

42. Calexico Chamber of Commerce, "Regulations at Crossing of International Boundary at the Port of Calexico, California," n.d., file 54410/331G, Record Group 85: Records of the Immigration and Naturalization Service, [hereafter cited as RG 85], National Archives and Records Administration, Washington, D.C. [hereafter cited as NARA I].

43. García, *Desert Immigrants*, 7. For a discussion of the raiding activities of Mexican revolutionaries on mines and oil fields in Mexico and the United States, see Hall and Coerver, *Revolution on the Border*.

44. In 1913, Victoriano Huerta, chief of staff to President Francisco Madero, assumed office in a military coup and ordered Madero's assassination. His military dictatorship galvanized Revolutionary forces against him, and he fled the country a year later. Huerta's resignation, however, did not bring peace to Mexico, as Revolutionary forces splintered into rival factions, battling one another for control of the state well after Revolutionary leader Venustiano Carranza assumed the presidency in 1917. See St. John, "Line in the Sand," 200.

45. Ibid., 200, 206, 216.

46. Acting in retaliation against Wilson's withdrawal of support for a Villa-led government in Mexico, Pancho Villa and his troops killed sixteen Americans traveling on a train in northern Mexico in January 1916. Several months later, they crossed the border into New Mexico and killed another seventeen Ameri-

cans. See Johnson, *Revolution in Texas,* 138–42. On the complex relationship between the Villistas and the borderlands, see St. John, "Line in the Sand," 211–17; and Romo, *Ringside Seat to a Revolution.*

47. Briggs, *For the Welfare of Wage Earners,* 164; St. John, "Line in the Sand," 231; Ralph J. Totten, Consul General at Large, El Paso, Texas, "Report on Conditions on the Mexican Border," 20 January 1918, file 54152/11, RG 85, NARA I.

48. Capitalizing on anti-American sentiments in the aftermath of Pershing's expedition, the German foreign minister, Arthur Zimmerman, proposed an alliance that, in the event of a German victory, promised the restoration of Texas and much of the Southwest to Mexico. Along with Germany's declaration of unrestricted submarine warfare, the telegram fueled anti-German sentiment, garnered popular support for the war, and led President Wilson to abandon neutrality for war.

49. García, *Desert Immigrants,* 7.

50. Romo, *Ringside Seat to a Revolution,* 7.

51. The U.S. Public Health Service refused to conduct the quarantine, arguing that it was an extreme measure. See Romo, *Ringside Seat to a Revolution,* 233.

52. During this inspection, city officials found two cases of typhus, and one incidence each of measles, rheumatism, tuberculosis, and chicken pox. Those who were found to be ill were forced to take vinegar and kerosene baths, shave their heads, and burn all of their clothing. See Romo, *Ringside Seat to a Revolution,* 231, 234, 235.

53. Ibid., 243.

54. Metz, *Border,* 233.

55. *Immigration Act of February 5, 1917,* Public Law 64-301, *U.S. Statutes at Large* 874 (1917): 39; *Entry and Departures Control Act,* Public Law 65, *U.S. Statutes at Large* 559 (1918): 40.

56. As an omnibus bill, the Immigration Act of 1917 became the foundation of this nation's immigration law for the next thirty-five years. While the Immigration Acts of 1921 and 1924 added pivotal features to this nation's immigration law, the Immigration Act of 1917 continued to serve as the basic outline or organizational structure. See Fitzgerald, *The Face of the Nation,* 129, 132.

57. For a history of the literacy test, see Higham, *Strangers in the Land.*

58. Ibid., 190–93; Divine, *American Immigration Policy,* 5.

59. Briggs, "For the Welfare of Wage Earners," 164.

60. Preston, *Aliens and Dissenters;* Briggs, "For the Welfare of Wage Earners," 164; Divine, *American Immigration Policy,* 8.

61. Under the Immigration Act of 1917, Congress decided not to waive the head tax (increased to $8) and the new literacy test for Mexican immigrants, as it had in the Immigration Acts of 1903 and 1907. See Cardoso, *Mexican Emigration,* 46.

62. Ibid.

63. Ibid.

64. Reisler, *By the Sweat of Their Brow*, 24.

65. Indeed, those whose only offense was entry without inspection were granted what the agency termed "voluntary return" to Mexico. See "Report of Supervising Inspector, District No. 23," in U.S. Bureau of Immigration, *Annual Report of the Commissioner General of Immigration to the Secretary of Labor for the fiscal year ended 1917*, 227. The agency relied on this procedure as a cost-saving measure, particularly in its enforcement of the Passport Act. See George J. Harris, Assistant Supervising Inspector to Commissioner General, 27 August 1918, file 54410/331A, RG 85, NARA I. Later, this procedure came to be known as "voluntary departure."

66. The report also stated: "Hundreds of aliens who arrive at the border hungry and penniless, were literally forced to cross the international line in search of food and work, it being their philosophy apparently that whatever happened their plight could be no worse and, luck with them, might be materially bettered. The drastic provisions of the present immigration act have led to the creation of a new and thriving industry, if by such a term it may be dignified, having for its object the illegal introduction into the United States of Mexican aliens on a wholesale scale by means of organized efforts." "Report of Supervising Inspector, Mexican Border District," in U.S. Bureau of Immigration, *Annual Report of the Commissioner General of Immigration to the Secretary of Labor for the fiscal year ended 1918*, 317–19.

67. House Committee on Foreign Affairs, *Control of Travel from and into the United States*, 65th Cong., 2nd sess., 1918, H. Doc., 4–5.

68. *Entry and Departures Control Act*, Public Law 65, *U.S. Statutes at Large* 559 (1918): 40; Executive Order no. 2932 (implementing Act of 22 May 1918), 18 August 1918, *Code of Federal Regulation*. The law also created criminal penalties—a maximum fine of $10,000 and prison sentence of twenty years—for violation of the Passport Act.

69. For a history of the passport, see Torpey, *The Invention of the Passport*.

70. Kang, "The Legal Construction of the Borderlands," 31–41.

71. Ralph J. Totten, Consul General at Large, El Paso, Texas, "Report on Conditions on the Mexican Border," 20 January 1918, 12, file 54152/11, RG 85, NARA I.

72. Ibid.

73. Ibid., 3.

74. Ibid., 8, 16.

75. Ibid., 15.

76. Ibid., 2.

77. Ibid., 8.

78. Ibid., 8–9.

79. U.S. Bureau of Immigration, *Annual Report of the Commissioner General of Immigration to the Secretary of Labor for the fiscal year ended 1920*, 700, as cited by Hall and Coerver, *Revolution on the Border*.

80. As historian Kelly Lytle Hernandez argues, U.S. diplomatic relations with Mexico played a pivotal role in the design and implementation of Operation Wetback in 1954, which resulted in the deportation of approximately one million Mexican nationals. This essay reveals that these binational efforts extended to immigration admissions policies, not just enforcement policies, dating back to the early twentieth century. See Lytle Hernandez, "The Crimes and Consequences of Illegal Immigration," 421–44.

81. Ralph J. Totten, Consul General at Large, El Paso, Texas, "Report on Conditions on the Mexican Border," 20 January 1918, 6, file 54152/11, RG 85, NARA I.

82. Ibid., 11.

83. See, e.g., González, *Mexican Consuls and Labor Organizing*; Lytle Hernandez, "Entangling Bodies and Borders"; Kirstein, *Anglo over Bracero*; Scruggs, "The United States, Mexico, and the Wetbacks"; Craig, *The Bracero Program*; Guglielmo, "Fighting for Caucasian Rights," 1212–37.

84. The Bracero Program, e.g., would not have been possible without Mexican consent. For one of the best accounts of Mexico's role in the formation of the Bracero Program, see Kirstein, *Anglo over Bracero*.

85. Some of the correspondents and their interests: W. J. Palmer, DeGraff and Palmer, New York (notions and dry goods), 16 April 1917, file 55601/684, RG 85, NARA I; Philip Carey Company, Cincinnati, Ohio (roofing company), 31 March 1917, ibid.; H. L. Greene, Amalgamated Paint Company, New York, to Department of Labor, 26 March 1917, ibid.; J. G. Park, Plumber and Tinsmith, London, Ontario, 31 March 1917, ibid.; S. Wallace Dempsey, U.S. House of Representatives, to the Secretary of the Treasury, 31 May 1917, ibid.; Guy Carleton Lee, President, National Society for Broader Education, Carlisle, Pennsylvania, 23 May 1917, ibid.; and Michael W. Davis Jr. to Department of State, 22 May 1917, ibid. See also Bukowczyk et al., *Permeable Border*.

86. On the supporters and opponents of immigration restriction in the Southwest, see Montejano, *Anglos and Mexicans in the Making of Texas*, 182–86.

87. Ralph J. Totten, Consul General at Large, El Paso, Texas, "Report on Conditions on the Mexican Border," 20 January 1918, 17, file 54152/11, RG 85, NARA I.

88. Reisler, *By the Sweat of Their Brow*.

89. See, e.g., Blocker, American Consul, Eagle Pass, to Secretary of State, 6 December 1917, file 54152/1E, RG 85, NARA I; and unsigned memorandum, 2 January 1918, ibid.

90. Ruiz, *From Out of the Shadows*, 12.

91. Alvey A. Adee, Second Assistant Secretary of State, to Anthony Caminetti, Commissioner General, 24 January 1918, file 54152/1G, RG 85, NARA I (this letter pertains to Japanese merchants living on the Mexican side of border who wished to cross the border to purchase goods); F. W. Berkshire, Supervising Inspector, El Paso, to Chief, Division of Passport Control, 9 September 1918, file 54410/331B, ibid. Merchants were exempted from the exclusionary provisions applied to Japanese (the Gentleman's Agreement of 1907) and Chinese (the Chinese Exclusion Act of 1882) immigrants. The McCreary Amendment of 1893, however, placed strict evidentiary requirements upon Chinese merchants reentering the United States. On Japanese exclusion, see Daniels, *The Politics of Prejudice*; on Chinese exclusion and the McCreary Amendment, see Salyer, *Laws Harsh as Tigers*.

92. In a telegram to Senator Hiram Johnson, C. K. Clarke, general manager of the Imperial Irrigation District, wrote, "Owing to our geographic location practically all our canal and levee system is in Mexico, but the resulting damage account of suspension of work will be to American farms and farmers." C. K. Clarke, General Manager, Imperial Irrigation District, to Senator Hiram Johnson, 19 November 1917, file 54152/1E, RG 85, NARA I.

93. Telegram to Frank L. Polk, received 10 December 1917, file 54152/1E, RG 85, NARA I.

94. Grosvenor Calkins, for Duquesne Mining and Reduction Company, to Louis F. Post, Assistant Secretary of Labor, 17 January 1918, file 54152/1G, RG 85, NARA I.

95. F. W. Berkshire, Supervising Inspector, El Paso, to Commissioner General, 1 January 1918, file 54152/1F, RG 85, NARA I.

96. George J. Harris, Acting Supervising Inspector, El Paso, to Commissioner General, 10 January 1918, file 54152/1G, RG 85, NARA I; Dr. J. A. Wallace to Department of State, Bureau of Citizenship, 10 January 1918, ibid.

97. Alvey A. Adee, Second Assistant Secretary of State, to Anthony Caminetti, Commissioner General, 11 April 1918, file 54152/1J, RG 85, NARA I.

98. A. A. Musgrove, Inspector in Charge, Calexico, California, to Supervising Inspector, Mexican Border District, 12 April 1918, file 54152/1J, RG 85, NARA I.

99. Prohibitionists, however, opposed any relaxation of passport regulations for those desirous of crossing the border into Mexico, which they called "a moral plague spot menacing soldiers and civilians alike." See Charles C. Selegman, President, Los Angeles Ministerial Alliance, to Robert Lansing, Secretary of State, 23 November 1917, file 54152/1E, RG 85, NARA I; W. B. Wheeler, General Counsel, Anti-Saloon League of America, to Raymond Fosdick, War Department, 4 April 1918, file 54152/1J, ibid.; T. A. Storey, Executive Secretary, Interdepartmental Social Hygiene Board, to Bureau of Immigration, 6 March 1920, file 54410/331F, ibid. For an account of how Prohibition impacted

border closing times in three different border communities, see Buffington, "Prohibition in the Borderlands."

100. Ralph J. Totten, Consul General at Large, El Paso, Texas, "Report on Conditions on the Mexican Border," 20 January 1918, 17, file 54152/11, RG 85, NARA I.

101. Anthony Caminetti, Commissioner General, to Supervising Inspector, Mexican Border District, 31 August 1918, file 54410/331A, RG 85, NARA I.

102. Reisler, *By the Sweat of Their Brow.*

103. U.S. Bureau of Immigration, *Annual Report of the Commissioner General of Immigration to the Secretary of Labor for the fiscal year ended 1919.*

104. Prior to the issuance of the *Code of Federal Regulations,* agency interpretations of federal immigration statutes were published as the *Immigration Rules.*

105. "Confidential Instructions for the Guidance of Officials Connected with the Administration of the Act of May 22, 1918," July 1918, file 54410/331, RG 85, NARA I.

106. J. E. Trout, Inspector in Charge, Laredo, Texas, to Supervising Inspector, El Paso, 23 November 1917 (citing a Department of State telegram), file 54152/1E, RG 85, NARA I.

107. Foreign Permits Office, Division of Passport Control, State Department, to Inspectors in Charge, 6 September 1918, file 54410/331A, RG 85, NARA I.

108. Gerard D. Reilly, Acting Solicitor of Labor, Memorandum for the Acting Commissioner of Immigration and Naturalization, 15 April 1937, file 55883/600, RG 85, NARA I. Holders of Section 13 certificates were exempted from the head tax because the Bureau realized that it would be unreasonable for them to pay the tax upon each entry.

109. R. W. Flournoy, Acting Chief, Bureau of Citizenship, Department of State, to A. W. Parker, Law Clerk, Immigration and Naturalization Service, 30 November 1917, file 54152/1E, RG 85, NARA I.

110. Indeed, in his report, Totten expressed great concern that supposedly innocent, yet poor, Mexican border-crossers might be persuaded to act on behalf of the enemy for money. He wrote, "Yet any one of these peons [border crossers] would carry messages, maps or any other kind of information for a few cents." Ralph J. Totten, Consul General at Large, El Paso, Texas, "Report on Conditions on the Mexican Border," 20 January 1918, 15, file 54152/11, RG 85, NARA I.

111. A. Warner Parker, Law Officer, Department of State, to Supervising Inspector, El Paso, 6 December 1917, file 54152/1E, RG 85, NARA I.

112. J. E. Trout, Inspector in Charge, Laredo, to Supervising Inspector, El Paso District, 23 November 1917, file 54152/1E, RG 85, NARA I.

113. George J. Harris, Acting Supervising Inspector, El Paso, to Commissioner General, 27 November 1917, file 54152/1E, RG 85, NARA I. Historians David

Lorey and Oscar Martínez explain that border towns experienced economic booms during Prohibition. Small businessmen moved their operations south of the line to evade the anti-saloon laws, while Chambers of Commerce in towns north of the border created a highly successful tourist industry, marketing their cities as gateways to the entertainment venues in Mexico. See Lorey, *The U.S.-Mexican Border in the Twentieth Century*; and Martínez, *Border Boom Town*.

114. F. W. Berkshire, Supervising Inspector, Mexican Border District, to Chief, Division of Passport Control, State Department, 22 September 1920, file 54410/331H, RG 85, NARA I.

115. F. W. Berkshire to Secretary of State, 6 November 1919, file 54410/331F, RG 85, NARA I.

116. In brief, institutional weaknesses (a lack of money, manpower, and material), a lack of political support among federal officials, and weak administrative supervision from the Bureau's central office in Washington, D.C., led southwestern Bureau of Immigration officials to revise the immigration laws for the benefit of local residents. For a fuller explanation of the political and institutional factors surrounding Bureau of Immigration operations in the Southwest, see Kang, "The Legal Construction of the Borderlands."

117. A. J. Milliken, Inspector in Charge, Nogales, Arizona, to Supervising Inspector, El Paso, 3 January 1918, file 54152/1F, RG 85, NARA I.

118. Alvey A. Adee, Second Assistant Secretary of State, to Anthony Caminetti, Commissioner General, 30 August 1918, file 54152/1L, RG 85, NARA I.

119. R. M. Cousar, Inspector in Charge, Nogales, Arizona, to Supervising Inspector, Mexican Border District, 5 October 1920, file 54410/331I, RG 85, NARA I.

120. F. W. Berkshire to Commissioner General, 20 April 1918, file 54152/1J, RG 85, NARA I.

121. William Kettner, Congressman, Eleventh District, California, to Commissioner General, 22 October 1919, file 54410/331F, RG 85, NARA I.

122. H. M. Hubbard, Secretary, Building Trades Council of San Diego, to William B. Wilson, Secretary of Labor, 29 October 1919, file 54410/331F, RG 85, NARA I.

123. Juan B. Rojo, Chargé d'Affaires Ad Interim, Mexican Embassy, to Frank L. Polk, Acting Secretary of State, 1 July 1919, file 54261/276A, RG 85, NARA I; Fletcher, Under Secretary of State, to Secretary of Labor, 31 October 1921, file 54410/331J, RG 85, ibid.

124. J. E. Trout, Inspector in Charge, Laredo, Texas, to Supervising Inspector, El Paso, 12 February 1919, file 54410/331D, RG 85, NARA I.

125. A. A. Musgrove, Inspector in Charge, Calexico, California, to Supervising Inspector, Mexican Border District, 12 April 1918, file 54152/1J, RG 85, NARA I.

126. Clyde Campbell, Acting District Director, San Antonio, to Commissioner General, 6 January 1925, file 55601/684, RG 85, NARA I.

127. Pedersen and Dahl, "Alien Farmworkers and United States Immigration and Naturalization Laws," 51–52.

128. On the numbers crossing the borders, the commissioner general wrote: "Hundreds of thousands of aliens and citizens residing on either side of the boundary, mainly in towns contiguous thereto, cross and re-cross daily or periodically upon social or business errands. Treating each entry of these 'crossers' as a separate transaction and adding thereto all other transactions, the total volume of entrants is estimated to have been 27,000,000 for the past year." U.S. Bureau of Immigration, *Annual Report of the Commissioner General of Immigration to the Secretary of Labor for the fiscal year ended 1928*, 10.

129. Sánchez, *Becoming Mexican American*, 58.

# CAUGHT IN THE GAP

*The Transit Privilege
and North America's
Ambiguous Borders*

..........................................

Andrea Geiger

During the first years of the twentieth century, U.S. immigration officials along the U.S.-Mexico border became increasingly anxious about a new strategy being employed by a growing number of Japanese migrants to circumvent legal barriers erected by the U.S. government early in 1906 to bar them from the United States. Migrants who employed this strategy invoked their "transit privilege" under international law to enter the United States based on the assertion that they intended to transit the United States to travel to Canada. Maps found in the possession of the migrants who had invoked the privilege seemed only to confirm the suspicions of immigration officers that the migrants' real purpose was to remain in the United States. Although the migrants told officers that their intended destination was Canada, the maps showed railway routes only as far as Los Angeles or San Francisco. The arrest of four young Japanese men who had left their train in Denver in December 1907 and admitted to U.S. immigration officers that they had invoked the transit privilege at the Mexico-U.S. border to cross into the United States appeared only to prove the point. For $100 Mexican, they told the officers, a Mexican man had told them what to say and had provided them with railway tickets and instructions to leave the train at Denver, since that was a station thought not to be monitored by immigration officials.[1] Four represented the hundreds who invoked the transit privilege during the early years of the twentieth century to cross national borders that would otherwise have barred them, and many regarded their actions as justified, on the grounds that U.S. immigration law unfairly discriminated against Japanese.[2]

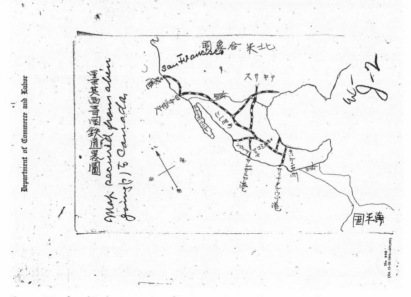

**Figure 1.** Map found in the possession of Japanese migrant. (From *Report of Marcus Braun*, U.S. Immigrant Inspector, 12 February 1907, exhibit B, in A8555, RG 85, NARA 1)

At a time when the United States and Canada were engaged in parallel efforts to regulate the borders to create their territories as racialized spaces that excluded Asians, the transit privilege emerged as one mechanism migrants could use to challenge the power of those borders to exclude certain immigrants. Although the international boundaries that transect North America often functioned as barriers to the realization of migrants' personal goals, at some stages of the Japanese migration the borders also became tools that migrants were able to use to achieve their objectives. Migrants understood that by crossing one border to access another they had available a wider range of options in relation to the second border, because the act of crossing the first border placed them in a different position vis-à-vis the second. The fact that the United States shared a border with both Canada and Mexico, in particular, created opportunities for Japanese migrants to negotiate one border in ways that would not have existed had it not been for the existence of the other. As Japanese migrants also realized, the two international borders that transect the North American continent, taken in concert, were permeable in ways that they were not when each was approached simply on its own terms. As a result, during the late nineteenth and early twentieth centuries, Japanese labor contractors and immigrants were able to take advantage of these opportunities to fulfill contractual obligations and reach destinations from which they would otherwise have been barred by the growing body of exclusionary laws in both Canada and the United States. The surprising power of the transit privilege to force the governments of both the United States and Canada to allow border crossings they would otherwise have chosen to impede allowed migrants to invoke the privilege repeatedly—to mitigate, to at least some degree, efforts on the part of both nations to erect a more impenetrable wall, and to circumvent at least some of the legal barriers they faced. The fact that the significance of the transit privilege remains obscured unless both international borders are taken into account makes clear the need to look beyond simple binational analyses of migration and to invoke instead a broader, transnational perspective to develop a more comprehensive understanding of the barriers and opportunities encountered by migrants along international boundaries.

Although both the United States and Canada attempted at various times to abrogate the transit privilege, it remained a point of vulnerability for both nations, one which neither was able to negate in its entirety. Extended under international law to citizens of friendly nations and recognized in treaties between such nations, the transit privilege operated as a badge of civilization which demonstrated the civilized status not only of those to whom it was granted, but also of the nation granting the privilege. Because international law was originally conceived of as a body of law to which only civilized nations subscribed, a nation's willingness to act according to its standards operated, in effect, as a measure of that country's entitlement to recognition as a civilized nation.[3] To deny the transit privilege, as a result, would not only have contravened the United States' or Canada's obligations under international law, it would also have undermined the rationale put forward by each nation for excluding Japanese immigrants to begin with, to the extent that that rationale depended on the nation characterizing itself as more civilized than the one from whence the immigrants they sought to bar originated.[4] Because the Meiji government also understood the transit privilege as a mark of civilization, it vigorously defended the right of Japanese to transit both the United States and Canada, despite its efforts in other areas to curb illegal and extralegal migration by its nationals, to avoid tarnishing Japan's image as a newly "civilized" nation, as measured by late-nineteenth-century North American and European standards.[5]

Attempts by Japanese migrants to use the transit privilege to avoid or subvert efforts by the United States and Canada to exclude them, as a result, often put Japanese migrants at odds not only with U.S. and Canadian immigration officials, but also with their own government. More concerned with maintaining the prerogatives of class than with challenging racial divides, and anxious to avoid the possibility that its subjects would become the object of exclusionary laws like those directed at Chinese immigrants, in 1900 the Meiji government first agreed to restrict the number of passports it issued for Canada and the United States.[6] Japanese migrants, however, were not always willing to comply with the restrictions imposed on them by their own government. Although the Meiji government discouraged any activity that might mark Japanese as undesirable or "illegal"—part of a larger effort to prove to Western nations Japan's status as a modern and civilized nation deserving of equal treatment—Meiji diplomats encouraged U.S. and Canadian authorities to strictly interpret the conditions attached to the passports that were issued to the emigrant laborers they feared might tarnish Japan's reputation as a modern and newly civilized nation in the eyes of the West.[7]

### Immigrant Strategies: Invoking the Transit Privilege at Canadian Ports

Although Japanese migrants invoked the transit privilege at both the U.S.-Canada and the U.S.-Mexico border, the practice first came to be used on a regular basis along Canada's western ocean boundary, where Japanese migrants invoked it to transit Canada after arriving at Canadian ports by ship in order to place themselves in a more favorable position in relation the U.S.-Canada border. The Meiji government first made clear its determination to defend the right of its subjects to invoke the transit privilege in 1901, in response to British Columbia's efforts to pass one of a series of Natal Acts—so named because they were modeled after legislation first adopted in the Colony of Natal—that required every prospective immigrant to demonstrate the ability "to read and write the English or some European language."[8] Although the Dominion government disallowed each Act as it was passed, on the instructions of the British Colonial Office, it was the British Colonial Secretary who had first recommended a literacy test, based on his belief that the Meiji government could be persuaded not to object to an educational test.[9] Meiji diplomats, however, immediately saw through the purported neutrality of the Act and objected to it on the grounds that it unfairly discriminated against Japanese subjects. Meiji government representatives regarded the Natal Acts as objectionable, however, less because they limited the direct entry of migrant laborers into Canada than because they interfered with the ability of other Japanese subjects to invoke the transit privilege. The Natal Acts were "high-handed measures," Meiji officials declared, that "totally deprived [Japanese] of their treaty right of free entry into Canada" on what should be understood as "an international highway, both by land and water."[10] Particularly offensive was the fact that the Natal Acts threatened to "most injuriously interfere with the free movement of all classes," calling into question the civilized status not just of immigrant laborers—something Meiji officials were willing to concede based on their own class biases— but also that of upper-class Japanese and, by extension, the tremendous effort Japan had made to prove itself the equal of Western nations.[11] In the words of the British Colonial Office, it was not "the practical exclusion of Japanese to which the [Meiji] government objects, but their exclusion *ad nominatim*, which specifically stamps the whole nation as undesirable persons."[12] In short, to deny the transit privilege to Japanese as a whole was to mark the entire nation as less than civilized in the eyes of Meiji government leaders.

Notwithstanding the repeated disallowance of each version of the Natal Act by the Dominion government, officials in British Columbia made every effort to enforce the Acts during the time that they were in force, resisting any order from the Dominion government that they desist. After B.C. officials arrested nineteen Japanese laborers employed by the Great Northern Railway to erect a fence on the Canadian side of the border near Blaine, Washington, in 1902, for example, the B.C. government refused to release them even after word was received that the Natal Act under which the arrest was made had been disallowed several days earlier.[13] As the *Vancouver Daily Province* noted with some irony, this put B.C. authorities in the peculiar position of prosecuting the Japanese they had arrested under an Act that was no longer in existence, leaving, in the newspaper's words, "a large hole in the provincial government's case."[14] Even during the time that each Natal Act was in force, however, B.C. officials struggled with the question of whether it applied to Japanese immigrants who entered Canada in transit to the United States. Given the vigorous protest that the Meiji government had made against any interference with its subjects' right of transit, British Columbia had conceded that Japanese migrants who did not intend to remain in Canada need only declare as much to avoid the literacy test, so long as they also paid a fee. The ability to invoke the transit privilege to avoid the Natal Acts, in the opinion of the *Vancouver Daily Province*, rendered the Acts "worthless" and "farcical in [their] application" even during those periods when each was in force.[15] B.C.'s efforts to pass a Natal Act ended only when the issue had been forced into the courts by two Japanese migrants who refused, in February 1908, either to take the literacy test or to return to their point of embarkation in the United States.[16] Four days after their arrest, the B.C. Supreme Court ordered their release, noting that the 1907 Treaty of Commerce and Navigation between Japan and Great Britain, like its predecessors, provided that the subjects of both nations "shall have full liberty to enter, travel or reside in any part of the dominions and possessions of the other." As a provincial government, the B.C. Supreme Court ruled, British Columbia lacked the power to interfere with the privileges afforded to Japanese nationals under the treaty.[17]

Difficulties faced by British Columbia in denying the transit privilege, together with an increase in the number of Japanese migrants arriving in the United States after that country's annexation of Hawaii in 1900, also generated considerable anxiety among U.S. officials, who were equally as determined as B.C. legislators to exclude Japanese and other Asian migrants. The efforts of U.S. authorities to bar Japanese migrants traveling to the mainland from Hawaii by restricting the entry of contract laborers at U.S. ports were increasingly undermined by the actions of those migrants in traveling to Vancouver and then applying to enter the United States across the U.S.-Canada border after having invoked the transit privilege to enter Canada. There was more than one reason why travel to the United States in transit through Canada was a sound strategic choice both for Japanese migrants traveling to North America directly from Japan and for transmigrants traveling to the mainland from Hawaii. In the absence of exclusionary legislation barring migration directly from Japan, both U.S. and Canadian immigration authorities relied heavily on medical examinations to exclude individuals who could be characterized as undesirable. By 1906, both Canada and the United States had enacted immigration laws that barred all who were "afflicted with a loathsome disease," or who were deemed likely to become a public charge.[18] Where literacy tests had failed, medical examinations promised to provide a mechanism for excluding Asian immigrants in particular, given the association of "Oriental" immigration with disease, both in the popular imagination and in the minds of immigration officials.[19]

Although both Canada and the United States sought to identify and exclude those who suffered from certain categories of disease, Canada permitted migrants with an excludable disease that was deemed treatable to remain in Canada to undergo treatment. Japanese migrants who arrived in Canada with passports for the United States were first examined by U.S. immigration officials stationed at Canadian ports. Those who were rejected by U.S. officials were turned over to Canadian officers, who permitted any with treatable conditions to remain in Canada, with the result that only migrants who were regarded as seriously ill by both U.S. and Canadian officials were required to return to Japan. For that reason, migrants bound for the United States increasingly made the strategic choice to travel to the United States through Canada, in order to reduce the risk that they would be deported to Japan if they failed the medical examination or were refused entry into the United States on some other grounds.[20]

U.S. officials, however, suspected that instead of staying in Canada, a majority of the Japanese immigrants who had been refused entry to the United States simply reapplied to enter the country once they had undergone treatment in Canada. In the words of one Immigration Bureau official, Japanese immigrants knew that by entering the United States in transit through Canada they could, in effect, "secure a double opportunity of entering the United States, that is, if rejected, they will not immediately be deported to Japan."[21] Determined to force the steamship companies that actively promoted labor migration to the North American mainland from both Hawaii and Japan to comply with the restrictions the United States sought to impose on Japanese labor immigration, U.S. regulations made each steamship company responsible for returning any migrant who had been refused entry into the United States to the port where his trip had originated, at the company's own expense.[22] Canadian law, in contrast, did not require the "trans-oceanic deportation" of immigrants who arrived in Canada intending to go on to the United States but who were refused entry by U.S. officials. Once the primacy of the transit privilege had been affirmed in connection with the Natal Acts, moreover, Canada also no longer sought to preclude migrants who did not intend to stay in Canada from landing at Canadian ports in transit to other destinations.[23] U.S. policy providing for the return of excluded migrants to the place where their trip had originated, in short, combined with the transit privilege to give migrants who arrived at the U.S. border either a way to avoid being returned to their country of origin if they were refused entry to the United States, or the option of remaining in Canada, where they could reapply to enter the United States.

Concerns on the part of U.S. officials that some migrants might apply a second time to enter the United States after receiving treatment, however, went beyond simply assuring that no one afflicted with a contagious disease entered the United States. Not only did U.S. immigration officers fear that those who were "diseased" might enter the United States, but they were also afraid that even migrants who had received treatment in Canada might attempt to enter. Those who had received treatment and no longer showed any signs of disease, in other words, remained implicitly marked as diseased in the minds of immigration officials. Even if the migrants were denied entry at the U.S.-Canada border a second time, U.S. immigration officials remained convinced that they did not just have a second opportunity to enter the United States, but rather—for those migrants willing to cross the border covertly—they had multiple opportunities to cross the Canada-U.S. border.[24] Most such crossings, they believed, occurred along a fifty-mile stretch between Blaine, Washington, and the foothills of the Cascade Mountains, where the existence of a "vast forest with numerous roads" and several railway bridges across the fast-running Nooksack River offered more than one way to cross the border undetected.[25] The forests were so dense with new foliage in springtime, one official complained, that it was all but impossible to see more than twenty feet in any direction.[26] Concern about the potential for the clandestine entry of both goods and people across the international boundary was further heightened by the many small islands that dotted the waters between Canada and the United States in the Puget Sound and the Gulf of Georgia. "No other place in the United States," one immigration inspector declared, "furnishes as many advantages for smuggling as the Puget Sound with its multitude of small islands."[27]

The danger seemingly inherent in the local landscape was compounded by the indifference of local residents on both sides of the U.S.-Canada border, in whose minds the international boundary appears to have signified far less than it did in the minds of both U.S. and Canadian government officials. U.S. immigration officers, on the one hand, complained that the residents of Blaine, Washington, were "exceedingly unwilling" to provide information about Japanese and other migrants who appeared in town after having crossed the border illegally.[28] Canadian officials, in turn, complained that B.C. residents north of the border turned a blind eye to illegal migration, and instead made a tidy profit guiding Japanese and other migrants into the United States along one or another of the fifteen trails in the area that were not monitored by immigration officials.[29]

Because the United States was able to exclude Japanese migrants only on the grounds that they were diseased or were likely to become a public charge, regardless of the destination designated on their passports, the U.S. Congress acted in February 1907 to authorize the U.S. president to bar immigrants with passports that did not expressly designate the United States as a country to which their own government permitted them to travel.[30] Pursuant to his authority under the February 1907 Act, President Theodore Roosevelt issued an Executive Order on March 14, 1907, expressly barring Japanese and Korean migrants who held passports for Mexico, Hawaii, or Canada from entering the United States. Like earlier measures taken to restrict immigration, the March 1907 Executive Order combined with the general bar against contract labor that had been in place since 1885 to redirect still greater numbers of Japanese migrants north to British Columbia.[31] In the fall of 1907, Canadian authorities estimated that just a third of the 4,811 Japanese who arrived in Canada during the first eight months of that year had come directly from Japan; the other two-thirds had come by way of Hawaii.[32] Canadians attributed the sudden increase in the number of Japanese migrants arriving in British Columbia directly to the refusal of U.S. immigration officials to continue to admit migrants with passports for Hawaii to the U.S. mainland.[33] Also a factor explaining increased migration to British Columbia from Honolulu, U.S. and Canadian authorities agreed, was the role played by the steamship companies, boardinghouse keepers, and employment agencies, all of which continued to encourage Japanese labor migrants to seek work on the mainland, in order to maximize their own profits. They also advised migrants leaving Hawaii for the U.S. mainland to travel through Canada in order to take advantage of the transit privilege.[34]

In the fall of 1907, continuing concerns on the part of U.S. Immigration Bureau officials about the use Japanese migrants were able to make of the transit privilege to position themselves advantageously in relation to the U.S.-Canada border led U.S. Immigration Inspector Marcus Braun to advocate that the U.S. government enter into a "treaty with Canada under which rejections by United States officers will be regarded as rejections under Canadian law."[35] The U.S. commissioner general of immigration dismissed Braun's suggestions, insisting that there was no evidence that Japanese migrants who remained in Canada for treatment later entered the United States illegally, and that the measures Braun proposed would only interfere with the free flow of commerce. The U.S. commissioner general understood, as Braun did not, that the U.S. government's real goal was to construct not an impenetrable wall, but a racialized filter along its boundaries—one that would allow the entry of needed goods and labor while excluding those who threatened the race-based labor hierarchy that ordered social relations in the American West. It was enough, in the U.S. commissioner general's view, for railway companies—when asked— to return migrants who had been denied entry to the United States to "points remote from the Canadian border, so as to discourage their clandestine entry after having been rejected."[36]

In November 1907, U.S. authorities succeeded in persuading Canadian officials to comply with a change in policy that would—in effect— deny U.S.-bound migrants the ability to invoke the transit privilege across Canada upon arrival at Canadian ports. Although U.S. immigration officers stationed at B.C. ports had, up to that time, been willing to examine U.S.-bound passengers when they landed at Canadian ports, turning them over to Canadian officials for treatment only if they did not pass inspection, they now refused to inspect migrants who carried passports for the United States, with the result that Canadian officials also refused landing to the migrants, making it necessary for them to remain on board the vessels that carried them until they could be inspected at a U.S. port. Despite its willingness to limit passports to particular countries—itself a key to the effective implementation of the new policy—the Meiji government objected to the uneven application of the new rule, complaining that the former practice was still applied to immigrants from European countries who arrived at Atlantic ports.[37] Arguing against the application of the new policy to Japanese migrants, the Japanese consul in Vancouver, B.C., protested that the United States was not entitled to insist that U.S.-bound passengers remain on board when ships stopped at B.C. ports. There existed no treaty between Japan and Canada, he pointed out, restricting landing in Canada only to those with passports for Canada. Japanese subjects were thus entitled to exercise the privilege of transit and to enter Canada when they arrived at Canadian ports regardless of their final destination.[38] U.S. steamship company officials joined the Japanese consul in his defense of Canadian sovereignty, arguing that when their ships were in Canadian ports, they also were subject only to Canadian jurisdiction and, therefore, as long as they had no U.S.-bound passengers on board when they entered U.S. waters, they had no obligation to provide manifests listing U.S.-bound passengers to U.S. authorities.[39] U.S. government efforts to monitor U.S.-bound passengers while their ships were in Canadian ports, U.S. steamship company officials argued, interfered both with the companies' ability to compete on equal terms with the Canadian Pacific Railway's steamship line, which was able to bring migrants bound for the United States to Canada without such monitoring, and with Canadian sovereignty—an argument, ironically, that the Canadian government itself declined to make.[40]

Although U.S. authorities prevailed in their efforts to limit use of the transit privilege by U.S.-bound migrants who arrived at Canadian ports, they were forced to concede that while the Executive Order of March 14, 1907, barred Japanese migrants with passports for Canada, Mexico, or Hawaii from the United States, the U.S. power to deny them the right to transit U.S. territory remained in doubt. On its face, the March 14, 1907, Order permitted U.S. immigration officers to refuse transit to those who were excludable as immigrants, even if they had no intention of remaining in the United States, but the United States could not abrogate the transit privilege in cases where the migrant was not otherwise excludable without violating international law and its treaties with Japan. As U.S. Immigration Bureau attorneys eventually conceded, this meant that even after March 14, 1907, the Bureau could not prevent Japanese migrants from traveling through U.S. ports or across the United States by rail, even if they did not have passports marked for the United States.[41]

### Immigrant Strategies: Invoking the Transit Privilege at the U.S.-Mexico Border

Much as the Executive Order of March 1907 redirected some Japanese migrants arriving at U.S. Pacific coast ports north to Canada, it also encouraged others to go south to Mexico, since the Mexico-U.S. border offered the same kinds of opportunities as the Canada-U.S. border did, and more. Although the Meiji government had begun to restrict the number of passports issued for Canada and the United States as early as 1900, it made no parallel effort during the early years of the twentieth century to restrict the number of passports issued to other North American destinations.[42] As Meiji government restrictions on the issuance of passports to Canada and the United States continued to tighten, emigration to Mexico increasingly offered many Japanese emigrants the only chance they had to obtain a passport to any North American destination. To obtain a passport to Mexico, however, emigrants had to show that they were guaranteed work when they arrived. In most cases, this meant entering into a labor contract, since Mexico, in contrast to the United States and Canada, continued to encourage contract laborers, who were recruited by emigration companies on behalf of private enterprises to facilitate the development of Mexico's industrial and agricultural infrastructure. Still another strategy employed by Japanese migrants after March 14, 1907, was to obtain a passport for Peru and then travel north to Mexico and apply for admission to the United States from there, since the March 1907 Order excluded entry into the United States for those with passports for Mexico, but not for those with passports for Peru.[43] Both were effective strategies because, as was the case at the U.S.-Canada border, migrants turned away by U.S. officials at the U.S.-Mexico border were required only to return to Mexico. Migrants arriving at Mexican ports also had a range of other options, including remaining in Mexico as immigrants, crossing Mexico's northern border into the United States surreptitiously, or traveling south to countries such as Peru or Brazil. Traveling to Mexico also held out the possibility of invoking the transit privilege to enter the United States in transit to Canada. Once in the United States, migrants had the option either of completing their journey or, alternatively, discontinuing it en route and remaining in the United States, either temporarily or permanently. For all these reasons, Mexico became the destination that offered the greatest number of alternatives to immigrants bound for all parts of

North America during the first years of the twentieth century. In fact, U.S. immigration officials would ultimately conclude that more Japanese entered the United States through Mexico during the first eight years of the twentieth century than through Canada.[44]

Some emigration companies went so far as to use the proximity of Mexico to the United States as a recruitment tool, telling potential recruits that they could easily enter the United States from Mexico.[45] Labor emigration companies also sometimes actively encouraged the migrants to break their contracts and migrate to the United States. This allowed the emigration companies not only to recruit new groups of migrants who would then require passage to Mexico, but it also allowed them to demand payment of the 100 to 150 yen penalty that was imposed when emigrants abrogated their original labor contract in Japan. In 1909, for example, the *Chuo Shimbun* reported that Tokyo District Court prosecutors were conducting an investigation of such practices by the Dairiku Emigration Company, which had sent over 3,800 emigrants to Mexico in recent years.[46] Although some Japanese migrants went to Mexico intending to complete their contracts, others arrived in Mexico with the express intention of immigrating to the United States. For example, Kusakabe Dengo, who had twice failed the trachoma examination in Japan, with the result that he was unable to obtain passage to Canada or the United States from any steamship company, admitted to U.S. immigration officers in 1906 that he had entered into a contract to work at a coal mine in Mexico because traveling to Mexico provided an alternate way to reach the United States.[47]

Before the Executive Order of March 14, 1907, most Japanese immigrants who arrived at the U.S.-Mexico border first attempted to enter the United States legally. Prior to that date, it was not illegal for Japanese migrants who had passports for Mexico or for Peru to immigrate to the United States, and only those who were excludable on medical grounds or because they were deemed likely to become a public charge had any reason to turn to clandestine means to cross the U.S. boundary with Mexico.[48] Because contract laborers had been barred for several decades, Japanese immigrants recognized that it was necessary to avoid giving the impression that they had come to Mexico as contract laborers, and they took care to present themselves as students or businessmen.[49] Only if they were denied entry into the United States by U.S. officials did Japanese immigrants resort to clandestine means to enter the United States. Most made that journey by rail, traveling in the water tanks of locomotives, or on foot, wading across the Rio Grande at night.[50] The Order of March 14, 1907, however, drove virtually all Japanese migration north across the Mexico-U.S. border underground. In Braun's words, Japanese migrants had crossed that boundary northward legally "in a continuous stream" prior to March 14, and "surreptitiously ever since."[51] Ironically, whereas it was the thick foliage along the Canadian border that seemed to pose a threat because of what it obscured, along the U.S.-Mexico border, it was the dry desert landscape that appeared to pose a threat because of what it revealed: enforcement was made more difficult along the southern border by the fact that immigration inspectors, in their dark blue uniforms, could be spotted from miles away.[52]

After March 14, 1907, Japanese migrants who had been denied passports permitting them to travel to the United States by the Meiji government turned to a new strategy: asserting a right under international law to enter the United States across its border with Mexico in transit to Canada. In addition to using the right to transit Mexico to minimize the risk that they would be deported to Japan if they were not admitted to the United States, once in Mexico, Japanese migrants also had the option of utilizing their right to enter the United States in transit to Canada to cross a border that would otherwise have barred them as migrants holding passports only for Mexico and not the United States. Migrants who employed this strategy as a way of immigrating to and remaining in the United States discontinued their journey en route, leaving the train at some predetermined point, where they redeemed the unused portion of their tickets. U.S. border officials indignantly described the invocation of the transit privilege by Japanese migrant as "a mere subterfuge to get into the United States," but they could do little to prevent it without violating international law.[53] In 1908, U.S. authorities considered requiring migrants to transit the United States in special barred railroad cars, but concluded that this plan was not economically feasible, since it would have required at least thirty migrants to travel at a time, and it would also have required the U.S. government to give railroad companies the power to use force to prevent escape, something the government was unwilling to do.[54]

Determined though it was to find a mutually agreeable solution to the problem of illegal immigration, the Meiji government regarded the restrictions imposed on its subjects by the U.S. government in the spring of

1907 as acts of discrimination that unfairly targeted Japan.[55] The issue was not, in Japan's view, that the U.S. government was not entitled to exclude any general categories of immigrants that it wanted to exclude, but that Japan should be treated in the same way as any other civilized country.[56] In an effort to mollify the complaints by the Meiji government that its nationals were being unfairly singled out, immigration inspectors along the U.S.-Mexico border were cautioned to avoid any action that "in any manner, . . . in fact or in appearance, could be construed as a discrimination against such aliens."[57]

Although Meiji government representatives endeavored to ensure that Japanese subjects were not singled out for investigation or otherwise discriminated against by U.S. officials, Japanese associations in the United States shunned those who used the transit privilege to enter and remain there. According to reports in a Japanese-language paper in San Francisco, for example, when a group of Japanese immigrants in transit to Canada escaped from their train in Los Angeles on May 3, 1907, and turned to the local Japanese association for assistance, the association refused to grant them any aid.[58] Migrants who chose to invoke the transit privilege to enter and remain in the United States, in contrast, often saw their actions as justified acts of defiance against an unjust law that unfairly discriminated against them. R. L. Pruett, an interpreter for the Immigration Service in El Paso, Texas, who was fluent in Japanese and who had lived in Japan for many years, reported in June 1907 that hundreds of Japanese immigrants had told him that "the Executive order which discriminates against us was meant [only] to satisfy a few people in San Francisco."[59] Other Japanese migrants deliberately defied U.S. officials' assumptions regarding their intentions in seeking to transit the United States to Canada. Two Japanese migrants who presented themselves to immigration officials in El Paso on April 9, 1907, for example, described themselves as fishermen in possession of enough funds to transit the United States to Vancouver, B.C., and made it clear that they considered their case a test case, which triggered a quick telegram by border officials to Washington, D.C., seeking instructions.[60] For his part, another Japanese migrant who invoked the transit privilege when he was admitted at El Paso on February 26, 1908, made sure that U.S. officials noted that he left the United States at Portal, North Dakota, a few days later.[61]

U.S. officials nevertheless remained convinced that the United States and not Canada was the real destination of most Japanese migrants who invoked the transit privilege. In an effort to ascertain whether a given individual's real reason for traveling to Mexico was to enter and remain in the United States, U.S. immigration inspectors along the U.S.-Mexico border examined maps and guidebooks in the immigrants' possession to determine what their intentions were. Braun concluded that the fact that "many" Japanese laborers arriving in Mexico had slips of paper with the names and addresses of Japanese contacts in the United States in their possession was "conclusive evidence" that they intended to go on to the United States even before they arrived in Mexico.[62] More persuasive are the maps recovered from some immigrants showing railroad routes across the border into the United States and to California, but not through to Canada. Even Pruett, who was largely sympathetic to the Japanese migrants he examined, reported that a number of the immigrants he spoke with arrived carrying compasses and Japanese-English conversation books along with maps of the United States.[63]

Although there is no question that some Japanese migrants had such materials in their possession, there was also reflected in the descriptions of the evidence obtained by U.S. border officials a definite tendency to exaggerate the significance of what the immigrants carried. According to Braun, for example, many Japanese migrants had a copy of a Japanese-language pamphlet published by the Tôyô Imin Gaisha with them when they arrived in Mexico. In Braun's words, although it was "ostensibly a 'Guidebook for Immigrants to Mexico,'" it was really a "guide book in a rough way to points within the Continental United States."[64] A copy of the guidebook in question still exists in U.S. immigration records. Although two pages are missing from the copy that was attached as an exhibit to Braun's report, nothing in the original Japanese reflects that the pamphlet was intended to serve as a guide to destinations in the United States. It is just what it purports to be: a guide to travel within Mexico. A similar tendency to exaggerate evidence was reflected in the discrepancy between Braun's estimate that thousands of Japanese immigrants were making their way north across the U.S.-Mexico border in violation of the March 1907 Executive Order, and the number of those actually arrested during the two and half months after the order went into effect—just thirty-one individuals.[65] In December 1907, even the U.S. ambassador to Japan complained about the tendency of border officials to exaggerate the num-

ber of illegal immigrants, complaining that Bureau of Immigration estimates were inconsistent with Japanese statistics showing the number of
migrants who had left Japan for Mexico in recent years.[66]

### Caught in the Gap: Interstitial Spaces

As Canada and the United States took steps to tighten immigration restrictions in response to efforts by Japanese migrants to utilize the transit
privilege to cross national borders that would otherwise have barred them,
migrants were also sometimes caught in the gaps between the shifting
sets of legal regulations developed by each nation in an effort to counter
the effects of the privilege. As a result, migrants were sometimes rendered illegal not because it was their intention to violate the transit privilege or to evade the immigration laws of either the United States or
Canada, but because they found themselves trapped in the interstices
between two different systems of law which overlapped or contradicted
one another in ways that rendered migrants "illegal" regardless of their
own intentions.

In June 1908, for example, Tatsumi Matsutaro was caught in such a
bind when he entered the United States at Eagle Pass, Texas, in transit
from Mexico to Canada. Unable to deny Japanese migrants the privilege of
transit altogether, the United States had acted in October 1907 to require
that certain categories of immigrants seeking to exercise the transit privilege post a $500 bond that was forfeited if they did not leave the United
States within twenty days.[67] Tatsumi had complied with these requirements and posted a bond. When he reached the Canadian border at Blaine,
Washington, however, Tatsumi was turned back based on the recent Order
in Council issued by the Dominion government which prohibited the
entry of immigrants into Canada, "unless arriving by a continuous journey from the country of their birth or citizenship on tickets purchased
before leaving that country."[68] That order, originally issued in 1906, was
incorporated into Canada's Immigration Act early in 1908 partly to cut off
further immigration to Canada through Hawaii.[69] As a result, any immigrant arriving in Canada in transit through the United States—bonded or
not—was, by definition, "debarred and . . . rejected on arrival at the Canadian frontier."[70] By virtue of Tatsumi's failure to leave the United States
and to enter Canada, however, he was also immediately in violation of U.S.
law and illegally in the United States, regardless of what his next step

proved to be. Lacking the funds to travel by railroad all the way back to the U.S.-Mexico border, Tatsumi instead traveled from Blaine to Seattle to try to obtain the funds he needed to prevent forfeiture of the bond. In Seattle, already an illegal immigrant and unable to obtain the travel money he needed to return to Mexico, Tatsumi disappeared.[71] Ironically, as U.S. immigration officials themselves noted, only by first becoming a Mexican citizen could Tatsumi have legally entered Canada in transit through the United States, as long as he did not interrupt his railway journey along the way.[72] The continuous passage rule, in effect, had made it impossible to exercise the transit privilege across any other state's territory in order to reach Canada, except in the limited situation where a migrant was traveling directly from his or her country of origin by continuous journey.

Unable to attack the transit privilege directly, both Canada and the United States had found ways to burden it to such a degree as to make it impractical for most migrants to utilize. An indirect approach was necessary in order to allow both countries to maintain their claim to status as "civilized" nations that honored the terms of the international treaties that bound them. Because the power and jurisdictional space of Canada and the United States, as nation-states, was necessarily bounded, efforts by both nations to determine their racial composition were concentrated, in particular, on the national borders that defined them. National borders, however, are also international borders, which permitted migrants traveling across international space to use the transit privilege to penetrate these borders in ways not intended by either government, until existing international agreements were replaced by more comprehensive immigration legislation. Until that time, migrants were able to use inconsistencies in the laws of the United States, Canada, and Mexico, together with the transit privilege, to avoid or subvert efforts by the United States and Canada to exclude them. Migrants were aided in these efforts by private entities whose interest in commerce and the free movement of goods and labor across national boundaries diverged from those of the state. Ironically, however, the Meiji government's conciliatory policy of accommodating and even anticipating the racially discriminatory demands of the U.S. and Canadian governments allowed both nations to mark Japanese subjects as excludable in some of the very kinds of ways the Japanese government had tried to avoid. The determination of Japanese migrants to pursue individual goals, regardless of the dictates of their own government, and their ability to utilize the transit privilege to take advantage of the gaps that existed between national and international law, ensured that the exclusionary measures passed by the United States and Canada during the first decade of the twentieth century were never perfectly implemented. Japanese migrants' utilization of the transit privilege to position themselves more favorably in relation to both international borders, moreover, makes clear the importance of locating borderlands histories within a larger continental and transnational framework so as not to obscure crucial elements of the stories of such migrations, and to permit a fuller understanding of the complex mix of obstacle and opportunity that such boundaries represented.

### Notes

1. H. Sterling, Acting Inspector in Charge, Denver, Colorado, to Commissioner General of Immigration, Washington, D.C., 19 March 1908, Records of the Immigration and Naturalization Service, Series A, Subject Correspondence Files, pt. 2, Mexican Immigration, 1906–30, no. A8555 [hereafter cited as A8555], Record Group 85: Records of the Immigration and Naturalization Service [hereafter cited as RG 85], National Archives and Records Administration, Washington, D.C. [hereafter cited as NARA I].

2. R. L. Pruett, U.S. Immigration Interpreter, El Paso, to F. P. Sargent, Commissioner General of Immigration, Washington, D.C., 11 June 1907, A8555, RG 85, NARA I; R. L. Pruett, U.S. Immigration Interpreter, El Paso, to Marcus Braun, New York, 18 June 1907, ibid.

3. For a description of international law as a compact among "civilized" nations, see Fitzpatrick, "Terminal Legality," 9–25.

4. Charles Earl, Solicitor, U.S. Immigration Service, Memorandum, 28 March 1907 (conceding that the United States could not abrogate the transit privilege if the migrant was not otherwise excludable without violating its treaties with Japan), A8555, RG 85, NARA I.

5. In the wake of the imposition of unequal treaties on Japan by Western nations following Commodore Perry's arrival in 1854, Meiji leaders concluded that "modernization"—the importation of Western technology, culture, and civic institutions—was key to meeting its goals both of resisting Western encroachment and of earning for Japan recognition as a nation equal in status to those of the West. The Meiji government, in the words of one scholar, was determined "to rid Japan of the humiliating shackles of being treated as an uncivilized people and to regain control over its own destiny" (Hayashida, "Identity, Race, and the Blood Ideology of Japan," 64). The Meiji government,

which lifted the bar on labor emigration in 1885, regarded labor emigration itself as a marker of that country's status as a modern, civilized nation (Wakatsuki, "Japanese Emigration to the United States," 400).

6. Canada, Parliament, House of Commons, *Sessional Papers 1902*, Paper no. 54, "Report of the Royal Commission on Chinese and Japanese Immigration," 330 (testimony of Alexander R. Milne, C.B., Collector of Customs at Victoria, B.C.); F. P. Sargent to President of the United States, 2 January 1907 (reporting that Saito Miko, Japanese consul general in Hawaii, had told him that "the general policy of his government was opposed to the settlement of the mainland of any considerable number of Japanese laborers, such government wishing to avoid conditions regarding Japanese of a character similar to those which had, in 1882 and 1884, brought about the laws excluding the Chinese laborers"), A8555, RG 85, NARA I.

7. See U.S. Department of State, *Report of the Honorable S. Morris on Japanese Immigration and Alleged Discriminatory Legislation against Japanese Residents in the United States.*

8. *Vancouver Daily Province*, 23 and 26 January 1901.

9. Canada, Parliament, House of Commons, *Sessional Papers, 1907–1908*, Paper no. 74b, 18, "J. Chamberlain to Earl of Aberdeen, Governor General, Canada, 20 July 1898."

10. Canada, Parliament, House of Commons, *Sessional Papers, 1907–1908*, Paper no. 74b, "Kato, H.I.J.M. Minister to the Court of St. James, to Marquis of Salisbury, 3 August 1898."

11. Canada, Parliament, House of Commons, *Sessional Papers, 1907–1908*, Paper no. 74b, "Tatszgoro [sic] Nosse to Governor General, 25 June 1902" (referring to the Natal Acts as "these obnoxious Bills").

12. Canada, Parliament, House of Commons, *Sessional Papers, 1907–1908*, Paper no. 74b, "Report of the Committee of the Privy Council, approved by the Governor General, 21 September 1900."

13. *Victoria Daily Colonist*, 18 December 1902.

14. Ibid., 12 January 1903.

15. Ibid.

16. Clipping from *The Evening Journal*, 17 February 1908, in file 9309, pt. 1, vol. 83, Record Group 76: Records of the Department of Employment and Immigration [hereafter cited as RG 76], Library and Archives Canada [hereafter cited as LAC].

17. *In re Nakane and Okazake*, [1908] 9 Ed. 7 (Hunter, C.J.), [1908] 13 B.C.R. 370 (Full Court).

18. Letter dated 19 December 1907 (probably G. L. Milne), Victoria, B.C., in file 9309, pt. 1, vol. 83, RG 76, LAC.

19. Shah, *Contagious Divides*, 2, 133; Canada, Parliament, House of Commons,

*Sessional Papers 1907–1908,* Paper no. 74b, p. 46 (petition describing Japanese and Chinese immigrants as "a menace to health"). Medical examinations were expressly regarded by some U.S. officials as a practical way to reduce the number of immigrants admitted to the United States. In October 1906, e.g., an immigration officer based in Hawaii suggested to the U.S. Immigration commissioner that stricter medical examinations were one way to limit travel from Hawaii to the mainland: as many as one out of ten migrants could be detained, he suggested, on the ground that they were carriers of a contagious disease, or, failing that, held for further diagnosis. Abraham E. Smith, U.S. Consul, Victoria, B.C., to Assistant Secretary of State, Washington, D.C., 19 September 1907, A8555, RG 85, NARA I.

20. Japanese consular officials insisted that Japanese exercise of the transit privilege through Canada was an economic benefit to British Columbians. See Canada, Parliament, House of Commons, *Sessional Papers 1907–1908,* Paper no. 74b, "T. Nosse to Sir Wilfrid Laurier, 18 January 1907."

21. Commissioner General, Bureau of Immigration and Naturalization, Washington, D.C., *Digest of, and Comment Upon, Report of Immigrant Inspector Marcus Braun, dated September 20, 1907* [hereafter cited as "Comment on Braun Report"], 9 October 1907, A8555, RG 85, NARA I. See also Canada, *Report of the Royal Commission Appointed to Inquire into the Methods by Which Oriental Labourers Have Been Induced to Come to Canada,* 64–65.

22. Charles Earl, Solicitor, Memorandum, 28 March 1907, A8555, RG 85, NARA I.

23. Oscar S. Straus, Secretary of Commerce and Labor, to Elihu Root, Secretary of State, 30 December 1907, A8555, RG 85, NARA I.

24. John H. Clark, Commissioner, U.S. Immigration Service, Montreal, to F. P. Sargent, 26 June 1907, A8555, RG 85, NARA I.

25. John H. Sargent, Inspector in Charge, Seattle, Washington, to F. P. Sargent, 19 September 1907, A8555, RG 85, NARA I; Charles L. Babcock, Immigrant Inspector, Port of Vancouver, B.C., to F. P. Sargent, 7 October 1907, ibid.

26. Charles L. Babcock to F. P. Sargent, 7 October 1907, A8555, RG 85, NARA I; John H. Clark to F. P. Sargent, 26 June 1907, ibid.

27. P. L. Prentis, Inspector in Charge, U.S. Immigration Service, Vancouver, B.C., to John H. Clark, 27 July 1907, A8555, RG 85, NARA I.

28. Charles L. Babcock to F. P. Sargent, 28 September 1907, A8555, RG 85, NARA I.

29. *Vancouver Daily Province,* 17 October 1900. Chilliwack residents, the *Province* reported, charged $25 to take migrants into the United States alone or in pairs, and $10 to $15 per person as part of a larger group.

30. Act of February 20, 1907, c. 1134, 34 stat. 898.

31. Executive Order no. m63.m (14 March 1907); *Contract Labor Act, U.S. Statutes at Large* (1885, amended 1891): c. 165, 23 stat. 332 (26 February 1885).

32. Canada, *Report of the Royal Commission Appointed to Inquire into the Methods by Which Oriental Labourers Have Been Induced to Come to Canada*, 55.

33. *Ottawa Free Press*, 5 July 1907.

34. Abraham E. Smith, U.S. Consul, Victoria, B.C., to U.S. Assistant Secretary of State, 19 September 1907, A8555, RG 85, NARA I; Canada, *Report of the Royal Commission Appointed to Inquire into the Methods by Which Oriental Labourers Have Been Induced to Come to Canada*, 55–63.

35. "Comment on Braun Report," 9 October 1907, A8555, RG 85, NARA I.

36. Ibid.

37. T. Nosse, Consul General of Japan, Ottawa, Canada, to U.S. Inspector of Immigration, Montreal, Quebec, 10 December 1907, A8555, RG 85, NARA I.

38. S. Morikawa, Consul of Japan, Vancouver, B.C., 27 November 1907, file 9309, pt. I, vol. 83, RG 76, LAC.

39. Charles Earl, Solicitor, Memorandum, 28 March 1907, A8555, RG 85, NARA I.

40. A. Stewart, Manager, Dodwell & Co., Ltd., to John H. Clark, 31 July 1907, A8555, RG 85, NARA I.

41. Charles Earl, Solicitor, Memorandum, 28 March 1907, A8555, RG 85, NARA I.

42. Emil Engelcke, Inspector in Charge, San Diego, California, to William H. Chadney, Chinese Inspector, Calexico, California, 23 April 1907, A8555, RG 85, NARA I.

43. Interview with Kawamoto Shinji, 30 April 1908, County Jail, El Paso, Texas, A8555, RG 85, NARA I.

44. *Report of Marcus Braun, Immigrant Inspector* [hereafter cited as "Braun Report"], 12 February 1907, A8555, RG 85, NARA I. It should be noted Japanese migrants were not the only focus of concern of U.S. immigration officers along the U.S.-Mexico border. Also of concern were Chinese immigrants, and "southeastern Europeans, such as Greeks, Italians, Southern Slavs from the Balcan [*sic*], Russian Jews and some Italians from South America" (ibid.). The Mexican government supported the United States' efforts to strictly enforce the border, because enforcement prevented Mexican rebels from fleeing to the United States so as to avoid Mexican authorities (see "Braun Report," 10 June 1907, A8555, RG 85, NARA I).

45. W. J. Maher, Inspector in Charge, Eagle Pass, Texas, to F. P. Sargent, 15 March 1907, A8555, RG 85, NARA I.

46. *Chuo Shimbun*, 9 December 1909, translation enclosed in letter from T. J. O'Brien, U.S. Ambassador, Tokyo, Japan, to Secretary of State, Washington, D.C., 10 December 1909, A8555, RG 85, NARA I.

47. Ito, *Issei*, 70.

48. Marcus Braun to F. P. Sargent, 10 June 1907, A8555, RG 85, NARA I.

49. F. H. Larned, Acting Commissioner General, Bureau of Immigration and

Naturalization, to Assistant Secretary of Commerce and Labor, 30 July 1908, A8555, RG 85, NARA I.

50. R. L. Pruett to Marcus Braun, 18 June 1907, A8555, RG 85, NARA I.

51. "Braun Report," 12 February 1907, A8555, RG 85, NARA I. Taken together, the Gentlemen's Agreements into which Japan entered with both the United States and Canada later in 1907 exacerbated this effect by further restricting the number of Japanese immigrants admissible to each country.

52. "Braun Report," 10 June 1907, pp. 17–18, A8555, RG 85, NARA I.

53. Marcus Braun to F. P. Sargent, 10 June 1907, A8555, RG 85, NARA I.

54. Attorney, Southern Pacific Company, to F. P. Sargent, 18 March 1908, A8555, RG 85, NARA I.

55. R. L. Pruett to Marcus Braun, Immigration Service, New York, 18 June 1907 (reporting on remarks made by Kamada Sannosuke, the Meiji government representative sent to investigate conditions affecting Japanese in Mexico), A8555, RG 85, NARA I.

56. "Comment on Braun Report," 9 October 1907, A8555, RG 85, NARA I.

57. F. P. Sargent re Enforcement of Department Circular No. 147, 14 May 1907, A8555, RG 85, NARA I.

58. Francis W. McFarland, Inspector in Charge, to F. P. Sargent., 20 May 1907 (in re an article in an unnamed San Francisco newspaper, dated 3 May 1907 and translated by Yoneshima, Immigration Interpreter at El Paso), A8555, RG 85, NARA I.

59. R. L. Pruett to F. P. Sargent, 11 June, 1907, A8555, RG 85, NARA I.

60. Marcus Braun, Immigrant Inspector, Eagle Pass, Texas, to Commissioner General of Immigration, Washington, D.C., 13 April 1907, A8555, RG 85, NARA I.

61. Luther C. Steward, Supervising Inspector, U.S. Immigration Service, San Antonio, Texas, to F. P. Sargent, 16 March 1909, A8555, RG 85, NARA I.

62. Marcus Braun to F. P. Sargent, 10 June 1907, A8555, RG 85, NARA I.

63. "Braun Report," 12 February 1907, Exhibit B (Report of R. L. Pruett), A8555, RG 85, NARA I.

64. "Comment on Braun Report," 9 October 1907, Exhibit K, A8555, RG 85, NARA I. The name of the pamphlet, "Hokubei mekishikokoku tankô yuki imin ôbô annai," the revised edition of which was published in *Meiji* 39 (1906) by the emigration company Tôyô Imin Gaisha, is more correctly translated as "Guidebook for Immigrants Going to Work in Mexico's Coal Mines."

65. *Japanese Aliens Arrested Prior to June 1, 1907, as Being in the United States in Violation of Executive Order of March 14, 1907*, A8555, RG 85, NARA I. Of the thirty-one Japanese arrested, one was deported to Mexico, twenty-nine were deported to Japan, and one escaped (ibid.).

66. See Exhibit B: Thomas J. O'Brien, U.S. Ambassador, Tokyo, Dispatch no. 120, 2 January 1908, enclosure no. 1: Memorandum from Foreign Office dated 30 December 1907, in U.S. Department of State, *Report of the Honorable S. Morris on Japanese Immigration and Alleged Discriminatory Legislation against Japanese Residents in the United States.*

67. Department of Commerce and Labor, Bureau of Immigration and Naturalization, *Regulations Relating to the Transit of Japanese and Korean Laborers through the Continental Territory of the United States*, 31 October 1907, A8555, RG 85, NARA I.

68. M. Berkohing, Supervising Inspector, Immigration Service, San Antonio, Texas, to Larned, 14 May 1908, A8555, RG 85, NARA I.

69. Roy et al., *Mutual Hostages*, 11. The continuous passage rule was also intended to bar immigration from India; see, e.g., Johnston, *The Voyage of the* Komagata Maru, 4.

70. Superintendent of Immigration, Department of the Interior, Ottawa, Canada, to John H. Clark, U.S. Immigration Commissioner, Montreal, Canada, 25 April 1908, A8555, RG 85, NARA I.

71. Luther C. Steward, Acting Supervising Inspector, San Antonio, Texas, to F. P. Sargent, 13 April 1908, A8555, RG 85, NARA I.

72. Emmett J. Wallace, Acting Commissioner of Immigration, Montreal, to F. P. Sargent, 18 March 1908, A8555, RG 85, NARA I.

## PART IV

...........................................

*Border Representation*

*and National Identity*

## THE WELCOMING VOICE
## OF THE SOUTHLAND

*American Tourism across
the U.S.-Mexico Border,
1880–1940*

..........................................

Catherine Cocks

In the summer of 1919, a young Langston Hughes spent several weeks in Toluca, Mexico, with his father. The idea of Mexico fascinated the teenager: "A land where there were no white folks to draw the color line, and no tenements with rent always due—just mountains and sun and cacti: Mexico!" His father, James Hughes, had abandoned the United States and his son more than ten years earlier to escape the racism that prevented so many African Americans from making a decent living. He was not alone in doing so, and not alone in going to Mexico. That country had represented the promise of freedom and racial egalitarianism for black Americans ever since it abolished slavery in 1829, a promise renewed when the Revolutionary governments of the 1920s threw down the gauntlet of *mestizaje* before North American and European white supremacy.[1]

The elder Hughes did well for himself, practicing law, managing German- and American-owned mines and factories, and buying property in Toluca and Mexico City. Yet, despite their shared anger at American inequality, the son refused to settle permanently in Mexico as his father wished. The casual racism of the three "cream-colored" sisters who managed his father's Mexico City properties—the uncultivated were always, to them, " '*muy indio*' "—did not escape his notice. The low wages and poor lodgings his father provided to the indigenous Mexicans who tended his house and livestock offended the youth. Perhaps the sharpest blow was his tightfisted father's contempt for the improvidence of mestizo Mexicans and African Americans, the same charge so often leveled at both groups by whites. Though drawn differently, the color line still existed south of the border, and in making the most of that difference, Hughes's father had not escaped but become the landlord owning "tenements with the rent always due."[2]

Disillusioned, that fall the teenager boarded the train to return to Cleveland to finish high school. "During the trip to the border, several American whites on the train mistook me for a Mexican, and some of them even spoke to me in Spanish, since I am of a copper-brown complexion, with hair that can be made quite slick and shiny if it has enough pomade on it in the Mexican fashion." Hughes used this confusion to buy a seat and berth in the sleeper car, accommodations normally denied to African Americans in the southern United States. Then, in St. Louis, he tried to get an ice cream: "The clerk said, 'Are you a Mexican or a Negro?' I said: 'Why?' 'Because if you're a Mexican, I'll serve you,' he said. 'If you're colored, I won't.' 'I'm colored,' I replied. The clerk turned to wait on someone else. I knew I was home in the U.S.A."[3]

On one level, this account of the first of two visits Langston Hughes made to his father in Mexico (he returned in 1920 and stayed through the summer of 1921) tells a story by now familiar to scholars of the U.S.-Mexico border, a story about national racism and borderlands hybridity in which leaving the United States means escaping, if not all racism, then at least the one-drop variety enforced there. Crossing the line produces a critical ambiguity that can undermine the certainties of white supremacy in the United States. But that is not the only story Hughes can tell us. In poking fun at his own teenage fantasy of a raceless, rent-free Mexico, he suggests that we might do well to understand him as a tourist, one among a growing number of Americans eagerly journeying to Mexico, or longing to do so, in the first half of the twentieth century. As a writer whose poetry often reworked the racial romanticism that drew so many Americans—most of them white—to Mexico and other Latin American countries, and as an astute observer of racial follies, Hughes guides us to see what we thought we knew in a new light.[4]

Hughes's wry portrayal of his illusions about Mexico and of the unsettling experience of travel between the United States and its southern neighbor prompts the question of how much influence a major purveyor of such fantasies—the tourist industry—had on the experience of border-crossing. Packaging these dreams as "the welcoming voice of the Southland,"[5] the tourist industry sold a realm of exotic landscapes and Latin and African peoples that encompassed and transcended Mexico, while simultaneously offering a respite from the U.S. racial-national order and an increasingly explicit critique of it. In popularizing this critique as a set of cultural possibilities rather than political demands, travel writers and tour operators played an unrecognized role in making a romantic valuation of non-white peoples and cultures, for the first time, a majority, rather than minority, point of view.

The history of American tourism in Mexico offers considerable insight into this remarkable shift in race thinking for two reasons. First, like Hollywood in the films that Brégent-Heald discusses, the tourist industry invested heavily in the production and circulation both of American fantasies and of the racial-cultural possibilities made available by the Mexican national project after 1920. Second, the patterns of mobility and encounter that tourist businesses manufactured brought a range of people together in ways that sometimes reinforced and sometimes exceeded the racial-national distinctiveness symbolized by the border. The result was not always—or even usually—a progressive critique of these bonds in the contemporary anti-racist mode, but neither was it a simple reproduction of triumphalist American white supremacy. Rather, governments, tourist businesses, and travelers actively worked and reworked these terms and their relationships in pursuit of political, economic, and aesthetic aims that, disparate as they were, ultimately contributed to the transmutation of white supremacy by racial romanticism into cultural pluralism—the claim that human differences form not an evolutionary hierarchy but a series of variegated gardens.[6]

In the remainder of this essay, I first defend my characterization of Hughes as a tourist and define my key term, "racial romanticism." I then sketch the ways in which U.S. tourism in Mexico began to rearticulate race and nation on both sides of the border in the early twentieth century. Finally, I explore the impact of the tourist industry's romantic view of Mexico and the idea of a transnational "Southland" on the international border.

## Tourism and Racial Romanticism

The young man who would in a few years become one of the leading voices of the Harlem Renaissance and a lifelong critic of race and class inequity was hardly the typical American tourist in Mexico. Yet Hughes's adolescent fantasy of that nation rehearsed themes common to travel literature addressed in the first instance to those paler and richer than he: an alluringly foreign landscape beyond the reign of U.S.-style white supremacy. Delicately avoiding the specifics, Gates Tours in 1896 appealed to its customers by offering "a civilization differing in all things from our own, with a people whose manners and customs are strange and unknown to Americans." Ten years later, the traveler William Seymour Edwards wrote, "The moment we crossed the Rio Grande we changed instantly from American twentieth century civilization to mediaeval [sic] Latin-Indian." Edwards also noted that the train's black porter had a Mexican sweetheart at every station. "There is no color line in Mexico," he wrote. Indulging a more romantic idiom in 1919, the Canadian Agnes Laut described Mexico as "a sort of lotus land, where far wanderers would come to enjoy their heart's desire and peace and forgetfulness of care"—if only Mexico's people would cease fighting each other.[7]

That such typical ideas also structured the desires of so atypical a traveler as Hughes demands a more complex accounting of race and nation in cross-border tourism than simply condemning its reinforcement of stereotypes and exempting him from American racism because he was a victim of it. Notably, although Hughes's experience in crossing the border exemplifies the unsettling possibilities border scholars have celebrated in recent years, he chose not to live there: " 'I'm colored,' I replied." Spurning the material success his father had gained by abandoning his blackness but trading on his Americanness in Mexico, the son moved in the fall of 1921 to Harlem, "the greatest Negro city in the world." There, and during long sojourns at sea and in Europe, he wrote some of the best-known literary expressions of an insistently African American aesthetic to come out of the Harlem Renaissance. He also continued to travel in the Americas, making common cause with other poets and artists who, like him, challenged white supremacy by celebrating their African heritage. Identity, not hybridity, structured his art and his politics.[8]

Hughes's affirmation of his racial identity and his frequent travels again can tell two stories—one about the strategic essentialisms and alliances common among colonized peoples in the early twentieth century, and another, less often told, about the role that tourist border-crossings may have had in reshaping the national-racial order. The fact that the poet's youthful fantasies of Mexico were similar to the ones that circulated in tourist agency brochures and in mainstream travel sketches ought to make us curious about both the content of that similarity and the effects of such travel on more privileged travelers, even if they themselves never questioned their white supremacy. Asking this question challenges the common assumption that white American tourists always simply reproduced racism in their forays abroad. It poses the possibility that tourism in the early twentieth century, although a creature of existing inequities, also created a set of economic and social relationships that allowed the rearticulation of race and nation—though not necessarily in the way that Hughes and his allies might have hoped.[9]

To turn to the case at hand, we know a great deal about white Americans' racism toward Mexicans and U.S. citizens of Mexican descent in these years of racial segregation, corporate agriculture, and rising immigration from Mexico. Equally well known is the "enormous vogue of things Mexican" among American artists and writers in the 1920s and 1930s, a period when Mexico's revolution signaled to many cultural radicals the birth of a society springing organically from American soil and reuniting the body and soul sundered by Anglo-American civilization. (Harlem was in vogue in these years, too, for similar reasons; it was no accident that Mexican artist Miguel Covarrubias designed the cover of Langston Hughes's first book.) The coexistence of discrimination and appropriation of Mexican culture can only partly be explained by social and regional differences among white Americans, for travel literature about Mexico—in forms as diverse as guidebooks, magazine articles, advertising, postcards, and films—translated the radical vogue into a popular fad with a national circulation.[10]

This "vogue" was a twentieth-century upsurge of racial romanticism, a phenomenon with roots in the eighteenth-century Romantic assertion of particularity, emotion, and nature, in opposition to Enlightenment universality, reason, and civilization. The *racial* romanticism of the 1920s and 1930s affirmed conventional notions of race-difference but insisted that each race brought its own gifts to the grand project of civilization. Accepting a racial taxonomy designed to produce white supremacy, racial romantics reversed its hierarchy to insist on the supreme value of spiritual, natural, sensual life—that is, non-white, "primitive" life—as against the artificiality and materialism of civilization. Anti-colonial and anti-racist activists the world over deployed this reversal in their struggles for national independence and civil and political rights. Modernists and bohemians used it in their attack on metropolitan conventions and constraints. And the tourist industry used it to sell tours, train tickets, cruises, and postcards, but, above all, the idea of "the Southland"—"essentially the land of festival," where order is joyously overturned all the time.[11]

## Tourism and Nation

Domestic and international tourism played an important role in producing and transforming the relationship among borders, belonging, and mobility over the course of the nineteenth and twentieth centuries. As Michel Hogue, Andrea Geiger, S. Deborah Kang, and Bethel Saler and Carolyn Podruchny argue in this volume, efforts to determine who belonged where required techniques such as the census, racial categories, and Indian reserves, but also new mechanisms such as visas, passports, and national genealogies for parsing different kinds of travelers and mobilities in relation to the nation. The increased policing of borders and border-crossing after 1900 and the growing distinctiveness of tourists from other travelers were aspects of the same process—the solidification of the nation-state as the globally dominant political unit.[12]

Long before scholars began calling our attention to the ideological function of national culture and its failures at the border, tourist entrepreneurs recognized nationality, and its limits, as a commercial opportunity. One of the chief functions of domestic pleasure travel was, quite literally, to construct a national landscape, to make nationality visible and visitable. A landscape embodying the nation was as crucial to solidifying the bond between territory and people as were official institutions like citizenship laws, or semi-official ones like a national literature and art. The person who traveled national circuits ideally acquired the proper understanding of and respect for national unity: "The thought sweeps over us—vast is this continent of ours, yet this is my country. . . . My joy in all this beauty is my right." This function of tourism was particularly important in the Americas, where settler states struggled to generate national unity in the painfully obvious absence of the pillars of nineteenth-century nationalist theory: clear territorial boundaries, ancient origins, and ethnic homogeneity. Among many other nation-building initiatives, Canada, the United States, and Mexico all heavily subsidized the construction of railroads. Primarily intended to facilitate the transportation of freight and settlers, the railroads at once began serving pleasure travel as well, by building hotels, advertising the new accessibility of national wonders, and offering organized tours.[13]

As this point suggests, traveling for colonization and traveling for pleasure were not always as distinct as scholars have assumed. The historic mobility of the continent's settler societies means that travel, for centuries, entailed seizing opportunity in lands incipiently or newly national. This fact has implications for conceptualizing tourism. Most definitions of tourism have shallow historical roots and attempt to categorize travelers by their activities in the present moment. Most histories of Western leisure travel offer the Grand Tour and imperial expansion as the modern industry's Adam and Eve. But pleasure travel in the Americas grew out of colonization, not the Grand Tour; though certainly imperial, its end goal through at least the nineteenth century was not simply mastery, but belonging—making new places home. The case of Mexico in the late nineteenth century demonstrates the ambiguity. During the Porfiriato (1876–1911), tens of thousands of Americans arrived in Mexico looking to buy or manage mines and plantations, but they also visited cathedrals and collected serapes along the way. Literally or metaphorically, these visitors descended from two and a half centuries of colonists, filibusters, and land speculators. But they were also tourists.[14]

American expatriates and would-be investors, and the friends and family members who visited them, stimulated the creation of the earliest organized American tours to Mexico. Following the models available in the United States, Canada, and Europe, the managers of Mexican railroads and local entrepreneurs quickly developed passenger services such as guided tours and publications advertising scenic and historic sights. Early tourist promoters clearly understood and fostered the link between pleasure travel and investment and settlement. One 1899 *Los Angeles Times* article, for example, detailed the commercial opportunities, the quality of labor, and the cost of land in and around the Mexican city of Guadalajara and then concluded, "The traveler will seek in vain for a scene on which nature has lavished her beauty in greater profusion." Indeed, Southern California bet its future on the symbiosis between tourism and development and won big time.[15]

The rise of tourism to its present economic and cultural importance was not just the inevitable outcome of colonization and the expansion of corporate capitalism, however. Mexico's participation in the World's Fairs demonstrates that the nationalist anti-imperialism characteristic of the early twentieth century was equally important in the development of tourism, especially in making some places more attractive than others. Whereas Canada and the United States suffered mainly from an imputed lack of originality as mere outposts of civilization, Mexico also confronted the potent force of the Black Legend and white supremacy. Beginning with the 1876 Philadelphia Exposition, Mexican government officials deliberately used the World's Fairs first to portray Mexico as thoroughly European, and later to challenge some aspects of the Eurocentric and white supremacist narratives of national success. Mexico's exhibits were also intended to encourage foreign investment, and they did, especially among Americans. For President Porfirio Díaz (1876–1911), strengthening the nation and attracting foreign investment were two sides of the same coin, but his opponents thought that coin was loaded in favor of outsiders.[16]

By the time Langston Hughes arrived in Mexico in 1919, a bloody revolution had toppled Díaz and brought his opponents to power. Like the former dictator, the Revolutionary presidents made Mexico's economic development a top priority, but with an important difference. They sought to prevent the extensive ownership of Mexican resources and industry by foreigners, particularly Americans. At the same time that the government reasserted ownership of the nation's key natural resources and enacted measures to support Mexican-owned enterprises, it began to distinguish between tourists and business investors in a new way. In the 1920s and 1930s, tourism planners deliberately targeted people seeking exotic experiences and hand-made pottery for a few weeks, not those seeking cheap labor and railroads, mines, and oil wells for long-term investment. Just as American officials, with a flourish of paperwork, made Mexican migrant laborers into immigrants, Mexican officials began identifying, tracking, and tallying "tourists," in order to encourage these welcome visitors even as they discouraged others—by, for example, mandating Mexican ownership of businesses on national soil and the employment of a certain percentage of Mexicans. Creating a distinct category for tourists—and Mexico was not alone in doing so in this period—was more than simply an administrative convenience; it constituted a decisive moment in the emergence of the modern nation-state.[17]

Drawing the line between business travelers and tourists thus underscored national borders, and because such borders posed increasingly starkly the question of who belonged where, they inevitably had racial meanings. Here again, Langston Hughes can be our guide. The youth came to Mexico to visit his father, not to see the sights. But while there, he had every intention of going to bullfights and of boating on the canals of Xochimilco in Mexico City, and he heartily resented his father's forcing him to spend most of his time studying bookkeeping in a cold, bare hacienda in Toluca. The bitter quarrels between father and son over whether the latter was merely a tourist, or a prospective resident, had everything to do with their conflicting articulations of race and nation. While the father successfully used his U.S. nationality to overcome the stigma of his race, the son insisted on embracing his blackness. Returning to Jim Crow America was to claim proudly his race *and* his nation, to deny that the United States was a white man's country.[18] Being a tourist in Mexico affirmed his African American identity, just as it would affirm for many white Americans their national-racial superiority: the whole point is to go home again.

After the Revolution, the Mexican government committed itself to widening the distance between colonization and tourism on this very basis— American tourists were welcome to visit and enjoy, but never belong to a mestizo nation, the birthplace of "the integral race" of tomorrow, a showplace for "the Anglo-Saxons [who] are gradually becoming more a part of yesterday." Emphasizing Mexico's triumphal racial syncretism, the Revolutionary governments greatly elaborated upon earlier official uses of "Aztec" history and architecture, preserved archaeological sites and enhanced their accessibility, and encouraged and promoted selected aspects of the nation's indigenous and rural mestizo cultures, particularly handcrafts, music, and dance. This official sponsorship served the purpose of "forjando patria"—forging a nation out of Mexico's many regional and ethnic groups. Indeed, tourists' interest in these deliberate stagings of culture proved their vitality in constructing the Mexican nation as unique among others. As President Pascual Ortiz Rubio put it in 1932, Mexicans were "eager and anxious to have foreigners learn that truth about the nation, knowing full well that in that way—and in that way only—can Mexico gain in prestige and gain for itself its rightful place among the foremost nations of the world."[19]

This project required making border peoples and places more national, while simultaneously easing travel and border-crossing for temporary visitors. Indeed, promoters believed that more northerners would travel south of the border if they knew things were really different down there— if Tijuana was not a recently built hodgepodge of bars, brothels, and shops selling souvenir silver spoons made in Connecticut, but an "ancient town . . . typically Latin in appearance," with "a wealth of things to entrance the tourist from 'the states.' Indian pottery, Mexican curios, drawn work . . . , a thousand things seldom if ever seen in the shop windows of [the United States]." By 1941, Mexican and American efforts to solidify a cultural border in the absence of a natural one were paying off. Dismissing the "artificialities of geographical boundaries," one American traveler wrote: "But the spiritual borders . . . There is a different feeling, evasive of definition, but inescapable to the inward sense." Nationalizing the borders enabled the nation to sort out desirable from undesirable travelers; spiritualizing them encouraged the right kind of visitors, those in search of "a different feeling" instead of a silver mine.[20]

This brief glance at the politics of tourism between Mexico and the United States suggests that portraying American pleasure travel in Mexico as merely imperialism on vacation, as an exercise in the racist perversion of an authentic Mexican culture, is inadequate. Americans and Mexicans—whatever their color—actively engaged common ideas about race and nation as they encountered each other. Comfortably certain of their own racial-national superiority, wealthy white American tourists nevertheless flocked southward in growing numbers, at the same time that Mexican anti-imperial nationalists celebrated their differences from the colossus of the North. In part by self-consciously developing and promoting Mexican culture, the Revolutionary governments compelled U.S.-owned businesses and U.S. tourists to respect Mexican sovereignty and national distinctiveness. Inextricably embedded in the unequal relationship between the two states, the American tourist trade nevertheless responded to Mexican initiatives and made that country's nationalist cultural program an international attraction.[21]

### "The Welcoming Voice of the Southland"

At the same time that the United States and Mexico deployed passports and visas, immigration restrictions and employment requirements, and songs and dances to enforce their differences, tourist entrepreneurs described a Southland that transcended the international border.[22] To give one example, the depictions of a dancing *china poblana* and a guitar-playing *charro* in Daniel Ramirez's 1935 advertisement for his Mexico City tour service look very similar to those that adorned the pages of the *San Diego Union*'s 1924 New Year's Day edition. Both turn Mexican national symbols to commercial ends—the first entrepreneurial, the second an exuberant exercise in regional boosterism; both address American consumers. California citrus growers adorned their shipping crates with images of coquettish Mexican maidens; Mexican officials selected similar (but suitably indigenized) images for tourist posters. Such images engaged a wide range of daydreamers, travelers, workers, and entrepreneurs —from Langston Hughes, to the now nameless visitor who preserved a postcard of a Mexico City cigarette vendor decked out as a charro, to the Lake Chapala fishermen eager to rent their boats to serape-hunting tourists.[23] The deployment of such images maps a tourist Southland within which the differences claimed by nations came to serve the cause of a transnational—but rarely anti-national—racial romanticism.

Understanding the effect of the creation of the "Southland" on the international border and on the national-racial order it was made to define means taking American tourists seriously, as people deliberately seeking to experience difference—which is to say, as cosmopolitans. Doing so does not require crediting them with the kind of progressive multiculturalism that some have celebrated as the result of borderlands hybridity. Rather, it means acknowledging that racism and cosmopolitanism could be, and often were, compatible and that their historical relationship was nothing like dialectical. From this perspective, tourist collecting, for example, can be seen as a form of transculturation, a transformation of all parties to cultural exchange that is not necessarily equally welcome or beneficial. Casting the relationship between tourist and host in this way directs us to ask, not about the perversion of an authentic culture, but about the effects of a new market on existing social relations. What happened when cultural nationalist projects expanded the market for handmade Mexican pottery and lace north of the border? The white American woman who sought her own uniquely patterned serape, or who made a Mexican luncheon for her bridge club, scarcely rushed into the vanguard of the struggle for national self-determination or racial equality. Yet she enacted, on a small scale, what had become one of the pillars of Mexican nationalism in the early twentieth

**Figure 1.** Advertisement for the Ramirez Tour Company, Mexico City. (From *Lands of Romance*, August 1935, 34)

**Figure 2.** Drawing of the *charro* and *china poblana*. (From "Historical Scenes Greet Motorists Who Speed along on Highways, Once Mountain Trails Trod Only by Pioneering Padres and Burros," *San Diego Union*, Automotive Section, 2 November 1924. Courtesy of the *San Diego Union-Tribune*)

**Figure 3.** La Reina brand, California Fruit Labels Collection. (Courtesy of the Department of Special Collections, Charles E. Young Research Library, University of California, Los Angeles)

**Figure 4.** "Visit Mexico" poster by Jorge González Camarena, Department of Tourism, Mexico, ca. 1940–50. (Courtesy of Library of Congress, Prints and Photographs Division, reproduction number LC-USZC4-4356)

century—the desirability of non-white culture—and her purchases contributed to the viability of artisanal practices identified with indigenous minorities, but now also with the entire Mexican nation.[24] In the context of political movements against racism and imperialism, tourist cosmopolitanism was one means by which racial romanticism could become an alternative to white supremacy, not just a soft-hearted variant of it.

This slow and uncertain shift appears in the changing meanings of common stereotypes. Popular American travel writing portrayed Mexicans as embodying a potent blend of Latin and Indian racial traits, including indolence, passion, cruelty, Catholic piety, and a childlike but powerful connection with nature and the divine. This set of characteristics hardly changed at all between 1880 and 1940, yet more and more often in the twentieth century, travel writing began to echo Langston Hughes's dream of Mexico as an escape from white supremacy—one in which white tourists were advised to admire the stereotypical Mexican for his supposed lack of their own Anglo-Saxon traits. This convergence stemmed not from mass tourist conversion to Hughes's anti-racist socialism, but rather, at least in part, from the travel industry's eager embrace of aspects of Mexico's nationalist cultural program.[25]

To demonstrate, I will focus on just one of these traits, laziness. An article otherwise devoted to the pleasures of boating on Mexico City's canals noted the presence of "that gentleman of leisure, the Mexican laborer. . . . While he is rolling and smoking countless cigarettes the sun smiles and the dew falls alike on weed and on sprouting seed; and if the harvest be small, whose the blame? 'Quien sabe?'" An editorial in the American expatriate journal *Modern Mexico* countered: "A hustling northerner suddenly dropped down among a more slow-going Latin race is apt to mistake deliberate methods for poor methods."[26] Although both passages express the common racial stereotype, they are not equally racist. The gentle scolding of the "hustling northerner" in the second example hints at the direction of change.

As business travel and tourism grew more distinct, travel writers increasingly portrayed the supposedly inherent Latin love of leisure as an opportunity—indeed, an invitation—for the traveler to lay down the burden of white supremacy. Having described in some detail the hard-working beggars, street vendors, and fishermen in the coastal town of Mazatlán, for example, the writer Clifford Gessler assured his readers in

1941 that "the easeful spirit of the West Coast ports conquers even North American restlessness." The reputed indolence of southern peoples made tourism, as distinct from colonization or investment, possible and desirable. As Arthur W. Page put it (after reassuring his readers that the opening battles of the Revolution were nothing to worry about), "Everyone ought to go to Mexico, for in that Republic you will find all the time there is, and if our share thereof is not enough almost anyone there will have some to spare which he will gladly give away. To those people whose time is money, therefore, a trip into Mexico is a bargain."[27]

This rehearsal of the usual stereotypes fed white supremacy, but it also perpetuated the long-standing romantic critique of the cold, materialist efficiency of Anglo-Americans. The idea that Latin Americans had a superior degree of spirituality and hedonism was neither new nor unique to travel writing. Indeed, by the early twentieth century, this opposition characterized anti-racist nationalist movements around the world. The Cuban nationalist and longtime U.S. resident José Martí made the distinction central to his clarion call to "Nuestra América" to resist the oppression of the United States of America in the 1880s. The Argentine intellectual José Enrique Rodó and the Mexican official and ideologue José Vasconcelos also integrated these racial distinctions into their works, *Ariel* (1900) and *La Raza Cósmica* (1925), respectively. Though few white American tourists may have read these particular writings, the ideas about Latinness that they expressed circulated widely in the English-speaking world, in movies and advertisements as well as travel writing. The unalienated Latin combination of spirit and sensuality—or as the American writer Waldo Frank put it, the "kind of *wholeness* that only the Hispanic countries seem still able to produce"—was precisely what travel businesses sold. What has often been described as an anti-modern anxiety about the burdens of white supremacy was, to a greater or lesser degree, a response to Latin American racial-national ideology and other romantic critiques.[28]

Importantly, the rejuvenation through racial-national transculturation that many American tourists sought in Mexico was also available within the United States, especially in Southern California, one of the main attractions of the emerging Southland. As one fictional standard-bearer declared in the novel *The Lure of San Francisco*: " 'I'm a Californian. I was born here and even if I haven't Spanish blood in my veins, I have the spirit of the old padres.'. . . The open-hearted hospitality of the Spaniards is canonical law throughout the West." Evoking the childlike love of leisure attributed to Latins, another elegist wrote, "The true Californian plays at living, and perhaps, nay, no doubt, this is the better way to live!" The vastly successful promotion of Southern California as an earthly Eden turned on the revalorization of childishness, leisure, and self-indulgence, qualities long associated with non-white peoples living in warm climates. This exemplar of border hybridity was the creature of Southern California's regional boosters, whose deft appropriation of Californio property and culture is well known.[29]

The similarity of American travel literature on California and Mexico highlights the success of the tourist industry in creating the transnational Southland as a place where cold-blooded Anglos and hot-blooded Latins could meet and mingle, to the benefit of both. The Anglos got in touch with their feelings, and the Latins earned dollars and pride. The existence of this realm had a real effect in promoting the romantic view of race, even though it largely reproduced standard-issue racism. For example, the Southland played an important but largely unrecognized role in what is often referred to as the sexual revolution in the United States. Changes in gender roles and sexual mores in the first half of the twentieth century occurred in part because of the gradual revalorization of just these traits that had earlier been associated with people of color.[30] The accounts of American travelers illustrate their eager incorporation of Mexican culture to this end.

"Writing in these artificial bepainted days," marveled G. Cunningham Terry in 1928, "it is difficult to describe women so beautiful, unique and natural," referring to the indigenous women in the state of Oaxaca, in Mexico. He lauded them as the embodiment of modern womanhood— "amazons" and "feminists" who controlled the family wealth uninhibited by their spineless men. The same women symbolized regional unity for the Oaxacan elite, whose female members often had themselves photographed wearing the characteristic lace headdresses of the Tehuanas. Tehuanas then found themselves uprooted via type photographs and postcards to serve the centralizing Mexican state, whereupon they became useful for a group of American women teachers participating in a six-week summer course at the Universidad Nacional Autónoma de México, who demonstrated their appreciation of things Mexican by imitating the wealthy Oaxaqueñas who imitated the elite Tehuanas. As if to complete the circuit, the Los Angeles–area theater owner Bess Garner imported a Tehuana headdress to be worn by the Mexican American actresses performing Mexican customs in plays intended to diminish white racial prejudice. Authentically feminine, attractively indigenous, genuinely Mexican, the symbolic Tehuana powerfully enacted the Revolutionary modernization project, which preserved tradition as a tool for asserting nationality in an international frame. All the parties to this complex process of transculturation both performed essential difference and made it negotiable currency, a currency American tourists were eager to acquire. In doing so, they imported a bit of the Mexican national project—with all its ambiguities—into their own sense of self, and they exported to Mexico the international recognition its leaders craved.[31]

The example of the U.S. journalist Emma Lindsay Squier makes Mexico's participation in the international reconstruction of gender and sexual norms during this era even clearer. Like a long line of imperial women travelers, she understood herself to be an ambassador of modern female freedoms. Her plan to visit Mexico in the early 1930s posed something of a challenge to female respectability: "I was looked upon as a mild sort of heroine, 'going into a country like Mexico, all alone!' " In one town, she tried to help two aspiring Mexican flappers trim their bobs more stylishly (the barber defeated them). More typically, she burnished the contrast between her own slender, blonde independence and the plump, brunette maternity of Mexican women. In one clichéd passage on the existence of a double standard for men and women, the ability to travel notably stands in for sexual self-determination. The freedom of Mexican men to take lovers, Squier remarked, "made us understand a little more fully the vast gulf between the American woman, with her casual independence and her nonchalant habits of going anywhere, any time, and the Mexican woman who still lives in the shadow of the Moorish harem." But Squier did not always find in favor of American modernity, and her criticisms expressed the racial romanticism typical of the time. In Mexico, after all, there were no "puritanical repressions," and she had come there seeking the flush of passion she first experienced as a girl reciting poetry before an appreciative Mexican audience. It is hardly surprising that Squier drew on her travels to publish several articles in popular women's magazines, in which she rendered "Indian" myths as tales of heterosexual romance—fairy tales for modern girls. The travails and triumphs of the Mexican maidens legitimized and limited the American woman's liberty, just as idealized *indígenas* and brazen *gringas* did for *la chica moderna*.[32]

## Conclusion

The circuits of desire that tourist businesses fostered and tourists traveled constructed a Southland where chilly northerners could warm their blood and southerners could assert their pride and make some money. Its geography defined by romantic racialism, this region existed within the United States, Mexico, and other American nations and transcended, without ever erasing, their borders. Like its philosophical cousin, white supremacy, romantic racialism often served nationalist aims and imperialist desires. Yet to the extent that the tourist industry responded to anti-imperial nationalist projects by valorizing difference as the possibility for pleasure, it also may have opened the door to critiques of white supremacy. The political limits of such a critique are obvious, as is the continued racism of white American tourists in Mexico and elsewhere.[33] But to treat the increasing circulation of such romantic ideas about race—and their material consequences, from tours to handmade pottery and textiles—as if they had no effect simply because they did not eliminate white supremacy or economic inequality is to believe that the development of the global tourist South in a century of decolonization and the defeat of legal segregation means nothing. Even though structural inequities persist—and tourism aids and abets them—the desirability of culture within and across national boundaries offers considerable political opportunities to those who would level the disparities. Often in spite of themselves, and with no guarantee of a good outcome, tourists' itineraries open up multiple occasions for working and reworking the borders that divide and join us.

## Notes

Thanks to the members of the 2006–7 Clements Center symposium for their constructive criticism of early rough drafts of this essay. I am especially grateful to Bethel Saler for believing in its potential, and to Ben Johnson and Andy Graybill for giving me the opportunity to realize it. Ben Johnson read this essay many more times than even a volume editor should have to, and he and the anonymous reviewers must be credited with its successes; its failures are mine alone. The

School for Advanced Research and the Huntington Library generously supported the research for the project of which this essay constitutes one part.

1. Hughes, *Autobiography: The Big Sea*, 53, 56. On African Americans in Mexico, see Jacoby, "Between North and South"; Kelley, "Mexico in His Head"; Mc-Broome, "Harvests of Gold"; and Horne, *Black and Brown*. But see also González Navarro, *Los extranjeros en México y los mexicanos en el extranjero* (500–10), on Mexican efforts to encourage white immigration and discourage that of Asians and African Americans. On Mexican *mestizaje* as a challenge to white supremacy, see Vasconcelos, *La raza cósmica/The Cosmic Race*, 9–16.

2. Hughes, *Autobiography: The Big Sea*, 55–58 (quotation on 56). The charge of improvidence cut especially deeply because James Hughes often leveled it at his son's college-educated mother, who struggled to support her two sons as a waitress and domestic.

3. Hughes, *Autobiography: The Big Sea*, 62–63. The status and racial identity of Mexicans in the United States in the early twentieth century were ambiguous and regionally specific; see Foley, *The White Scourge*; Guglielmo, *White on Arrival*; Johnson, *Revolution in Texas*; Mitchell, *Coyote Nation*. Some African Americans claimed to be "Latin" (often Cuban) to evade Jim Crow; see Jacoby, "Between North and South," 211.

4. The 1919 and 1920–21 visits were actually Hughes's second and third; he first went as a small child when his parents attempted to reconcile (see Hughes, *Autobiography: The Big Sea*, 39). On race, the border, and hybridity, see Jacoby, "Between North and South"; Horne, *Black and Brown*; Anzaldúa, *Borderlands/La Frontera*; García Canclini, *Hybrid Cultures*; Staudt and Spener, "The View from the Frontier"; Truett and Young, "Making Transnational History." On the greater fluidity of race in Latin America, see Appelbaum, Macpherson, and Rosemblatt, "Introduction: Racial Nations," 9. I ask those who object to my casting of Hughes as a tourist to consider Paul Gilroy's point about "the folly of assigning uncoerced or recreational travel experiences only to whites" (see his *The Black Atlantic*, 133); my understanding of Hughes's reworking of racial tropes relies on Hutchinson, *The Harlem Renaissance in Black and White*, 1–28.

5. "The World's Progress/To the South," 57. In this magazine article, the term "Southland" referred to southern destinations (especially California) generally, not to Mexico specifically; as will become clear, this generality is the point. Moreover, the larger project of which this essay is a part includes Southern California, Florida, and the Caribbean.

6. See Brégent-Heald, "Projecting the In-Between," this volume; Sadowski-Smith, "Introduction: Border Studies, Diaspora, and Theories of Globalization," esp. 13; Hoganson, *Consumers' Imperium*. On the relationship between race and culture, see Stoler, "Racial Histories and Their Regimes of Truth."

Rouse ("Mexican Migration and the Social Space of Postmodernism") makes the case for the postmodernity of contemporary immigration. I argue that twentieth-century tourism similarly constituted a circuit that must be examined as a distinct kind of culture-making across national boundaries, even though its social effects cannot be presumed to be progressive. The present essay relies chiefly on travel writing published in English in the United States; my larger project will draw on Mexican and Caribbean sources.

7. Gates's "Third [1896] Tour through Mexico," 4, DeGolyer Library, Southern Methodist University, Dallas; Edwards, *On the Mexican Highlands,* 44, 50; Laut, "Mexico, the Land of Desire," 43.

8. Hughes, *Autobiography: The Big Sea,* 53, 63, 70–71; Berry, *Langston Hughes,* 23–26, 120–26. On the Harlem Renaissance, see Lewis, *When Harlem Was in Vogue,* and Hutchinson, *The Harlem Renaissance in Black and White*; on traveling and alliances, see Gilroy, *The Black Atlantic,* and Stephens, *Black Empire.* I do not mean to argue that Hughes's politics and art were limited to celebrating African heritage; he was a committed socialist and cosmopolitan intellectual. As Carrie Tirado Bramen argues in *The Uses of Variety* (72–74) for other thinkers, these commitments were not necessarily at odds with identitarian claims.

9. Cooper, *Colonialism in Question*; Chatterjee, *Nationalist Thought and the Colonial World*; Stephens, *Black Empire.* In arguing for taking tourism seriously as a form of cultural contact, I draw on Pratt, *Imperial Eyes,* and Buzard, *The Beaten Track.* The specific point about American racism has a more abstract counterpart in the way that scholars often tacitly conceptualize tourism as a form of encounter that leaves tourists unchanged but devastates the hosts (e.g., see Löbbermann, " 'Making Strange' in Tourism"). The ruthless critique of tourism's complicity in exploitation and racism (nowhere better expressed than in Jamaica Kincaid's *A Small Place*) fails to undermine the practice—in part because staying home is no solution. One way out of this impasse is to examine specific instances of tourism for the kinds of opportunities and relationships they create, instead of assuming that we already know. Anthropologists and sociologists have taken the lead in this kind of work, and I would also like to thank the three listeners who called in to question the orthodox critique of American tourism that Marguerite S. Shaffer and I presented on the *Odysseys* radio program, 14 July 2004.

10. Johnson, *Revolution in Texas*; Foley, *White Scourge*; Weber, "Scarce More Than Apes"; Anderson, "What's To Be Done with 'Em?"; Delpar, *The Enormous Vogue of Things Mexican*; Oles, *South of the Border.* On the book cover, see Berry, *Langston Hughes,* 64. On racism and appropriation, see Lott, *Love and Theft*; and Hoganson, *Consumers' Imperium.* I cite guidebooks and magazine articles throughout this essay; advertisements for and columns on trips to

Latin American destinations appeared with increasing regularity in the major newspapers; see, e.g., "Where to Go for Winter for Rest, Recreation, or Sport," *New York Times*, 4 January 1903, WRI; Grace Kingsley, "A Mexican Luncheon a la Hollywood," *Los Angeles Times*, 12 September 1926, 17; and Mexico cruises advertisement in the *New York Times*, 8 December 1935, XX14. Mexican postcard collections at the Mandeville Special Collections Library, University of California, San Diego; Department of Special Collections, University Research Library, University of California, Los Angeles; and the Autry National Center of the American West attest to the considerable circulation of Mexican scenes. The American Film Institute Catalog lists more than four hundred movies about Mexico, the U.S.-Mexico border, and Mexicans that were made between 1911 and 1940; see Brégeant-Heald, "Projecting the In-Between," this volume, for an account of their themes. Although not all of these films featured the racial romanticism I emphasize, plot summaries indicate that many did.

11. Terry, "The Imperious Amazons of Mexico," 23 (quotation). On racial romanticism, see Löwy and Sayre, *Romanticism against the Tide of Modernity*; Moses, *The Golden Age of Black Nationalism*; Young, *Colonial Desire*; Chatterjee, *Nationalist Thought and the Colonial World*; Kuper, *Culture*, 23–46; Torgovnick, *Gone Primitive*. On festival (more commonly "carnival"), see Stallybrass and White, *The Politics and Poetics of Transgression*, 6–19.

12. On passports, see Torpey, *The Invention of the Passport*.

13. Curtis, "An Old Town of the New World," 316 (quotation); Curtis had this feeling of righteous ownership on viewing the Hopi town of Oraibi. On tourism, nationalism, and development, see Shaffer, *See America First*; Sears, *Sacred Places*; Koshar, "What Ought to Be Seen"; Buzard, *The Beaten Track*; Buzard, "Culture for Export"; Berger, *Development of Mexico's Tourism Industry*; Jasen, *Wild Things*; Dawson, *Selling British Columbia*; and Cocks, *Doing the Town*, 106–42.

14. Franklin and Crang, "The Trouble with Tourism and Travel Theory"; Adler, "Origins of Sightseeing." Brown (*Inventing New England*, 16) offers a brief etymology of "tourist"; Berger (*Development of Mexico's Tourism Industry*, 124n16) offers only a brief definition. The literature on imperialist tourism emphasizes the foreignness of the visitors; my point is that in settler societies, tourism was for a long time a step along the way to being at home, and the moment in which it largely ceases to be so is an important one. (That U.S. retirees are now increasingly seeking homes in Mexico and Central America is another interesting turning point.) The anthropological critique of the assumed isomorphism of place and culture, combined with this history, should compel a reconceptualization of tourism as a cultural practice.

15. A. C. Shafer, "Guadalajara. Interesting Facts and Figures about That Mexican

City," *Los Angeles Times*, 19 November 1899, 14 (quotation). For railroad promotions, see Mexican National Railroad, *Mexico: Tropical Tours to Toltec Towns*. The Gates Tours brochures (at the DeGolyer Library, Southern Methodist University) for 1896, 1904, 1907, and 1911 all offered visits to plantations as well as historic and cultural attractions. For a representative selection of American tourist materials, see Boardman, *Destination México*. On the symbiosis between tourism and development, see Jasen, *Wild Things*, 4, 6–7; Dawson, *Selling British Columbia*, 15–42; Cocks, *Doing the Town*, 106–42; and Kropp, *California Vieja*.

16. Tenorio-Trillo, *Mexico at the World's Fairs*.

17. Berger, *Development of Mexico's Tourism Industry*, 11–26 and passim; although she tracks the debate among Mexico's tourism promoters over how to define and regulate tourists, Berger does not connect it to a larger history of travel. See also Samaniego López, "Formación y consolidación de las organizaciones obreras en Baja California"; the fact that Mexico could not sustain these nationalist economic measures against foreign pressure does not obviate their political and symbolic importance. On U.S. immigration officials and tourist visas, see Kang, "Crossing the Line," this volume; on passports, see Mongia, "Race, Nationality, Mobility."

18. Hughes, *Autobiography: The Big Sea*, 53, 56, 59–60, 65, 70–71; see also Berry, *Langston Hughes*, 19–20, 23–26. On the affirmation of Americanness through consumption of the foreign, see Hoganson, *Consumers' Imperium*.

19. Vasconcelos, *La raza cósmica / The Cosmic Race*, 20 ("the integral race"); Manuel Gamio, *Forjando Patria* ("forjando patria"). President Pascual Ortiz Rubio (called "Rubio") is quoted in *Real Mexico* (April 1932, 5), the organ of the Consolidated Railroad and Pullman Company Tourist Service, published by the City of Mexico. See also Berger, *The Development of Mexico's Tourism Industry*, 61–62; Saragoza, "The Selling of Mexico"; Vaughn and Lewis, *The Eagle and the Virgin*; and Lombardo de Ruiz, "Estudio preliminar." I reject the idea that performing culture makes it inauthentic, a classic (and much critiqued) element in the denigration of tourism (see Boorstin, *The Image*, 103; and in response, Kirshenblatt-Gimblett, *Destination Culture*).

20. On Tijuana, Piñera Ramos, *Historia de Tijuana*; St. John, "Selling the Border"; Schantz, "The Mexicali Rose and Tijuana Brass." On silver spoons, Lester G. Bradley interview, 17, Oral History Collection, San Diego Historical Society; on "ancient town," see "Thousands of Tourists Visit Quaint Mexican Town Yearly," *San Diego Union*, 1 January 1920, 8; on spiritual borders, see Gessler, *Pattern of Mexico*, 1–2. The opposition between white Americans and mestizo Mexicans of course ignores the existence of mixed-race and non-white Americans, including those of Mexican or other Latin American descent.

21. Berger, *Development of Mexico's Tourism Industry*, 23–24, 104; Saragoza, "The Selling of Mexico," 99–100; Moreno, *Yankee Don't Go Home!*

22. See the "The World's Progress/To the South," 57.

23. See " 'Mexico City' with Ramirez Sightseeing Tours," advertisement in *Lands of Romance*, August 1935, 34 (top of page); "Historical Scenes Greet Motorists Who Speed along on Highways, Once Mountain Trails Trod Only by Pioneering Padres and Burros," *San Diego Union*, Automotive Section, 2 November 1924, n.p. (the charro and china poblana are at lower right). Images from the California citrus growers' boxes are from the La Reina and Esperanza brands, in Collection of California Fruit Labels, Department of Special Collections, University Research Library, University of California, Los Angeles; the "Visit Mexico" poster was produced by the Tourist Department of the Mexican Government, and is in the collection of the Library of Congress Prints and Photographs Division, Washington, D.C.; for the cigarette vendor postcard, see Album, Trip to Mexico, photo no. 67 (left), DeGolyer Library, Southern Methodist University; on the Lake Chapala fishermen, see Norma Berryman as told to I. M. Dunn, "Serape Hunting in the Mexican Wilds," 22.

24. For a similar argument, see Hoganson, *Consumers' Imperium*, 6–12. Fernando Ortiz (*Contrapunteo cubano del tabaco y el azucar*) coined the term "transculturation," which for him described the mutual transformation of Europeans and Africans as they mingled in the Americas, a process deeply implicated in shaping race, gender, and nationality, and obviously neither voluntary nor egalitarian. Mary Louise Pratt (*Imperial Eyes*) revived the term to explore the mutual reshaping of European explorers and indigenous peoples. Examples: Berryman, "Serape Hunting in the Mexican Wilds," 22; Duval, "Luncheon a la Mexicana," 27–28; see also Bsumek, "Exchanging Places."

25. Hughes, *Autobiography: The Big Sea*, 53; Pike, *The United States and Latin America*; Saragoza, "The Selling of Mexico," 99–100. See also Hutchinson, *The Harlem Renaissance in Black and White*, 1–28, for a similar argument about scholarly judgments of the Harlem Renaissance.

26. J. Torrey Connor, "On the Viga Canal: The Journey by Waterway to the Chinampas" (editorial), *Los Angeles Times*, 5 November 1899, 4–5. See also Flandrau, *Viva Mexico!*, 43–45; Squier, *Gringa*, 40, 50, 123, 172.

27. Gessler, *Pattern of Mexico*, 52; Page, "Our Nearest Latin Neighbor," 113.

28. Martí, *Our America*; Rotker, "The (Political) Exile Gaze in Martí's Writing on the United States"; Pike, *The United States and Latin America*, 193–220; Reid, *Spanish American Images of the United States*, esp. 120–23; Vasconcelos, *La raza cósmica/The Cosmic Race*; Chatterjee, *Nationalist Thought and the Colonial World*. On "wholeness," see Frank, *America Hispana*, 267 (emphasis in

the original); appropriately, Frank was lionizing José Martí in this passage. See also note 10.

29. Potter and Gray, *The Lure of San Francisco*, 14; MacFarlane, "California the Land of Promise," 44; Kropp, *California Vieja*; Deverell, *Whitewashed Adobe*; Culver, "Promoting the Pacific Borderlands." I write about this revalorization more fully in "The Pleasures of Degeneration." Mexican officials were well aware of Southern California's success; see Berger, *Development of Mexico's Tourism Industry*, 15.

30. For a critique of the usual story of the sexual revolution, see Cocks, "Rethinking Sexuality in the Progressive Era." On the interrelationship among ideologies of race, gender, and sexuality, see Carter, *The Heart of Whiteness*, and my own paper in progress, "Warm, Voluptuous Scenes of Tropic Lands."

31. Terry, "The Imperious Amazons of Mexico," 24; Poole, "An Image of 'Our Indian'"; Townley, "Six Glorious Weeks at America's Oldest School!" 12–14. On Garner, see Garcia, *A World of Its Own*, 121–54. Tehuanas have not lost their power as symbols of progressive politics; see Taylor, "Malinche and Matriarchal Utopia."

32. Squier, *Gringa*, 9, 33, 79–80, 97, 4–5; for legends, see ibid., 44, 125. See also Olcott, Vaughn, and Cano, *Sex in Revolution*; Rubenstein, "The War on *Las Pelonas*"; Muñoz, *Cuerpo, representación y poder*; Olcott, *Revolutionary Women in Postrevolutionary Mexico*; Walton, "American Girls and French *Jeunes Filles*"; Mills, *Discourses of Difference*; Barlow, "The Modern Girl around the World." On modernization, see Vaughn, "Modernizing Patriarchy, State Policies, Rural Households, and Women in Mexico."

33. On African American artists in Mexico during the Cold War and their critique of white tourists, see, e.g., Schreiber, "Dislocations of Cold War Cultures." Heath Bowman and Stirling Dickinson (*Mexican Odyssey*, 115, 129, 131, 135, 146, 192) simultaneously critique white American tourists (almost always women) for their racism and also endorse the most banal stereotypes of southern laziness, while spending most of their time lying on the beach.

# PROJECTING THE IN-BETWEEN

*Cinematic Representations of
Borderlands and Borders in
North America, 1908–1940*

.........................................

Dominique Brégent-Heald

As the previous essays in this collection demonstrate, cultural and polit-ical borders are transnational points of convergence and divergence. Borderlands function as sites for intercultural encounters and asymmetri-cal social interactions, for human and animal mobility, and for commerce and trade. Yet borders are also divisive places of conflict, coercion, and competition. As such, the tension between contact and collision charac-terizes the histories of North American border zones. Hence, one cannot conceptualize borders as static spaces, but rather as fluid locations. While the analysis of textual evidence is fundamental to understanding the shift-ing meanings of boundaries and borderlands, visual culture also sheds light on the past by providing a lens through which to observe those mercurial constructions of the border regions within the popular imagi-nary. As such, film can function as an "unconscious historian," distorting the past no more or less than archival evidence.[1]

Indeed, from the initial novelty of reproducing lifelike motion, the U.S. film industry has evolved into both a mass entertainment industry and a hegemonic and imperialist cultural institution. During cinema's forma-tive years, audiences reveled in film's ability to "show" rather than "tell." As the novelty of filmed images waned by the early 1900s, filmmakers increasingly used the medium to tell stories. From roughly 1915 on, film production centralized in Southern California and, over the next decade or so, the industry consolidated into the studio system—or what anthro-pologist Hortense Powdermaker labeled a "dream factory." By 1930, the five major and three minor studios formed an oligopoly that controlled the production, distribution, and exhibition of film product.[2] As corporate entities, the studios' primary function was to turn a profit, but in the process they created works of cultural and social magnitude that enjoyed worldwide distribution. Since the industry sought a mass undifferentiated audience, both foreign and domestic, Hollywood promoted film as a universal language while it simultaneously exported Americanized cultural commodities.[3]

Beginning in the early 1900s, the U.S. film industry produced and exported hundreds of motion pictures set on or about the physical edges of the United States. As the nation's premier mass media industry and the incontrovertible leader in the international film industry, Hollywood films, with their far-reaching appeal, likely helped shape popular conceptions of North America's borders not only domestically, but also throughout much of the world. Typically, films set in the U.S.-Mexico border region take place in the territories of northern Mexico and in the U.S. states bordering Mexico, namely California, Arizona, Texas, and New Mexico. Meanwhile, films set in the U.S.-Canada borderlands characteristically unfold in the Pacific Northwest, in the region along the 49th parallel, or in the Klondike. With the exception of Niagara Falls, Canadian-themed border films infrequently take place in states or provinces in eastern North America.

Despite the iconographic differences within and between the various regions situated on the margins of the United States, Hollywood films approached the North American border zones in similar ways: screening the tension between closed borders and open borderlands by dramatizing the process by which dynamic frontiers became borders—lines that separate and define while nevertheless maintaining the fluid characteristics of borderlands. Although the quantity of films set in the U.S.-Mexico border region exceeds the number of motion pictures with Canadian border settings, a comparative examination of Hollywood representations of borders and borderlands in North America challenges notions of national exceptionalism.

While not an exhaustive survey of border films, this essay highlights the multiple ways that the mainstream U.S. film industry popularized many of the struggles and encounters between interconnected border communities from the 1850s through the 1930s. With this goal in mind, I have divided this essay into two broad sections. First, I focus on films set in the frontier and borderlands regions of the Southwest and Northwest. The temporal and geographic liminality of these frontier and borderlands films projected myths about nation-state formation and the unresolved, residual tensions left therein. Second, I examine border films that positioned the borders as danger zones or as passageways for the extralegal movement of people and goods. Borders appear as criminal havens and, alternatively, as places of law, order, and justice. Perceived anxieties about ruptures in the nation-state projected on the silver screen reinforced the tangible desire for stricter enforcement along the borders that the United States shares with both Canada and Mexico.

**Part I: Ambiguous Frontiers and Romantic Borderlands**

In "The Significance of the Frontier in American History," Frederick Jackson Turner positioned Anglo-American westward expansion as the pinnacle stage in the evolution of the American nation-state, exemplified by democratic ideals and rugged individualism. As David M. Wrobel argues, Turner's thesis was symptomatic of the broader psychological anxieties surrounding a frontier-less American democracy during the 1890s, a decade marked by economic uncertainty, social unrest, and political strife. By the early twentieth century, however, a wistful romanticization of the Old West had supplanted the heightened level of apprehension.[4] Artists, writers, western boosters, and tourism proponents popularized frontier mythology by linking it to such ideologies as American exceptionalism, anti-modernism, and Anglo-Saxon masculinity.

The embryonic film industry further fueled nostalgia for the frontier by fashioning what Richard Slotkin calls "mythic space"—"an imaged landscape which evokes authentic places and times, but which becomes, in the end, completely identified with the fictions created about it."[5] In particular, Western films of the silent period delineated "a myth of national origin" for the United States.[6] The production of Western and Indian subject films surged in 1908–9 as pioneering film companies appropriated the conventions of late-nineteenth-century dime novels and Wild West shows, which would have been familiar to audiences. Moreover, with their distinctive iconography and subject matter, cowboy pictures, frontier dramas, and Indian pictures proliferated as part of the domestic film industry's strategy to counter the preponderance of European imports.[7]

Although the Chicago-based Selig Polyscope Company and Essanay Film Manufacturing Company led the way in the production of Westerns, it was D. W. Griffith who facilitated film's transformation from a "cinema of attractions to one based on narrative integration," while working as a director for the Biograph Company of New York City between 1908 and 1913.[8] Griffith's source material during his tenure at Biograph was eclectic. Nevertheless, several films featured frontier and borderland settings. Though filmed along the Hudson River, the narrative of *The Fight for Freedom: A Story of the Arid Southwest* (1908) unfolds in the region in between Mexico and the United States. This one-reel film opens at a saloon on the Mexican side of the border, where a group of cowboys is playing poker. A fight ensues when Pedro accuses another man of cheating. In the melee, Pedro accidentally kills the man. The sheriff arrives and a wounded Pedro escapes to his home, with the police and local vigilantes in pursuit. Following a violent chase, which results in the death of his wife, Juanita, Pedro is "seized, bound, and carried to prison to meet his inevitable." The film exhibits the chase melodrama format typical of the period. Yet while early Western pictures characteristically featured triangular relationships between Anglo-American protagonists, villains, and damsels-in-distress, *The Fight for Freedom* blurs the line between "good" and "evil." As a murderer, Pedro is not a hero, but neither is he the heavy—the cheater's death was unintentional. Moreover, if the film's moral message is that crime should be punished, the ambiguities of the film make one "question the justice of fate."[9]

The ambiguity within *The Fight for Freedom* is also present in *The Greaser's Gauntlet* (1908), which similarly deals with themes of redemption and interracial attraction in the borderlands of the U.S. Southwest and northern Mexico. Like Pedro in *The Fight for Freedom,* Jose is a "handsome young Mexican" who finds trouble at a card game in a border town when he is falsely accused of stealing a roll of money from a cowboy. The crowd at the saloon decides to lynch Jose, but at the last minute Mildred, the fiancée of a local engineer, saves his life. In return, Jose pledges to come to her aid should the need arise in the future. Hopelessly in love with Mildred, Jose turns to a life of drinking and crime. Nevertheless, he keeps his promise to the now married Mildred by rescuing her from the advances of one of her husband's assistant engineers. The film concludes with Jose returning home to the Sierra Madre mountains of Mexico a changed man.[10]

By 1910, an estimated one out of every five films released in the United States could be classified as a Western, a broad category of films that included frontier dramas, cowboy pictures, and Northwestern melodramas.[11] Responding to audience demand, exhibitors included at least one Western picture in their programs. Meanwhile, the center of film production in the United States was gradually relocating from the Northeast and Midwest to Southern California, which provided a more authentic topographical background for Western subject films.[12] In the process, Westerns increasingly followed what Scott Simmon calls a Plains Wars model, in which cowboys, cavalries, and wagon-train pioneers battled bloodthirsty Apache, Comanche, and Sioux warriors.[13] Westerns were typically set in the "Far West"—geographically located in the western interior of North America—and historically situated in the "Old West," that is, in the period of Anglo-American westward expansion through to the end of the Plains Wars, or roughly the 1840s through the 1890s.

During the early cinema period, U.S.-based film studios produced a considerable number of features set in the northwestern borderlands of North America, which formed a distinct cinematic cycle known as the Northwestern melodrama.[14] In 1908, Griffith directed *The Ingrate: A Tale of the North Woods*, about a trapper and his wife who live in a remote log cabin in the Canadian North Woods. One day, the trapper stumbles upon a hunter lost in the forest and brings him back to his home to recover. The hunter covets the trapper's beautiful wife. He returns to the woods and hides a bear trap on the trail with the intention of doing away with the kind trapper. Back at the cabin, the hunter tries to overpower the wife, but she manages to escape. After his wife finds him and releases him from the bear trap, the maimed trapper manages to overpower the hunter and throws him into the river, where he drowns.[15] The Biograph bulletin, a promotional flyer distributed to exhibitors and trade journals, emphasizes the picturesque qualities of the film's sylvan setting, despite its violent plot. The synopsis characterizes the North Woods as a secluded environment lacking the corruption and materialism connected with modern living; the married couple in *The Ingrate* is described as "carefree and happy, far from the maddening crowd."[16]

Biograph was not unique in its romanticization of the northwestern frontier of the mid- to late nineteenth century, as other U.S. film companies released fur trade or Northwestern melodramas. The idealization of the primordial hinterlands of North America was broadly an outcome of the interrelated cultural and ideological movements of romanticism, anti-modernism, and primitivism—a reaction to the rapid pace of industrialization and urbanization during the late nineteenth and early twentieth centuries. Films set in the amorphous northwest borderlands, such as Lubin's *A Romance of the Fur Country* (1908) or Selig's *In the Great Northwest* (1910), typically depicted the region and fur trade society as a barbarous forerunner to civilization. As Bethel Saler and Carol Podruchny argue in this volume, popular American histories of the fur trade pictured it as a colorful predecessor to nationhood in the Turnerian evolution from savagery to agrarian settlement. Yet although fur trappers frequently appear as uncivilized brutes, who embraced Native customs and consorted with Native or mixed-race peoples, they are simultaneously celebrated as freewheeling, nomadic, and hypermasculine individualists.

The diegesis of most films set in the Northwest is rooted in the historical period of civilizing the frontier, when Anglo-Canadian interests from the East, primarily agriculture, mining, and railroad industries, consolidated their power in the transnational West, thereby destroying the previous social orders established by Native and Métis communities, as well as the French colonial regime. In these films, trading posts characteristically appear as contact zones for asymmetrical intercultural/racial encounters between Anglo-Saxon Mounties, Native peoples, Métis, and French Canadians.[17] As such, Mounties functioned as go-betweens in the march toward civilization. These romantic masculine heroes of the North Woods symbolized Anglo-Saxon imperial authority, while their intrepid adventures in the sublime wilderness simultaneously positioned them outside the bounds of civil society.[18] Therefore, pictures set in the northwestern frontier praised the actions of those Anglo-Canadians who tamed the wilderness and conquered Native peoples, while paradoxically lamenting the demise of unbridled nature, the "vanishing Indian," and the passing of a more fluid social order.[19]

The closing of the frontier in the United States and the lore of the Gold Rush era also precipitated romanticized constructions of Alaska as "the last frontier"—a seemingly limitless authentic and natural wilderness for rugged male adventurers. American popular fiction writers of the early twentieth century, most notably James Oliver Curwood, Jack London, and Rex Beach, staged their masculine-centered narratives in the Klondike region. As Susan Kollin demonstrates, the repeated border-crossings of American protagonists in their writings ultimately erased the distinction between Alaska and the Canadian Yukon.[20] The erasure or blurring of the national boundary in the Klondike facilitated the incorporation of this resource-rich region into the capitalist economy of the United States while denying Canadian sovereignty in the Far North.

The U.S. film industry recurrently released films inspired by the novels and short stories of these popular adventure writers that both evoked a romanticized image of the Great White North and obfuscated the Yukon-Alaska boundary.[21] For example, there were three film versions of Rex Beach's 1908 novel *The Barrier*. The narrative unfolds during the 1890s in a fictional mining settlement called Flambeau, located along the Yukon-Alaskan border, which is booming with gold rush fever. The U.S. Army sends in a detachment under the command of Lieutenant Burrell to maintain order. Necia, who is apparently the daughter of a white prospector and an Indian woman, falls in love with the chivalrous lieutenant despite her mother's warnings not to fall in love with a white man. Burrell, however, struggles with his feelings for Necia—as a Southerner, he has been raised to observe racial divides. As it turns out, however, Necia is white; her father had changed her identity in order to protect himself from the law. She and Burrell thus live happily ever after. The barrier thus refers to not only a physical border, but also to the racial and social divide between the two lovers on North America's last frontier.

Indeed, films set in the borderlands and frontiers of North America frequently included characters with dual Native and European ancestry. As Michel Hogue establishes in his essay in this volume, the ambiguous nationality of mixed-race communities in the transnational West defied national efforts to impose discrete territorial boundaries. Similarly, the *mestizo* peoples of the U.S. Southwest and "Greater Mexico" not only dwell in this in-between region, but their hybrid identities embody the very dualism that underpins the borderlands.[22] One of the first films to introduce a borderlands *mestiza* character was D. W. Griffith's one-reel adaptation of Helen Hunt Jackson's 1884 novel *Ramona*. Griffith filmed *Ramona: A Story of the White Man's Injustice to the Indian* (1910) in

**Figure 1.** Still from *The Barrier*, directed by Edgar Lewis (State Rights, 1917). (Courtesy of New York Public Library)

Ventura County while he and his company wintered in Southern California. Canadian-born Mary Pickford played Ramona, who as a child had been adopted into the wealthy Moreno household. She falls in love with Alessandro, a Luiseño Indian temporarily employed as a sheep-shearer at the Moreno ranch. Upon discovering the romance, Señora Moreno banishes Alessandro and reveals to Ramona that her mother was Indian. Renouncing her *criolla* identity and embracing her "Indian blood," she and Alessandro marry. Their lives together, however, are filled with misery and hardship, as Anglo-Americans repeatedly drive them off their land. Ultimately, a white settler kills Alessandro and Ramona reunites with Felipe, the Señora's son, who takes her back to the ranch.[23]

Helen Hunt Jackson had written *Ramona* to shame the United States into reforming its policies toward Native peoples.[24] The thrust of Jackson's novel concentrates on the dispossession of the California Mission Indians. At the same time, both the novel and the film dramatize the destruction of the remaining vestiges of the Spanish colonial system. The story of Ramona unfolds in the "multicultural borderlands of the U.S. Southwest" during the 1870s, when Anglo-American capitalist expansion

**Figure 2.** Still from *Ramona*, directed by D. W. Griffith (Biograph Co., 1910). (Courtesy of Library of Congress)

displaced the *californios*.[25] José Martí, the Cuban poet and independence leader who translated the novel into Spanish, thus called its mestiza protagonist a symbol of his vision of "Our America"; Ramona represented a transnational, interracial, and intercultural collectivity that transcends the imperialist project of the United States.[26]

Although the novel was highly successful, its sentimental aspects overshadowed the potential of its critique. The book's impact on Indian reform was equally negligible. Characteristically, readers responded to Jackson's utopian vision of Franciscan missions and pastoral haciendas. Dubbed "The Ramona Myth," this idealized vision of the region's Castilian heritage and the *rancho* era not only lured tourists, attracted tract development, and promoted a Mission Revival aesthetic, it also reinvented California's public identity and memory.[27] As Catherine Cocks demonstrates in her essay, the tourism industry on both sides of the border similarly helped fashion the transnational identity of "the Southland," which promoted the rise of what she calls "racial romanticism." Borderlands served as desirable tourist destinations where Anglo-Americans could encounter the unique *fronterizo* culture.

The imagined preindustrial landscape of the Canadian Northwest and the Yukon-Alaskan borderlands in many ways paralleled the cinematic romanticization of the pastoral Spanish borderlands.[28] Promotional materials for the film *Ramona* emphasized the scenic beauty and authenticity of its setting. According to the Biograph bulletin, the film re-creates "the house wherein Ramona lived with its vine-clad verandas; the inner-court, which is a veritable paradise, the little chapel amid the trees, the huge cross, and the bells from old Spain are all apparently just as Mrs. Jackson saw them, and while the very air breathes romance there is a pious solemnity about the place that is awe-inspiring."[29]

Filmmakers, who in the 1910s had moved their operations to the West Coast, similarly embraced a rose-tinted vision of the region's Hispanic past. Hollywood released a number of Spanish borderlands films between 1910 and 1940 endorsing a particular vision of the Southwest, which Carey McWilliams later termed "Spanish Fantasy Heritage."[30] For example, films featuring the characters of Zorro and the Cisco Kid, chivalrous bandits fighting on behalf of the downtrodden, romanticized the region.[31] Furthermore, *Robin Hood of El Dorado* (1936) dramatized the story of the legendary Joaquín Murrieta and his band of desperadoes, held responsible for a series of robberies and murders in the California borderlands during the 1850s.[32] The Murrieta legend consequently represents either resistance to Anglo-American conquest or banditry.[33] Regardless, these "gay caballero" films did not depict the Spanish borderlands as a contested terrain, but rather reinvented the region as a pastoral Arcadia. Spanish borderlands films not only established a connection between the new Anglo-American elite and the former Castilian dons, they also glossed over histories of brutal conquest and existing discrimination toward persons of Mexican descent living in the Southwest.

Mainstream film productions thus both upheld and challenged popular images of frontiers and borderlands. On the one hand, the films represent the processes of western capitalist expansion and Indian removal at work on multiple and diverse frontiers that were parallel zones of intercultural contact and conflict.[34] On the other hand, the border landscapes in the emergent Western genre functioned as shibboleths for national myths and Anglo-American identity-formation. Borderlands and frontiers appear perpetually ensconced in Turner's evolutionary conception of the West—trapped in the moment of incorporation into the nation-state.

**Figure 3.** Still from *Robin Hood of El Dorado*, directed by William A. Wellman (Loew's, 1936). (Courtesy of New York Public Library)

While most of these films wax nostalgic for the irreversible past and lost landscapes, ultimately, the cinematic borderlands, whether they represented the North or South, created a "usable past" that affirmed modern Americanism and the imagining of a (white Anglo-Saxon Protestant) national identity.[35]

### Porous and Precarious Perimeters

Films set in North America's frontiers or borderlands frequently coded these in-between regions as sanctuaries from modern industrial society and as male proving grounds for rugged individualism. Moreover, the marked presence of Native and mixed-race (mestizo and Métis) peoples enabled transracial and transcultural interactions and relationships that had the potential to destabilize national boundaries. The U.S. borders with Mexico and Canada concurrently figured as precarious locales, populated by dangerous revolutionaries, smugglers, gunrunners, whiskey traders, outlaws, fugitives, and spies. Consequently, these violent and blood-stained border spaces require policing by law enforcement agents. The frequent depiction of trans-boundary criminal activities heightened concerns regarding lax control over both borders, thereby helping to create the perceived need to curb their permeability. Border films focused on the importance of securing boundaries as linear divides between order and chaos.

While early Westerns frequently romanticized the ambiguous borderlands and frontiers of North America, along with their preindustrial inhabitants, other motion pictures presented a counter-narrative that focused on the importance of solidifying boundaries in order to achieve Turnerian progress. As the synopsis for *On the Border* (1909), a Western subject film that takes place in the early 1860s along the Mexican border, states: "The class of humanity that flock to the borderland of civilization are always of an adventurous nature, the kind of people who dislike conventions and long for freedom, and very often we find the lawless element predominating."[36]

In Western films set in the southwestern frontier, *mexicanos* frequently filled the role of the melodramatic villain. Western films correspondingly demonized other marginalized racial groups, namely "half-breeds" and "bloodthirsty Indians," who often operated in cahoots with mexicanos to menace the expanding Anglo-American settler population. For example, in *In Old Arizona* (1909), after a young woman from the East rebuffs his advances, a Mexican man induces "hostile Indians" to attack both her and her escort as they travel through the desert. Soldiers from the nearby military post, however, arrive in time to capture the assailants.[37]

The on-screen vilification of Mexicans was not without precedent. As early as the sixteenth century, the English along with the Dutch slandered the Spaniards, claiming that their imperial rivals were barbaric and racially impure, giving rise to the so-called Black Legend, which then migrated to Spain's New World colonies. Animosity toward Mexicans intensified as expansionist fervor gripped the American republic during the mid-nineteenth century. Mexico's defeat following the Mexican-American War did little to curtail racial hatred and damaging depictions of Mexicans in the Anglo-American popular consciousness. The term "greaser," which emerged with the rise of Anglo-American "conquest fiction" during the nineteenth century and continued with early twentieth-century Western pulp fiction, equated Mexican males with violence as a way to bolster Anglo-American racial superiority and justify the conquest of the Southwest.[38]

The villainous mexicano stereotype in southwest border films intensified following the onset the Mexican Revolution in 1910. The emergence of Southern California as the epicenter of film production in the United States coincided with Mexico's Revolutionary period (1910–20). Not only did this facilitate the ability of filmmakers to record the Revolutionary events occurring in the southwest border region, it also provided exciting source material for feature films. The narratives of many Revolution-themed films unfolded in the U.S.-Mexican border region. By their very nature, borders are spaces of friction and are thus particularly sensitive to certain moments of upheaval, as was evidenced during Mexico's Revolutionary period.[39] Yet in dramatizing this unstable period in Mexican history, most films overlooked the Revolutionaries' drive for democratic reform and instead sensationalized the violence, which repeatedly spilled north of the boundary.

The Philadelphia-based Lubin Company released a series of Mexican War pictures filmed throughout the Southwest, including in such border towns as El Paso and Nogales.[40] *The Mexican Spy* (1913), a dramatic story of the army life of both Mexico and the United States, was promoted as a "highly sensational border picture," which is "based on the supposition that the border between Mexico and the United States is in a state of warfare." The film, directed by Wilbert Melville, centers on Tom, a colonel's son who redeems his gambling ways and enlists in the army. His regiment is ordered to the border, where tensions are running high between the United States and the Republic of Mexico. Mexican troops attack Tom's wagon, but he emerges victorious and is appointed a lieutenant due to his bravery.[41]

Other films similarly reinforced the desirability of a strong military presence along the border. In Romaine Fielding's *An Adventure on the Mexican Border* (1913), filmed in Nogales, U.S. troops are stationed on the boundary, "with a view to protecting the International line and the citizens of the United States," while on the other side, Mexican soldiers "were camped to do likewise for their country." An attractive senorita enters into this tense situation, and captivates both a Mexican captain and a U.S. lieutenant. The Mexican captain wins her hand via "quiet love and kindness," while "the irrepressible, impassionate United States trooper tries to take the senorita's heart by storm." To punish his rival, the American lies to his commanding officer and "nearly causes international complications" by bringing the U.S. regiment into conflict with the Mexican troops. Regretting his actions, the lieutenant delivers the captain from jail, returns him to his fiancée, and awaits punishment.[42]

In addition to praising the film's realistic atmosphere, the reviewer for the *Moving Picture World* noted the unconventionality of its story, which "does not make a gingerbread hero of an American lieutenant and an impossible victim of a Mexican."[43] Yet, following a series of diplomatic crises, motion pictures increasingly presented an unambiguous portrayal of cross-border violence. Bilateral relations between Mexico and the United States deteriorated due to President Woodrow Wilson's intervention in the Mexican Revolution during the Tampico Affair (1914), Pancho Villa's Columbus Raid (1916), the subsequent Punitive Expedition of 1916–17, and the disclosure of the Zimmerman Telegram in early 1917.

Much of Hollywood's output during these years added to the bilateral strain by portraying the U.S.-Mexican border as a hazardous crossroads teeming with marauding *bandidos*, who often preyed upon Anglo-American women.[44] As early as 1914, Harry B. Ott, the *New York Dramatic Mirror*'s correspondent in Chihuahua, warned U.S. producers that exhibitors in Mexico "complain loudly of the deluge of films which have flooded the American market recently in which Mexicans are always portrayed as villains and dastardly characters." He went on: "There is hardly a shipment of pictures received nowadays in which at least one of these objectionable pictures is not to be found. . . . Does the American public demand such unfaithful portrayals of a friendly people? We believe not. Then why produce them."[45]

Hollywood's denigrating and sexualized representations of Mexico, Mexican nationals, and the Mexico-U.S. border region affronted Mexican audiences on both sides of the border. Mexican protests peaked with the release of Paramount's *Her Husband's Trademark* (1922). In the film, Gloria Swanson stars as Lois Miller, the trophy wife of a wealthy American industrialist named James Berkeley. While accompanying her husband to Mexico, where he is conducting business, Lois reunites with her former suitor, Allan Franklin. A gang of Mexican bandits descends upon the trio and kills Berkeley in the attack. They attempt to kidnap Lois, but Allan rescues her and they escape back across the border. The brutality and racism of this sequence prompted the Mexican government to implement a temporary embargo on the importation and exhibition of films distributed by Paramount Pictures. Moreover, President Álvaro Obregón threatened to boycott all Hollywood output should such offensive stereotypes persist.[46] However, a concerted effort to remove negative characterizations would not occur until the Second World War period, due to the strategic importance of Pan-American unity.

While perhaps not as vociferous as representations of the Mexican border in this period, motion pictures nonetheless depicted the regions along the U.S.-Canadian border as unsafe spaces. Northwestern melodramas of the silent period routinely juxtaposed a romantic vision of the landscape with violence, depicting the region as a primal environment teeming with murder, lust, greed, and criminality. Largely unmanned, the U.S.-Canadian border region had in fact been used by rustlers, outlaws, fugitives, and whiskey traders as a convenient escape route. Sir John A. Macdonald, Canada's first prime minister, thus established the Royal Northwest Mounted Police in 1873 to not only bring law and order to the western interior, but to police the frontier between the American and Canadian Northwest.[47] Likewise, the Mounted Police invariably restore law and order in Canadian-themed films. For example, Mounties track down fugitives in such films as *In Defiance of the Law* (1914), *Until They Get Me* (1917), and *South of Northern Lights* (1922); chase whiskey runners in *Heléne of the North* (1915); and hunt down fur smugglers in *Out of the Snows* (1920) and *The Challenge of the Law* (1920).

*The Cattle Thieves* (1909), one of the first American non-actualities shot on location in Canada, was publicized as the first film to introduce "to the American public the heroes of the NORTHWEST MOUNTED POLICE." The film centers on the triangular relationship between a Mountie, his sweetheart, and a treacherous French "half-breed" leader of a gang of cattle rustlers.[48] Like the mestizos of the southwest borderlands, motion pictures often characterized the Métis as duplicitous and treacherous. The film industry developed a tradition of presenting men and women of mixed Native and European parentage as tragic victims of their parents' transgression, as objects of unfulfilled desire or as volatile sexual forces, or some combination thereof. As Susan Courtney argues, miscegenous fantasies within American cinematic practice expressed the dominant apprehension concerning the loss of an imagined racial, cultural, national, and linguistic "purity," while at the same time offering a means to negotiate those anxieties.[49]

While Canada's Northwest Mounted Police perpetually secured the 49th parallel by pacifying Indians, half-breeds, and criminals, on the U.S.-Mexico border, cowboys and rangers subdued Indians, mestizos, Mexicans, and outlaws. The popular image of the Mounties as the police officers of the northwestern frontier served as a filmic model for representations of the Texas Rangers on the southwestern frontier.[50] In *The Ranger and the Girl* (1910), which Lubin promoted as "a spirited story of the Texas-Mexican frontier," Captain "Bud" Carver is "a member of the famous band of Texans whose exploits have made them the equals of the Canadian Northwest Mounted Police."[51] Subsequently, motion pictures routinely represented the Mexican border region as a dangerous locale, which necessitated pacification at the hands of the Anglo-American rangers. For example, the Texas Rangers police the Rio Grande in *Keith of the Border* (1918), *Pure Grit* (1923), *The Web of the Law* (1923), and *Border Justice* (1925).

Whether set in the northwest or southwest borderlands, Anglo-Saxon protagonists policed the vulnerable and exposed edges of their respective nations from a host of threats, such as rustlers and outlaws. *The Cattle Thieves* (1908) was one of the earliest films about cattle rustling, which would become a common motif in border-themed Westerns. Though cattle thieves operated in the Western U.S.–Canadian borderlands, an expansive open range that proved difficult to police, rustling appears as a plot device more frequently in films set in the southwest border region.[52] Films presented bandits either as Robin Hood–type heroes or as ruthless villains, which reinforced the slipperiness of such categories as legality and illegality in the border region.[53] For example, in *The Scarlet Brand* (1932), rustlers terrorize the U.S.-Mexico border region; the villains trick an itinerant cowhand named Bud Bryson into rustling cattle for them. The irate ranchers capture Bud and brand him. Bud manages to escape, with the help of a man named Slim, and tries to prove his innocence while running from a lynch mob. Slim, it turns out, had been working as an undercover detective for the Cattlemen's Association. He not only clears Bud's name, but also apprehends the real rustlers. Meanwhile, in *The Cyclone Ranger* (1935), the Pecos Kid is the leader of a band of cattle rustlers on the Mexican border. Although he is an outlaw, he does not engage in such violent crimes as kidnapping or murder. In the film, the

Pecos Kid prevents his former associates from stealing cattle from a ranch owned by a blind Mexican grandmother.

The smuggling of cattle from Mexico across the border to the United States and vice versa in films dramatizes the contested nature of land and cattle rights in the transnational West, particularly as the cattle industry consolidated into large ranches reined in by national boundaries during the late nineteenth and early twentieth centuries. As Rachel St. John shows in her essay, the borderlands of the U.S. Southwest and Mexico's northern territories supported a transnational ranching industry, which became bifurcated into two distinct U.S. and Mexican ranching regimes defined by customs duties, ports of entry, and fences. As a result, state authorities were more concerned with regulating the trans-border traffic of the cattle herds than monitoring the border-crossing habits of individuals.

In addition to rustling, films represented the border badlands of the Southwest and the sylvan borderlands of the Northwest as temporary places of refuge for a variety of fugitives and criminals. A common storyline in border films centers on outlaws who commit crimes in border regions knowing that, since the law cannot cross an international borderline, as long as they escape to the other side before the authorities catch up, they may get away with stealing or murder. As such, the function of the northern and southern national boundaries as lines of separation is destabilized. The division between innocence and freedom on the one hand, and criminality on the other, appears fluid. No longer is one's culpability connected to the criminal act, but rather it depends on which side of the line one is standing.

In *Border Brigands* (1935), for instance, a ruthless American bandit named Conyda and his gang terrorize a Canadian community along the 49th parallel. Taking a leave of absence from the Mounted Police, Buck Barry, played by Buck Jones, a popular cowboy film star of the 1920s and 1930s, crosses the border. Pretending to be an American six-shooter, Buck successfully infiltrates the gang. His identity revealed, the film concludes with a shoot-out at the border, between Conyda and his gang on the one hand, and Buck and the Mounties on the other. The Mounties prevail, and by repelling the American outlaws they have secured the border and restored order to their community. As the head commissioner of the Mounted Police informed his men, "It is simply a question of who's going to run this community: a despicable outlaw who'll stop at nothing to satisfy his lustful desire, or, the decent forces of law and order." The commissioner here outlines the competing elements at play on the U.S.-Canadian boundary: the "lustful" American side versus the righteous Canadian side, each struggling for control over their shared border.⁵⁴ Alternatively, in *Border Caballero* (1936), the Mexican side functions as a disorderly criminal haven, while the United States stands for law and order. Tex Weaver is a G-man who goes undercover and joins a gang of border bandits, who are planning a series of bank robberies. When Tex is killed in action, his friend Tim Ross, played by sagebrush hero Tim Mc-Coy, joins the Department of Justice. Disguised as a Mexican, he heads south of the border and manages to bring down the gang.⁵⁵

The frequent depiction of trans-boundary criminal activities such as rustling and robberies, coded border areas as porous and problematic, thereby helping to create the perceived need to curb their permeability. Frequently, border films also responded to more specific social and economic anxieties prevalent at the time of their production and exhibition. During the Prohibition era (1919–33), a cycle of films emerged that centered on gangsters who used the borders to transport alcohol or narcotics into the United States. *Up and Going* (1922), *Channing of the Northwest* (1922), and *Over the Border* (1922), focused on Mounties who successfully foil bootleggers who had been smuggling hooch into the United States via the Canadian border. Meanwhile, in *The Unknown Ranger* (1920), *Quicksands* (1923), and *Hands across the Border* (1926), narcotics smuggling rings operate along the Mexican border, until federal or state authorities apprehend the criminals in question.

Throughout the 1920s and into the 1930s, other Hollywood films focused on subduing a perceived racial threat—the smuggling of Chinese and Mexican laborers. Federal authorities in the United States had linked the trafficking of illegal substances, particularly the opium trade, with the unlawful cross-border immigration of Chinese workers. Responding to a North American climate of racism and nativism, Chinese-smuggling films similarly positioned the borders as both economic and racial divides, whose vulnerability necessitated enforcement on behalf of Anglo-American/Canadian authorities. In *The Cyclone* (1920), a gang of smugglers illegally transport Chinese laborers across the Canadian border into the United States but are thwarted when a Mounted Police officer apprehends the leader of the gang at his headquarters in Vancouver's Chinatown. Two years later, in *Sky High* (1922), Tom Mix plays a U.S. immigration officer whose duty is to "capture the smugglers of Chinese coolies and prevent the Orientals from crossing the [Mexican] border" into the United States.[56]

By the 1930s, the on-screen racialization of borders indicated a new concern over the smuggling of Mexican laborers across the U.S.-Mexican border. Prior to the First World War, there were no restrictions imposed on non-Asians crossing the U.S.-Mexican border. Even with the passage of the wartime Immigration Act of 1917 and the Passport Act of 1918, as S. Deborah Kang demonstrates in her essay here, enforcement of policies regulating the border remained lax. The booming agricultural industry of the Southwest necessitated a pool of cheap farm labor, and since Mexican migrants fulfilled that need, cotton and food growers called for a relatively open border. With the onset of the Great Depression, however, record-high unemployment among Anglo-Americans intensified their racial hostility, as seen in the deportation of hundreds of thousands of ethnic Mexicans, many of whom were actually U.S. citizens, between 1929 and 1935. Agriculturalists, who perennially complained of worker shortages, particularly at harvest time, brought in Mexican labor. As a result, the Immigration Service now seized nearly five times the number of suspected undocumented immigrants in the Mexican border region than along the Canadian border.[57]

Films focusing on the extralegal entry of Mexican migrants typically position the laborers as pawns in elaborate smuggling schemes, which were often carried out by air as opposed to physically crossing the border. For example, in *Soldiers of the Storm* (1933) a small California town next to the Mexican border opens its first airport and becomes a convenient location for a narcotics and illegal-alien smuggling ring. A U.S. Border Patrol officer, who happens to be a daring aviator, goes undercover and brings down the smugglers.[58] Furthermore, in *Secret Service of the Air* (1939) Ronald Reagan stars as Lieutenant Brass Bancroft, a former military pilot who joins the Secret Service (it was the first in a series of four films he would do in this role). For his first assignment, Brass is sent to the Mexican border to investigate a gang of smugglers who illegally transport Mexican migrants into the United States on planes. The pilots are instructed to release their cargo, that is, the Mexican laborers, at the first sign of trouble, which is conveyed in a scene early on in the film. After winning the trust of the ringleader, Brass is hired as one of the pilots, and eventually succeeds in bringing down the smuggling ring.

As *Secret Service of the Air* and *Soldiers of the Storm* indicate, border films during the 1930s increasingly featured protagonists who were representatives of U.S. federal authority, such as Border Patrol officers, customs and immigration agents, or G-men. For example, *On the Border* (1930), *Skull and Crown* (1935), and *The Border Patrolman* (1936) all feature border patrol agents, while federal agents are the protagonists in *God's Country and the Man* (1931), *The Lone Defender* (1934), and *El Diablo Rides* (1939). The increased appearance of heroic federal agents during this period is linked to a variety of factors. In 1934, following a thirty-year moralistic tirade against the so-called corruptive influence of movies, the Motion Pictures Producers and Distributors Association (MPPDA) strengthened the Production Code, a set of moral standards to govern film content. To enforce filmmakers' compliance with these rules, the MPPDA established the Production Code Administration (PCA), which remained in operation until its official dismantling in 1968. Under this framework of self-censorship, motion pictures had to make clear to audiences that crime does not pay. Subsequently, actors such as James Cagney and Edward G. Robinson, who had played gangsters in *Public Enemy* (1931) and *Little Caesar* (1930), migrated to the other side of the law in *G-Men* (1935) and *Bullets or Ballots* (1936), respectively.[59] The prevalence of G-men could also indirectly be due to J. Edgar Hoover's efforts to promote a positive public image of the FBI. Furthermore, valiant images of federal agents represented the injection of New Deal social consciousness by many of Hollywood's left-liberal filmmakers in the 1930s and into the early 1940s.

Many of these crime-themed border films and Westerns were themselves on the edge of respectable filmmaking. Small production companies had emerged in the early 1930s to provide a sizable quantity of low-budget films and serials, to provide audiences with more value for their dwindling entertainment budget. To that end, the major studios correspondingly maintained "B" units.[60] Though relegated to the second half of a double bill, B-Westerns, for instance, were popular in rural and small-town communities as well as with recent working-class immigrants in urban areas. Unlike A-Westerns, which were invariably period epics, B-Westerns typically took place at the time of their production and exhibition, and typically addressed current social and economic concerns from a populist perspective.[61]

Beginning in the late 1930s, a cycle of B-Westerns appeared that depicted America's long, permeable borders as ideal refuges for Axis spies and saboteurs, who then used the unguarded borders as convenient portals of entry into the United States. Though democracy ultimately prevails at the conclusion of these films, the presence of enemy agents upon America's doorstep fostered a sense that the United States was under threat. For example, *Border G-Man* (1938), *Pals of the Saddle* (1938), and *Death Rides the Range* (1940) focus on the espionage and sabotage on the U.S.-Mexican border, while *Valley of Hunted Men* (1942) features Nazi POWs who escape across the Canadian border into the neutral United States.

Still, as Miguel Ángel González-Quiroga contends in his essay, cooperation and conflict frequently go hand in hand along the border. While such films coded the Canadian and Mexican borders as places of instability, the border zones could offer opportunities to depict transnational collaboration. With the integrity of the United States under threat from perceived and actual Axis subversion, the FDR administration shored up hemispheric defenses and strengthened America's relationships with both Canada and Mexico. American feature films released during the period of the Second World War routinely reinforced bilateral amity and the theme of cooperation. For example, in *Unseen Enemy* (1942) two high-ranking Nazi naval officers escape from a POW camp on the Canadian border and arrive at a San Francisco café, a rendezvous point for the area's Axis spy ring. The enemy agents attempt to solicit a crew to staff a Japanese ship docked in the San Francisco harbor for a daring raid on U.S. shipping interests on the Pacific coast. However, a U.S. government agent and a Canadian intelligence officer work together to bring the Nazi mob to justice. Furthermore, American feature films released during the years of the Second World War routinely depicted Canada as a valued friend and vital ally of the United States by featuring Canadian protagonists, played by such virile stars as James Cagney, Errol Flynn, and Randolph Scott, who appeared as staunch partners in the project of continental defense.[62]

Likewise, although Hollywood films positioned the U.S.-Mexican border as an Achilles' heel—that is, as a location where the United States was susceptible to Axis incursion—films emphasized the importance of

**Figure 4.** Still from *Unseen Enemy*, directed by John Rawlins (Universal Pictures, 1942). (Courtesy of New York Public Library)

teamwork between U.S. and Mexican authorities. Under the aegis of the Good Neighbor policy (1935–45), the Motion Picture Division of the Office of the Coordinator of Inter-American Affairs promoted the mutual benefits of inter-American kinship by encouraging Hollywood productions with Latin American themes and sponsoring goodwill tours. Moreover, beginning in 1939, the Nazis restricted the importation of Hollywood pictures in those European countries it controlled. The loss of this key foreign market augmented the value of the Latin American market in general and Mexico in particular. As a result, though Hollywood motion pictures in the period from the mid-1930s to the mid-1940s continued to portray the U.S.-Mexico border region as a precarious perimeter, films nevertheless aimed to depict Mexican nationals in a sympathetic light.

The most perceptible transformation was the absence of "greasers" or bandidos in border films. For example, in *Arizona Gang Busters* (1940), Captain Juan Rodriguez of the Mexican National Police poses as the border bandit Gringo in order to infiltrate a gang engaged in war-related smuggling, espionage, and sabotage activities along the U.S.-Mexican border. Upon scrutinizing the script, Joseph Breen, head of the Production Code Administration, recommended that the film avoid typecasting any Mexican nationals as "heavies," and urged that "their characterization be changed to American renegades, in order to avoid offense to the Mexican government."[63]

In 1941, the Production Code Administration hired Addison Durland to scrupulously monitor scripts and completed films to ensure that they did not undermine the goals of the Good Neighbor policy. For example, in *Below the Border* (1942), the Rough Riders avenge the killing of a fellow U.S. marshal and clean up Border City, a town terrorized by a group of gun-crazy bandits. Since the narrative unfolds in Mexico, Durland was concerned that the appearance of Mexican henchmen would forestall the film's release south of the border. To eliminate any danger of offending the sensibilities of "our Mexican neighbors," Durland ordered script changes to ensure that no Mexicans were portrayed as "heavies" or members of the outlaw band. He also urged the producer to apply great care in depicting the costumes, makeup, dialogue, mannerisms, and general behavior of all Mexican characterizations, as well as to avoid excessive use of broken English or the mispronunciation of Spanish words.[64] Ultimately, Durland's recommendations were followed, and the final production contained "nothing that could reasonably offend our neighbors to the south."[65]

### Conclusion

Between the early 1900s and the 1940s, the Canadian and Mexican borders served as prominent geographic settings for American motion pictures. Filmmakers translated onto the silver screen many of the tensions and themes that the contributors to this collection of essays examine. First, films set on borderlands and frontiers grapple with the myth of the frontier, specifically the formation of nation-states via the construction of boundaries, and the unresolved, residual tensions left therein. Second, border films depicted the border zones as porous, which enabled the trans-boundary exchange of illicit goods and human and animal mobility. On-screen criminal activities within the permeable border zones created conflict, but also necessitated cooperation among the various law enforcement agents charged with policing the borders. More than mere images, Hollywood thus offered, to borrow Norma Iglesias's phrase, "social representations," which shifted according to the state of America's relationships with its neighbors.[66] These representations both reinforced and challenged the dominant myths about Mexico and Canada, as well as the border each nation shares with the United States.

## Notes

1. Rollins, Introduction to *Hollywood as Historian*, 4.
2. The rise of Classical Hollywood and the studio system is too complex to recount in detail here. See Bordwell, Thompson, and Staiger, *The Classical Hollywood Cinema*.
3. Richard Maltby calls the contradiction between business interests and the sociocultural implications of film the "commercial aesthetic" (see Maltby, *Hollywood Cinema*, 15).
4. Wrobel, *The End of American Exceptionalism*, 3.
5. Slotkin, *Gunfighter Nation*, 233.
6. Wexman, "The Family on the Land," 130.
7. Abel, *The Red Rooster Scare*, 151–74.
8. Gunning, *D. W. Griffith and the Origins of Narrative Film*, 35.
9. D. W. Griffith is likely the director of this film; see "The Fight for Freedom," reprinted in Bowser, *Biograph Bulletins*, 2.
10. "The Greaser's Gauntlet," reprinted in Bowser, *Biograph Bulletins*, 9. For a discussion on the film, see Alonzo, "From Derision to Desire."
11. Anderson, "The Role of the Western Film Genre in Industry Competition," 19–26.
12. Bowser, *The Transformation of Cinema*, 169.
13. Simmon, *The Invention of the Western Film*, 44.
14. Langman, *American Film Cycles*, xvi–xvii.
15. "The Ingrate," reprinted in Bowser, *Biograph Bulletins*, 38. Biograph released another version of this film in 1912 called *In the North Woods*. Griffith also directed *A Woman's Way: A Romance of the Canadian Woods* in 1908, which similarly features an attractive female victim and a predatory trapper.
16. "The Ingrate," reprinted in Bowser, *Biograph Bulletins*, 38.
17. E.g., *The Call of the North* (1914), *The Primal Lure* (1916), and *The Law of the Great Northwest* (1918).
18. Brégent-Heald, "Primitive Encounters," 64.
19. Renato Rosaldo terms this process "imperialist nostalgia," wherein the colonizers destroy the cultures of the Other and then yearns for what they have vanquished (see Rosaldo, *Culture and Truth*, 70).
20. See Kollin, *Nature's State*, 59–90.
21. Between 1910 and 1940, there were over ninety films adapted from Cur-

wood's writings, and approximately fifty each based on stories by London and Beach.

22. José Límon uses the term "Greater Mexico" in his *American Encounters*. On hybridity and the borderlands, see Anzaldúa, *Borderlands / La Frontera*.

23. In the ending of the novel, Felipe and Ramona move to Mexico. "Ramona," reprinted in Bowser, *Biograph Bulletins*, 197. There have been three subsequent film adaptations of the novel in the United States, in 1916, 1928, and 1936.

24. See Mathes, *Helen Hunt Jackson and Her Indian Reform Legacy*.

25. Irwin, "*Ramona* and Postnationalist American Studies," 541.

26. See Gillman, "*Ramona* in 'Our America,'" 91–111.

27. See DeLyser, *Ramona Memories*; Noriega, "Birth of the Southwest," 203–26; and Thomas, "Harvesting Ramona's Garden," 119–57.

28. Herbert Eugene Bolton popularized the term "Spanish Borderlands" to define "the regions between Florida and California, now belonging to the United States, over which Spain held sway for centuries" (see Bolton, *The Spanish Borderlands*, vii).

29. "Ramona," reprinted in Bowser, *Biograph Bulletins*, 197.

30. McWilliams, *Southern California Country*.

31. Zorro films include *The Mark of Zorro* (1920); *Don Q, Son of Zorro* (1925); *The Bold Caballero* (1936); and *The Mark of Zorro* (1940). The Cisco Kid films include *In Old Arizona* (1929); *The Cisco Kid* (1931); *The Return of the Cisco Kid* (1939); *The Cisco Kid and the Lady* (1939); *The Gay Caballero* (1940); and *Romance of the Rio Grande* (1941).

32. The Murrieta legend also appeared on the silver screen in *The Avenger* (1931), remade as *Vengeance of the West* (1942), and *The Gay Defender* (1927).

33. Irwin, "Toward a Border Gnosis of the Borderlands," 523.

34. See Cronon, Miles, and Gitlin, "Becoming West," 3–27.

35. Abel, *Americanizing the Movies and "Movie-Mad" Audiences*, 4, 62.

36. *Moving Picture World*, 27 November 1909, 773.

37. *Moving Picture World*, 23 January 1909, 7. *The Indian Scout's Vengeance* (1909) features a similar plot.

38. See Pettit, *Images of the Mexican American in Fiction and Film*.

39. Hall and Coerver, *Revolution on the Border*, 3.

40. Some of these films include *The Mexican Revolutionist* (1912); *Down on the Rio Grande* (1913); *A Mexican Tragedy* (1913); *A Girl Spy in Mexico* (1913); and *The Clod* (1913).

41. *Moving Picture World*, 28 December 1912, 1268; *New York Dramatic Mirror*, 22 January 1913, 29.

42. *Moving Picture World*, 8 March 1913, 1018; 15 March 1913, 1113.

43. *Moving Picture World*, 29 March 1913, 1336.

44. E.g., *The Grandee's Ring* (1915); *The Brand of Cowardice* (1916); *Lieutenant Danny, U.S.A.* (1916); and *The Border Wireless* (1918).

45. *New York Dramatic Mirror*, 14 October 1914, 28. Some examples of films with villainous Mexican rebels include *The Mexican's Last Raid* (1914); *'Cross the Mexican Line* (1914); and *Captured by Mexicans* (1914).

46. See Serna, "As a Mexican I Feel It's My Duty," 225–44.

47. Walden, *Visions of Order*, 117.

48. *Moving Picture World*, 6 November 1909, 632, 655.

49. Courtney, *Hollywood Fantasies of Miscegenation*, 9.

50. For a historical comparison of the Northwest Mounted Police and the Texas Rangers, see Graybill, *Policing the Great Plains*.

51. *Moving Picture World*, 5 March 1910, 354, 351.

52. Some examples of cattle rustling films include *Sunrise Trail* (1931); *Beyond the Rockies* (1932); *Arizona Badman* (1935); *Borderland* (1937); and *Land of the Six Guns* (1940).

53. See White, "Outlaw Gangs of the Middle Border," 387–408.

54. *O'Malley of the Mounted* (1936) and *Fighting Mad* (1939) deal with a similar theme.

55. See also *Oklahoma Cyclone* (1930) and *Border Law* (1931).

56. *Motion Picture News* (12 December 1921), reprinted in Jensen, *The Amazing Tom Mix*, 169. See also *Roarin' Broncs* (1927); *Hair-Trigger Casey* (1936); and *Shadows of the Orient* (1937). *Speed Wild* (1925) and *Border Phantom* (Luby, Republic Pictures, 1936) specifically focus on the cross-border trade of Chinese "picture brides" across the Mexican border into the United States.

57. Ngai, *Impossible Subjects*, 70.

58. See also *Criminals of the Air* (1937).

59. Munby, *Public Enemies, Public Heroes*, 110.

60. See Flynn and McCarthy, "The Economic Imperative."

61. See Stanfield, *Horse Opera*; and also his *Hollywood, Westerns, and the 1930s*.

62. See James Cagney in *Captains of the Clouds* (1942), Errol Flynn in *Northern Pursuit* (1943), and Randolph Scott in *Corvette K-225* (1943).

63. Joseph Breen to Sigmund Neufeld (producer of the film), 5 August 1940, Motion Picture Association of America, Production Code Administration Records [hereafter cited as MPAA/PCA], Academy of Motion Picture Arts and Sciences, Margaret Herrick Library [hereafter cited as AMPAS].

64. Addison Durland to R. E. Pirschel, Great Western Productions, Inc., 11 December 1941, MPAA/PCA, AMPAS.

65. Addison Durland to R. E. Pirschel, Great Western Productions, Inc., 13 January 1941, MPAA/PCA, AMPAS.

66. Iglesias, "Border Representations," 183.

# GLASS CURTAINS AND STORIED LANDSCAPES

*The Fur Trade, National*
*Boundaries, and Historians*

........................................

Bethel Saler and
Carolyn Podruchny

It may be unusual to find an essay about the historiography of the fur trade in a collection that considers the history of national borders. At first glance, national borders should play a very small part in the history of the fur trade because most of it occurred before the border dividing Canada from the United States was firmly drawn. Yet, this essay explores how historians' national consciousness informed their rendering of North American fur trade history. Rather than studying the fur trade on its own geographic terms, many scholars have cast the fur trade as the birthing place of one transcontinental nation and a regional footnote of another. Such national distinctions underscore how historians contribute to the formation of borders as ideas and spaces that reinforce the authority of the nation-state. In representing borders usually implicitly in their narratives, fur trade historians, however, also take part in a more ambivalent discourse about the construction of national borders that similarly captivated the writers of tourist literature, explored by Catherine Cocks, and the makers of border films, analyzed by Dominique Brégent-Heald—essays that precede this article. Collectively, the North American fur trade histories written by Canadian and American scholars form an unresolved and open-ended literature that, while often reaffirming national borders, also reveals a subject in which national borders constitute only one of many overlapping territorial spaces—spaces that factored into the contingent understandings and political power of national divides. The fur trade as subject, like tourist literature and border films, offers a site to unravel the historical and distinct cultural meanings articulated by people when they creatively narrated border spaces.

The fur trade comprised a trade of fur pelts, primarily beaver, produced by Aboriginal people, and material goods produced in Europe. Western Europeans initiated the trade informally in the first half of the sixteenth century, and it became the major commerce in the colony of New France from the early seventeenth century onward.[1] The British began to trade for furs in North America when the Crown chartered the Hudson's Bay Company in 1670. After the British conquest of New France in 1763, the Montreal-based trade continued in small partnerships that eventually merged into the North West Company in 1779. The Jay Treaty of 1794 secured the lands south of the Great Lakes for the United States, and in 1818 the 49th parallel was established as the northern boundary of the Louisiana Purchase, separating the United States from what would become Canada up to the Rocky Mountains. Although all were allowed to trade on either side of this border, providing they paid taxes, American traders attempted to drive away Canadian traders from the areas immediately south of the line. In 1808 John Jacob Astor established the American Fur Company, and later other subsidiary companies. An 1817 Act of Congress excluded foreign traders from U.S. territory, after which the American Fur Company dominated the U.S. trade until its demise in 1850. In 1821 the North West Company merged with the Hudson's Bay Company, and in 1870 the company transferred much of its land to the newly created Canadian nation, continuing its operations in the Far North until the Second World War.

Though Britain and the United States set national boundaries cutting through the Great Lakes region in 1785, Native, European, and Euro-American residents continued to adhere to the diverse and long-standing geographies of the North American fur trade. American politicians sought this boundary as a means of removing the British military from their posts on the American side of the border (a process not fully realized until 1796), and of forcing British inhabitants living on now American soil to assume U.S. national allegiances and identities. By setting this new U.S.-Canadian boundary, the U.S. Congress put into motion centripetal forces intrinsic to the formation of any nation-state: they promoted popular and territorial cohesion, insisted on loyalty from its new residents, and encouraged people to look inward, to invest themselves and their communities with a national consciousness. Yet other centrifugal forces influenced local inhabitants' territorial allegiances, distracting them with different ideas about how to view the land on which they lived, worked, and traveled. In the case of the fur trade, it produced its own territoriality of trading posts and Native hunting camps and of commercial centers in Montreal and London. Moreover, Aboriginal conceptions of territoriality continued to shape localized fur trade landscapes, ideas of territoriality that conflicted with the new Northern U.S.–British North America boundary line and the land-tenure systems of the new European settler communities.

The first part of this essay considers how much of United States and Canadian fur trade historiography has implied the inevitability and stability of national borders and bordered states by invoking national myths of state-making. Because American and Canadian national origin stories are discrete, the two national historiographies of the fur trade situate it in very different ways within their national narratives. At the same time, not all works fall into this categorization. Some fur trade histories have revealed alternative historical and geographic imaginings that challenge the universality and exclusivity of nation-state-centered histories.[2] This fur trade historiography makes clear that one group's historical geography, or "storied landscapes," as Colin Calloway has termed it, cannot serve to explain other peoples' experiences in and understanding of the same space.[3]

Following this theme, the second part of this essay argues that the history of the North American fur trade at different points in time and place and for different groups of people encompassed alternative definitions of territory and community to those of the nation-state. Because of its central narrative of cultural encounter, the fur trade brought together a diversity of people who imagined the geographic worlds they inhabited in distinct ways. These insights are important to the study of borderlands because they expose the fractured and contingent meanings of national borders—they did not exist in all circumstances for all people. Further, the sweep of time and scale of the North American fur trade, stretching from the sixteenth through the twentieth centuries and representing overlapping local, regional, national, and international enterprises, reveals the transience and vulnerability of national and imperial state borders to the dictates and interpretations of other political spaces.

## Of National Historiographies and Glass Curtains

Although the United States and Canadian border did not interfere in the various operations of the North American fur trade until late in the game, nationalist attitudes are particularly pronounced in much of its written history, and many fur trade scholars in each country have shuttered their view of stories from the other side of their national divides. The disparate interpretations of the fur trade in Canada and the United States serve the different national narratives. The fur trade scholarship in the United States is a less substantial body of literature than that produced in English Canada. In contrast to the central place that Canadian historians have given the fur trade in their national development, American scholars have not considered the trade a particularly important factor in the rise of their nation. Whether explicitly or not, historians have relegated the fur trade to a transient and regional phenomenon. Racially mixed and multinational trading populations offer colorful and exceptional stories to the mutually informing main narratives of American agrarian settlement and urban development spreading across the continent.

Americans' privileging of agrarian settlement in their nationalist origin story expressed the particular late-eighteenth-century context of their forays into nation-state formation. Unlike Canada, the United States formed its national identity in rebellion against the British Empire. Their union of settler states dedicated to still protean notions of modern republican governance represented a resounding ideological break from their former colonial history. No longer living in an imperial space defined by subjection to a monarch, Anglo-Americans perceived themselves as members of a collectively "owned," territorially defined, nation. Lockean republican theory posited that the most basic job of the state was to protect property; and Americans initially assumed property ownership as a fundamental criterion for political membership and of settled permanent life.

Landed property owners such as farmers manifested the idea of a property-based territoriality. Farmers represented the interior of the nation, the settled parts or those in the process of being cultivated. Moreover, though Revolutionaries disputed a future of manufacturing versus agricultural-based economies, a romantic faith in the rejuvenating powers of an agrarian economy and farmers as the model citizens became a core part of national mythology by the early nineteenth century.[4] In all these ways, (legal) agrarian settlement realized the republican territorially based identity of the American nation-state. The fur trade, in contrast, held a decidedly colonial legacy: it took place in lands inhabited by Aboriginal peoples, it was both mobile and transitory, and it was a reminder of the messier reality of competing and confusing claims of Indian and French colonial possession undermining the state's idealized assertions of sovereignty.

Popular history representations of the fur trade as a colorful and fleeting antecedent to permanent, that is, *real* American settlement can find no better founding father than the early nineteenth-century author Washington Irving. After securing acclaim in Europe during a long sojourn, Irving returned to his native land and turned his hand to chronicling the romance of the American West. He wrote three books in quick succession in the mid-1830s. First he recounted his own travels across U.S. Indian Territory (present-day Oklahoma) in *A Tour of the Prairies* (1835). Then, over the next two years, Irving wrote two books about fur trading and exploration in the Pacific Northwest: *Astoria* (1836), about fur magnate John Jacob Astor's failed attempt in 1810–12 to capture a part of the Columbia River trade, and *The Adventures of Captain Bonneville* (1837), an account of the thrilling explorations of Captain Bonneville, whose "rambling kind of enterprise, had strangely engrafted the trapper and hunter upon the soldier."[5] Astor, the financier of both his own company's and Bonneville's Pacific Northwest expeditions, supplied Irving with his entire archive of the Astoria venture. Since most of this material consisted of business papers, Irving looked for social insights and comparable experiences in the journals of other explorers in the same region, and in the case of the second book, he relied on the notes and maps of Captain Bonneville.[6] Out of this careful, evidentiary research, Irving hoped to narrate the "the stories of these Sinbads of the wilderness," and to capture "[their] perilous adventures and hair-breadth escapes among the Indians."[7] He declared that the importance of their adventures lay in the historic role performed by fur traders generally, as "pioneers and precursors of civilization." First French, then British, and finally American traders laid open "the hidden secrets of the wilderness leading the way to remote regions of beauty and fertility that might have remained unexplored for ages, and beckoning after them the slow and pausing steps of agriculture and civilization."[8]

Almost fifty years after Irving's fur trade writings, the historian Frederick Jackson Turner published *The Character and Influence of the Indian Trade in Wisconsin* (1891), which claimed a professional academic imprimatur to speak for the nation, including the narrative of the fur trade as a necessary savagery in the evolution toward agrarian civilization. Turner viewed the trader as "the pathfinder for civilization,"[9] but not *of* it. *The Character and Influence of the Indian Trade in Wisconsin*, Turner's first published monograph and his dissertation, foreshadowed his famous "frontier thesis" by situating this localized exchange economy as an early stage in the ineluctable progression of American settlement in Wisconsin, toward soil cultivation and, finally, the manufacturing-based economy of his present day. Euro-American property ownership and agrarian settlement were the signifiers of permanent society—in other words, of "civilization." Fur traders and trappers, on the other hand, with their mobile hunting life, dependence on finite animal supplies, and their infamous habits of adopting Native customs and relationships, embodied an oppositional Euro-American "barbarism."[10]

Much of American fur trade historiography over the twentieth century has followed Turner's lead of constructing fur traders and trappers as "precursors" in an American advance westward that inevitably eclipsed their mobile exchange economies. A sense of doom hangs over this interpretation of the American fur trade, as well as a centralizing pull toward an established, coherent United States. American fur trade historians falling under this "spell of inevitability" run into the problem of claiming national importance for a subject both transient and counter to the central developments of agriculture and manufacturing.[11]

The first line of defense has been for scholars to extol traders' importance as pathfinders and explorers. Trappers living west of the Mississippi River in the 1830s and 1840s, according to Sydney Greenbie's *Furs to Furrows* (1939), were "always some 500 miles ahead of the army, the missionaries, and the land-hungry pioneers, showing them the way."[12] Robert G. Cleland in 1950 insisted on a "reckless breed" of trapper and trader in the American Southwest, such that "the feet of the nation walked his half-obliterated trails, the course of empire followed his solitary pathways to the western seas."[13] In the 1960s, Walter O'Meara maintained that fur traders and trappers, not "the people of the covered wagons or the bearded forty-niners . . . led the westward march of the frontier." These men "were the true spearheads of Manifest Destiny."[14] Richard Dillon highlighted in 1975 that the early California trade provided a path later followed by the Gold Rush and railroads, and in a 1997 monograph, Robert Utley called fur traders "the point men, the advance guard, of a nation unfolding westward, geographically and politically."[15]

A few studies of the American fur trade, though, have made much bolder claims to national significance. Such scholarship has argued that, at different points in time, trading matters and national or imperial concerns were inseparable. The fate of the fur trade and the nation-state or empire, in other words, was one and the same. David Lavender's *Fist in the Wilderness* (1964), for example, depicts John Jacob Astor's attempts to monopolize the fur trade in the American portions of the Great Lakes as a critical part of a national effort to free the United States finally from the yoke of British economic dependence. John C. Phillips and J. W. Smurr's masterful two-volume *The Fur Trade* (1961) presents nearly two centuries of the North American fur trade as a story of imperial competition among European and American nations. Though endowing the fur trade with greater weight than most histories, the imperial or republican nation-state still holds center stage as the master subject.[16] This view imposes a progressive narrative of nation-state formation on a subject not wholly within or subsumed by the national political community. While policies of imperial and national governments affected the fur trade, other distinct dynamics, such as international markets, local agendas, and Indian politics, also determined its course. By the same token, the fur trade only inconsistently and in combination with other international and local factors influenced the shape of national and imperial politics.

By far the most common fate of the fur trade within American historiography has been its subordination as a topic of regional, rather than national importance. The majority of the American fur trade scholarship has focused on parts of the Great Lakes/Midwest region (including Missouri), the Southern Rockies, the Southwest, and the Pacific Northwest. This fact in and of itself does not presume regionalism, however. Graduate programs in American history, professional organizations, journal editorial boards, academic publishers, and many fur trade historians themselves have reinforced the idea of the regional particularity of the American fur trade. That is, regions are constructed categories in the work of scholars as well as many other groups and individuals—including boosters, politicians, and local residents—wishing for various reasons to cohere and distinguish a particular area. Those areas also exist in a relational role to the master subject of the nation-state. In the spaces of the fur trade, however, European, Euro-American, and mixed-race traders and their Native exchange partners more often operated in geographic worlds defined by labor, kin, culture, natural environment, and company affiliations than from a self-conscious notion of region or nation.

Ironically, much of fur trade scholarship pigeonholed as regionally specific challenges the coherence of the nation-state and its centrality in trading narratives. Both the Pacific Northwest and the Southwest regions, for example, long were imperial battlegrounds among a host of European powers and the United States well after the latter had established its independence. American imperial conflicts with other nations lie at the center of accounts of the Southwest fur trade such as Gloria Griffen Cline's *Exploring the Great Basin* (1963) and David Weber's *Taos Traders* (1969). And similarly, imperial competition and the overlapping sovereign claims of numerous nations frame Pacific Northwest fur trade scholarship such as James Ronda's *Astoria and Empire* (1990) and James Gibson's *Otter Skins, Boston Ships, and China Goods* (1992), to name just two. In this way, these "regional" fur trade literatures raise numerous points of national significance: the transitory nature of empires and their boundaries; the United States' domestic imperial history; and the diverse ways that European, Euro-American, and Native inhabitants resisted, ignored, or gave shape to territorial borders at the local level.

In marked contrast to American historiography, English Canadian national histories depict the fur trade as a cornerstone in the development of the Canadian nation-state.[17] In one sense, this contrast originates in the different patterns of British colonization in these two parts of North America, differences that speak also of geographic distinctions. The lower thirteen British colonies in North America attracted a vastly larger European immigration than Canada and built diverse economies out of the environments endemic to particular Atlantic colonies. The geographic and climatic shift northward to Canada drops the total arable land, from the small number of 19 percent of the continental United States, to the minuscule amount of 5 percent of the landmass of Canada. This fact, combined with the smaller settler population, meant that agricultural settlement in Canada occurred at a slower pace and over more limited terrain than in the United States. At the same time, the small percentages of arable land in *both* countries correspond with the importance of extractive industries such as lumber, mining, (fur/hide) hunting, and fishing in the growth of both national economies. Particularly in the beginnings of European mercantile empires in North America, new colonies were expected to supply ready markets for finished goods, and staple or raw products to their respective European centers of empire. Thus, in the lower thirteen British colonies of North America, fur trading as well as other extractive industries mixed collectively with animal husbandry and staple and diversified farming in distinctive patterns that yielded different regional economies.

The powerful, republican associations of national independence with domestic manufacturing and agriculture, however, have tied those two forms of economy to the emergence of the American nation-state in ways not true of the fur trade. In contrast, English Canadian national histories do not emphasize a rupture with their colonial past, but on the contrary, envision their nation as organically developing within the French and British empires in North America. This tie between colony and nation-state in Canadian histories meant that chroniclers depicted the fur trade as introducing civilization into northern wilderness, not as a precursor thereof. Alexander Ross, for instance, an early nineteenth-century Scottish migrant, lifelong fur trader, and a founding citizen of the multiracial Red River colony (in present-day Winnipeg, Manitoba), wrote about his trading adventures and settled life at Red River as forays of progress in a wilderness. Ross's book *The Red River Settlement* (1856) described that colony as an island of civility in vast oceans of savage forest and prairie, and he implied that trading furs and establishing a line of posts along canoe routes were acts of civilization.[18] Subsequent narrators of western Canada reinforced Ross's view of the fur trade as foundational to this early national nucleus, as in the classic works of W. L. Morton's *Manitoba: A History* (1957) and George F. G. Stanley's *The Birth of Western Canada* (1961).[19]

Paralleling the influence of Frederick Jackson Turner on American fur trade historiography, the scholarship of Harold Adams Innis critically shaped Canadian fur trade historiography and the concomitant central place of the fur trade in the formation of the Canadian nation. In *The Fur Trade in Canada* (1930), Innis asserted that "the present Dominion emerged not in spite of geography but because of it. The significance of the fur trade consisted in its determination of the geographic framework."[20] In other words, the main posts of the Hudson's Bay Company and North West Company became the geographic framework for the western and northern part of the Canadian nation. Innis framed his study in nationalist terms by portraying furs as one of the staple economies that shaped the country's political borders. In the east, the main staple exploited by merchants was cod, and the geographic extent of the cod fisheries served as the geographic imprint for the Maritime Provinces. The exploitation of wheat did the same for central and western Canada. Innis argued that the successive economies that were built on various staples provided the chronological framework for the emergence of the Canadian nation. The fur trade and the nascent Dominion of Canada, Innis believed, spread across the continent long before the Americans.[21]

Innis's work was underscored by one of the pillars of Canadian history —Donald Creighton—whose 1937 *Commercial Empire of the Saint Lawrence* proposed that Canadian history could be best understood as an expansion westward of the fur trade, which built the architecture for the later east-west trading of other staples. Creighton argued that Canadian economic and national development derived from the gradual exploitation of key staple products—fur, timber, and wheat—by colonial merchants in the major metropolitan centers along the St. Lawrence River system. The staple products were sold to major European cities, creating a transatlantic and transcontinental economy that undermined the continentalism implicit in Turner's frontier thesis. In *Canada: A Story of Challenge* (1953), J. M. S. Careless extended the staples and Laurentian theses by exploring the consequences of metropolitan areas exploiting regional hinterlands. Although the exploitation of staples occurred within regions, the flow of harvested products, laborers, and goods between the resource-rich regional hinterlands and the heartland of mercantile trade, manufacturing, and political governance (which eventually became the Quebec City–Windsor corridor of central Canada) made the staples theory a story of nation-building.

Up to the 1970s, scholars followed Innis's interpretation of the fur trade as a central resource industry and an important first step in the building of the Canadian nation. This robust historiography has been well studied. As early as 1973, L. G. Thomas published a comprehensive literature review of what he termed "the fur trade era," observing that most English Canadian work only covered the period from 1763 to 1870 and focused exclusively on the West and North of Canada.[22] These histories, mainly concerned with business and empire, focused on fur trade companies that located their stories primarily in the early Canadian Northwest, that is, the Hudson's Bay Company and North West Company. The volume devoted to the fur trade in the Canadian Centenary Series, E. E. Rich's *The Fur Trade and the Northwest to 1857* (1967), is divided equally among the histories of the North West Company, the Hudson's Bay Company, and the reconstituted company after these two merged in 1821. The biographies of fur trade explorers, another popular topic in this classic historiography, supported the nationalist framework by celebrating great men who overcame severe tests of their strength and fortitude to bring commerce and civilization to the Indians and map the wilderness for the British and later Canadian empire. Marjorie Wilkins Campbell's *The Nor'westers: The Fight for the Fur Trade* (1954), *The North West Company* (1957), and *McGillivray, Lord of the Northwest* (1962) are perfect exemplars.

The 1970s witnessed a broad shift in fur trade historiography that paralleled developments in other historical fields for the writing of social history "from the ground up." Scholars became interested in the everyday lives of ordinary people and turned their attention away from great men and top-down perspectives on nation-building to community studies focused on women, families, workers, and Aboriginal people. Their work constituted a revolutionary change in the questions scholars asked about the trade, and in the sources they used. It also brought out new dimensions and perspectives on the trade, suggesting the diverse workforces and social geographies contributing to this broad subject. In 1980, for instance, two groundbreaking studies appeared that showed the centrality of family, marriage, and women's roles within the formation of trading economies in Canada. Sylvia Van Kirk's *Many Tender Ties* (1980) highlighted that key roles of Native and Métis women in trade relationships as wives, cultural brokers, and traders. At the same time, Jennifer S. H. Brown's *Strangers in Blood* (1980) traced the new family structures and complicated racial politics emerging from Hudson's Bay Fur Trade Company employees' marriages with Native peoples. Others have explored the labor history of the fur trade in comparative studies of the American Fur Company and the Hudson's Bay Company, looking at servant resistance to master authority and examining the wide cultural variety of laborers, including French Canadians, Orcadians, Iroquois, Métis, and Algonquians.[23]

In tandem with these new social histories, scholars started to take seriously Native peoples' particular perspectives of the fur trade. Combining research techniques from history and anthropology, a renewed ethnohistorical literature invigorated fur trade investigations by transforming representations of Aboriginal people from mono-dimensional, passive characters to full-scale trading partners with their own particular histories. Such Native-centered histories revealed the cultural beliefs and customs, including ideas of territoriality, influencing Indian peoples' participation in the trade. Arthur Ray's 1974 *Indians in the Fur Trade*, which led the way in Canada, pursued the question of why Aboriginal people entered the fur trade and what they gained from it. His later work with Donald Freeman in *"Give Us Good Measure"* (1978), and books by Robin Fisher, Toby Morantz, and Paul Thistle, to name a few, have generally shown that Native peoples were neither pawns in the trade or dependent on European trade goods, nor were their economic and social systems rapidly and radically transformed by contact with Europeans.[24] Instead, these scholars showed that Europeans accommodated to Aboriginal trading systems and, concomitantly, to their notions of space.

Similar American ethnohistorical studies reaped textured new histories of Indian peoples and also new attention to the fur trade, particularly within colonial American history.[25] Innovative "colonial-era" scholarship over the last twenty-five years has brought attention to distinctive Aboriginal epistemologies about land and trading, such as Calvin Martin's *Keepers of the Game* (1979), William Cronon's *Changes in the Land* (1983), Richard White's *Roots of Dependency* (1983) and, later, *The Middle Ground* (1991), Bruce White's many articles, Kathryn E. Holland Braunds's *Deerskins and Duffels* (1996), and Colin Calloway's *One Vast Winter Count* (2003).

The rise of ethnohistorical explorations of the fur trade in Canada and the United States also garnered new notice to the children of European traders and Native women—the Métis, or mixed-race, peoples. This group first received extensive attention in 1945 with Marcel Giraud's *Les Métis canadien*, which considered them as a step between savagery and civilization. After doctoral dissertations by Fritz Pannekoek and John Foster, both completed in 1973, studies of multiethnic families gained momentum. Jacqueline Peterson's 1980 dissertation, "The People In Between," which examined the ethnogenesis of the Métis in the Great Lakes region, asked when and how ethnically distinct Métis communities emerged. Peterson and Brown's edited collection *The New Peoples: Being and Becoming Métis* (1985) quickly carved out Métis studies as a stable field of inquiry, and remains the most widely cited work on Métis history to date, despite the recent explosion in the field.[26]

In the United States, the same regionally based Métis studies abound, revealing the complexity of identities, customs, and social spaces outside of and existing simultaneously with dominant national, racial, and cultural definitions. In her study of the lower Missouri River, Tanis Thorne chose the metaphor "many hands" for the title of her book on "the interrelationships of French Creoles and Central Siouan tribes" and the localized fur trade they cultivated. Such a metaphor, Thorne explains, refers to "the various human relationships that cross and often transcend cultural, ethnic or national boundaries."[27] Susan Sleeper-Smith and Lucy Eldersveld Murphy have also explored the strategies with which Euro-American and Indian fur trade communities in parts of the Midwest retained local distinctiveness and resisted social disintegration in the face of an imposition of dominant Anglo-American customs and racial and spatial identities. In *Indian Women and French Men* (2001), for example, Sleeper-Smith charts the critical power of female-dominated, Catholic, Indian (and eventually also Métis) kin networks in southwest Michigan and northwest Indiana to minimize incursions of American market forces and to ward off removal from their homelands. Similarly, in *A Gathering of Rivers* (2000), Lucy Eldersveld Murphy demonstrates the ways that both Wisconsin Indian and French-Indian trading peoples diversified their production to adapt to a dominant American market economy, while also shaping their local portion of that national economy. Their expansion of their maple sugar yield and their fabrication of Indian keepsakes, beadwork, and weaving for the tourist trade all marked their region with their separate (counter-national) heritage and selfhood. In contrast to these midwestern stories of persistence of alternative identities and spatial definition, John C. Jackson's investigation of Pacific Northwest Métis in the eighteenth and nineteenth centuries, in *The Children of the Fur Trade* (1995), focuses on the ephemerality of a people who disappeared from record in the face of more rigidly defined borders and national identities.

For scholars of borderlands, these studies of racially mixed and Indian fur trading communities intimate alternative social geographies operating simultaneously with those of the nation-state. The full implications of these border-challenging facets, however, largely have gone unrealized until recently. While U.S. and Canadian historians have provided a wealth of suggestive community and regional studies of Native and Métis or mixed-race peoples in the fur trade, national borders still implicitly frame depictions of these communities. The border between Canada and the United States seems to act like a glass curtain. Scholars of the fur trade do not pay any attention to it, yet they seem to be unable to pass through it.

Although the focus on the history of Aboriginal peoples often fosters a centrifugal model of geographic imaginings, very few studies span the Canadian and American border, and the divide between Canada and the United States looms as a divide for subjects and sources. Scholars situated in Canada write about Natives situated in Canada and generally confine their reviews to scholars and topics in Canada. This disturbing tendency shutters fur trade scholars on either side of the border.

In Canada, the falling out of fashion of fur trade history has compounded this trend. The best social and cultural history on the fur trade has shifted from university academics to federal employees working at National Historic Sites administered by the Parks Canada Agency, such as at Lower Fort Garry in Manitoba, Rocky Mountain House in Alberta, and Fort Langley in British Columbia.[28] The work of these federally employed historians, anthropologists, and archaeologists is exceptional, but they are required by their government mandate to reinforce the nationalism of the fur trade scholarship.[29] Thus, they interpret Canadian historical sites for a Canadian national public out of the relevant historical sources and the material culture found at those sites. In other words, historic sites and public commemorations have followed academic developments in emphasizing the agency of Aboriginal people and women and revealing the multivocality of the past, yet it is always presented within the guidelines of Canadian national heritage commemoration.

A few studies in both Canadian and U.S. Aboriginal history deserve special note for highlighting the border challenges raised by the North American fur trade as a subject by focusing specifically on transnational geographies peculiar to some of these "counter-national" populations.[30] In a very early example of such a counter-viewpoint, the anthropologist Oscar Lewis's notable study *The Effects of White Contact upon Blackfoot*

*Culture* (1942) assumes the territoriality of the Blackfoots rather than that of the United States, and thus he looks equally at the different Canadian and American policies on the Indian trade. In so doing, Lewis emphasized how the Blackfoots lived on both sides of the international line, their group identities not exclusively determined by one side or the other.

The most recent examinations of Métis have gone to the greatest lengths to dispel the exclusive nationalist framing in fur trade studies. Such awareness is probably tied to the fact that national borders profoundly shape Métis political identity, given that the Canadian government recognizes the Métis as a distinct Aboriginal group and constitutionally protects their (as yet undefined) rights, while the U.S. government does not.[31] A surge of community studies, including Diane Payment's *"The Free People—Otipemisiwak"* (1990), Pannekoek's *A Snug Little Flock* (1991), Gerhard En's *Homeland to Hinterland* (1996), Nicole St-Onge's *Saint-Laurent* (2004), and Michel Hogue's article in this volume, all illustrate the great variety of the Métis experience and imply that their findings are not restricted to north of the 49th parallel. Worthy of special note for its transcendence of borders, Heather Devine's *The People Who Own Themselves* (2004) illustrates the journey of a Métis family across nations and generations from seventeenth-century France to an Alberta reserve in the twentieth century. Tracing her ancestral genealogy, Devine chronicles 250 years of border-crossing by the Desjarlais family. By the same token, this family journey in time and space also illustrates the historicity of borders as they disappear and morph into new political boundaries and internal borders within the nation. The Desjarlais traveled from early modern France to the St. Lawrence Valley under the French regime, to colonial Louisiana, St. Louis, the Missouri region, the American Southwest, the Red River settlement, and finally to the reserves of the central Albertan Plains.

Despite recent work in ethnohistory and indigenous studies, much of the scholarship on the fur trade has been indirectly but profoundly shaped by national borders. Scholars based in Canada have featured the fur trade as the conception of the Canadian dominion, rooted in a mercantilist economy of resource extraction on the edges of empire, while scholars based in the United States have dismissed the fur trade as a small stumble on the path of the inexorable tsunami of republican civilization. The reduction of the multi-scaled topic of the fur trade to solely national narra-

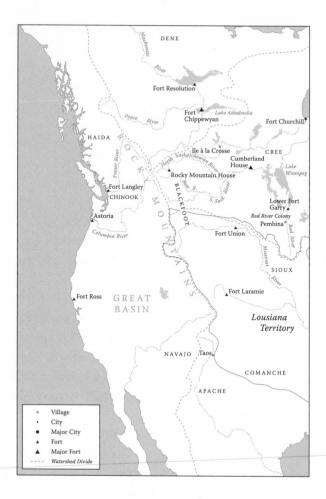

Map legend:

- ○ Village
- · City
- ● Major City
- ▴ Fort
- ▲ Major Fort
- ---- Watershed Divide

tives reflects the central focus on the nation-state within the production of history. But, as we shall see in the following section, scholars who have been particularly sensitive to the geographic organization of the fur trade have provided models for overcoming this form of nationalism. The fur trade as a historical subject provides an excellent model for thinking in more capacious and contingent terms about the many layers and scales of historical borders within which people interact, including but not exclusive to national borders.

## Storied Landscapes

Nature, culture, and time all colluded in the formation of particular historical fur trade landscapes. On the most primary level, environmental

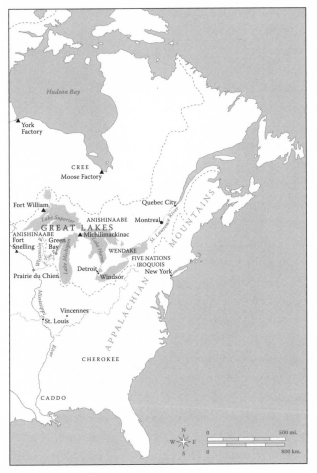

**Map 1.**
Geographies of
the fur trade. (Map
by Ezra Zeitler)

conditions gave shape to economic and social spaces dedicated to the
hunting and preparation of wild animal skins and furs. Many natural
factors collectively contributed to the peculiarities and advantages of different fur trade regions, including geomorphology, geology, biology, lati-
tude, altitude, and climate. For example, it is no accident that the beaver
fur trade spread along waterways in boreal forests. Not only were rivers
and streams important for human travel, but beavers inhabited water
courses bordered by forests or areas with ample deciduous trees and
shrubs. Arthur Ray early on highlighted the importance of the physical
characteristics of landscape when exploring Aboriginal and European encounters in *Indians in the Fur Trade* (1974). In a more recent study, Theodore Binnema's *Common and Contested Ground* (2001) grants the envi-

ronment equal and interdependent subject status with the human population in the history of the Northwestern Plains.[32]

Aboriginal notions of territoriality also prefigured and fundamentally shaped fur trade landscapes. Jacqueline Peterson and John Afinson observe that "the fur trade, properly phrased, was an 'Indian trade,' and the many new trading landscapes that European-descent and native people formed either originated in or were inflected by older Aboriginal ways of thinking about territory."[33] Indian geographies spoke of histories stretching back to ancient periods of North America, and of social dynamism propelled by shifting tribal identities, alliances, trade routes, kinship ties, and migrations. Helen Tanner has shown how Native trading networks linked together most of North America well before Europeans arrived on the continent: these "major trade routes of North America" ran along "the waterways, supplemented by footpaths through river valleys, across portages and mountain passes, and along ridges and bluffs of rugged terrain. The largest communication system covered the Mississippi River valley, embracing all the territory between the Appalachian Mountains and the Rockies."[34]

The crisscrossing networks of Native North American exchanges reflected conceptions of territoriality markedly different from the property-based notions of nation-states. Instead, as Jeanne Kay and Patricia Albers have demonstrated, networks of social relations as well as different sorts of usages premised Native construction of territory. In other words, Indian peoples defined a territory according to both relations among the groups who lived there and the social activities carried out within a place. Neutral territory, exclusive and shared hunting grounds and farmland, multivillage regions, sacred ceremonial sites, and ancestral burial grounds all described specific relationships and undertakings—such as alliances, hereditary enemies, labor, kinship, and worship.[35] Such a conception of territoriality defined by associations produced spaces that were by nature changeable and fluid, rather than permanent or fixed. The historian Colin Calloway, for example, explains that counter to the delimiting and permanent or fixed geometry of European mapping, Native maps "did not rely on fixed points within a bounded space, but on patterns of intersecting lines."[36] Similarly, Keith Goulet, a Cree from northern Saskatchewan, has explored this conceptual difference between territory as a separate or alienated object versus territory as embodying animate social relationships and activity/use. Goulet points out that European nations and cartographers were unlike the Crees, because they created and drew boundaries, borders, and lines on maps that defined their claims, company territories, and empires. In contrast, Crees saw their communities as open-ended, not contained by defined edges. Centralized core settlements were surrounded by villages and hunting camps, which spread out along waterways and into the bush until they touched the resources used by others.[37]

These tangible matters of social relations and usage that distinguished and defined Native spaces reflected root epistemologies structuring all parts of their cultural and material lives.[38] Conceptions of territoriality constitute ideological maps of a society's cultural logic and social identity. The anthropologist Keith Basso, for example, has shown comprehensive ties between territoriality and culture at all levels of Apache consciousness, asserting that "Apache conceptions of land reach deeply into other cultural spheres, including conceptions of wisdom, notions of morality, politeness and tact in forms of spoken discourse, and certain conventional ways of imagining and interpreting the Apache tribal past."[39] Alfred Jacob Miller's painting "The Rendezvous Near Green River, Oregon" gives us a hint of the rich communities and trading patterns Euro-American fur traders would have encountered on the Northwest Great Plains.

As European colonials formed trading economies with Aboriginal peoples, they gave shape to new local geographies that, while built on prior Aboriginal ideas of territoriality, also were distinct from them. Kay and Albers have outlined the main factors that generated a fur trade territoriality in and around Indian lands. First, a profit-driven international market for furs fostered competition over and circulation of trade goods, which led to shifting relations among neighboring tribal groups and between Native peoples and European American traders. Aboriginal communities closest to European colonies, settlements, and trading posts often became middlemen in the trade, especially when local fur-bearing animals became extinct, and reoriented their economies and alliances to funneling furs and trade goods between the continental interior and European mercantilist centers, as did the Wendats (Hurons) trading with French Canadians and the "Homeguard Cree" (as they came to be known) trading with the Hudson's Bay Company. Second, trading entrepôts drew together different trading peoples. Tribes from widely scattered regions

**Figure 1.** "The Rendezvous near Green River, Oregon / Rendez-vous près de la rivière Verte, dans l'Oregon," by Alfred Jacob Miller, 1867. (Library and Archives Canada, Acc. 1946-146-1, Repro. c-000439. Gift of Mrs. J. B. Jardine)

came together at European centers, such as Montreal, Michilimackinac, and Grand Portage, to trade with the Europeans and with each other. In the Pacific Northwest a pidgeon language called Chinook Jargon emerged from the medley of languages that met in the trade. Third, ethnically mixed villages reoriented social relations and social spaces within Indian country.[40] In places like Prairie du Chien in Wisconsin, Pembina in North Dakota, and Ile à la Crosse in Saskatchewan, the meeting of diverse peoples and their mixed-heritage offspring led to new communities that developed their own alliances, material culture, and even language (such as Michif) distinct from the Aboriginal societies all around them.

Driven by transnational political and economic forces at one end of the spectrum and the vagaries of local politics and European-Indian exchanges at the other, the North American fur trade operated simultaneously on multiple planes.[41] When speaking of fur trade geographies, therefore, one has to distinguish among many spatial scopes that ranged from macro views of global and hemispheric-wide economies to discrete company geographies that contributed to the shape of regional and local trading realms. The broad canvases of global and hemispheric views of the fur trade challenge the too common tendency to see everything in terms of discrete nation-states. A global perspective displays the pattern of international economy and trade, highlighting the spread of mercantile capitalism and the connections among people separated by vast distances and vastly different cosmologies. This approach has appealed particularly to historians of empire and to those developing an Atlantic world paradigm.[42] Narrowing from the global to hemispheric perspective renders a fur trade geography encompassing the whole of North America, or the northern Atlantic world, depending on orientation. Viewing how the trade operated across North America or the northern Atlantic as a whole promotes comparative analysis of European exploitation of North American resources, and of the continental and oceanic trading patterns of both European merchants and Native peoples. Although few scholars have taken such a large-scale approach, it is a promising line of inquiry to destabilize nationalist and single-nation imperial perspectives.[43]

Contracting from the hemispheric, one encounters the most common frame within North American fur trade historiography: the regions within which different fur trade companies operated. Both French and British imperial administrations tried to control the movement and spheres of fur trade ventures in North America, in keeping with the rules of mercantilism. For example, by a royal charter of 1670, the Hudson's Bay Company acquired trading rights to all lands draining into Hudson Bay, a vast area that encompassed the homelands of most Subarctic peoples, many Woodlands peoples, and some Plains peoples. With a British monopoly over former French and Dutch fur trade regions by the end of the French and Indian War (1763), however, the Hudson's Bay Company's declared jurisdiction on paper meant little to competing British and Anglo-American companies. The North West Company, the Hudson's Bay Company's greatest rival before their merger in 1821, held no charter but, rather, aggressively sought trading relationships with Aboriginal people and established its posts along major waterways, notably the Great Lakes, Lake Winnipeg, Lake Athabasca, and the St. Lawrence, Saskatchewan, Red, Mississippi, Missouri, Peace, and Columbia rivers. Leading up to and after the War of 1812, the New Yorker John Jacob Astor's American Fur Company, as well as his short-lived Pacific Fur Company, attempted to seize the fur trade south of the northern American boundary. The success of companies' geographic ambitions, however, also depended to a large extent on the material factor of available travel routes, rather than abstract thoughts about national boundaries; the most common means was the canoe, but as the nineteenth century progressed, the fur trade relied more and more on York boats, sloops, horse trails, and Red River cart trails. The

**Figure 2.** "Hudson's Bay Company Canoe—Nipigon River (Ontario)," by Frederick Arthur Verner, 1900. (Library and Archives Canada, Repro. c-094104)

territories of each of the above-mentioned companies shifted with the depletion of fur-bearing animals; they engaged in an ongoing and mobile competition along waterways and Aboriginal trails into new regions still rich in furs. Frederick Arthur Verner's painting "Hudson's Bay Company Canoe" illustrates the smallest scale of trading—trading without even leaving one's canoe.

All of the above fur trade geographies, like a Russian nesting doll, blended into the next toward the decentralized base of action of the trading posts. Post life was enacted locally, both within the post communities and among neighboring posts and Aboriginal communities.[44] The size of the post and its consequence in the trade determined its impact on the surrounding areas; important posts had higher European populations and a greater impact on the landscape and surrounding societies, while smaller posts left a fainter imprint. European traders attempted to control their small world within fur trade posts. The immediate interests of European colonial offices and American federal agencies governing empire differed substantially from those of fur trade businessmen in Montreal or New York, and from the men contracted to transport furs and goods, work at the posts, and collect furs directly from Aboriginal trappers. Living in Indian homelands, traders formed familiar Europeanized safe spaces for themselves in the face of the demographic dominance and cultural differences of their Native hosts. In Cole Harris's words, they created "islands of relative security" by setting up defense systems, such as palisades. This stark geography imposed by the European traders "was a minimal construction of nodes and circuits intended to facilitate trade in an isolated corner of the world, and to make connections to distant managers and markets."[45]

Aboriginal communities remained self-governing in these fur trade landscapes, and it was company men at isolated posts who depended on their Indian neighbors and exchange partners for meat, fish, produce, gum for their canoes, guidance, and protection. European and Euro-American traders also established unions of different lengths with Native women, giving rise to a mixed-race population within the fur trade that further complicated the pulls of localized interests shaping an area. The immediate and contingent politics of community that determine how people inhabit places was, in the open-ended sphere of trading posts and Indian villages, a many-headed phenomenon. As Jennifer S. H. Brown has elaborated, "the trade was built upon and spawned a broad spectrum of Aboriginal, mixed, and newcomer communities that related with one another in diverse, complex ways that changed over time."[46] Moreover, these multiple, interacting communities were mobile and seasonal. Trading posts, often distant from each other, represented points of conflict, exchange, and social activity within otherwise decentralized and centrifugal trading worlds. It was here, at the local level, that the diverse peoples of the fur trade chose whether and how to accommodate to changing imperial, national, and company boundaries. The fluid and varied notions of space and place allowed those in the fur trade to configure ideas about race in novel and unexpected ways. One of the most unusual expressions of this fluidity was freemen who, on leaving the fur trade service, remained in fur trade territory without joining Aboriginal communities. These men lived either independently or in small, mobile communities of like-minded souls, eking out a living from a variety of economic strategies that could include trapping, trading, hunting, fishing, gathering, farming, and small-scale manufacturing of pemmican, canoes, moccasins, and other necessities of fur trade life. Undoubtedly, some freemen and their Native wives became the proto-generation of Métis, but others developed distinct communities—places and ways of using space that did not make their way into the historical record and did not survive the exigencies of time.

## The Limits of National Histories

Although the shadow of the nation-state frames a great deal of the American and Canadian fur trade historiographies over the past century, the subject itself defies easy compartmentalization to a single dynamic, like national or imperial politics. The North American fur trade is an umbrella term referring to a myriad of historically and geographically specific, localized exchange economies, which brought together Europeans, Euro-Americans, and Aboriginal peoples and fostered dynamic social, economic, and political relationships among them. Additionally, the fur trade operated along many spatial levels often simultaneously—global, hemispheric, national, regional, central trading towns, rendezvous sites, local company posts, and Indian camps. Because the fur trade encompassed such a wide spectrum of geographic spheres, and because it involved culturally and politically diverse peoples with alternative identities to national ones, it stands as a critique of the limitations of national histories. The North American fur trade illustrates the nuanced and multiple ways that people inhabited and formed their histories in spaces not exclusively and sometimes not at all shaped by the dynamics of the nation-state.

Nations tend to create centripetal forces in their societies, drawing people together into a common identity. National identities express the fictive kinship of people in the interior of a state, not at the edges, and state borders reinforce the distinctiveness of that interior from its neighbors. The fur trade operated along multiple layers of interconnected spaces that included national boundaries but also expanded into international capitalist networks and transnational trading companies, and narrowed to culturally counter-national spaces at the regional and local levels. Thus, pre-existing physical and Aboriginal geographies, commercial interests, local dynamics surrounding fur trade posts, and new kin ties all pulled against nationalist forces. Indeed, the North American fur trade fostered open-ended cultural constructions as European, Euro-American, mixed-race, and Native people accommodated, adopted, created, and resisted cultural change to varying degrees and formed a diverse range of communities and associations. Nonetheless, the diverging paths of historiography of the fur trade on either side of the Canada-U.S. border clearly show how nationalist consciousnesses has circumscribed historical interpretation despite innovative ethnohistorical approaches and a much better sense of the reflexive, progressive teleology of nation-state-centered histories. This article seeks to remind historians that history need not be teleological. Territoriality and situated identities in North America must be studied as though the creation of the American and Canadian nations and the border between them did not exist—that is, right up until the point when they did come into being. Even after that point, a wide variety of dynamics beyond governmental assertions constructed the historically contingent and multiple understandings of borders among culturally and politically diverse populations in both Canada and the United States. It is time to shatter the glass curtain.

## Notes

1. See Turgeon, "Le temps des pêches lointaines"; and Pope, "The Practice of Portage in the Early Modern North Atlantic."
2. The strongest counter to nationalist biases in fur trade historiography are the published proceedings of the first eight North American Fur Trade Conferences. See Morgan et al., *Aspects of the Fur Trade*; Bolus, *People and Pelts*; Judd and Ray, *Old Trails and New Directions*; Buckley, *Rendezvous*; Trigger, Morantz, and Dechene, *Le Castor Fait Tout*; Brown, Eccles, and Heldman, *The Fur Trade Revisited*; Fiske, Sleeper-Smith, and Wicken, *New Faces of the Fur Trade*; and Johnson, *Aboriginal People and the Fur Trade*. Rhoda Gilman and Carolyn Gilman provided a superb recounting of these conferences and a description of these proceedings in a keynote address at the Ninth North American Fur Trade Conference in St. Louis in May 2006.
3. Calloway, *One Vast Winter Count*, 7–17.
4. See McCoy, *The Elusive Republic*, for a discussion of this romantic view of the yeoman farmer.
5. Irving, *Three Western Narratives*, 629.
6. Irving explained in his introduction to *The Adventures of Captain Bonneville* that Bonneville had attempted to write up his memoirs, producing a "mass of manuscript, which he subsequently put at my [Irving's] disposal, to fit it for publication and bring it before the world" (see Irving, *Three Western Narratives*, 632).
7. Irving, *Three Western Narratives*, 179.
8. Ibid., 180, 183.
9. Turner, *The Character and Influence of the Indian Trade in Wisconsin*, 558.
10. In *Regeneration through Violence*, Richard Slotkin makes the distinction between Euro-Americans who adopted Native customs, dress, language, etc. and lived among Indian peoples, and Native people themselves. Characters

like Daniel Boone could and did return to "civilized" life after a time. At the same time, in his article "Neither White nor Red," Colin Calloway has explored how the nineteenth-century U.S. literary descriptor of "renegade" referred to "someone who abandoned white society to live with Indians" (43). In both cases, a subtle distinction is implied between Euro-American savagery and Indian "savagery."

11. Clifford, *Routes*, 329. Nearly thirty years ago, the Western historian Howard R. Lamar challenged American historians to stop letting national myths direct their interpretation of the fur trade. More specifically, he argued that traders and trappers are "myth's victim," maintaining that frontier historians "have neglected a dual tradition of trade and mercantile capitalism by overstressing the mythic figures of explorers, pioneers and settlers." Lamar cogently attacked the prevailing belief among historians that the fur trade had been a temporary phenomenon that had quickly receded, by showing that there had been an extremely long history of North American exchange economies, stretching back to a prehistoric trade among Indian peoples and later encompassing Indian-European trading networks that flourished from 1600 to 1850. Moreover, far from disappearing by 1850, Euro-American traders and trappers merely diversified into any range of capitalist endeavors, becoming merchandisers or hostelers after animal supplies dwindled and federal authorities segregated their Indian partners on reservations. See Lamar, *The Trader on the American Frontier* (quote on 17).

12. Greenbie, *Furs to Furrows*, 2.

13. Cleland, *This Reckless Breed of Men*, 5.

14. O'Meara, *Daughters of the Country*, 8.

15. To offer a few more examples of this pervasive interpretation of fur traders as "pathfinders and precursors": historian Nathaniel Hale succinctly captured the distinctive value of the fur trade in the progress of European-descent settlement of North America by arguing that the trade had "sustained the colonies along the Atlantic seaboard until they could be rooted in agriculture," and that it was "a controlling factor in the westward movement of our population" (see Hale, *Pelts and Palisades*, vii). More recently, Michael Golay collapses earlier distinctions between self-interested fur traders and those early adventurers/pathbreakers who presumed more selfless aims, and celebrates "the transformational power of American energy" in the push wrought by individual traders, missionaries, and explorers for an American empire in the Pacific Northwest (see Golay, *The Tide of Empire*, xiii).

16. Duara, *Rescuing History from the Nation*, 27.

17. Likewise, Quebec historians portraying New France as the golden age of French Canadian independence pair agriculture and the fur trade as twin economic pillars to the success of the colony, but debate the relative impor-

tance of each. The influence of Quebec nationalism on fur trade historiography, and more broadly on the writing of Quebec history, has a long and complex history and is outside the parameters of this essay. The rupture of the Conquest, and the replacement of one colonial regime with another, created distinct patterns in the imagining of a national history, and the place of the fur trade within it, that deserve a detailed study not possible in the confines of this volume. For recent work on nationalism and historiography in Quebec, see Rudin, *Making History in Twentieth-Century Quebec*; and Fecteau, "Between Scientific Enquiry and the Search for a Nation," 641–86.

18. *Dictionary of Canadian Biography Online*, s.v. "Ross, Alexander," by Fritz Pannekoek, http://www.biographi.ca/009004-119.01-e.php?&id_nbr=4167 &interval=25&&PHPSESSID=ckq5ieaokql75cg27ln2viks67.

19. For a detailed examination of the historiography of Manitoba history, see Bumsted, "The Quest for a Usable Founder."

20. Innis, *The Fur Trade in Canada*, 393.

21. Innis has been the focus for much historiographical and cultural commentary, most recently in the Acland and Buxton, *Harold Innis in the New Century*.

22. Thomas, "Historiography of the Fur Trade Era"; see also Payne, "Fur Trade Historiography."

23. See Judd, "Native Labour and Social Stratification in the Hudson's Bay Company's Northern Department"; Swagerty and Wilson, "Faithful Service under Different Flags"; Nicks, "Orkneymen in the HBC"; Skinner, "The Sinews of Empire"; Burley, *Servants of the Honourable Company*; Podruchny, *Making the Voyageur World*; Allaire, "Les engagements pour la traite des fourrures"; Allaire, "Fur Trade Engages"; Dechêne, *Habitants and Merchants in Seventeenth-Century Montreal*, 117–24; Greer, "Fur-Trade Labour and Lower Canadian Agrarian Structures"; Grabowski and St.-Onge, "Montreal Iroquois Engagés in the Western Fur Trade"; Nicks, "The Iroquois and Fur Trade in Western Canada"; and Karamanski, "The Iroquois and the Fur Trade of the Far West."

24. See Fisher, *Contact and Conflict*; Francis and Mortantz, *Partners in Furs*; and Thistle, *Indian-European Trade Relations in the Lower Saskatchewan River Region to 1840*. For historiographical articles exploring the work on Indians in the fur trade, see Tanner, "The End of Fur Trade History"; and Peterson and Anfinson, "The Indian in the Fur Trade."

25. For a few examples, see Merrell, *The Indians' New World*; Usner, *Indians, Settlers, and Slaves in a Frontier Exchange Economy*; Norton, *The Fur Trade in Colonial New York*; Merchant, *Ecological Revolutions*; and Merwick, *Possessing Albany*.

26. For bibliographies on much of this literature, see Barkwell, Dorion, and Préfontaine, *Metis Legacy*, 273–505; and Pannekoek, "Metis Studies."

27. Thorne, *The Many Hands of My Relations*, 9.

28. Payne, "Fur Trade Social History and the Public Historian," 482.

29. For their mandate, see the Parks Canada Web site, http://www.pc.gc.ca/agen/index_E.asp.

30. For further discussion of counter-national identities, see Clifford, *Routes*, chapter 12, "Fort Ross Meditation," 299–348; and Lloyd, "Nationalisms against the State," 173–98.

31. Trends in Métis historiography are outlined in Pannekoek, "Metis Studies."

32. This tradition has been carried on by Victor Lytwyn (see *The Fur Trade of the Little North*) and Cole Harris (*The Resettlement of British Columbia*).

33. Peterson and Afinson, "The Indian and the Fur Trade," 1.

34. Tanner, *The Settling of North America*, 28–29.

35. Albers and Kay, "Sharing the Land."

36. Calloway, *One Vast Winter Count*, 11.

37. Goulet, "The Cumberland Cree Nehinuw Concept of Land."

38. E.g., Keith Goulet is writing his doctoral dissertation at the University of Regina on Cree Nehinuw concepts of land, exploring how animate and inanimate objects shaped the way people viewed land. The idea of "root epistemologies" of cultures originates from Marilyn Strathern, *The Gender of the Gift*.

39. Basso, *Wisdom Sits in Places*, xv.

40. Albers and Kay, "Sharing the Land."

41. For a similar way of conceptualizing landscape as "spaces of power," see Mann, *The Sources of Social Power*, 1:1–33; and Mancke, "Spaces of Power in the Early Modern Northeast."

42. See, e.g., Eccles, "The Fur Trade and Eighteenth-Century Imperialism"; and Bailyn, "The Idea of Atlantic History."

43. A good example of a hemispheric approach to colonial history is Greer and Bilinkoff, *Colonial Saints*.

44. For a couple of examples of studies of individual posts, see Parker, *Emporium of the North*; and Mitchell, *Fort Timiskaming and the Fur Trade*.

45. Harris, *The Resettlement of British Columbia*, 32–42 (quotes on 34, 42).

46. Brown, "Noms et métaphores dans l'historiographie métisse." Brown's translation, personal communication.

# BIBLIOGRAPHY

..........................................

## Archival Collections

CANADA

British Columbia Provincial Archives, Victoria (BC Archives)
    GR-0435: Department of Fisheries Records
    GR-0446: Provincial Game Warden Records
    GR-1378: Commercial Fisheries Branch Records
    Library and Archives Canada, Ottawa (LAC)
    Record Group 10: Records of the Department of Indian Affairs
        Black (Western) Series
    Record Group 13: Records of the Department of Justice
    Record Group 15: Records of the Department of the Interior
        Dominion Lands Branch Files
    Record Group 23: Records of the Department of Fisheries and Oceans
    Record Group 76: Records of the Department of Employment and
    Immigration
Provincial Archives of Manitoba (PAM)
    Adams George Archibald Papers
    Alexander Morris Papers
Saint-Boniface Historical Society, Saint Boniface, Manitoba (SBSH)
    Roman Catholic Archdiocese of Saint-Boniface, Alexandre-Antonin Taché
    Papers
Saskatchewan Archives Board, Regina, Saskatchewan
    Musée de Willow Bunch Papers
University of British Columbia Special Collections, Vancouver (UBC)
    International Pacific Salmon Fisheries Commission Collection (IPSFC)

MEXICO

Archivo General del Estado de Nuevo León, Monterrey
    Estadísticas, Montemorelos
Archivo General del Estado de Sonora, Hermosillo, Sonora

UNITED STATES

Academy of Motion Picture Arts and Sciences, Margaret Herrick Library, Beverly
Hills, California (AMPAS)
Motion Picture Association of America, Production Code Administration
Records (MPAA/PCA)
Arizona Historical Society–Southern Arizona Division, Tucson, Arizona
(AHS–SAD)
Bernice Cosulich Papers
Slaughter Financial Papers
Autry National Center of the American West, Los Angeles, California
Mexican Postcard Collection
Beinecke Rare Book and Manuscript Library, Yale University, New Haven,
Connecticut
James Weldon Johnson Collection in the Yale Collection of American
Literature
Mifflin Wistar Gibbs Papers concerning Victoria, British Columbia
Western Americana Collection
Samuel Anderson Papers
G. Clinton Gardner Papers
George Gibbs Notebooks of Scientific Observations of the Pacific North-
west
Joseph Smith Harris Papers
Van Bokkelen, John J. H., Letter to the Honorable James Douglas,
17 January 1856
Center for Pacific Northwest Studies, Western Washington University,
Bellingham
Alaska Packers' Association Collection
Daughters of the Republic of Texas Library, San Antonio, Texas
James Lincoln Papers
DeGolyer Library, Southern Methodist University, Dallas, Texas
Tourist Album, Mexico, 1925
Gates Tours brochures, 1896, 1904, 1907, and 1911
Library of Congress, Prints and Photographs Division, Washington, D.C.
"Visit Mexico" (poster)
Mandeville Special Collections Library, University of California, San Diego
Denton Ranch Collection
Tijuana Photograph Postcard Collection
Montana Historical Society Research Center, Helena (MHS)
William W. Alderson papers

Thomas J. Bogy Diary
Merrill G. Burlingame Writings, 1803–1938
Ben Kline Reminiscence
Samuel O'Connell Papers
National Archives and Records Administration, College Park, Maryland
(NARA II)
    Record Group 76: Records of the United States–Mexico Claims
    Commission
National Archives and Records Administration, Washington, D.C. (NARA I)
    Record Group 26: Records of the U.S. Coast Guard
        Records of the Revenue Cutter Service and its Predecessors
    Record Group 59: Records of the U.S. Department of State
        Microfilm M165: Consular Dispatches, Monterrey, 1849–1906
        Microfilm M283: Despatches from United States Consul in Nogales,
        1889–1906
    Record Group 75: Records of the Bureau of Indian Affairs
        Microfilm M234: Letters Received by the Office of Indian Affairs
    Record Group 85: Records of the Immigration and Naturalization Service
        Microfilm 8555: Series A, Subject Correspondence Files, pt. 2, Mexican
        Immigration, 1906–30
    Record Group 94: Records of the Adjutant General's Office
        Microfilm M666: Letters Received by the Adjutant General's Office
        (Main Series), 1871–80
National Archives and Records Administration, Pacific Alaska Region, Seattle
    Record Group 36: Records of the U.S. Customs Service
        Letters to the Secretary of the Treasury, 1898–99, Puget Sound Collec-
        tion District
National Archives and Records Administration, Rocky Mountain Region, Denver
    Record Group 75: Records of the Bureau of Indian Affairs
        Records of the Fort Belknap Indian Agency
Pimeria Alta Historical Society, Nogales, Arizona (PAHS)
    Ephemera Files
San Diego Historical Society, San Diego, California
    Oral History Collection
        Lester G. Bradley interview
Sherman Library, Corona Del Mar, California (SL)
    Colorado River Land Company Papers (CRLC Papers)
University of Arizona, Special Collections, Tucson (UASC)
    Francis Henry Hereford Papers
    San Rafael Cattle Company Papers (SRCC Papers)

University of California, Los Angeles, University Research Library, Department
    of Special Collections
        Collection of California Fruit Labels, ca. 1905–49
        Collection of Mexican Postcards, 1899–1933
University of Texas, Austin
    Benson Latin American Collection
        Presbyterian Church in the United States of America, Board of Foreign
        Missions, Correspondence and Reports, 1833–1911
    Center for American History
        Gilbert Kingsbury Papers and Memoirs
        J. B. Lacoste Papers
        John Twohig Papers
        John Z. Leyendecker Papers
        Joseph Kleiber Papers
        Matamoros Archives
University of Washington Libraries, Special Collections, Seattle (uw Libraries)
    John Pease Babcock Papers
Canada Department of Marine and Fisheries, Correspondence Incoming
    Miller Freeman Papers
    Microfiche T2701–27: Marine Hospital Annual Reports, 1874–1912, cis
    U.S. Exec Branch Microfiche T-2701–27
    Microfilm A171: U.S. Bureau of Indian Affairs, Records of the Washington
    Territory Superintendency of Indian Affairs, 1853–74
    Microfilm A1265: Records Relating to the Northwest Boundary, 1853–1901
    Microfilm A2573: [Author Unknown], *Guidebook to British Columbia*
    James Gilchrist Swan Papers, 1833–1909
Washington State Archives, Olympia (wsa)
    Department of Fisheries, Administration (dfa)
    Governor Clarence Martin Papers
        Subject Files
    Governor Louis Hart Papers
        Subject Files

## Filmography

*An Adventure on the Mexican Border*. Directed by Romaine Fielding. General Film
    Co., 1913.
*Arizona Badman*. Directed by S. Roy Luby. State Rights, 1935.
*Arizona Gang Busters*. Directed by Peter Stewart. Producers Releasing Corp.,
    1940.
*The Avenger*. Directed by Roy William Neill. Columbia Pictures Corp., 1931.

*The Barrier*. Directed by Edgar Lewis. State Rights, 1917.

*The Barrier*. Directed by George Hill. Metro–Goldwyn–Mayer Distributing Corp., 1926.

*The Barrier*. Directed by Lesley Selander. Paramount Pictures, Inc., 1937.

*Below the Border*. Directed by Howard P. Bretherton. Monogram Pictures Corp., 1942.

*Beyond the Rockies*. Directed by Fred Allen. RKO Pathé Pictures Inc., 1932.

*The Bold Caballero*. Directed by Wells Root. Republic Pictures Corp., 1936.

*Border Brigands*. Directed by Nick Grinde. Universal Pictures Corp., 1935.

*Border Caballero*. Directed by Sam Newfield. Puritan Pictures Corp., 1936.

*Border G-Man*. Directed by David Howard. RKO Radio Pictures, Inc., 1938.

*Border Justice*. Directed by B. Reeves Eason. Independent Pictures Corp., 1925.

*Border Law*. Directed by Louis King. Columbia Pictures Corp., 1931.

*The Border Patrolman*. Directed by David Howard. Principal Productions, Inc.; Twentieth Century–Fox Film Corp., 1936.

*Border Phantom*. Directed by S. Roy Luby. Republic Pictures Corp., 1936.

*The Border Wireless*. Directed by William S. Hart. Famous Players–Lasky Corp.; Artcraft Pictures, 1918.

*Borderland*. Directed by Nate Watt. Paramount Pictures, Inc., 1937.

*The Brand of Cowardice*. Directed by John W. Noble. Metro Pictures Corp., 1916.

*The Call of the North*. Directed by Oscar Apfel. State Rights, 1914.

*Captains of the Clouds*. Directed by Michael Curtiz. Warner Bros. Pictures, Inc., 1942.

*Captured by Mexicans*. General Film Co., 1914.

*The Cattle Thieves*. Kalem Co., 1909.

*The Challenge of the Law*. Directed by Scott Dunlap. Fox Film Corp., 1920.

*Channing of the Northwest*. Directed by Ralph Ince. Select Pictures, 1922.

*The Cisco Kid*. Directed by Irving Cummings. Fox Film Corp., 1931.

*The Cisco Kid and the Lady*. Directed by Herbert I. Leeds. Twentieth Century–Fox Film Corp., 1939.

*The Clod*. Directed by Romaine Fielding. General Film Co., 1913.

*Corvette K-225*. Directed by Richard Rosson. Universal Pictures Co., Inc., 1943.

*Criminals of the Air*. Directed by C. C. Coleman Jr. Columbia Pictures Corp. of California, Ltd., 1937.

*'Cross the Mexican Line*. Universal Film Mfg. Co., 1914.

*The Cyclone Ranger*. Directed by Bob Hill. Spectrum Pictures Corp.; State Rights, 1935.

*Death Rides the Range*. Directed by Sam Newfield. State Rights, 1940.

*Don Q, Son of Zorro*. Directed by Donald Crisp. United Artists Corp., 1925.

*Down on the Rio Grande*. Directed by Wilbert Melville. General Film Co., 1913.

*El Diablo Rides*. Directed by Ira S. Webb. State Rights, 1939.

*The Fight for Freedom: A Story of the Arid Southwest*. Directed by D. W. Griffith. American Mutoscope and Biograph Co., 1908.

*Fighting Mad*. Directed by Sam Newfield. Monogram Pictures Corp., 1939.

*The Gay Caballero*. Directed by Otto Brower. Twentieth Century–Fox Film Corp., 1940.

*The Gay Defender*. Directed by Gregory La Cava. Paramount Famous Lasky Corp., 1927.

*A Girl Spy in Mexico*. Directed by Romaine Fielding. General Film Co., 1913.

*God's Country and the Man*. Directed by J. P. McCarthy. State Rights; Syndicate Pictures Corp., 1931.

*The Grandee's Ring*. Picture Playhouse Film Co., 1915.

*The Greaser's Gauntlet*. Directed by D. W. Griffith. American Mutoscope and Biograph Co., 1908.

*Hair-Trigger Casey*. Directed by Harry Fraser. Atlantic Pictures Corp., 1936.

*Hands Across the Border*. Directed by David Kirkland. Film Booking Offices of America, 1926.

*Heléne of the North*. Directed by J. Searle Dawley. Paramount Pictures Corp., 1915.

*Her Husband's Trademark*. Directed by Sam Wood. Paramount Pictures, 1922.

*In Defiance of the Law*. Directed by Colin Campbell. General Film Co., 1914.

*In Old Arizona*. Selig Polyscope Co., 1909.

*In Old Arizona*. Directed by Raoul Walsh. Fox Film Corp., 1929.

*In the Great Northwest*. Selig Polyscope Co., 1910.

*In the North Woods*. Directed by D. W. Griffith. Biograph Co., 1912.

*The Indian Scout's Vengeance*. Kalem Co., 1909.

*The Ingrate: A Tale of the North Woods*. Directed by D. W. Griffith. American Mutoscope and Biograph Co., 1908.

*Keith of the Border*. Directed by Clifford Smith. Triangle Distributing Corp., 1918.

*Land of the Six Guns*. Directed by Raymond K. Johnson. Monogram Pictures Corp., 1940.

*The Law of the Great Northwest*. Directed by Raymond Wells. Triangle Distributing Corp., 1918.

*Lieutenant Danny U.S.A.* Directed by Walter Edwards. Triangle Film Corp., 1916.

*The Lone Defender*. Directed by Richard Thorpe. State Rights, 1934.

*The Mark of Zorro*. Directed by Fred Niblo. United Artists Corp., 1920.

*The Mark of Zorro*. Directed by Rouben Mamoulian. Twentieth Century–Fox Film Corp., 1940.

*The Mexican Revolutionist*. Directed by Wilbert Melville. General Film Co., 1912.

*The Mexican Spy*. Directed by Wilbert Melville. General Film Co., 1913.

*A Mexican Tragedy*. Directed by Wilbert Melville. General Film Co., 1913.

*The Mexican's Last Raid*. Universal Film Mfg. Co., 1914.

*Northern Pursuit*. Directed by Raoul Walsh. Warner Bros. Pictures, Inc., 1943.

*Oklahoma Cyclone.* Directed by J. P. McCarthy. Tiffany Productions, 1930.

*O'Malley of the Mounted.* Directed by David Howard. Twentieth Century–Fox
    Film Corp., 1936.

*On the Border.* Selig Polyscope Co., 1909.

*On the Border.* Directed by William McGann. Warner Bros. Pictures, Inc., 1930.

*Out of the Snows.* Directed by Ralph Ince. Select Pictures Corp., 1920.

*Over the Border.* Directed by Penrhyn Stanlaws. Famous Players–Lasky Corp.,
    1922.

*Pals of the Saddle.* Directed by George Sherman. Republic Pictures Corp., 1938.

*The Primal Lure.* Directed by William S. Hart. Triangle Film Corp., 1916.

*Pure Grit.* Directed by Nat Ross. Universal Pictures, 1923.

*Quicksands.* Directed by Jack Conway. American Releasing Corp.; Paramount
    Famous Lasky Corp., 1923.

*Ramona: A Story of the White Man's Injustice to the Indian.* Directed by D. W.
    Griffith. Bioscope Co., 1910.

*Ramona.* Directed by Donald Crisp. State Rights, 1916.

*Ramona.* Directed by Edwin Carewe. United Artists Corp., 1928.

*Ramona.* Directed by Henry King. Twentieth Century–Fox Film Corp., 1936.

*The Ranger and the Girl.* Lubin Mfg. Co., 1910.

*The Return of the Cisco Kid.* Directed by Herbert I. Leeds. Twentieth Century–Fox
    Film Corp., 1939.

*Roarin' Broncs.* Directed by Richard Thorpe. Pathé Exchange, Inc., 1927.

*Robin Hood of El Dorado.* Directed by William A. Wellman. Loew's, Inc., 1936.

*A Romance of the Fur Country.* S. Lubin, 1908.

*Romance of the Rio Grande.* Directed by Herbert I. Leeds. Twentieth Century–Fox
    Film Corp., 1941.

*The Scarlet Brand.* Directed by J. P. McGowan. Big 4 Film Corp., 1932.

*Secret Service of the Air.* Directed by Noel Smith. Warner Bros. Pictures, Inc.,
    1939.

*Shadows of the Orient.* Directed by Burt Lynnwood. Empire Film Distributors;
    Monogram Pictures Corp., 1937.

*Skull and Crown.* Directed by Elmer Clifton. Reliable Pictures Corp.; State Rights,
    1935.

*Sky High.* Directed by Lynn Reynolds. Fox Film Corp., 1922.

*Soldiers of the Storm.* Directed by D. Ross Lederman. Columbia Pictures Corp.,
    1933.

*South of Northern Lights.* Directed by Neal Hart. William Steiner Productions,
    1922.

*Speed Wild.* Directed by Harry Garson. Film Booking Offices of America, 1925.

*Sunrise Trail.* Directed by J. P. McCarthy. Tiffany Productions, Inc., 1931.

*The Unknown Ranger.* Aywon Film Corp.; State Rights, 1920.

*Until They Get Me.* Directed by Frank Borzage. Triangle Distributing Corp., 1917.

*Unseen Enemy.* Directed by John Rawlins. Universal Pictures Co., Inc., 1942.

*Up and Going.* Directed by Lynn Reynolds. Fox Film Corp., 1922.

*Valley of Hunted Men.* Directed by John English. Republic Pictures Corp., 1942.

*Vengeance of the West.* Directed by Lambert Hillyer. Columbia Pictures Corp., 1942.

*The Web of the Law.* Directed by Tom Gibson. American Releasing Corp., 1923.

*A Woman's Way: A Romance of the Canadian Woods.* Directed by D. W. Griffith. American Mutoscope and Biograph Co., 1908.

## References

Abel, Richard. *Americanizing the Movies and "Movie-Mad" Audiences, 1910–1914.* Berkeley: University of California Press, 2006.

——. *The Red Rooster Scare: Making Cinema American, 1900–1910.* Berkeley: University of California Press, 1999.

Acland, Charles R., and William J. Buxton, eds. *Harold Innis in the New Century.* Montreal: McGill-Queen's University Press, 1999.

Acuna, Rodolfo. *Occupied America: The Chicano's Struggle toward Liberation.* San Francisco: Canfield Press, 1972.

Adelman, Jeremy, and Stephen Aron. "From Borderlands to Borders: Empires, Nation-States, and the Peoples in between in North American History." *American Historical Review* 104, no. 3 (1999): 814–41.

Adler, Judith. "Origins of Sightseeing." *Annals of Tourism Research* 16, no. 1 (1989): 7–29.

Agnew, John. "The Territorial Trap." *Review of International Political Economy* 1, no. 1 (1994): 53–80.

Aguirre, Yjinio F. "The Last of the Dons." *Journal of Arizona History* 10, no. 4 (1969): 239–55.

Albers, Patricia C. "Changing Patterns of Ethnicity in the Northeastern Plains, 1780–1870." In *History, Power, and Identity: Ethnogenesis in the Americas, 1492–1992,* edited by Jonathan D. Hill, 90–118. Iowa City: University of Iowa Press, 1996.

Albers, Patricia, and Jeanne Kay. "Sharing the Land: A Study in American Indian Territoriality." In *A Cultural Geography of North American Indians,* edited by Thomas E. Ross and Tyrel G. Moore, 47–91. Boulder, Colo.: Westview Press, 1987.

Allaire, Gratien. "Fur Trade Engages, 1701–1745." In *Rendezvous: Selected Papers of the Fourth North American Fur Trade Conference,* edited by Thomas C. Buckley, 15–26. St. Paul, Minn.: The Conference, 1984.

——. "Les engagements pour la traite des fourrures: Évaluation de la documentation." *Revue d'Histoire de l'Amérique Française* 34, no. 1 (1980): 3–26.

Almaguer, Tomás. *Racial Fault Lines: The Historical Origins of White Supremacy in California*. Berkeley: University of California Press, 1994.

Alonzo, Juan. "From Derision to Desire: The 'Greaser' in Stephen Crane's Mexican Stories and D. W. Griffith's Early Westerns." *Western American Literature* 38, no. 4 (2004): 374–401.

Álvarez, Robert R. *Familia: Migration and Adaptation in Alta and Baja California, 1800–1975*. Berkeley: University of California Press, 1987.

——. "The Mexican-U.S. Border: The Making of an Anthropology of Borderlands." *Annual Review of Anthropology* 24 (1995): 447–70.

Ames, Kenneth M., and Herbert D. G. Maschner. *Peoples of the Northwest Coast: Their Archaeology and Prehistory*. New York: Thames and Hudson, 1999.

Anderson, Mark C. "What's to Be Done with 'Em?: Images of Mexican Cultural Backwardness, Racial Limitations, and Moral Decrepitude in the United States Press, 1913–1915." *Mexican Studies / Estudios Mexicanos* 14, no. 1 (1998): 23–70.

Anderson, Robert. "The Role of the Western Film Genre in Industry Competition, 1907–1911." *Journal of the University Film Association* 31, no. 2 (1970): 19–26.

Andreas, Peter. *Border Games: Policing the U.S.-Mexico Divide*. Ithaca, N.Y.: Cornell University Press, 2000.

Anzaldúa, Gloria. *Borderlands / La Frontera: The New Mestiza*. San Francisco: Spinsters/Aunt Lute Press, 1987.

Appelbaum, Nancy P., Anne S. Macpherson, and Karin Alejandra Rosemblatt. "Introduction: Racial Nations." In *Race and Nation in Modern Latin America*, edited by Nancy P. Appelbaum, Anne S. Macpherson, and Karin Alejandra Rosemblatt, 1–31. Chapel Hill: University of North Carolina Press, 2003.

Aron, Stephen. *American Confluence: The Missouri Frontier from Borderland to Border State*. Bloomington: Indiana University Press, 2006.

Asher, Brad. *Beyond the Reservation: Indians, Settlers, and the Law in Washington Territory, 1853–1889*. Norman: University of Oklahoma Press, 1999.

Bahre, Conrad Joseph. *A Legacy of Change: Historic Human Impact on Vegetation in the Arizona Borderlands*. Tucson: University of Arizona Press, 1991.

Bailyn, Bernard. "The Idea of Atlantic History." *Itinerario* 20, no. 1 (1996): 19–44.

Bancroft, Hubert Howe. *History of Washington, Idaho, and Montana, 1845–1889*. San Francisco: The History Company, 1890.

Barkwell, Lawrence J., Leah Dorion, and Darren Préfontaine, eds. *Metis Legacy: A Metis Historiography and Annotated Bibliography*. Winnipeg, Man.: Pemmican Publications, 2001.

Barlow, Tani E. "The Modern Girl around the World: A Research Agenda and Preliminary Findings." *Gender & History* 17, no. 2 (2005): 245–94.

Barrera, Mario. *Race and Class in the Southwest: A Theory of Racial Inequality.* Notre Dame, Ind.: University of Notre Dame Press, 1979.

Basso, Keith H. *Wisdom Sits in Places: Landscape and Language among the Western Apache.* Albuquerque: University of New Mexico Press, 1996.

Bastian, Jean Pierre. "Las sociedades protestantes y la oposición a Porfirio Díaz en México, 1877–1911." In *Protestantes, liberales, y francmasones: Sociedades de ideas y modernidad en América Latina, siglo XIX,* edited by Jean Pierre Bastian, 132–64. México, D.F.: Fondo de Cultura Económica, 1990.

———. *Los disidentes: Sociedades protestantes y revolución en México, 1872–1911.* México, D.F.: Fondo de Cultura Económica; El Colegio de México, 1989.

Baud, Michiel, and Willem Van Schendel. "Toward a Comparative History of Borderlands." *Journal of World History* 8, no. 2 (1997): 211–42.

Bayly, C. A., Sven Beckert, Matthew Connelly, Isabel Hofmeyr, Wendy Kozol, and Patricia Seed. "On Transnational History." AHR Conversation. *American Historical Review* III, no. 5 (2006): 1440–64.

Beal, R. F., J. E. Foster, and Louise Zuk. *The Métis Hivernement Settlement at Buffalo Lake, 1872–1877.* Edmonton, Alb.: Historic Sites and Provincial Museums, 1987.

Bender, Thomas. *A Nation among Nations: America's Place in World History.* New York: Norton, 2006.

———, ed. *Rethinking American History in a Global Age.* Berkeley: University of California Press, 2002.

Bennett, John W., and Seena B. Kohl. *Settling the Canadian-American West, 1890–1915: Pioneer Adaptation and Community Building.* Lincoln: University of Nebraska Press, 1995.

Berger, Dina. *Development of Mexico's Tourism Industry: Pyramids by Day, Martinis by Night.* New York: Palgrave Macmillan, 2006.

Berry, Faith. *Langston Hughes: Before and Beyond Harlem.* New York: Citadel Press, 1983.

Berryman, Norma, as told to I. M. Dunn. "Serape Hunting in the Mexican Wilds." *Lands of Romance,* April 1936, 22–23.

Binnema, Theodore. *Common and Contested Ground: A Human and Environmental History of the Northwestern Plains.* Norman: University of Oklahoma Press, 2001

Boardman, Andrea. *Destination México: "A Foreign Land a Step Away": U.S. Tourism in Mexico, 1880s–1950s.* Dallas: DeGolyer Library, Southern Methodist University, 2001.

Bolton, Herbert E. *The Spanish Borderlands: A Chronicle of Old Florida and the Southwest.* 1921. Reprint, Albuquerque: University of New Mexico Press, 1996.

Bolus, Malvina, ed. *People and Pelts: Selected Papers of the Second North American Fur Trade Conference*. Winnipeg, Man.: Peguis Publishers, 1972.

Boorstin, Daniel J. *The Image: A Guide to Pseudo-Events in America*. 1961. 25th anniversary ed. New York: Atheneum, 1987.

Bordwell, David, Janet Staiger, and Kristin Thompson. *The Classical Hollywood Cinema: Film Style and Mode of Production to 1960*. New York: Routledge, 1985.

Bosch García, Carlos. *Historia de las relaciones entre México y los Estados Unidos, 1819–1848*. México, D.F.: Universidad Autónoma de México, 1961.

Bowman, Heath, and Stirling Dickinson. *Mexican Odyssey*. Chicago: Willet, Clark & Co., 1936.

Bowser, Eileen, ed. *Biograph Bulletins, 1908–1912*. New York: Octagon Books, 1973.

——. *The Transformation of Cinema, 1907–1915*. History of the American Cinema, vol. 2. New York: Scribner, 1990.

Bowsfield, Hartwell, ed. *Fort Victoria Letters, 1846–1851*. Winnipeg, Man.: Hudson's Bay Record Society, 1979.

Boyd, Consuelo. "Twenty Years to Nogales: The Building of the Guaymas-Nogales Railroad," *Journal of Arizona History* 22, no. 3 (1981): 295–324.

Boyd, Robert. *The Coming of the Spirit of Pestilence: Introduced Infectious Diseases and Population Decline among Northwest Coast Indians, 1774–1874*. Seattle: University of Washington Press, 1999.

Bradfute, Richard Wells. *The Court of Private Land Claims: The Adjudication of Spanish and Mexican Land Grant Titles, 1891–1904*. Albuquerque: University of New Mexico Press, 1975.

Bramen, Carrie Tirado. *The Uses of Variety: Modern Americanism and the Quest for National Distinctiveness*. Cambridge, Mass.: Harvard University Press, 2000.

Braund, Kathryn E. Holland. *Deerskins and Duffels: The Creek Indian Trade with Anglo-America, 1685–1815*. Lincoln: University of Nebraska Press, 1993.

Brebner, John Bartlet. *North Atlantic Triangle: The Interplay of Canada, the United States, and Great Britain*. New Haven, Conn.: Yale University Press, 1945.

Breen, David H. *The Canadian Prairie West and the Ranching Frontier, 1874–1924*. Toronto: University of Toronto Press, 1983.

——. "The Turner Thesis and the Canadian West: A Closer Look at the Ranching Frontier." In *Essays on Western History in Honour of Lewis Gwynne Thomas*, edited by Lewis H. Thomas, 147–56. Edmonton: University of Alberta Press, 1976.

Brégent-Heald, Dominique. "Primitive Encounters: Film and Tourism in the North American West." *Western Historical Quarterly* 38, no. 1 (2007): 47–67.

Brendan, Piers. *Thomas Cook: 150 Years of Popular Tourism*. London: Secker and Warburg, 1991.

Briggs, Lawrence John. "For the Welfare of Wage Earners: Immigration Policy and the Labor Department, 1913–1921." Ph.D. diss., Syracuse University, 1995.

Brooks, James. *Captives and Cousins: Slavery, Kinship, and Community in the Southwest Borderlands*. Chapel Hill: University of North Carolina Press, 2002.

Brown, Dona. *Inventing New England: Regional Tourism in the Nineteenth Century*. Washington, D.C.: Smithsonian Institution Press, 1995.

Brown, Jennifer S. H. "The Blind Men and the Elephant: Fur Trade History Revisited." In *Proceedings of the Fort Chipewyan and Fort Vermilion Bicentennial Conference*, edited by Patricia A. McCormack and R. Geoffrey Ironside, 15–19. Edmonton: Boreal Institute for Northern Studies, University of Alberta, 1990.

——. "Fur Trade as Centrifuge: Familial Dispersal and Offspring Identity in Two Company Contexts." In *North American Indian Anthropology: Essays on Society and Culture*, edited by Raymond J. DeMallie and Alfonso Ortiz, 197–219. Norman: University of Oklahoma Press, 1994.

——. "Noms et métaphors dans l'historiographie métisse: anciennes catégories et nouvelles perspectives." *Recherches Amerindiennes au Quebec*, vol. 37, nos. 2–3 (2007): 7–14.

——. "Partial Truths: A Closer Look at Fur Trade Marriage." In *From Rupert's Land to Canada*, edited by Theodore Binnema, Gerhard J. Ens, and R. C. Macleod, 59–80. Edmonton: University of Alberta Press, 2001.

——. *Strangers in Blood: Fur Trade Company Families in Indian Country*. Vancouver: University of British Columbia Press, 1980.

Brown, Jennifer S. H., W. J. Eccles, and Donald P. Heldman, eds. *The Fur Trade Revisited: Selected Papers of the Sixth North American Fur Trade Conference, Mackinac Island, Michigan, 1991*. East Lansing: Michigan State University Press; Mackinac Island: Mackinac State Historic Parks, 1994.

Brown, Jennifer S. H., and Theresa Schenk. "Métis, Mestizo, and Mixed-Blood." In *A Companion to American Indian History*, edited by Philip J. Deloria and Neal Salisbury, 321–38. Malden, Mass.: Blackwell Publishing, 2002.

Brown, Jennifer S. H., and Elizabeth Vibert, eds. *Reading beyond Words: Contexts for Native History*. 2nd ed. Peterborough, Ont.: Broadview Press, 2003.

Browne, J. Ross. *Adventures in Apache Country: A Tour through Arizona and Sonora, 1864*. 1869. Reprint, Tucson: University of Arizona Press, 1974.

Bsumek, Erika Marie. "Exchanging Places: Virtual Tourism, Vicarious Travel, and the Consumption of Southwest Indian Artifacts." In *The Culture of Tourism, The Tourism of Culture: Selling the Past to the Present in the American Southwest*, edited by Hal K. Rothman, 118–39. Albuquerque: University of New Mexico Press, 2003.

Buckley, Thomas C. *Rendezvous: Selected Papers of the Fourth North American Fur Trade Conference, 1981*. St. Paul, Minn.: North American Fur Trade Conference, 1984.

Buffington, "Prohibition in the Borderlands: National Government-Border Community Relations." *Pacific Historical Review* 63 (February 1993): 19–38.

Bukowczyk, John J., Nora Faires, David R. Smith, and Randy William Widdis. *Permeable Border: The Great Lakes Basin as Transnational Region, 1650–1990*. Pittsburgh: University of Pittsburgh Press, 2005.

Bumsted, J. M. "The Quest for a Usable Founder: Lord Selkirk and Manitoba Historians, 1856–1923." *Manitoba History*, no. 2 (1981): 2–7.

Burley, Edith I. *Servants of the Honourable Company: Work, Discipline, and Conflict in the Hudson's Bay Company, 1770–1879*. Toronto: Oxford University Press, 1997.

Burlingame, Merrill G. *The Montana Frontier*. 1942. Reprint, Bozeman, Mont.: Big Sky Books, 1980.

Buzard, James. *The Beaten Track: European Tourism, Literature, and the Ways to "Culture," 1800–1918*. Oxford: Oxford University Press, 1993.

——. "Culture for Export: Tourism and Autoethnography in Postwar Britain." In *Being Elsewhere: Tourism, Consumer Culture, and Identity in Modern Europe and North America*, edited by Shelley Baranowski and Ellen Furlough, 299–319. Ann Arbor: University of Michigan Press, 2001.

Calavita, Kitty. "Collisions at the Intersection of Gender, Race, and Class: Enforcing the Chinese Exclusion Laws." *Law and Society Review*, no. 40 (2006): 249–82.

Calloway, Colin. "Neither White nor Red: White Renegades on the American Indian Frontier." *Western Historical Quarterly* 17, no. 1 (1986): 43–66.

——. *One Vast Winter Count: The Native American West before Lewis and Clark*. Lincoln: University of Nebraska Press, 2003.

Calvert, Robert A., and Arnoldo De León. *The History of Texas*. Arlington Heights, Ill.: Harlan Davison, 1990.

Camou Healy, Ernesto. *De rancheros, poquiteros, orejanos y criollos: Los productores ganaderos de Sonora y el mercado internacional*. Hermosillo, Sonora: Centro de Investigación en Alimentación y Desarrollo, 1998.

Campbell, Marjorie Wilkins. *McGillivray, Lord of the Northwest*. Vancouver: Clark, Irwin, 1962.

——. *The North West Company*. Toronto: Macmillan, 1957.

——. *The Nor'westers: The Fight for the Fur Trade*. Toronto: Macmillan, 1954.

Canada. *Report of the Royal Commission Appointed to Inquire into the Methods by Which Oriental Labourers Have Been Induced to Come to Canada*. By W. L. Mackenzie King, C.M.G., Commissioner. Ottawa: Government Printing Bureau, 1908.

Canada. Department of Fisheries. *Annual Report, 1930–31*. Ottawa: Department of Fisheries, 1931.

Canada. Department of Indian Affairs. *Annual Report of the Department of Indian Affairs*. 57 vols. Ottawa: Department of Indian Affairs, 1880–19 .

Canada. Department of Marine and Fisheries. *Annual Report,* 1900; 1909–10. Ottawa: Department of Marine and Fisheries, 1901, 1910.

——. Fisheries Branch. *Annual Report,* 1927–28; 1929–30. Ottawa: Department of Marine and Fisheries, 1928; 1930.

Canada. Parliament. House of Commons. *Sessional Papers.* [1876, 1885, 1902, 1907–8.] Ottawa: Maclean, Rogers & Co., 1876; 1885; 1902; 1908.

Cardoso, Lawrence A. *Mexican Emigration to the United States, 1897–1931: Socio-economic Patterns.* Tucson: University of Arizona Press, 1980.

Careless, J. M. S. *Canada: A Story of Challenge.* Cambridge: Cambridge University Press, 1953.

Carter, Julian B. *The Heart of Whiteness: Normal Sexuality and Race in America, 1880–1940.* Durham, N.C.: Duke University Press, 2007.

Carter, Sarah. *Aboriginal Peoples and Colonizers of Western Canada to 1900.* Toronto: University of Toronto Press, 1999.

Ceballos, Alfredo Félix Buenrostro, ed. *Memoria del Segundo Congreso Internacional sobre fronteras en Iberoamérica.* Mexicali: Universidad Autónoma de Baja California, 1991.

Ceballos, Manuel Ramírez. *Encuentro en la frontera: mexicanos y norteamericanos en un espacio común.* México, D.F.: El Colegio de México, Centro de Estudios Históricos; Tijuana, Baja California: El Colegio de la Frontera Norte; Ciudad Victoria: Universidad Autónoma de Tamaulipas, 2001.

Ceballos, Manuel Ramírez, and Oscar J. Martínez. "Conflict and Accommodation on the U.S.-Mexican Border, 1848–1911." In *Myths, Misdeeds, and Misunderstandings: The Roots of Conflict in U.S.-Mexican Relations,* edited by Jaime E. Rodríguez O. and Kathryn Vincent, 135–57. Wilmington, Del.: SR Books, 1997.

Cerutti, Mario. *Burguesía, capitales e industria en el norte de México: Monterrey y su ámbito regional (1850–1910).* Monterrey: Facultad de Filosofía y Letras, Universidad Autónoma de Nuevo León, 1989.

Cerutti, Mario, and Miguel Ángel González Quiroga. *El norte de México y Texas (1848–1880): Comercio, capitales y trabajadores en una economía de frontera.* México, D.F.: Instituto Mora, 1999.

——. *Frontera e historia económica: Texas y el Norte de México (1850–1865).* México, D.F.: Instituto Mora; Universidad Autónoma Metropolitana, 1993.

Chabot, Frederick C. *With the Makers of San Antonio.* San Antonio: Artes Gráficas, 1937.

Chan, Sucheng. "European and Asian Immigration into the United States in Comparative Perspective, 1820–1920s." In *Immigration Reconsidered: History, Sociology, and Politics,* edited by Virginia Yans-McLaughlin. New York: Oxford University Press, 1990.

Chance, Joseph. *Jose Maria de Jesus Carvajal: The Life and Times of a Mexican Revolutionary.* San Antonio: Trinity University Press, 2006.

Chaplin, Joyce. *Subject Matter: Technology, the Body, and Science on the Anglo-American Frontier*. Cambridge, Mass.: Harvard University Press, 2001.

Chatterjee, Partha. *Nationalist Thought and the Colonial World: A Derivative Discourse*. 1986. Reprint, Minneapolis: University of Minnesota Press, 1993.

Chester, Charles C. *Conservation across Borders: Biodiversity in an Interdependent World*. Washington, D.C.: Island Press, 2006.

Cleland, Robert Glass. *This Reckless Breed of Men: The Trappers and Fur Traders of the Southwest*. New York: Knopf, 1950.

Clifford, James. *Routes: Travel and Translation in the Late Twentieth Century*. Cambridge, Mass.: Harvard University Press, 1997.

Cline, Gloria Griffen. *Exploring the Great Basin*. Norman: University of Oklahoma Press, 1963.

Cocks, Catherine. *Doing the Town: The Rise of Urban Tourism in the United States, 1850–1915*. Berkeley: University of California Press, 2001.

——. "The Pleasures of Degeneration: Climate, Race, and the Origins of the Global Tourist South in the Americas." *Discourse*, edited by Hsuan Hsu and Mark Feldman, 29, no. 2–3 (spring and fall 2007): 215–35.

——. "Rethinking Sexuality in the Progressive Era." *Journal of the Gilded Age and Progressive Era* 5, no. 2 (2006): 94–118.

——. " 'Warm, Voluptuous Scenes of Tropic Lands': Sex, Race, and Tourism in the Southland, 1880–1940." Paper presented at the conference Connexions: Histories of Race and Sex in North America, New York University, 7–8 November 2008.

Collins, June. "John Fornsby: The Personal Document of a Coast Salish Indian." In *Indians of the Urban Northwest*, by Marian W. Smith. 1949. Reprint, New York: AMS, 1969.

Cook, Ramsay, ed. *The Maple Leaf Forever: Essays on Nationalism and Politics in Canada*. Toronto: Macmillan, 1971.

Coolidge, Dane. *Old California Cowboys*. New York: E. P. Dutton and Co., 1939.

Cooper, Frederick. *Colonialism in Question: Theory, Knowledge, History*. Berkeley: University of California Press, 2005.

Cosío Villegas, Daniel. *Historia moderna de México*. Vol. 5–6, *El Porfiriato: La vida política exterior, parte segunda*. México, D.F.: Editorial Hermes, 1974.

Courtney, Susan. *Hollywood Fantasies of Miscegenation: Spectacular Narratives of Gender and Race, 1903–1967*. Princeton, N.J.: Princeton University Press, 2004.

Cowie, Isaac. *The Company of Adventurers: A Narrative of Seven Years in the Service of the Hudson's Bay Company during 1867–1874 on the Great Buffalo Plains*. Toronto: William Briggs, 1913.

Craig, Richard B. *The Bracero Program: Interest Groups and Foreign Policy*. Austin: University of Texas Press, 1971.

Creighton, Donald. *The Empire of the St. Lawrence: A Study in Commerce and Politics, 1760–1850.* Toronto: Ryerson Press, 1937.

Crews, Litha. "The Know-Nothing Party in Texas." Master's thesis, University of Texas at Austin, 1925.

Crisp, James E. "Race, Revolution, and the Texas Republic: Toward a Reinterpretation." In *The Texas Military Experience from the Texas Revolution through World War II,* edited by Joseph G. Dawson III, 32–48. College Station: Texas A&M University Press, 1995.

Cronon, William. *Changes in the Land: Indians, Colonists, and the Ecology of New England.* New York: Hill and Wang, 1983.

——. *Nature's Metropolis: Chicago and the Great West.* New York: W. W. Norton, 1991.

Cronon, William, George Miles, and Jay Gitlin. "Becoming West: Toward a New Meaning for Western History." In *Under and Open Sky: Rethinking America's Western Past,* edited by William Cronon, George Miles, and Jay Gitlin, 3–27. New York: W. W. Norton, 1992.

Cueva Perus, Marcos. "Fronteras y representaciones fronterizas: Aproximaciones comparativas entre Estados Unidos y América Latina." *Estudios Fronterizos* 6, no. 11 (2005): 9–38.

Culver, Lawrence. "Promoting the Pacific Borderlands: Leisure and Labor in Southern California, 1870–1950." In *Land of Necessity: Consumer Culture in the United States–Mexico Borderlands,* edited by Alexis McCrossen. Durham, N.C.: Duke University Press, 2009.

Curtis, Natalie. "An Old Town of the New World." *Travel* 8, no. 5 (1905): 315–16.

Daniels, Roger. *The Politics of Prejudice: The Anti-Japanese Movement in California and the Struggle for Japanese Exclusion.* Berkeley: University of California Press, 1962.

Dawson, Michael. *Selling British Columbia: Tourism and Consumer Culture, 1890–1970.* Vancouver: University of British Columbia Press, 2004.

Dechêne, Louise. *Habitants and Merchants in Seventeenth-Century Montreal.* Montreal: McGill-Queen's University Press, 1992. Originally published as *Habitants et marchands de Montréal au XVIIe siècle* (Paris: Editions Plon, 1974).

Deering, Fremont B. *The Border Boys with the Mexican Rangers.* New York: Hurst & Co., 1911.

De Leon, Arnoldo. *La comunidad tejana, 1836–1900.* México, D.F.: Fondo de Cultura Económica, 1988.

Delgado, Grace. "In the Age of Exclusion: Race, Region, and Chinese Identity in the Making of the Arizona-Sonora Borderlands, 1863–1943." PhD diss., University of California, Los Angeles, 2000.

Delpar, Helen. *The Enormous Vogue of Things Mexican: Cultural Relations between the United States and Mexico, 1920–1935.* Tuscaloosa: Alabama University Press, 1992.

DeLyser, Dydia. *Ramona Memories: Tourism and the Shaping of Southern California.* Minneapolis: University of Minnesota Press, 2005.

Dempsey, Hugh A. *Firewater: The Impact of the Whisky Trade on the Blackfoot Nation.* Calgary, Alb.: Fifth House, 2002.

Deverell, William. *Whitewashed Adobe: The Rise of Los Angeles and the Remaking of Its Mexican Past.* Berkeley: University of California, 2004.

Devine, Heather. *The People Who Own Themselves: Aboriginal Ethnogenesis in a Canadian Family, 1660–1900.* Calgary, Alb.: University of Calgary Press, 2004.

Dillon, Richard H. *Siskiyou Trail: The Hudson's Bay Company Route to California.* New York: McGraw-Hill, 1975.

Divine, Robert A. *American Immigration Policy, 1924–1952.* New Haven, Conn.: Yale University Press, 1957.

Dobak, William A. "Killing the Canadian Buffalo, 1821–1881." *Western Historical Quarterly* 27, no. 1 (1996): 33–52.

Dorsey, Kurkpatrick. *The Dawn of Conservation Diplomacy: U.S.-Canadian Wildlife Protection Treaties in the Progressive Era.* Seattle: University of Washington Press, 1998.

Duara, Prasenjit. *Rescuing History from the Nation: Questioning Narratives of Modern China.* Chicago: University of Chicago Press, 1995.

Dunae, Patrick A. *Gentlemen Emigrants: From the British Public Schools to the Canadian Frontier.* Vancouver, B.C.: Douglas & McIntyre, 1981.

Duval, Gloria. "Luncheon a la Mexicana." *Lands of Romance*, August 1935, 27.

Earman, Sam, B. J. O. L. McPherson, F. M. Philips, S. Ralser, and J. M. Herrin. "Hydrologic Framework and Groundwater Characteristics, San Bernardino Valley, Arizona and Sonora." Paper presented at Session 175: Hydrogeologic Framework and Basin Hydrology of the Desert Southwestern United States, of the annual meeting of the Geologic Society of America, October 29, 2002. Available online at http://gsa.confex.com/gsa/2002AM/finalprogram/abstract_45184.htm (accessed February 25, 2007).

Eccles, W. J. "The Fur Trade and Eighteenth-Century Imperialism." *William and Mary Quarterly*, 3rd ser., 40, no. 3 (1983): 341–62.

Editorial, *Modern Mexico* 7, no. 3 (1899): 4.

Edwards, G. Thomas, and Carlos A. Schwantes, eds. *Experiences in a Promised Land: Essays in Pacific Northwest History.* Seattle: University of Washington Press, 1986.

Edwards, William Seymour. *On the Mexican Highlands, with a Passing Glance of Cuba.* Cincinnati: Press of Jennings and Graham, 1906.

Eells, Myron. *The Indians of Puget Sound.* Edited by George Castile. Seattle: University of Washington Press, 1985.

Ens, Gerhard J. "The Border, The Buffalo, and the Métis of Montana." In *The Borderlands of the American and Canadian Wests: Essays on the Regional History of the Forty-Ninth Parallel,* edited by Sterling Evans, 139–54. Lincoln: University of Nebraska Press, 2006.

——. *Homeland to Hinterland: The Changing Worlds of the Red River Metis in the Nineteenth Century.* Toronto: University of Toronto Press, 1996.

Erwin, Allen A. *The Southwest of John Horton Slaughter, 1841–1922: Pioneer Cattle-man and Trail-driver of Texas, the Pecos, and Arizona, and Sheriff of Tombstone.* Spokane, Wash.: Arthur H. Clark Co., 1997.

Ettinger, Patrick. "Imaginary Lines: Border Enforcement and the Origins of Undocumented Immigration, 1882–1930." PhD diss., Indiana University, 2000.

——. " 'We Sometimes Wonder What They Will Spring on Us Next': Immigrants and Border Enforcement in the American West, 1882–1930." *Western Historical Quarterly* 37, no. 2 (2006): 159–81.

Evans, Sterling, ed. *The Borderlands of the American and Canadian Wests: Essays on the Regional History of the 49th Parallel.* Lincoln: University of Nebraska Press, 2006.

——. *Bound in Twine: The History and Ecology of the Henequen-Wheat Complex for Mexico and the American and Canadian Plains, 1880–1950.* College Station: Texas A&M University Press, 2007.

Evenden, Matthew D. *Fish versus Power: An Environmental History of the Fraser River.* New York: Cambridge University Press, 2004.

Fairchild, Amy. *Science at the Borders: Immigrant Medical Inspection and the Shaping of the Modern Industrial Labor Force.* Baltimore: Johns Hopkins University Press, 2003.

Faragher, John Mack. Commentary, delivered at the conference on Bridging National Borders in North America, Clements Center for Southwest History, Dallas, Texas, 2007. In author's possession.

Fecteau, Jean-Marie. "Between Scientific Enquiry and the Search for a Nation: Quebec Historiography as Seen by Ronald Rudin." *Canadian Historical Review* 80 (December 1999): 641–92.

Ficken, Robert E. *Unsettled Boundaries: Fraser Gold and the British-American Northwest.* Pullman: Washington State University Press, 2003.

Findlay, John M., and Ken S. Coates, eds. *Parallel Destinies: Canadian-American Relations West of the Rockies.* Seattle: University of Washington Press, 2002.

Fisher, Robin. *Contact and Conflict: Indian-European Relations in British Columbia, 1774–1890.* Vancouver: University of British Columbia Press, 1977.

Fiske, Jo-Anne, Susan Sleeper-Smith, and William Wicken, eds. *New Faces of the Fur Trade: Select Papers of the Seventh North American Fur Trade Conference, Halifax, Nova Scotia, 1995.* East Lansing: Michigan State University Press, 1998.

Fitzgerald, Keith. *The Face of the Nation: Immigration, the State, and the National Identity.* Stanford, Calif.: Stanford University Press, 1996.

Fitzpatrick, Peter. "Terminal Legality: Imperialism and the (De)composition of Law." In *Law, History, and Colonialism: The Reach of Empire*, edited by Diane Kirby, 9–25. Manchester: Manchester University Press, 2001.

Flandrau, Charles. *Viva Mexico!* New York: D. Appleton & Co., 1909.

Flynn, Charles, and Todd McCarthy. "The Economic Imperative: Why Was the B Movie Necessary?" In *Kings of the Bs: Working within the Hollywood System: An Anthology of Film History and Criticism*, edited by Todd McCarthy and Charles Flynn, 13–43. New York: E. P. Dutton, 1975.

Foley, Neil, ed. *Reflexiones: New Directions in Mexican American Studies, 1997.* Austin: CMAS Books, 1998.

——. *The White Scourge: Mexicans, Blacks, and Poor Whites in Texas Cotton Culture.* Berkeley: University of California Press, 1997.

Fong, Lawrence Michael. "Sojourners and Settlers: The Chinese Experience in Arizona." *Journal of Arizona History* 21, no. 3 (1980): 1–30.

Ford, John Salmon. *Rip Ford's Texas.* Edited by Stephen B. Oates. 1987. Reprint, Austin: University of Texas Press, 2004.

Foster, John E. "The Country-born in the Red River Settlement, 1820–1850." PhD diss., University of Alberta, 1973.

——. "The Plains Metis." In *Native Peoples: The Canadian Experience*, edited by R. Bruce Morrison and C. Roderick Wilson, 414–43. 2nd ed. Toronto: McClelland and Stewart, 1995.

Foster, Martha Harroun. *We Know Who We Are: Métis Identity in a Montana Community.* Norman: University of Oklahoma Press, 2006.

Fowler, Gene, and Bill Crawford. *Border Radio: Quacks, Yodelers, Pitchmen, Psychics, and Other Amazing Broadcasters of the American Airwaves.* Austin: Texas Monthly Press, 1987.

Fox, Claire. *The Fence and the River: Culture and Politics at the U.S.-Mexico Border.* Minneapolis: University of Minnesota Press, 1999.

Francis, Daniel, and Toby Mortanz. *Partners in Furs: A History of the Fur Trade in Eastern James Bay, 1600–1870.* Montreal: McGill-Queen's University Press, 1983.

Frank, Waldo. *America Hispana: A Portrait and a Prospect.* London: Charles Scribner's Sons, 1932.

Franklin, Adrian, and Mike Crang. "The Trouble with Tourism and Travel Theory." *Tourist Studies* 1, no. 1 (2001): 5–22.

Friesen, Gerald. *The Canadian Prairies: A History.* Lincoln: University of Nebraska Press, 1984.

Frink, Maurice, W. Turrentine Jackson, and Agnes Wright Spring. *When Grass Was King: Contributions to the Western Range Cattle Industry.* Boulder: University of Colorado Press, 1956.

Galeana, Patricia. "Presentación." In *Nuestra Frontera Norte,* edited by Patricia Galeana, 7–14. México, D.F.: Archivo General de la Nación, 1999.

——, ed. *Nuestra Frontera Norte*. México, D.F.: Archivo General de la Nación, 1999.

Gamio, Manuel. *Forjando Patria*. México, D.F.: Porrúa Hermanos, 1916.

García, María Cristina. *Seeking Refuge: Central American Migration to Mexico, the United States, and Canada*. Berkeley: University of California Press, 2006.

García, Mario T. *Desert Immigrants: The Mexicans of El Paso, 1880–1920*. New Haven, Conn.: Yale University Press, 1981.

Garcia, Matt. *A World of Its Own: Race, Labor, and Citrus in the Making of Greater Los Angeles, 1900–1970*. Chapel Hill: University of North Carolina Press, 2001.

García Canclini, Néstor. *Hybrid Cultures: Strategies for Entering and Leaving Modernity*. Foreword by Renato Rosaldo, translated by Christopher L. Chiappari and Silvia L. López. 1990. Reprint, Minneapolis: University of Minnesota Press, 1995.

García Cantú, Gastón. *Las invasiones norteamericanas en México*. México, D.F.: Ediciones Era, 1971.

García Martínez, Bernardo. "El espacio del (des)encuentro." In *Encuentro en la frontera: Mexicanos y norteamericanos en un espacio común*, edited by Manuel Ceballos Ramírez, 19–51. México, D.F.: El Colegio de México, Centro de Estudios Históricos; Tijuana, Baja California: El Colegio de la Frontera Norte; Ciudad Victoria: Universidad Autónoma de Tamaulipas, 2001.

Garretson, Charles Edwin. "A History of the Washington Superintendency of Indian Affairs." Master's thesis, University of Washington, 1962.

Gehlbach, Frederick R. *Mountain Islands and Desert Seas: A Natural History of the U.S.-Mexican Borderlands*. College Station: Texas A&M Press, 1983.

Gessler, Clifford. *Pattern of Mexico*. New York: D. Appleton-Century Co., 1941.

Gibbs, George. *Tribes of Western Washington and Northwestern Oregon*. Washington, D.C.: Government Printing Office, 1877.

Gibson, James R. *Otter Skins, Boston Ships, and China Goods: The Maritime Fur Trade of the Northwest Coast, 1785–1841*. Seattle: University of Washington Press, 1992.

Gillman, Susan. "*Ramona* in 'Our America.'" In *José Martí's "Our America": From National to Hemispheric Cultural Studies*, edited by Jeffrey Belnap and Raúl Fernandez, 91–111. Durham, N.C.: Duke University Press, 1998.

Gilroy, Paul, *The Black Atlantic: Modernity and Double Consciousness*. Cambridge, Mass.: Harvard University Press, 1993.

Giraud, Marcel. *The Métis in the Canadian West*. Translated by George Woodcock. 2 vols. Edmonton: University of Alberta Press, 1986. Originally published as *Les Métis canadien: Son rôle dans l'histoire des provinces de l'ouest* (Paris: Institut d'Ethnologie, 1945).

Golay, Michael. *The Tide of Empire: America's March to the Pacific*. Hoboken, N.J.: Wiley, 2003.

Goldfrap, John Henry. *The Border Boys with the Texas Rangers*. New York: Hurst & Co., 1912.

González, Gilbert G. *Mexican Consuls and Labor Organizing*. Austin: University of Texas Press, 1999.

González Navarro, Moisés. *Anatomía del poder en México, 1848–1853*. México, D.F.: El Colegio de México, 1977.

———. *Los extranjeros en México y los mexicanos en el extranjero, 1821–1867, vol. 1*. México, D.F.: El Colegio de México, 1993.

Goodwin, Grenville, and Keith H. Basso. *Western Apache Raiding and Warfare*. Tucson: University of Arizona Press, 1971.

Goulet, Keith. "The Cumberland Cree Nehinuw Concept of Land." Paper presented at the Indigenous Knowledge Systems: International Symposium, University of Saskatchewan, Saskatoon, 2004.

Grabowski, Jan, and Nicole St.-Onge. "Montreal Iroquois Engagés in the Western Fur Trade, 1800–1821." In *From Rupert's Land to Canada: Essays in Honour of John E. Foster*, edited by Theodore Binnema, Gerhard J. Ens, and R. C. MacLeod, 23–58. Edmonton: University of Alberta Press, 2001.

Graf, LeRoy. "The Economic History of the Lower Rio Grande Valley, 1820–1875." PhD diss., Harvard University, 1942.

Graybill, Andrew R. *Policing the Great Plains: Rangers, Mounties, and the North American Frontier, 1875–1910*. Lincoln: University of Nebraska Press, 2007.

Green, Stanley C. "The Texas Revolution and the Rio Grande Border." In *The Texas Revolution on the Rio Grande: Bi-National Conference Proceedings, March 25, 2005*, 47–67. San Antonio: Daughters of the Republic of Texas Library at the Alamo, 2005.

Greenbie, Sydney. *Furs to Furrows: An Epic of Rugged Individualism*. Caldwell, Ida.: Caxton Printers, 1939.

Greer, Allan. "Fur-Trade Labour and Lower Canadian Agrarian Structures" [1981]. In *Historical Papers / The Canadian Historical Association*, by Canadian Historical Association Meeting, 197–214. Ottawa: CHA, 1981.

Greer, Allan, and Jodi Bilinkoff, eds. *Colonial Saints: Discovering the Holy in the Americas*. New York: Routledge, 2003.

Guglielmo, Thomas. "Fighting for Caucasian Rights: Mexicans, Mexican Americans, and the Transnational Struggle for Civil Rights in World War II Texas." *Journal of American History* 92, no. 4 (2006): 1212–37.

———. *White on Arrival: Italians, Race, Color, and Power in Chicago, 1890–1945*. Oxford: Oxford University Press, 2003.

Gunning, Tom. *D. W. Griffith and the Origins of Narrative Film: The Early Years at Biograph*. Urbana: University of Illinois Press, 1991.

Gutiérrez, David G., ed. *Between Two Worlds: Mexican Immigrants in the United States*. Wilmington, Del.: Scholarly Resources, 1996.

——. "Migration, Emergent Ethnicity, and the 'Third Space': The Shifting Politics of Nationalism in Greater Mexico." *Journal of American History* 86, no. 2 (1999): 481–517.

Gwyn, Richard. *The 49th Paradox: Canada in North America.* Toronto: McClelland and Stewart, 1985.

Haden, J. M. "Medical Topography and Diseases of Fort Steilacoom." In *Statistical Report on the Sickness and Mortality in the Army of the United States.* 34th Cong., 1st and 2nd sess., 1856, S. Exec. Doc., vol. 18, no. 96, 480–81.

Hadley, Diana. "Ranch Life, the Border Country, 1880–1940: The Way It Really Was." *Cochise Quarterly* 12, no. 1 (1982).

Hadley, Diana, and Thomas E. Sheridan. "Land Use History of the San Rafael Valley, Arizona (1540–1960)." General Technical Report RM-GTR-269. Fort Collins, Colo.: Rocky Mountain Forest and Range Experiment Station, U.S. Department of Agriculture, September 1995.

Hale, Nathaniel C. *Pelts and Palisades: The Story of Fur and the Rivalry for Pelts in Early America.* Richmond, Va.: Dietz Press, 1959.

Haley, J. Evetts. *Jeff Milton: A Good Man with a Gun.* Norman: University of Oklahoma Press, 1948.

Hall, Linda B., and Don M. Coerver. *Revolution on the Border: The United States and Mexico, 1910–1920.* Albuquerque: University of New Mexico Press, 1988.

Hamilton, Leonidas, ed. *Hamilton's Mexican Law: A Compilation of Mexican Legislation Affecting Foreigners, Rights of Foreigners, Commercial Law, Etc.* San Francisco, 1882.

Harmon, Alexandra. *Indians in the Making: Ethnic Identities and Indian Relations around Puget Sound.* Berkeley: University of California Press, 1999.

Harris, Cole. *Making Native Space: Colonialism, Resistance, and Reserves in British Columbia.* Vancouver: University of British Columbia Press, 2002.

——. *The Resettlement of British Columbia: Essays on Colonialism and Geographical Change.* Vancouver: University of British Columbia Press, 1997.

Hart, John M. *Empire and Revolution: The Americans in Mexico since the Civil War.* Berkeley: University of California Press, 2002.

——. *Revolutionary Mexico: The Coming and Process of the Mexican Revolution.* Berkeley: University of California Press, 1987.

Haskett, Bert. "Early History of the Cattle Industry in Arizona." *Arizona Historical Review* 6, no. 4 (1935): 3–42.

Hatfield, Shelley Bowen. *Chasing Shadows: Apaches and Yaquis along the United States–Mexico Border, 1876–1911.* Albuquerque: University of New Mexico Press, 1998.

Hayashida, Cullen Tadao. "Identity, Race, and the Blood Ideology of Japan." PhD diss., University of Washington, 1976.

Heath, Joseph. *Memoirs of Nisqually*. Edited by Lucille McDonald. Fairfield, Wash.: Ye Galleon Press, 1979.

Hendricks, William O. "Developing San Diego's Desert Empire." *Journal of San Diego History* 17, no. 3 (1971): 1–11.

——. "Guillermo Andrade and Land Development on the Mexican Colorado River Delta, 1874–1905." PhD diss., University of Southern California, 1967.

Herrera Pérez, Octavio. *El norte de Tamaulipas y la conformación de la frontera México–Estados Unidos, 1835–1855*. Ciudad Victoria: El Colegio de Tamaulipas, 2003.

Herrera Carrillo, Pablo. *Reconquista y colonización del valle de Mexicali y otros escritos paralelos*. Mexicali: Universidad Autónoma de Baja California, 2002.

Higham, Carol L., and Robert Thacker, eds. *One West, Two Myths: A Comparative Reader*. Calgary: University of Calgary Press, 2004.

——, eds. *One West, Two Myths II: Essays on Comparison*. Calgary: University of Calgary Press, 2006.

Higham, John. *Strangers in the Land: Patterns of American Nativism, 1860–1925*. New York: Atheneum, 1963.

Hoganson, Kristin L. *Consumers' Imperium: The Global Production of American Domesticity, 1865–1920*. Chapel Hill: University of North Carolina Press, 2007.

Holden, Robert H. *Mexico and the Survey of Public Lands: The Management of Modernization, 1876–1911*. DeKalb: Northern Illinois University Press, 1994.

Horne, Gerald. *Black and Brown: African Americas and the Mexican Revolution, 1910–1920*. New York: New York University Press, 2005.

Hornsby, Stephen J., and John G. Reid, eds. *New England and the Maritime Provinces: Connections and Comparisons*. Montreal: McGill-Queens University Press, 2006.

Hourie, Audreen, and Anne Carrière-Acco. "Metis Families." In *Metis Legacy II*, edited by Lawrence Barkwell, Leah M. Dorion, and Audreen Hourie, 56–63. Saskatoon, Sask.: Gabriel Dumont Institute and Pemmican Publications, 2006.

Hoxie, Frederick E. *Parading through History: The Making of the Crow Nation in America, 1805–1935*. Cambridge: Cambridge University Press, 1995.

Hu-DeHart, Evelyn. "Immigrants to a Developing Society: The Chinese in Northern Mexico, 1875–1932." *Journal of Arizona History* 21 (fall 1980): 49–86.

——. *Yaqui Resistance and Survival: The Struggle for Land and Autonomy, 1821–1910*. Madison: University of Wisconsin Press, 1984.

Hughes, Langston. *Autobiography: The Big Sea*. Edited with an introduction by Joseph McLaren. The Collected Works of Langston Hughes, vol. 13. Columbia: University of Missouri Press, 2002.

Hutchinson, George. *The Harlem Renaissance in Black and White*. Cambridge, Mass.: Harvard University Press, 1995.

Iglesias, Norma. "Border Representations: Border Cinema and Independent Video." In *Postborder City: Cultural Spaces of Bajalta California,* edited by Michael J. Dear and Gustavo Leclerc, 183–216. New York: Routledge, 2003.

Innis, Harold A. *The Fur Trade in Canada: An Introduction to Canadian Economic History.* Rev. ed. Toronto: University of Toronto Press, 1956. First published 1930 by Yale University Press.

"Intersections: Studies in the Canadian and American Great Plains." Special issue, *Great Plains Quarterly* 3, no. 1 (1983).

Irby, James A. "Line of the Rio Grande: War and Trade on the Confederate Frontier, 1861–1865." PhD diss., University of Georgia, 1969.

Irving, Washington. *The Adventures of Captain Bonneville, or, Scenes beyond the Rocky Mountains of the Far West.* London: R. Bentley, 1837.

———. *Astoria, or, Enterprise beyond the Rocky Mountains.* London: R. Bentley, 1836.

———. *Three Western Narratives.* New York: Library of America, 2004.

———. *A Tour of the Prairies.* Philadelphia: Carey, Lea, and Blanchard, 1835.

Irwin, Robert McKee. "*Ramona* and Postnationalist American Studies: On 'Our America' and the Mexican Borderlands." *American Quarterly* 55, no. 4 (2003): 539–67.

———. "Toward a Border Gnosis of the Borderlands: Joaquín Murieta and Nineteenth-Century U.S.-Mexico Border Culture." *Nepantla* 2, no. 3 (2001): 509–37.

Isenberg, Andrew C. *The Destruction of the Bison: An Environmental History, 1750–1920.* New York: Cambridge University Press, 2000.

Isern, Thomas D., and R. Bruce Shepard. "Paul F. Sharp." *Heritage of the Great Plains* 23, no. 1 (1990): 4–19.

———. "Paul F. Sharp and the Historiography of the North American Plains." Unpublished paper in author's possession.

Ito, Kazuo. *Issei: A History of Japanese Immigrants in North America.* Translated by Shinichiro Nakamura and Jean S. Gerard. Seattle: Japanese Community Service, 1973.

Jackson, John C. *Children of the Fur Trade: Forgotten Métis of the Pacific Northwest.* Missoula: Mountain Press Pub. Co., 1995.

Jacoby, Karl. "Between North and South: The Alternative Borderlands of William H. Ellis and the African American Colony of 1895." In *Continental Crossroads: Remapping U.S.-Mexico Borderlands History,* edited by Samuel Truett and Elliott Young, 209–40. Durham, N.C.: Duke University Press, 2004.

Jameson, Elizabeth, and Jeremy Mouat. "Telling Differences: The Forty-Ninth Parallel and Historiographies of the West and Nation." *Pacific Historical Review* 75, no. 2 (2006): 183–230.

Jasen, Patricia. *Wild Things: Nature, Culture, and Tourism in Ontario, 1790–1914.* Toronto: University of Toronto Press, 1995.

Jensen, Richard D. *The Amazing Tom Mix: The Most Famous Cowboy of the Movies.* Bloomington, Ind.: iUniverse, 2005.

Johnson, Benjamin Heber. *Revolution in Texas: How a Forgotten Rebellion and Its Bloody Suppression Turned Mexicans into Americans.* New Haven, Conn.: Yale University Press, 2003.

Johnson, Louise, ed. *Aboriginal People and the Fur Trade: Proceedings of the 8th North America Fur Trade Conference, Akwesasne.* Cornwall, Ont.: Akwesasne Notes Publishing, 2001.

Johnston, Hugh. *The Voyage of the* Komagata Maru: *The Sikh Challenge to Canada's Colour Bar.* Vancouver: University of British Columbia Press, 1989.

Jordan, Terry G. *North American Cattle-Ranching Frontiers: Origins, Diffusion, and Differentiation.* Albuquerque: University of New Mexico Press, 1993.

Judd, Carol M. "Native Labour and Social Stratification in the Hudson's Bay Company's Northern Department, 1770–1870." *Canadian Review of Sociology and Anthropology* 17, no. 4 (1980): 305–14.

Judd, Carol M., and Arthur J. Ray, eds. *Old Trails and New Directions: Papers of the Third North American Fur Trade Conference.* Toronto: University of Toronto Press, 1980.

Kang, S. Deborah. "The Legal Construction of the Borderlands: The INS, Immigration Law, and Immigration Rights on the U.S.-Mexico Border, 1917–1954." PhD diss., University of California, Berkeley, 2005.

Karamanski, Theodore J. "The Iroquois and the Fur Trade of the Far West." *The Beaver* (Spring 1982): 5–13.

Katz, Friedrich. *The Secret War in Mexico: Europe, the United States, and the Mexican Revolution.* Chicago: University of Chicago Press, 1981.

Kearney, Michael. "Borders and Boundaries of State and Self at the End of Empire." *Journal of Historical Sociology* 4, no. 1 (1991): 52–74.

Kelley, Sean. " 'Mexico in His Head': Slavery and the Texas-Mexico Border, 1810–1860." *Journal of Social History* 37, no. 3 (2004): 709–23.

Kelm, Mary-Ellen. *Colonizing Bodies: Aboriginal Health and Healing in British Columbia.* Vancouver: University of British Columbia Press, 1998.

Kerig, Dorothy Pierson. "Yankee Enclave: The Colorado River Land Company and Mexican Agrarian Reform in Baja California, 1902–1944." PhD diss., University of California, Irvine, 1988.

Kincaid, Jamaica. *A Small Place.* New York: Farrar, Straus, and Giroux, 1988.

Kirshenblatt-Gimblett, Barbara. *Destination Culture: Tourism, Museums, and Heritage.* Berkeley: University of California Press, 1998.

Kirstein, Peter Neil. *Anglo over Bracero: A History of the Mexican Workers in the United States from Roosevelt to Nixon.* San Francisco: R&E Research Associates, 1977.

Klingle, Matthew. *Emerald City: An Environmental History of Seattle.* New Haven, Conn.: Yale University Press, 2007.

Kleinman, Arthur. *The Illness Narratives: Suffering, Healing, and the Human Condition.* New York: Basic Books, 1988.

Kollin, Susan. *Nature's State: Imagining Alaska as the Last Frontier.* Chapel Hill: University of North Carolina Press, 2001.

Konrad, Victor. "The Borderlands of the United States and Canada in the Context of North American Development." *International Journal of Canadian Studies,* no. 4 (fall 1991): 77–95.

Koshar, Rudy. " 'What Ought to Be Seen': Tourists' Guidebooks and National Identities in Modern Germany and Europe." *Journal of Contemporary History* 33, no. 3 (1998): 323–40.

Kraut, Alan. *Silent Travelers: Germs, Genes, and the "Immigrant Menace."* Baltimore: Johns Hopkins University Press, 1994.

Kristof, Ladis. "The Nature of Frontiers and Boundaries." *Annals of the Association of American Geographers* 49, no. 3 (1959): 269–82.

Kropp, Phoebe. *California Vieja: Culture and Memory in a Modern American Place.* Berkeley: University of California Press, 2006.

Kuper, Adam. *Culture: The Anthropologists' Account.* Cambridge, Mass.: Harvard University Press, 2000.

Lackman, Howard. "George T. Howard." In *Handbook of Texas Online.* http://www.tshaonline.org/handbook/online/articles/HH/fho77.html.

LaDow, Beth. *The Medicine Line: Life and Death on a North American Borderland.* New York: Routledge, 2001.

Lamar, Howard R. *The Trader on the American Frontier: Myth's Victim.* College Station: Texas A&M University Press, 1977.

Langman, Larry. *American Film Cycles: The Silent Era.* Westport, Conn.: Greenwood Publishing, 1998.

Laut, Agnes C. "Mexico, the Land of Desire: Troubled and Troublous [sic] Mexico a Garden Spot of the World—The Enormous Possibilities for Good in Our Neighbor—Shall She Be Redeemed from the Toils of Her Plunderers and Thieves?" *Travel,* December 1919.

Lavender, David. *The Fist in the Wilderness.* Albuquerque: University of New Mexico Press, 1964.

Lee, Erika. *At America's Gates: Chinese Immigration during the Exclusion Era, 1882–1943.* Chapel Hill: University of North Carolina Press, 2003.

Lewis, Daniel. *Iron Horse Imperialism: The Southern Pacific of Mexico, 1880–1951.* Tucson: University of Arizona Press, 2007.

Lewis, David Levering. *When Harlem Was in Vogue.* New York: Oxford University Press, 1979.

Lewis, Oscar. *The Effects of White Contact upon Blackfoot Culture, with Special Reference to the Role of the Fur Trade.* New York: J. J. Augustin, 1942.

Limerick, Patricia Nelson. *The Legacy of Conquest: The Unbroken Past of the American West.* New York: Norton, 1987.

———. *Something in the Soil: Legacies and Reckonings in the New West.* New York: Norton, 2000.

Límón, José E. *American Encounters: Greater Mexico, the United States, and the Erotics of Culture.* Boston: Beacon Press, 1998.

Lipset, Seymour Martin. *Continental Divide: The Values and Institutions of the United States and Canada.* New York: Routledge, 1990.

Little, J. L. *Borderland Religion: The Emergence of an English-Canadian Identity, 1792–1852.* Toronto: University of Toronto Press, 2004.

Lloyd, David. "Nationalisms against the State." In *The Politics of Culture in the Shadow of Capital,* edited by Lisa Lowe and David Lloyd, 173–98. Durham, N.C.: Duke University Press, 1997.

Löbbermann, Dorothea. " 'Making Strange' in Tourism: Harlem through European Eyes in the 1920s and 1930s." In *Sites of Ethnicity: Europe and the Americas,* edited by William Boelhower, Rocío G. Davis, and Carmen Birkle, 63–78. Heidelberg, Germany: Universitätsverlag Winter, 2004.

Lombardo de Ruiz, Sonia. "Estudio preliminar." In vol. 1 of *El pasado prehispanico en la cultura nacional: Memoria Hemerografica, 1877–1911,* compiled by Sonia Lombardo de Ruiz, 21–47. México, D.F.: Instituto Nacional de Antropología e Historia, 1994.

Lorey, David. *The U.S.-Mexican Border in the Twentieth Century.* Wilmington, Del.: Scholarly Resources, 1999.

Los Super Seven. *Heard it on the X.* Telarc, 2005. Compact disc.

Lott, Eric. *Love and Theft: Blackface Minstrelsy and the American Working Class.* New York: Oxford University Press, 1993.

Loveridge, D. M., and Barry Potyondi. *From Wood Mountain to the Whitemud: A Historical Survey of the Grasslands National Park Area.* History and Archaeology, no. 67. Ottawa: Parks Canada, 1983.

Löwy, Michael, and Robert Sayre. *Romanticism against the Tide of Modernity.* Translated by Catherine Porter. Durham, N.C.: Duke University Press, 2001.

Lumsden, Ian, ed. *Close the 49th Parallel Etc.: The Americanization of Canada.* Toronto, 1973.

Lutz, John. "Inventing an Indian War: Canadian Indians and American Settlers in the Pacific West, 1854–1864." *Journal of the West* 38 (July 1999): 7–13.

———. "Making 'Indians' in British Columbia: Power, Race, and the Importance of Place." In *Power and Place in the North American West,* edited by Richard White and John M. Findlay, 61–84. Seattle: University of Washington Press, 1999.

———. "Work, Sex, and Death on the Great Thoroughfare: Annual Migrations of 'Canadian Indians' to the American Pacific Northwest." In *Parallel Destinies:*

Canadian-American Relations West of the Rockies, edited by John M. Findlay and Ken S. Coates, 80–103. Seattle: University of Washington Press, 2002.

Lytle Hernandez, Kathleen. "Entangling Bodies and Borders: Racial Profiling and the U.S. Border Patrol, 1924–1955." PhD diss., University of California, Los Angeles, 2002.

Lytwyn, Victor P. *The Fur Trade of the Little North: Indians, Peddlars, and English-men East of Lake Winnipeg, 1760–1821.* Winnipeg, Man.: Rupert's Land Research Centre, 1986.

MacFarlane, Peter Clark. "California the Land of Promise." *Sunset*, July 1914, 44.

MacLeod, Margaret Arnett, and W. L. Morton. *Cuthbert Grant of Grantown: Warden of the Plains of Red River.* Toronto: McClelland and Stewart Ltd., 1963.

Macleod, R. C. *The North-West Mounted Police and Law Enforcement, 1873–1905.* Toronto: University of Toronto Press, 1976.

Maier, Charles. "Consigning the Twentieth Century to History: Alternative Narratives for the Modern Era." *American Historical Review* 105, no. 3 (June 2000): 807–31.

Maltby, Richard. *Hollywood Cinema.* 2nd ed. Malden, Mass.: Blackwell Publishing, 2003.

Mancke, Elizabeth. "Spaces of Power in the Early Modern Northeast." In *New England and the Maritime Provinces: Connections and Comparisons*, edited by Stephen J. Hornsby and John G. Reid, 32–49. Montreal: McGill-Queen's University Press, 2005.

Mann, Michael. *The Sources of Power.* Vol. 1, *A History of Power from the Beginning to A.D. 1769.* Cambridge: Cambridge University Press, 1986.

Martí, José. *Our America: Writings on Latin America and the Struggle for Cuban Independence.* Translated by Elinor Randall with Juan de Onís and Roslyn Held Foner, edited and annotated by Philip S. Foner. New York: Monthly Review Press, 1977.

Martin, Calvin. *Keepers of the Game: Indian-Animal Relationships and the Fur Trade.* Berkeley: University of California Press, 1978.

Martínez, Oscar. *Border Boom Town: Ciudad Juárez since 1848.* Austin: University of Texas Press, 1978.

——. *Border People: Life and Society in the U.S.-Mexico Borderlands.* Tucson: University of Arizona Press, 1994.

——. *Troublesome Border.* 1988. Reprint, Tucson: University of Arizona Press, 2006.

Mathes, Valerie Sherer. *Helen Hunt Jackson and Her Indian Reform Legacy.* Austin: University of Texas Press, 1990.

Mayer, Arthur J. "San Antonio, Frontier Entrepôt." PhD diss., University of Texas at Austin, 1976.

McBroome, Delores Nason. "Harvests of Gold: African American Boosterism,

Agriculture, and Investment in Allensworth [California] and Little Liberia [Mexico]." In *Seeking El Dorado: African Americans in California*, edited by Lawrence B. deGraff, Kevin Mulroy, and Quintard Taylor, 149–78. Seattle: Autry Museum and the University of Washington Press, 2001.

McClain, Charles J. *In Search of Equality: The Chinese Struggle against Discrimination in Nineteenth-Century America*. Berkeley: University of California Press, 1994.

McClaran, Michael P., and Thomas R. Van Devender, eds. *The Desert Grassland*. Tucson: University of Arizona Press, 1995.

McCoy, Drew R. *The Elusive Republic: Political Economy in Jeffersonian America*. Chapel Hill: Institute of Early American History and Culture, University of North Carolina Press, 1980.

McCrady, David G. *Living with Strangers: The Nineteenth-Century Sioux and the Canadian-American Borderlands*. Lincoln: University of Nebraska Press, 2006.

McCrossen, Alexis. "Disrupting Boundaries: Consumer Capitalism and Culture in the U.S.-Mexico Borderlands." In *Land of Necessity*, edited by Alexis McCrossen. Durham, N.C.: Duke University Press, 2009.

——, ed. *Land of Necessity: Consumer Culture in the United States–Mexico Borderlands*. Durham, N.C.: Duke University Press, 2009.

McGreevy, Patrick. *The Wall of Mirrors: Nationalism and Perceptions of the Border at Niagara Falls*. Orono: University of Maine, 1991.

McKellar, William H., and George H. Hart. "Eradicating Cattle Ticks in California." *26th Annual Report of the Bureau of Animal Industry for the Year 1909*. Washington, D.C.: Government Printing Office, 1911.

McKeown, Adam. "Ritualization of Regulation: The Enforcement of Chinese Exclusion in the U.S. and China." *American Historical Review* 108, no. 2 (2003): 377–403.

McKinsey, Lauren, and Victor Konrad. *Borderland Reflections: The United States and Canada*. Orono: University of Maine, 1989.

McLachlan, Morag, ed. *The Fort Langley Journals, 1827–1830*. Vancouver: University of British Columbia Press, 1998.

McManus, Sheila. *The Line Which Separates: Race, Gender, and the Making of the Alberta-Montana Borderlands*. Edmonton: University of Alberta Press; Lincoln: University of Nebraska Press, 2005.

McNab, David T. "Metis Participation in the Treaty-Making Process in Ontario: A Reconnaissance." *Native Studies Review* 1, no. 2 (1985): 57–79.

McWilliams, Carey. *North from Mexico: The Spanish-Speaking People of the United States*. New edition, updated by Matt S. Meier. New York: Praeger, 1990.

——. *Southern California Country: An Island on the Land*. New York: Duell, Sloan & Pearce, 1946.

Meeks, Eric. "Cross-Ethnic Political Mobilization and Yaqui Identity Formation in Guadalupe, Arizona." In *Reflexiones: New Directions in Mexican American Studies, 1997*, edited by Neil Foley, 77–108. Austin: CMAS Books, 1998.

Merchant, Carolyn. *Ecological Revolutions: Nature, Gender, and Science in New England*. Chapel Hill: University of North Carolina Press, 1989.

Merrell, James H. *The Indians' New World: Catawbas and Their Neighbors from European Contact through the Era of Removal*. Chapel Hill: Institute of Early American History and Culture, University of North Carolina Press, 1989.

Merwick, Donna. *Possessing Albany, 1630–1710*. New York: Cambridge University Press, 1990.

Metz, León C. *Border: The U.S.-Mexico Line*. El Paso, Tex.: Mangan Books, 1989.

Mexican National Railroad. *Mexico: Tropical Tours to Toltec Towns, compliments of the Mexican National R. R. / The Shortest, Quickest, and Most Picturesque Route between Mexico and the United States*. Chicago: Knight, Leonard and Co., Printers, 1892.

Mexico City. *Real Mexico*, April 1932. Organ of the Consolidated Railroad and Pullman Company Tourist Service.

Migdal, Joel S., ed. *Boundaries and Belonging: States and Societies in the Struggle to Shape Identities and Local Practice*. Seattle: University of Washington Press, 2004.

Mignolo, Walter D. *Local Histories / Global Designs: Coloniality, Subaltern Knowledges, and Border Thinking*. Princeton, N.J.: Princeton University Press, 2000.

Miller, David, Dennis Smith, Joseph R. McGeshick, James Shanley, and Caleb Shields. *The History of the Assiniboine and Sioux Tribes of the Fort Peck Indian Reservations, Montana, 1800–2000*. Poplar, Mont.: Fort Peck Community College; Helena: Montana Historical Society Press, 2008.

Miller, Joseph, ed. *The Arizona Rangers*. New York: Hastings House, 1972.

Mills, Sara. *Discourses of Difference: An Analysis of Women's Travel Writing and Colonialism*. London: Routledge, 1993.

Mitchell, Elaine Allen. *Fort Timiskaming and the Fur Trade*. Toronto: University of Toronto Press, 1977.

Mitchell, Pablo. *Coyote Nation: Sexuality, Race, and Conquest in Modernizing New Mexico, 1880–1920*. Chicago: University of Chicago Press, 2005.

Mongia, Radhika Viyas. "Race, Nationality, Mobility: A History of the Passport." In *After the Imperial Turn: Thinking with and through the Nation*, edited by Antoinette Burton, 196–214. Durham, N.C.: Duke University Press, 2003.

Montejano, David. *Anglos and Mexicans in the Making of Texas, 1836–1986*. Austin: University of Texas Press, 1987.

Montoya, María E. *Translating Property: The Maxwell Land Grant and the Conflict over Land in the American West, 1840–1900*. Berkeley: University of California Press, 2002.

Mora-Torres. Juan. *The Making of the Mexican Border: The State, Capitalism, and Society in Nuevo León, 1848–1910*. Austin: University of Texas Press, 2001.

Moreno, Julio. *Yankee Don't Go Home!: Mexican Nationalism, American Business Culture, and the Shaping of Modern Mexico, 1920–1950*. Chapel Hill: University of North Carolina Press, 2003.

Morgan, Dale L., W. L. Morton, K. G. Davies et al., eds. *Aspects of the Fur Trade: Selected Papers of the 1965 North American Fur Trade Conference*. St. Paul: Minnesota Historical Society, 1967.

Morin, Gail. *Métis Families: A Genealogical Compendium*. 6 vols. Pawtucket, R.I.: Quintin Publications, 2001.

Morris, Peter S. "Regional Ideas and the Montana-Alberta Borderlands." *Geographical Review* 89, no. 4 (1999): 469–90.

Mortimer-Sandilands, Catriona. " 'The Geology Recognizes No Boundaries': Shifting Borders in Waterton Lakes National Park." In *The Borderlands of the American and Canadian Wests: Essays on the Regional History of the Forty-ninth Parallel*, edited by Sterling Evans, 309–33. Lincoln: University of Nebraska Press, 2006.

Morton, W. L. *Manitoba: A History*. Toronto: University of Toronto Press, 1957.

Moses, Wilson J. *The Golden Age of Black Nationalism, 1850–1925*. New York: Oxford University Press, 1978.

*Moving Picture World*. A weekly trade magazine published from 1907 to 1927.

Munby, Jonathan. *Public Enemies, Public Heroes: Screening the Gangster from Little Caesar to Touch of Evil*. Chicago: University of Chicago Press, 1999.

Muñoz, Elsa. *Cuerpo, representación y poder: México en los albores de la reconstrucción nacional, 1920–1934*. México, D.F.: Universidad Autónoma Metropolitana, 2002.

Murphy, Lucy Eldersveld. *A Gathering of Rivers: Indians, Métis, and Mining in the Western Great Lakes, 1737–1832*. Lincoln: University of Nebraska Press, 2000.

Nance, Joseph M. *After San Jacinto: The Texas-Mexican Frontier, 1836–1841*. Austin: University of Texas Press, 1963.

Nañez, Alfredo. *History of the Rio Grande Conference of the United Methodist Church*. Dallas: Bridwell Library, Southern Methodist University, 1980.

Nash, Linda. *Inescapable Ecologies: A History of Environment, Disease, and Knowledge*. Berkeley: University of California Press, 2006.

Ngai, Mae M. *Impossible Subjects: Illegal Aliens and the Making of Modern America*. Princeton, N.J.: Princeton University Press, 2004.

Nicks, John. "Orkneymen in the HBC, 1780–1821." In *Old Trails and New Directions: Papers of the Third North American Fur Trade Conference*, edited by Carol M. Judd and Arthur J. Ray, 102–26. Toronto: University of Toronto Press, 1980.

Nicks, Trudy. "The Iroquois and Fur Trade in Western Canada." In *Old Trails and*

*New Directions: Papers of the Third North American Fur Trade Conference*, edited by Carol M. Judd and Arthur J. Ray, 85–101. Toronto: University of Toronto Press, 1980.

Noriega, Chon A. "Birth of the Southwest: Social Protest, Tourism, and D. W. Griffith's *Ramona.*" In *The Birth of Whiteness: Race and the Emergence of U.S. Cinema*, edited by Daniel Bernardi, 203–26. New Brunswick, N.J.: Rutgers University Press, 1996.

Northrup, Cynthia Clark, and Elaine C. Prange Turney, eds. *Encyclopedia of Tariffs and Trade in U.S. History.* 3 vols. Westport, Conn.: Greenwood Press, 2003.

Northwest Territories. *Ordinances of the Northwest Territories.* Ottawa: Queen's Printer for Canada, 1877–.

Northwest Territories. Council. *Journal of the Council of the North-West Territories of Canada.* Regina, Sask.: Northwest Territories Council, 1877.

Norton, Thomas Elliot. *The Fur Trade in Colonial New York.* Madison: University of Wisconsin Press, 1974.

Nugent, Daniel. *Spent Cartridges of Revolution: An Anthropological History of Namiquipa, Chihuahua.* Chicago: University of Chicago Press, 1993.

Nugent, Paul. *Smugglers, Secessionists, and Loyal Citizens on the Ghana-Togo Frontier.* Athens: Ohio University Press, 2002.

Ochoa, Enrique C. "Investigación reciente en torno al norte de México y la región fronteriza entre Estados Unidos y México a partir del Porfiriato." *Revista Mexicana de Sociología* 53, no. 3 (1991): 351–68.

Olcott, Jocelyn. *Revolutionary Women in Postrevolutionary Mexico.* Durham, N.C.: Duke University Press, 2005.

Olcott, Jocelyn, Mary Kay Vaughn, and Gabriela Cano, eds. *Sex in Revolution: Gender, Politics, and Power in Modern Mexico.* Durham, N.C.: Duke University Press, 2006.

Oles, James. *South of the Border: Mexico in the American Imagination, 1914–1947.* Washington, D.C.: Smithsonian Institution Press, 1993.

O'Meara, Walter. *Daughters of the Country: The Women of the Fur Traders and Mountain Men.* New York: Harcourt, Brace and World, 1968.

Orsi, Robert. *Sunset Limited: The Southern Pacific Railroad and the Development of the American West, 1850–1930.* Berkeley: University of California Press, 2005.

Ortiz, Fernando. *Contrapunteo cubano del tabaco y el azúcar.* La Habana: J. Montero, 1940. Translated by Harriet de Onis as *Cuban Counterpoint* (New York: A. A. Knopf, 1947).

Ostler, Jeffrey. *The Plains Sioux and U.S. Colonialism from Lewis and Clark to Wounded Knee.* Cambridge: Cambridge University Press, 2004.

Page, Arthur W. "Our Nearest Latin Neighbor: Mexico Is a Country of Many Variations—Evidences of American Enterprise in Contrast with Old World Customs—Strawberries Every Day in the Year." *Travel*, January 1911.

Pannekoek, Fritz. "The Churches and the Social Structure in the Red River Area, 1818–70." PhD diss., Queen's University, 1973.

——. "Metis Studies: The Development of a Field and New Directions." In *From Rupert's Land to Canada: Essays in Honour of John E. Foster,* edited by Theodore Binnema, Gerhard J. Ens, and R. C. Macleod, 111–28. Edmonton: University of Alberta Press, 2001.

——. *A Snug Little Flock: The Social Origins of the Riel Resistance of 1869–1870.* Winnipeg, Man.: Watson and Dwyer Publishing, 1991.

Parker, James. *Emporium of the North: Fort Chipewyan and the Fur Trade to 1835.* Regina, Sask.: Canadian Plains Research Centre and Alberta Culture and Multiculturalism, 1987.

Payment, Diane. *"The Free People—Otipemisiwak," Batoche, Saskatchewan, 1870–1930.* Ottawa: National Historic Parks and Sites, 1990.

Payne, Michael. "Fur Trade Historiography: Past Conditions, Present Circumstances, and a Hint of Future Prospects." In *From Rupert's Land to Canada,* edited by Theodore Binnema, Gerhard J. Ens, and R. C. Macleod, 3–22. Edmonton: University of Alberta Press, 2001.

——. "Fur Trade Social History and the Public Historian: Some Other Recent Trends." In *The Fur Trade Revisited: Selected Papers of the Sixth North American Fur Trade Conference, Mackinac Island, Michigan, 1991,* edited by Jennifer S. H. Brown, W. J. Eccles, and Donald P. Heldman, 481–99. East Lansing: Michigan State University Press; Mackinac Island: Mackinac State Historic Parks, 1994.

Pedersen, Donald B., and Dale C. Dahl. "Alien Farmworkers and United States Immigration and Naturalization Laws." *Immigration and Nationality Law Review* 7 (1983–84): 51–52.

Peers, Laura, and Robert Coutts. "Aboriginal History and Historic Sites: The Shifting Ground." In *Gathering Places: Essays on Aboriginal and Fur Trade Histories in Honour of Jennifer S. H. Brown,* edited by Laura Peers and Carolyn Podruchny. Unpublished manuscript in author's possession.

Perales, Monica. "Smeltertown: A Biography of a Mexican-American Community, 1880–1973." PhD diss., Stanford University, 2004.

Perry, Adele. *On the Edge of Empire: Gender, Race, and the Making of British Columbia, 1849–1871.* Toronto: University of Toronto Press, 2001.

Peterson, Jacqueline. "Many Roads to Red River: Metis Genesis in the Great Lakes Region, 1680–1815." In *The New Peoples: Being and Becoming Metis in North America,* edited by Jacqueline Peterson and Jennifer S. H. Brown, 37–72. Winnipeg: University of Manitoba Press, 1985.

——. "The People In Between: Indian-White Marriage and the Genesis of a Métis Society and Culture in the Great Lakes Region, 1680–1830." PhD diss., University of Illinois, Chicago Circle, 1980.

Peterson, Jacqueline, and John Anfinson. "The Indian and the Fur Trade: A Review of Recent Literature." In *Scholars and the Indian Experience: Critical Reviews of Recent Writing in the Social Sciences*, edited by W. R. Swagerty, 223–57. Bloomington: Indiana University Press, 1984. A slightly revised version appeared in *Manitoba History* 10 (autumn 1985): 10–18.

Peterson, Jacqueline, and Jennifer S. H. Brown. "Introduction." In *The New Peoples: Being and Becoming Métis in North America*, edited by Jacqueline Peterson and Jennifer S. H. Brown, 3–16. Winnipeg: University of Manitoba Press, 1985.

——, eds. *The New Peoples: Being and Becoming Métis in North America*. Winnipeg: University of Manitoba Press, 1985.

Pettit, Arthur G. *Images of the Mexican American in Fiction and Film*. College Station: Texas A&M University Press, 1980.

Phillips, Paul C. *The Fur Trade*. With concluding chapters by J. W. Smurr. 2 vols. Norman: University of Oklahoma Press, 1961.

Pike, Fredrick B. *The United States and Latin America: Myths and Stereotypes of Civilization and Nature*. Austin: University of Texas Press, 1992.

Piñera Ramírez, David. "La historia de la frontera Mexico–Estados Unidos en el contexto de las fronteras en Iberoamerica." *Frontera Norte* 6, no. 11 (1994): 123–33.

Piñera Ramos, David, ed. *Historia de Tijuana: Semblanza general*. Tijuana: Centro de Investigaciones Históricas, UNAM-UABC, 1985.

Pitt, Leonard. *The Decline of the Californios: A Social History of the Spanish-Speaking Californians, 1846–1890*. Berkeley: University of California Press, 1966.

Podruchny, Carolyn. *Making the Voyageur World: Travelers and Traders in the North American Fur Trade*. Lincoln: University of Nebraska Press; Toronto: University of Toronto Press, 2006.

Poole, Deborah. "An Image of 'Our Indian': Type Photos and Racial Sentiments in Oaxaca, 1920–1940." *Hispanic American Historical Review* 84, no. 1 (2004): 37–82.

Pope, Peter. "The Practice of Portage in the Early Modern North Atlantic: Introduction to an Issue in Maritime Historical Anthropology." *Journal of the Canadian Historical Association*, n.s., 6 (1995): 19–41.

Potter, Elizabeth Gray, and Mabel Thayer Gray. *The Lure of San Francisco: A Romance amid Old Landmarks*. San Francisco: Paul Elder and Co., 1915.

Pratt, Mary Louise. *Imperial Eyes: Travel Writing and Transculturation*. New York: Routledge, 1992.

Preston, William. *Aliens and Dissenters: Federal Suppression of Radicals, 1903–1933*. Cambridge, Mass.: Harvard University Press, 1963.

Prucha, Francis Paul. *American Indian Policy in the Formative Years: The Indian*

*Trade and Intercourse Acts, 1790–1834.* Cambridge, Mass.: Harvard University Press, 1962.

Pulling, Hazel Adele. "California's Range Cattle Industry: Decimation of the Herds, 1870–1912." *Journal of San Diego History* 11, no. 1 (1965): 20–32.

Raibmon, Paige. *Authentic Indians: Episodes of Encounter from the Late Nineteenth-Century Northwest Coast.* Durham, N.C.: Duke University Press, 2005.

Ramirez, Bruno. "Canada in the United States: Perspectives on Migration and Continental History." *Journal of American Ethnic History* 20, no. 3 (2001): 50–70.

———. *Crossing the 49th Parallel: Migration from Canada to the United States.* Ithaca, N.Y.: Cornell University Press, 2001.

Ramírez, Nora E. "The Vaquero and Ranching in the Southwestern United States, 1600–1970." PhD diss., Indiana University, 1979.

Rankin, Melinda. *Twenty Years among the Mexicans: A Narrative of Missionary Labor.* Edited by Miguel Ángel González Quiroga and Timothy Bowman. Dallas: DeGolyer Library and William P. Clements Center for Southwest Studies, 2008.

Ray, Arthur J. *Indians in the Fur Trade: Their Roles as Hunters, Trappers, and Middlemen in the Lands Southwest of Hudson Bay, 1660–1870.* Toronto: University of Toronto Press, 1974.

Ray, Arthur J., and Donald Freeman. *"Give Us Good Measure": An Economic Analysis of Relations between the Indians and the Hudson's Bay Company before 1763.* Toronto: University of Toronto Press, 1978.

Ready, Alma. *Open Range and Hidden Silver: Arizona's Santa Cruz County.* Nogales: Pimeria Alta Historical Society, 1986.

Rees, Tony. *Arc of the Medicine Line: Mapping the World's Longest Undefended Border across the Western Plains.* Lincoln: University of Nebraska Press, 2008.

Reid, John T. *Spanish American Images of the United States, 1790–1960.* Gainesville: University Presses of Florida, 1977.

Reisler, Mark. *By the Sweat of Their Brow: Mexican Immigrant Labor in the United States, 1900–1940.* Westport, Conn.: Greenwood Press, 1976.

Reséndez, Andrés. *Changing National Identities at the Frontier: Texas and New Mexico, 1800–1850.* Cambridge: Cambridge University Press, 2005.

Rich, E. E. *The Fur Trade and the Northwest to 1857.* Toronto: McClelland and Stewart Ltd., 1967.

Rippy, J. Fred. "Border Troubles along the Rio Grande, 1848–1860." *Southwestern Historical Quarterly* 23, no. 2 (1919): 91–111.

———. *The United States and Mexico.* Rev. ed. New York: F. S. Crofts and Co., 1971.

Rivard, Ron, and Catherine Littlejohn. *The History of the Metis of Willow Bunch.* Saskatoon, Sask.: n.p., 2003.

Robbins, William G., Robert J. Frank, and Richard E. Ross, eds. *Regionalism and the Pacific Northwest.* Corvallis: Oregon State University Press, 1983.

Rollins, Peter C. Introduction to *Hollywood as Historian: American Film in a Cultural Contex*, edited by Peter C. Rollins, 1–8. Rev. ed. Lexington: University Press of Kentucky, 1998.

Romo, David. *Ringside Seat to a Revolution: An Underground Cultural History of El Paso and Juárez, 1893–1923*. El Paso: Cinco Puntos Press, 2005.

Ronda, James. *Astoria and Empire*. Lincoln: University of Nebraska Press, 1990.

Roos, John F. *Restoring Fraser River Salmon: A History of the International Pacific Salmon Fisheries Commission, 1937–1985*. Vancouver, B.C.: Pacific Salmon Commission, 1991.

Rosaldo, Renato. *Culture and Truth: The Remaking of Social Analysis*. Boston: Beacon Press, 1989.

Rosenberg, Charles. "Framing Disease: Illness, Society, and History." In *Framing Disease: Studies in Cultural History*, edited by Charles Rosenberg and Janet Golden, xiii–xxvi. New Brunswick, N.J.: Rutgers University Press, 1992.

Ross, Alexander. *Adventures of the First Settlers on the Oregon or Columbia River: Being a Narrative of the Expedition Fitted Out by John Jacob Astor, to Establish the "Pacific Fur Company;" With an Account of Some Indian Tribes on the Coast of the Pacific*. London: Smith, Elder & Co., 1849.

——. *The Fur Hunters of the Far West; A Narrative of Adventures in the Oregon and Rocky Mountains*. 2 vols. London: Smith, Elder and Co., 1855.

——. *The Red River Settlement: Its Rise, Process, and Present State. With Some Account of the Native Race and Its General History to the Present Day*. London: Smith, Elder & Co., 1856.

Rotker, Susana. "The (Political) Exile Gaze in Martí's Writing on the United States." In *José Martí's "Our America": From National to Hemispheric Cultural Studies*, edited by Jeffrey Belnap and Raúl Fernández, 58–76. Durham, N.C.: Duke University Press, 1998.

Rouse, Roger. "Mexican Migration and the Social Space of Postmodernism." In *Between Two Worlds: Mexican Immigrants in the United States*, edited by David G. Gutiérrez, 247–63. Wilmington, Del.: Scholarly Resources, 1996.

Roy, Patricia E., J. L. Granatstein, Masako Iino, and Hiroko Takamura. *Mutual Hostages: Canadians and Japanese during the Second World War*. Toronto: University of Toronto Press, 1990.

Rozum, Molly P. "Grasslands Grown: A Twentieth-Century Sense of Place on North America's Northern Prairies and Plains." PhD diss., University of North Carolina, Chapel Hill, 2001.

Rubenstein, Anne. "The War on *Las Pelonas*: Modern Women and Their Enemies, Mexico City, 1924." In *Sex in Revolution: Gender, Politics, and Power in Modern Mexico*, edited by Jocelyn Olcott, Mary Kay Vaughn, and Gabriela Cano, 57–80. Durham, N.C.: Duke University Press, 2006.

Rudin, Ronald. *Making History in Twentieth-Century Quebec.* Toronto: University of Toronto Press, 1997.

Ruíz, Ramón Eduardo. *The People of Sonora and Yankee Capitalists.* Tucson: University of Arizona Press, 1988.

Ruiz, Vicki. *From Out of the Shadows: Mexican Women in Twentieth-Century America.* New York: Oxford University Press, 1998.

Sadowski-Smith, Claudia. *Border Fictions: Globalization, Empire, and Writing at the Boundaries of the United States.* Charlottesville: University of Virginia Press, 2008.

——, ed. *Globalization on the Line: Culture, Capital, and Citizenship at U.S. Borders.* New York: Palgrave, 2002.

——. "Introduction: Border Studies, Diaspora, and Theories of Globalization." In *Globalization on the Line: Culture, Capital, and Citizenship at U.S. Borders,* edited by Claudia Sadowski-Smith, 1–27. New York: Palgrave, 2002.

Sage, Walter N. "Geographical and Cultural Aspects of the Five Canadas." Canadian Historical Association, *Report of the Annual Meeting* (1937): 28–34.

——. "Some Aspects of the Frontier in Canadian History." Canadian Historical Association, *Report of the Annual Meeting* (1928): 62–72.

Sahlins, Peter. *Boundaries: The Making of France and Spain in the Pyrenees.* Berkeley: University of California Press, 1989.

Saldívar, José David. *Border Matters: Remapping American Cultural Studies.* Berkeley: University of California Press, 1997.

Salyer, Lucy. *Laws Harsh as Tigers: Chinese Immigrants and the Shaping of Modern Immigration Law.* Chapel Hill: University of North Carolina Press, 1995.

Samaniego López, Marco Antonio. "Formación y consolidación de las organizaciones obreras en Baja California, 1920–1930." *Mexican Studies / Estudios Mexicanos* 14, no. 2 (1998): 329–62.

Sánchez, George J. *Becoming Mexican American: Ethnicity, Culture, and Identity in Chicano Los Angeles, 1900–1945.* New York: Oxford University Press, 1993.

Santleben, August. *A Texas Pioneer: Early Staging and Overland Freighting Days on the Frontiers of Texas and Mexico.* Edited by I. D. Affleck. New York: Neale Publishing Co., 1910.

Saragoza, Alex. "The Selling of Mexico: Tourism and the State, 1929–1952." In *Fragments of a Golden Age: The Politics of Culture in Mexico since 1940,* edited by Gilbert M. Joseph, Anne Rubenstein, and Eric Zolov, 91–115. Durham, N.C.: Duke University Press, 2001.

Saxton, Alexander. *The Indispensable Enemy: Labor and the Anti-Chinese Movement in California.* Berkeley: University of California Press, 1975.

Sayre, Nathan F. *Ranching, Endangered Species, and Urbanization in the Southwest: Species of Capital.* Tucson: University of Arizona Press, 2002.

Schantz, Eric Michael. "The Mexicali Rose and Tijuana Brass: Vice Tours of the United States–Mexico Border, 1910–1965." PhD diss., University of California, Los Angeles, 2001.

Schiavone Camacho, Julia. "Crossing Boundaries, Claiming a Homeland: The Mexican Chinese Transpacific Journey to Becoming Mexican, 1910s–1960s." Unpublished manuscript in possession of author.

Schreiber, Rebecca M. "Dislocations of Cold War Cultures: Exile, Transnationalism, and the Politics of Form." In *Imagining Our Americas: Toward a Transnational Frame*, edited by Sandhya Shukla and Heidi Tinsman, 282–312. Durham, N.C.: Duke University Press, 2007.

Schulze, Jeffrey. "Trans-Nations: Indians, Imagined Communities, and Borderlands Realities in the Twentieth Century." PhD diss., Southern Methodist University, 2008.

Schwantes, Carlos. *Radical Heritage: Labor, Socialism, and Reform in Washington and British Columbia, 1885–1917*. Seattle: University of Washington Press, 1979.

Scott, James C. *Seeing Like a State: How Certain Schemes to Improve the Human Condition Have Failed*. New Haven, Conn.: Yale University Press, 1998.

Scruggs, Otey. "The United States, Mexico, and the Wetbacks." *Pacific Historical Review* 30, no. 2 (1961): 149–64.

Sears, John F. *Sacred Places: American Tourist Attractions in the Nineteenth Century*. New York: Oxford University Press, 1989.

Seltz, Jennifer. "Embodying Nature: Health, Place, and Identity in Nineteenth-Century America." PhD diss., University of Washington, 2005.

Serna, Laura I. " 'As a Mexican I Feel It's My Duty': Citizenship, Censorship, and the Campaign against Derogatory Films in Mexico, 1922–1930." *The Americas* 63, no. 2 (2006): 225–44.

Shaffer, Marguerite S. *See America First: Tourism and National Identity, 1880–1940*. Washington, D.C.: Smithsonian Institution Press, 2001.

Shah, Nayan. *Contagious Divides: Epidemics and Race in San Francisco's Chinatown*. Berkeley: University of California Press, 2001.

Sharp, Paul F. *The Agrarian Revolt in Western Canada: A Survey Showing American Parallels*. Minneapolis: University of Minnesota Press, 1948.

——. "When Our West Moved North." *American Historical Review* 55, no. 2 (1950): 286–300.

——. *Whoop-Up Country: The Canadian-American West, 1865–1885*. 1955. Reprint, Norman: University of Oklahoma Press, 1973.

Shepard, R. Bruce. *Deemed Unsuitable: Blacks from Oklahoma Move to the Canadian Prairies in Search of Equality in the Early 20th Century Only to Find Racism in Their New Home*. Toronto: Umbrella Press, 1997.

Sheridan, Thomas E. *Arizona: A History*. Tucson: University of Arizona Press, 1995.

———. *Landscapes of Fraud: Mission Tumacácori, the Baca Float, and the Betrayal of the O'odham*. Tucson: University of Arizona Press, 2008.

———. *Los Tucsonenses: The Mexican Community in Tucson, 1854–1941*. Tucson: University of Arizona Press, 1986.

Simmon, Scott. *The Invention of the Western Film: A Cultural History of the Genre's First Half-Century*. Cambridge: Cambridge University Press, 2003.

Skinner, Clairborne. "The Sinews of Empire: The Voyageurs and the Carrying Trade of the *Pays d'en Haut*, 1681–1754." PhD diss., University of Illinois, Chicago, 1991.

Sleeper-Smith, Susan. *Indian Women and French Men: Rethinking Cultural Encounter in the Western Great Lakes*. Amherst: University of Massachusetts Press, 2001.

Slotkin, Richard. *Gunfighter Nation: The Myth of the Frontier in Twentieth-century America*. New York: Atheneum Press, 1992.

———. *Regeneration through Violence: The Mythology of the American Frontier*. Middleton, Conn.: Wesleyan University Press, 1973.

Smith, Cornelius C., Jr. *Emilio Kosterlitzky: Eagle of Sonora and the Southwest Border*. Glendale, Calif.: Arthur H. Clark Co., 1970.

Smith, Marian L. "Early Immigrant Inspection along the U.S.-Mexican Border." United States Citizenship and Immigration Services. http://uscis.gov/graphics/aboutus/history/articles/MBTEXT2.htm.

Smith, Marian W. *The Puyallup-Nisqually*. New York: Columbia University Press, 1940.

Sonnichsen, C. L. *Colonel Greene and the Copper Skyrocket; The Spectacular Rise and Fall of William Cornell Greene: Copper King, Cattle Baron, and Promoter Extraordinary in Mexico, the American Southwest, and the New York Financial District*. Tucson: University of Arizona Press, 1974.

Spicer, Edward H. *Cycles of Conquest: The Impact of Spain, Mexico, and the United States on the Indians of the Southwest, 1533–1960*. Tucson: University of Arizona Press, 1962.

Spiegelman, Art. "Those Dirty Little Comics." In *Tijuana Bibles: Art and Wit in America's Forbidden Funnies, 1930s–1950s*, edited by Bob Adelman. New York: Simon & Schuster, 1997.

Spry, Irene M. "The 'Private Adventurers' of Rupert's Land." In *The Developing West: Essays in Honor of Lewis H. Thomas*, edited by John E. Foster, 49–70. Edmonton: University of Alberta Press, 1983.

Squier, Emma Lindsay, *Gringa: An American Woman in Mexico*. Boston: Houghton Mifflin Co., 1934.

Stallybrass, Peter, and Allon White. *The Politics and Poetics of Transgression*. Ithaca, N.Y.: Cornell University Press, 1986.

Stanfield, Peter. *Hollywood, Westerns, and the 1930s: The Lost Trail*. Exeter, Devon, U.K.: University of Exeter Press, 2001.

———. *Horse Opera: The Strange History of the 1930s Singing Cowboy*. Urbana: University of Illinois Press, 2002.

Stanley, George F. G. *The Birth of Western Canada: A History of the Riel Rebellions*. Toronto: University of Toronto Press, 1961.

———, ed. *Mapping the Frontier*. Seattle: University of Washington Press, 1970.

———. "Western Canada and the Frontier Thesis." Canadian Historical Association, *Report of the Annual Meeting* (1940): 104–14.

Staudt, Kathleen, and David Spener. "The View from the Frontier: Theoretical Perspectives Undisciplined." In *The U.S.-Mexico Border: Transcending Divisions, Contesting Identities*, edited by Kathleen Staudt and David Spener, 3–33. Boulder, Colo.: Lynne Rienner Publishers, 1998.

Stegner, Wallace. *Wolf Willow: A History, a Story, and a Memory of the Last Plains Frontier*. 1955. Reprint, Lincoln: University of Nebraska Press, 1980.

Stephens, Michelle Ann. *Black Empire: The Masculine Global Imaginary of Caribbean Intellectuals in the United Sates, 1914–1962*. Durham, N.C.: Duke University Press, 2005.

Stern, Alexandra Minna. "Buildings, Boundaries, and Blood: Medicalization and Nation-building on the U.S.-Mexico Border, 1910–1930." *Hispanic American Historical Review* 79, no. 1 (1999): 41–81.

———. *Eugenic Nation: Faults and Frontiers of Better Breeding in Modern America*. Berkeley: University of California Press, 2005.

St. Germain, Jill. *Indian Treaty-Making Policy in the United States and Canada, 1867–1877*. Toronto: University of Toronto Press, 2001.

St. John, Rachel C. "Line in the Sand: The Desert Border between the United States and Mexico, 1848–1934." PhD diss., Stanford University, 2005.

———. "Selling the Border: Trading Land, Attracting Tourists, and Marketing American Consumption on the Baja California Border, 1900–1934." In *Land of Necessity: Consumer Capitalism and Culture in the United States–Mexico Borderlands*, edited by Alexis McCrossen. Durham, N.C.: Duke University Press, 2009.

Stoler, Ann Laura. *Carnal Knowledge and Imperial Power: Race and the Intimate in Colonial Rule*. Berkeley: University of California Press, 2002.

———. "Racial Histories and Their Regimes of Truth." *Political Power and Social Theory*, no. 11 (1997): 183–206.

St-Onge, Nicole. *Saint-Laurent, Manitoba: Evolving Métis Identities, 1850–1914*. Regina, Sask.: Canadian Plains Research Centre, University of Regina, 2004.

Strathern, Marilyn. *The Gender of the Gift: Problems with Women and Problems with Society in Melanesia*. Berkeley: University of California Press, 1988.

Stuart, Reginald. *Dispersed Relations: Americans and Canadians in Upper North America*. Baltimore: Johns Hopkins University Press, 2007.

Swagerty, William R., and Dick A. Wilson. "Faithful Service under Different Flags: A Socioeconomic Profile of the Columbia District, Hudson's Bay Company, and the Upper Missouri Outfit, American Fur Company, 1825–1835." In *The Fur Trade Revisited: Selected Papers of the Sixth North American Fur Trade Conference, Mackinac Island, Michigan, 1991*, edited by Jennifer S. H. Brown, W. J. Eccles, and Donald P. Heldman, 243–67. East Lansing: Michigan State University Press; Mackinac Island: Mackinac State Historic Parks, 1994.

Swan, James. *Almost out of the World: Scenes from Washington Territory*. Edited by William A. Katz. Tacoma: Washington State Historical Society, 1971.

——. *The Northwest Coast; or, Three Years' Residence in Washington Territory*. 1857. Reprint, Seattle: University of Washington Press, 1969.

Tanner, Adrian. "The End of Fur Trade History." *Queen's Quarterly* 90, no. 1 (1983): 176–91.

Tanner, Helen Hornbeck, ed. *The Settling of North America: The Atlas of the Great Migrations into North America from the Ice Age to the Present*. New York: Macmillan, 1995.

Taussig, F. W. *The Tariff History of the United States*. New York: G. P. Putnam's Sons, 1931.

Taylor, Alan. *The Divided Ground: Indians, Settlers, and the Northern Borderland of the American Revolution*. New York: Knopf, 2006.

Taylor, Analisa, "Malinche and Matriarchal Utopia: Gendered Visions of Indigeneity in Mexico." *Signs: Journal of Women in Culture and Society* 31, no. 3 (2000): 815–40.

Taylor, Joseph E., III. "The Historical Roots of the Canadian-American Salmon Wars." In *Parallel Destinies: Canadian-American Relations West of the Rockies*, edited by John M. Findlay and Ken S. Coates, 155–80. Seattle: University of Washington Press, 2002.

——. *Making Salmon: An Environmental History of the Northwest Fisheries Crisis*. Seattle: University of Washington Press, 1999.

Taylor, Paul Schuster. *An American-Mexican Frontier: Nueces County, Texas*. Chapel Hill: University of North Carolina Press, 1934.

Taylor, Peter. "The State as Container: Territoriality in the Modern World System." *Progress in Human Geography* 18, no. 2 (1994): 151–62.

Tenorio-Trillo, Mauricio. *Mexico at the World's Fairs: Crafting a Modern Nation*. Berkeley: University of California Press, 1996.

Terrazas y Basante, Marcela. "Colaboración y conflicto: Relaciones transfronterizas en el noreste mexicano." In *En busca de una nación soberana: Relaciones internacionales de México, siglos XIX y XX*, edited by Jorge A.Schiavón, Daniela Spenser, and Mario Vázquez Olivera, 127–56. México, D.F.: Secretaría de Relaciones Exteriores, Centro de Investigación y Docencia Económicas, 2006.

Terrill, Tom E. *The Tariff, Politics, and American Foreign Policy, 1874–1901*. Westport, Conn.: Greenwood Press, 1973.

Terry, G. Cunningham, "The Imperious Amazons of Mexico / On the Exotic Isthmus of Tehuantepec—America's Oldest Feminists—How the Zapotec Gods Are Honored." *Travel*, February 1928.

Thelen, David. "Mexico, the Latin North American Nation: A Conversation with Carlos Rico Ferrat." *Journal of American History* 86, no. 2 (1999): 467–80.

——. "Of Audiences, Borderlands, and Comparisons: Toward the Internationalization of American History." *Journal of American History* 79, no. 2 (1992): 432–62.

——. "Rethinking History and the Nation-State: Mexico and the United States." *Journal of American History* 86, no. 2 (1999): 438–52.

"The World's Progress / To the South." *The Four-Track News* [later *Travel*], January 1905, 57.

Thistle, John. " 'As Free of Fish as a Billiard Ball Is of Hair': Dealing with Depletion in the Pacific Halibut Fishery, 1899–1924," *B.C. Studies*, no. 142/143 (2004): 105–25.

Thistle, Paul C. *Indian-European Trade Relations in the Lower Saskatchewan River Region to 1840*. Winnipeg: University of Manitoba Press, 1986.

Thomas, David Hurst. "Harvesting Ramona's Garden: Life in California's Mythical Mission Past." In *The Spanish Borderlands in Pan-American Perspective*, edited by David Hurst Thomas, 119–57. Columbian Consequences, vol. 3. Washington, D.C.: Smithsonian Institution Press, 1991.

Thomas, L. G. "Historiography of the Fur Trade Era." In *A Region of the Mind*, edited by Richard Allen, 73–85. Regina, Sask.: Canadian Plains Research Centre, 1973.

Thomas, Lewis H., ed. *Essays on Western History in Honour of Lewis Gwynne Thomas*. Edmonton: University of Alberta Press, 1976.

Thompson, Jerry. *Mexican Texans in the Union Army*. El Paso, Tex.: Western Press, 1986.

——. *Vaqueros in Blue and Gray*. Austin, Tex.: Presidial Press, 1976.

Thorne, Tanis C. *The Many Hands of My Relations: French and Indians on the Lower Missouri*. Columbia: University of Missouri Press, 1996.

Thrush, Coll. "City of the Changers: Indigenous People and the Transformation of Seattle's Watersheds." *Pacific Historical Review* 75, no. 1 (2006): 89–117.

——. *Native Seattle: Histories from the Crossing-Over Place*. Seattle: University of Washington Press, 2007.

Tichenor, Daniel J. *Dividing Lines: The Politics of Immigration Control in America.* Princeton, N.J.: Princeton University Press, 2002.

Tinker Salas, Miguel. *In the Shadow of the Eagles: Sonora and the Transformation of the Border during the Porfiriato.* Berkeley: University of California Press, 1997.

Tolmie, William Fraser. *The Journals of William Fraser Tolmie, Physician and Fur Trader.* Vancouver, B.C.: Mitchell Press, 1963.

Torgovnick, Marianna. *Gone Primitive: Savage Intellects, Modern Lives.* Chicago: University of Chicago Press, 1990.

Torpey, John C. *The Invention of the Passport: Surveillance, Citizenship, and the State.* New York: Cambridge University Press, 2000.

Tough, Frank. *"As Their Natural Resources Fail": Native Peoples and the Economic History of Northern Manitoba, 1870–1930.* Vancouver: University of British Columbia Press, 1996.

Tout, Otis B. *The First Thirty Years, 1901–1931: Being an Account of the Principal Events in the History of Imperial Valley, Southern California, U.S.A.* San Diego: Otis B. Tout, 1931.

Townley, Adele. "Six Glorious Weeks at America's Oldest School!" *Lands of Romance*, February 1936.

Traister, Bryce. "Border Shopping: American Studies and the Anti-Nation." In *Globalization on the Line: Culture, Citizenship, and Capital at U.S. Borders*, edited by Claudia Sadowski-Smith, 31–52. New York: Palgrave, 2002.

———. "Risking Nationalism: NAFTA and the Limits of the New American Studies." *Canadian Review of American Studies*, 27, no. 3 (1997): 191–205.

Trennert, Robert A., Jr. "The Southern Pacific Railroad of Mexico." *Pacific Historical Review* 35, no. 3 (1966): 265–84.

Trigger, Bruce G., Toby Morantz, and Louise Dechene, eds. *Le Castor Fait Tout: Selected Papers of the Fifth North American Fur Trade Conference, 1985.* Montreal: Lake St. Louis Historical Society, 1987.

Truett, Samuel. *Fugitive Landscapes: The Forgotten History of the U.S.-Mexico Borderlands.* New Haven, Conn.: Yale University Press, 2006.

———. "Neighbors by Nature: Rethinking Region, Nation, and Environmental History in the U.S.-Mexico Borderlands." *Environmental History* 2, no. 2 (1997): 160–78.

———. "Transnational Warrior: Emilio Kosterlitzky and the Transformation of the U.S.-Mexico Borderlands." In *Continental Crossroads: Remapping U.S.-Mexico Borderlands History*, ed. Samuel Truett and Elliot Young. Durham, N.C.: Duke University Press, 2004.

Truett, Samuel, and Elliott Young, eds. *Continental Crossroads: Remapping U.S.-Mexico Borderlands History.* Durham, N.C.: Duke University Press, 2004.

———. "Making Transnational History: Nations, Regions, and Borderlands." Introduction to *Continental Crossroads: Remapping U.S.-Mexico Borderlands History*, edited by Samuel Truett and Elliott Young, 1–32. Durham, N.C.: Duke University Press, 2004.

Turgeon, Laurier. "Le temps des pêches lointaines: Permanences et transformations (vers 1500–vers 1850)." In *Histoire des pêches maritimes en France*, edited by M. Mollat, 134–81. Toulouse: Privat, 1987.

Turner, Allen R. "Surveying the International Boundary: The Journal of George M. Dawson, 1873." *Saskatchewan History* 21, no. 1 (winter 1968): 1–23.

Turner, Frederick Jackson. *The Character and Influence of the Indian Trade in Wisconsin: A Study of the Trading Post as an Institution.* Johns Hopkins University Studies in Historical and Political Science, ser. 9, no. 11–12. Baltimore: Johns Hopkins University Press, 1891.

——. "The Significance of the Frontier in American History." Paper presented at the annual meeting of the American Historical Association, Chicago, 1893. Printed in the *Proceedings of the State Historical Society of Wisconsin*, December 14, 1893. Reprinted in John Mack Faragher, ed. *Rereading Frederick Jackson Turner.* New Haven, Conn.: Yale University Press, 1998.

Tyler, Ronnie C. "The Callahan Expedition of 1855: Indians or Negroes?" *Southwestern Historical Quarterly* 70 (April 1967): 574–85.

Tyrrell, Ian. *Transnational Nation: United States History in Global Perspective since 1879.* New York: Palgrave Macmillan, 2007.

United States. *Indian Affairs: Laws and Treaties.* Vol. 2., *Treaties.* Compiled and edited by Charles J. Kappler. Washington, D.C.: Government Printing Office, 1904.

——. *Revised Statutes of the United States.* 2nd ed. Washington, D.C.: Government Printing Office, 1878.

United States. Bureau of Animal Industry. *Annual Report of the Bureau of Animal Industry for the Year 1909.* Washington, D.C.: Government Printing Office, 1911.

United States. Bureau of Fisheries. *Report of the United States Commissioner of Fisheries for the Fiscal Year 1914.* Washington D.C.: Government Printing Office, 1915.

——. *Report of the United States Commissioner of Fisheries for the Fiscal Year 1920.* Washington, D.C.: Government Printing Office, 1921.

United States. Bureau of Indian Affairs. *Annual Report of the Commissioner of Indian Affairs to the Secretary of the Interior, 1851–1903.* Washington, D.C.: Government Printing Office, 1837–1968.

United States. Congress. *Congressional Record.* 51st Cong., 1st sess., 1889. Vol. 21, pt. 5.

United States. Court of Claims. *Duwamish et al. v. United States.* Seattle: Argus Press, 1933. 2 vols.

United States. Department of Labor. Bureau of Immigration. *Annual Report, fiscal year ended June 30, 1917.*

———. *Annual Report of the Commissioner General of Immigration to the Secretary of Labor for the fiscal year ended* . . . 20 vols. Washington, D.C.: Government Printing Office, 1914–32.

United States. Department of State. *Report of the Honorable S. Morris on Japanese Immigration and Alleged Discriminatory Legislation against Japanese Residents in the United States.* Washington, D.C.: Government Printing Office, 1921.

United States. Department of the Interior. *Report of the United States and Mexican Boundary Survey.* Made under the direction of the Secretary of the Interior by William H. Emory. 2 vols. 34th Cong., 1st sess., Senate Executive Document 108. Washington, D.C.: A. O. P. Nicholson, Printer, 1857.

United States. House. Committee on Foreign Affairs. *Control of Travel from and into the United States.* 65th Cong., 2nd sess., 1918. H. Rep. 485.

United States. Senate. "Survey and Remarking of the Boundary between the United States and Mexico West of the Rio Grande, 1891–1896." 55th Cong., 2nd sess., 1898. S. Doc. 247.

Usner, Daniel H. *Indians, Settlers, and Slaves in a Frontier Exchange Economy: The Lower Mississippi Valley before 1783.* Chapel Hill: Institute of Early American History and Culture, University of North Carolina Press, 1992.

Utley, Robert. *A Life Wild and Perilous: Mountain Men and the Paths to the Pacific.* New York: Henry Holt and Co., 1997.

Valenčius, Conevery Bolton. *The Health of the Country: How American Settlers Understood Themselves and Their Land.* New York: Basic Books, 2002.

Valerio-Jiménez, Omar. *Rio Grande Crossings: Identity and Nation along the Rio Grande, 1849–1880.* Durham, N.C.: Duke University Press, forthcoming.

Vanderwood, Paul J. *Juan Soldado: Rapist, Murderer, Martyr, Saint.* Durham, N.C.: Duke University Press, 2004.

Van Kirk, Sylvia. *Many Tender Ties: Women in Fur-Trade Society, 1670–1870.* Winnipeg, Man.: Watson & Dwyer Publishing Ltd., 1980.

Vasconcelos, José. *La raza cósmica / The Cosmic Race.* Translated by by Didier T. Jaén. Baltimore: Johns Hopkins University Press, 1997.

Vaughn, Mary Kay. "Modernizing Patriarchy, State Policies, Rural Households, and Women in Mexico, 1930–1940." In *Hidden Histories of Gender and the State in Latin America*, edited by Elizabeth Dore and Maxine Molyneux, 192–214. Durham, N.C.: Duke University Press, 2000.

Vaughn, Mary Kay, and Stephen E. Lewis, eds. *The Eagle and the Virgin: Nation and Cultural Revolution in Mexico, 1920–1940.* Durham, N.C.: Duke University Press, 2006.

Vibert, Elizabeth. *Traders' Tales: Narratives of Cultural Encounters in the Columbia Plateau, 1807–1846.* Norman: University of Oklahoma Press, 1997.

Vila, Pablo. *Crossing Borders, Reinforcing Borders: Social Categories, Metaphors, and Narrative Identities on the U.S.-Mexico Frontier.* Austin: University of Texas Press, 2000.

Wadewitz, Lissa. "After 1846: Native vs. Newcomer Cartographies in the Western Canada–U.S. Borderlands." Unpublished manuscript in possession of author.

——. "The Nature of Borders: Salmon and Boundaries in the Puget Sound / Georgia basin." PhD diss., UCLA, 2004.

——. "Pirates of the Salish Sea: Labor, Mobility, and Environment in the Transnational West." *Pacific Historical Review* 75, no. 4 (2006): 587–627.

Wakatsuki, Yasuo. "Japanese Emigration to the United States, 1866–1924: A Monograph." *Perspectives in American History*, no. 12 (1979): 389–516.

Walden, Keith. *Visions of Order: The Canadian Mounties in Symbol and Myth.* Toronto: Butterworths, 1982.

Waldram, James B., D. Ann Herring, and T. Kue Young. *Aboriginal Health in Canada: Historical, Cultural, and Epidemiological Perspectives.* Toronto: University of Toronto Press, 1995.

Walker, Henry Pickering, and Don Bufkin. *Historical Atlas of Arizona.* Norman: University of Oklahoma Press, 1979.

Walton, Whitney. "American Girls and French *Jeunes Filles*: Negotiating National Identities in Interwar France." *Gender & History* 17, no. 2 (2005): 325–53.

Walz, Eric. "The Issei Community in Maricopa County: Development and Persistence in the Valley of the Sun, 1900–1940." *Journal of Arizona History* 38, no. 1 (1997): 1–22.

Washington (State). Department of Fisheries. *Biennial Reports*, 1902; 1905–6; 1913–15; 1915–17; 1917–19; 1919–21; 1921–23; 1929–31. Olympia: Department of Fisheries, 1902; 1907; 1916; 1917; 1920; 1921; 1924; 1932.

Weber, David J. "Conflictos y acuerdos: Las fronteras hispanomexicanas y angloamericanas en su perspectiva histórica (1670–1853)." In *Encuentro en la frontera: Mexicanos y norteamericanos en un espacio común*, edited by Manuel Ceballos Ramírez, 55–89. México, D.F.: El Colegio de México, Centro de Estudios Históricos; Tijuana, Baja California: El Colegio de la Frontera Norte; Ciudad Victoria: Universidad Autónoma de Tamaulipas, 2001.

——. *La frontera norte de México, 1821–1846: El sudoeste norteamericano en su época mexicana.* México, D.F.: Fondo de Cultura Económica, 1988.

——. *The Mexican Frontier, 1821–1846: The American Southwest under Mexico.* Albuquerque: University of New Mexico Press, 1982.

——. " 'Scarce More Than Apes': Historical Roots of Anglo-American Stereotypes of Mexicans in the Border Region." In *New Spain's Far Northern Frontier: Essays on Spain in the American West, 1540–1921*, edited by David J. Weber, 295–307. Dallas: Southern Methodist University Press, 1979.

——. *The Spanish Frontier in North America.* New Haven, Conn.: Yale University Press, 1992.

——. *The Taos Trappers: The Fur Trade in the Far Southwest, 1540–1846.* Norman: University of Oklahoma Press, 1969.

——. "Turner, the Boltonians, and the Borderlands." *American Historical Review* 91, no. 1 (1986): 66–81.

Westrup, Tomás M. *Principios: Relato de la introducción del Evangelio en México.* Monterrey, Nuevo Léon: Enrique T. Westrup, 1948.

Wexman, Virginia Wright. "The Family on the Land: Race and Nationhood in Silent Westerns." In *The Birth of Whiteness: Race and the Emergence of U.S. Cinema,* edited by Daniel Bernardi, 129–69. New Brunswick, N.J.: Rutgers University Press, 1996.

White, Bruce M. "The Fear of Pillaging: Economic Folktales of the Great Lakes Fur Trade." In *The Fur Trade Revisited: Selected Papers of the Sixth North American Fur Trade Conference, Mackinac Island, Michigan, 1991,* edited by Jennifer S. H. Brown, W. J. Eccles, and Donald P. Heldman, 199–216. East Lansing: Michigan State University Press; Mackinac Island: Mackinac State Historic Parks, 1994.

——. "A Skilled Game of Exchange: Ojibwa Fur Trade Protocol." *Minnesota History* 50, no. 6 (1987): 229–40.

White, Richard, *"It's Your Misfortune and None of My Own": A New History of the American West.* Norman: University of Oklahoma Press, 1991.

——. *The Middle Ground: Indians, Empires, and Republics in the Great Lakes Region.* Cambridge: Cambridge University Press, 1991.

——. "The Nationalization of Nature." *Journal of American History* 86, no. 3 (1999): 976–86.

——. "Outlaw Gangs of the Middle Border: American Social Bandits." *Western Historical Quarterly* 12, no. 4 (1981): 387–408.

——. *The Roots of Dependency: Subsistence, Environment, and Social Change among the Choctaws, Pawnees, and Navajos.* Lincoln: University of Nebraska Press, 1983.

Widdis, Randy William. "Borders, Borderlands, and Canadian Identity: A Canadian Perspective." *International Journal of Canadian Studies* 15 (spring 1997): 49–66.

——. *With Scarcely a Ripple: Anglo-Canadian Migration into the United States and Western Canada, 1880–1920.* Montreal: McGill-Queen's University Press, 1998.

Wilkes, Charles. *Narrative of the United States Exploring Expedition during the Years 1838, 1839, 1840, 1841, 1842.* 5 vols. Philadelphia: Lea and Blanchard, 1845.

Wilkinson, Joseph B. *Laredo and the Rio Grande Frontier.* Austin: Jenkins Publishing Co., 1975.

Williams, Colin, and Anthony Smith. "The National Construction of Social Space." *Progress in Human Geography* 7 (1983): 502–18.

Williams, David L. "Prairies and Plains: The Leveling of Difference in Stegner's *Wolf Willow*." *American Review of Canadian Studies* 33, no. 4 (2003): 607–16.

Wright, Frederick G. "Indians of British Columbia." *West Shore*, September 1879, 263–65.

Wrobel, David M. *The End of American Exceptionalism: Frontier Anxiety from the Old West to the New Deal*. Lawrence: University Press of Kansas, 1993.

Wunder, John R. "The Chinese and the Courts in the Pacific Northwest: Justice Denied?" *Pacific Historical Review* 52 (May 1983): 191–211.

Young, Elliott. *Catarino Garza's Revolution on the Texas-Mexico Border*. Durham, N.C.: Duke University Press, 2004.

Young, Robert J. C. *Colonial Desire: Hybridity in Theory, Culture, and Race*. New York: Routledge, 1995.

Zamora, Emilio. *The World of the Mexican Worker in Texas*. College Station: Texas A&M University Press, 1993.

Zorrilla, Luis. *Historia de las relaciones entre México y Estados Unidos de América*. México, D.F.: Porrúa, 1965.

# CONTRIBUTORS

..........................................

**Dominique Brégent-Heald** is an assistant professor of history at Memorial University of Newfoundland, where she teaches courses in U.S. history and film history. She is currently writing a book on the U.S.-Mexican and U.S.-Canadian borders in film between 1908 and 1920.

**Catherine Cocks** is the author of *Doing the Town: The Rise of Urban Tourism in the United States, 1850–1915* (2001). She is currently researching the emergence of a resort region encompassing Southern California, Florida, the Caribbean, and Mexico, 1880–1940.

**Andrea Geiger** is an assistant professor of history at Simon Fraser University in Burnaby, B.C. She served as a reservation attorney for the Colville Tribes in northeastern Washington before launching her academic career and has recently completed a transnational history of early twentieth-century Japanese immigration to the North American West.

**Miguel Ángel González-Quiroga** is a professor of history at the Universidad Autónoma de Nuevo León in Mexico. He has co-authored two books and co-edited two others on the Texas-Mexico border region.

**Andrew R. Graybill** is an associate professor of history at the University of Nebraska, Lincoln, where he teaches courses on the United States, Canada, and the environment. He is the author of *Policing the Great Plains: Rangers, Mounties, and the North American Frontier, 1875–1910* (2007).

**Michel Hogue** is an assistant professor of history at Carleton University. His published work has appeared in *Montana, the Magazine of Western History*, and in anthologies on the Canadian-U.S. borderlands.

**Benjamin H. Johnson** is an associate professor of history and associate director of the Clements Center for Southwest Studies at Southern Methodist University. He is the author of *Revolution in Texas: How a Forgotten Rebellion and Its Bloody Suppression Turned Mexicans into Americans* (2003) and *Bordertown: The Odyssey of an American Place* (2008).

**S. Deborah Kang** holds an MA in jurisprudence and social policy and a PhD in history from the University of California, Berkeley. She is currently completing a manuscript, "The Legal Construction of the Borderlands: The INS, Immigration Law, and Immigrant Rights on the U.S.-Mexico Border, 1917–1954," that will provide one of the first comprehensive histories of the Immigration and Naturalization Service in the Southwest.

**Carolyn Podruchny** is an associate professor of history at York University in Toronto. She is the author of *Making the Voyageur World: Travelers and Traders in the North American Fur Trade* (2006).

**Bethel Saler** is an associate professor of history at Haverford College. She is the author of a book on early U.S. state-formation and the development of a domestic empire. Her other research interests include relations between North African states and the early American republic, and cultural aspects of the North American fur trade.

**Jennifer Seltz** teaches environmental history at Western Washington University. She received her PhD from the University of Washington and is working on a cultural and environmental history of disease and place in the nineteenth-century North American West.

**Rachel St. John** is an associate professor of history at Harvard University, where she teaches classes on western, environmental, borderlands, and nineteenth-century U.S. history. She is currently working on a book titled *Line in the Sand: The History of the Western U.S.–Mexico Border, 1848–1934.*

**Lissa Wadewitz** is an assistant professor of history and environmental studies at Linfield College, a liberal arts college in McMinnville, Oregon. She is currently working on a book that explores the impacts of both Native and newcomer borders on the salmon fishery of the Fraser River/Puget Sound area, to be titled *The Nature of Borders: Salmon and Boundaries in the Salish Sea.*

# INDEX

................................................

Italicized page numbers refer to maps, illustrations, and tables

crossing; "Borderlands"; Customs; 49th parallel (as Canadian border); Immigration; Medical Inspections; Nation-states; Ports of entry; Rio Grande (as Mexican border); Smuggling; Territoriality; Violence

*Border Boys, The*, 22

*Border Brigands* (film), 265–66

*Border Caballero* (film), 266

Border-crossing (migration), 7, 15–16; by American slaves to Mexico, 8, 35, 47; cards for, 184–87; by diseases, 91–115; effects of Mexicans', on Mexico, 8; by fish and animals, 6, 16, 18–19, 22–23, 116–64; vs. immigration, 169; by Indians, 18, 68, 91–115; lax rules concerning, in early days, 167, 178, 267; by Métis on Great Plains, 59–87, 289; of *mexicanidad*, 49; of Mexicans to the U.S., 8, 24, 46–49, 52, 53, 57n36, 167–98; novelists on Alaskan/Yukon, 255; as postmodern metaphor, 6; of scientific knowledge, 154; "transit privilege" used for, 199–217; U.S.'s westward, 13. *See also* Customs (and duties); Immigration; Labor needs; Medical inspections; Ports of entry; Tourism

*Border G-Man* (film), 269

*Border Justice* (film), 264

"Borderlands": becoming borders, 52–53, 117, 119–24, 128, 170–74, 178, 217; comparative accounts of, 3, 17, 20–24, 295; cooperation in Mexican-U.S., 33–58, *39, 119*, 269–70; historiography of, 4–25; Hollywood films' depiction of, 250–74; mixed-race, 17–18, 38–52, 59–87; tensions in salmon, 144–48; transnational character of, 167–88. *See also* Frontier

Borderlands Studies, 4–5

Border patrol. *See* Border(s): policing of

*Border Patrolman, The* (film), 268

Boundary Bay, 103

Bowman, Heath, 248n33

Bozeman Trail, 66

Bracero Program, 194n84

Bramen, Carrie Tirado, 244n8

Braun, Marcus, 208, 212, 214

Braund, Kathryn E. Holland, 286

Brazil, 210

Brebner, John Bartlet, 11

Breen, Joseph, 270–71

Brégent-Heald, Dominique, 20, 22, 24, 54n3, 227

British Columbia, 19; Asian immigration to, 202–4, 206–8; disease transmission and, 91–96, 98, 99, 101, 105–7, 109; salmon issues in, 141, 143, 145, 147, 149–54. *See also specific places*

British Empire: America's national identity established in opposition to, 278, 281; Canada's identity linked to, 13, 282–83, 289; Canadian-U.S. boundary disputes of, 27n22; fur trade and, 67, 276, 295; influence of, on American historiography, 4; Métis seen as citizens of, 73, 74, 80; on Spaniards, 260

Brown, Jennifer S. H., 285, 287, 297

Brownsville (Texas), 41, 42, 44, 50, 94, 178, 179

Buenavista Ranch, 123, 125

Buenos Aires Ranch, 122

Buffalo, 60, 62–65, 67, 68, 70–77, 78, 80, 81

*Bullets or Ballots* (film), 268

Bureau of Animal Industry (U.S.), 116–18, 129

Bureau of Immigration (Immigration Service; INS—U.S.), 167–70, 175–78, 180, 181, 183–88, 190n19, 208, 209, 213, 215, 267

Bush, George W., 1, 3
B-Westerns, 268–69

Cagney, James, 268, 269
Calexico (California), 180, 183, 186, 187
California: as "borderland," 4; cattle ranching in, 22, 116; gold rush in, 281; Hollywood films made in, 253, 256, 261; Hollywood films set in, 250, 256–57; as part of "Southland," 231, 235, 237, 239–41, 243n5. *See also* Baja California (Mexico); Hollywood films; *Specific places*
California Mission Indians, 256–57
Callahan Expedition, 35
Calloway, Colin, 277, 286, 292
Camargo (Mexico), 38
Cameron, Brewster, 123, 125–27, 130, 132
Cameron, Colin, 123, 125–27, 130
Caminetti, Anthony, 183
Camou family, 125
Campbell, Marjorie Wilkins, 285
Canada: disease transmission across borders of, 91–115; divisions within, 11; fur trade history in, 278, 282–89, 298–99, 300n17; historians of, 10–13, 27n30; identity of, linked to Britain, 13, 282–83, 289; immigration restrictions set by, 19, 201, 202, 204–10, 215–17, 221n51; Indian reservations in, 61, 80, 81; Indian treaties of, 77, 79–81; interconnectedness of, with U.S. and Mexico, 1, 11, 14; Métis on borderlands of, 19, 21–22, 58–87; Métis' rights in, 64, 73, 74, 76, 79–81, 289; national characteristics associated with, 11, 12, 15–16; salmon industry in, 141–64; transit privilege and, 19, 21–22, 199–217. *See also* 49th parallel (as Canadian border); French Canadians; Hudson's Bay Company; New France; North-West Mounted Police; *Specific provinces and places*
*Canada: A Story of Challenge* (Careless), 284
Canadian Dominion Lands Commission, 59
Canadian Pacific Railway, 209
Canales, Antonio, 35
Cananea (Sonora), 127, 131
Cananea Cattle Company, 131
Canning industry, 93, 145, 147, 148, 150, 152–54
Cano de los Rios, Elena, 127
Capitalism, 117, 171, 256, 287, 293, 294, 298
Cardoso, Lawrence A., 176
Careless, J. M. S., 284
Carranza, Venustiano, 191n44
Carvajal, José María, 37, 53
Carvajal Revolt (Merchant's War), 35–38, 43, 53
Cascade Mountains, 103
Catholic Church, 50, 60
Cattle ranching, 18, 22–23, 48, 92, 116–40. *See also* Smuggling: of cattle
*Cattle Thieves, The* (film), 263, 264
Cavazos, Sabas, 38
Cazneau, William L., 42
*Challenge of the Law, The* (film), 263
*Changes in the Land* (Cronon), 286
*Channing of the Northwest* (film), 266
*Character and Influence of the Indian Trade in Wisconsin, The* (Turner), 280
*Charros*, 235, 236
Cheyennes, 66
Chihuahua (Mexico), 5, 42, 45, 119, 122, 127, 262
*Children of the Fur Trade, The* (Jackson), 287
China: illegal immigrants from, 176, 266–67; migrants from, *146, 173*;

*Her Husband's Trademark* (film), 262–63

Hermosillo (Mexico), 132

Hernández, Alejo, 51

Hernández, Mariano, 43

Hernández, Vicente, 57n39

Herrera, Octavio, 35, 41

Hogue, Michel, 18, 230, 289

Hollywood films, 20, 22, 24, 54n3, 227, 249–75

*Homeland to Hinterland* (Ens), 289

Hoover, J. Edgar, 268

Houston (Texas), 40

Howard, George T., 42–43

Hudson's Bay Company (HBC): British charter for, 276; Canada assumes control of lands of, 59, 66, 276; land owned by, 61, 64–66, 284, 285, 295–96; merger of, with North West Company, 62, 276; traders with, 98, 113n43, 293

"Hudson's Bay Company Canoe" (Verner), 296, *296*

Huerta, Victoriano, 191n44

Hughes, James, 225–26, 228, 233

Hughes, Langston, 225–29, 232, 233, 235, 238, 243n4

Huron Indians, 293

Identities: formation of, 7, 18, 21, 23, 258–59; national, 9–10, 13, 16, 21, 52, 59–61, 278, 281–83, 287, 289, 298; non-national, 287, 298; porousness of, 6, 8; racial, 59–61, 65–66, 79, 80–82, 94, 226, 228, 233; regional, 53n1; transnational, in binational communities, 171–73, 178–79, 188. *See also* Mixed-race groups

Iglesias, Norma, 271

Ile à la Crosse (Saskatchewan), 294

Ilges, Guido, 75

Immigrants: defined, 169, 170; Mexi-

cans as, in U.S., 7, 168, 171–78, 229. *See also* Immigration; Refugees

Immigration: Canadian restrictions on, 19, 201, 204–10, 215–17, 221n51; Canadian-U.S., 28n40; Japanese use of "transit privilege" for, 199–217; local conditions as influencing federal administration of, 167–98; undocumented, 1, 10, 18, 19, 33, 134, 173, 176–77, 179–80, 199, 206–8, 210–12, 214–16, 266–68; U.S. restrictions on, 8, 19, 95, 168–71, 173, 175–79, 181, 183–84, 186–88, 190nn15, 19, 195n91, 199–202, 204–7, 213–17, 221n51, 267. *See also* Border-crossing; Head taxes; Labor needs; Literacy tests

Immigration Act (Canada, 1908), 215

Immigration Act (U.S., 1903), 171

Immigration Act (U.S., 1907), 171

Immigration Act (U.S., 1917), 168–70, 175–78, 181, 183–84, 186–88, 267

Immigration Act (U.S., 1924), 19

Immigration and Naturalization Service (INS). *See* Bureau of Immigration (U.S.)

Imperial Irrigation Project, 182

Imperialism. *See* Colonization; *Specific empires*

*In Defiance of the Law* (film), 263

Indian Affairs officials (U.S.), 67–70, 72–73, 80, 93, 98–99, 104–8

Indians: borderland cooperation of, with other races, 38; as cattle ranchers, 122; colonialisms experienced by Southwest, 5; effects of border-making on, 15, 21, 23, 53, 59–87, 277; effects of border-policing on, 8, 18; federal policies toward, 12, 61, 66–70, 72–76, 80, 81, 83n17, 93, 97–99, 102, 104–8, 119, 256–57; in fur trade, 15, 276, 279, 280, 282, 285–88, 292, 293–98; Hollywood films depicting,

making on, 8, 33–34; historians of, 5–7, 9–10, 12–13, 23; Hollywood films set in, 250, 252, 261–63; immigrants to, 8, 35, 47, 173, 210; industrialization in, 171–72, 181–82, 210; interconnectedness of, with U.S. and Canada, 1; land distribution and ownership in, 118, 124–27, 232; as less powerful than U.S., 9–10, 21; "prohibited zone" in, 126–27; slavery's abolition in, 8, 225; tourism in, 225–48, *236*, *237*; transit privilege and, 19, 21–22, 169, 210–15; U.S. immigration and deportation of Mexicans and, 194nn80, 84. *See also* Commerce; *Mestizaje*; Mexicans; Rio Grande (as Mexican border); *Specific places*

Mexico City (Mexico), 225; cross-border commerce and, 38, 40–41, 235, *236*, 238; as unable to police Texas-Mexico border, 34–35, 128–29, 132

Michif language, 294

Michilimackinac, 294

*Middle Ground, The* (White), 286

Migration. *See* Border-crossing

Milk River, 63, 68, 72–75

Miller, Alfred Jacob, 293

Milmo, Patricio, 44, 48

Milroy, R. H., 104–5

Mining, 93, 127, 171, 172, 182, 211, 254, 255, 283

Minnesota, 67

Missionaries, 18, 46, 49–53, 119

Mississippi River, 280, 292, 295

Missouri River, 63, 66, 287, 295

Mix, Tom, 267

Mixed-race groups, 16; on borderlands, 59–87, 100; cooperation among, in borderlands, 38–52, *39*, 53n1; in fur trade history, 278, 282, 297, 298; Hollywood depictions of, 254–57,

259, 263. *See also* Mestizos; Métis; Racial hybridity

*Modern Mexico*, 238

Montana: cattle ranching in, 23; Indian reservations in, 61, 66, 67, 69, 70, 72–76, 83n17; Métis in, 66–72, 81; railroad interests in, 68

Montemorelos region (Mexico), 47

Monterrey (Mexico), 5, 50; cross-border commerce with, 40–42, 44–46, 48

Montoya, María, 137n16

Montreal (Canada), 61, 294

Morantz, Toby, 286

Morris, Alexander, 70, 79

Morton, W. L., 283

Motion Pictures and Distributors Association (MPPDA), 268

Mouat, Jeremy, 11

Mount Baker, 103

Mounties. *See* North-West Mounted Police

*Moving Picture World*, 262

Murphy, Lucy Eldersveld, 287

Murrieta, Joaquín, 258

Musgrave, A. A., 187

NAFTA (North American Free Trade Agreement), 1, 9, 134

Nance, Joseph N., 40

National Historic Sites (Canada), 288

Nationalism: American, 9, 289–90; Canadian, 288, 289–90, 301n17. *See also* Nation-states

Nation-states: border fences as marking, 116–17; building of Mexican, 20, 225–48; characteristics of, 276–77; creation of, in opposition to racialized others, 22, 67, 199–217; expansion of, 3, 64–67; in historical scholarship, 1–10, 15, 20, 23–25, 53n2, 275–302; impact of, on fur trade, 60, 67; myths created by, 21, 225–48, 251–59, 271,

Chinook Jargon in, 294; early American writings about, 279; Hollywood films set in, 250–51; imperial contests over, 282; Métis in, 287; salmon migration routes in, *142. See also specific places*

Pacific Salmon Treaty (1985), 156

Page, Arthur W., 239

Palomas Land and Cattle Company, 127

Palominas (Mexico), 129

*Pals of the Saddle* (film), 269

Pan-American unity, 263, 269–71

Pannekoek, Fritz, 286, 289

Paramount Company, 262–63

Parker, Ely, 98

Parks Canada Agency, 288

Passport Act (Entry and Departures Control Act of 1918), 168–70, 175, 177, 178–79, 181, 183–84, 187, 188, 267

Passports, 202, 207, 208–10, 212, 234

Pastoralism: defined, 135n4. *See also* Cattle ranching

Pathfinders, 280–81, 285, 292

Payment, Diane, 289

Peace River, 295

Pembina (North Dakota), 62, 74, 294

Pembina River, 77

"People in Between, The" (Peterson), 286–87

*People Who Own Themselves, The* (Devine), 289

Perales, Monica, 172

Pérez, Ignacio, 120, 122

Pershing, John, 174

Peru, 210, 211

Peterson, Jacqueline, 286–87, 292

Philadelphia Exposition (1876), 232

Philippines, 175

Phillips, John C., 281

Pickford, Mary, 256

Piedras Negras (Mexico), 35, 48

Piegan Indians, 74, 83n17

Pinkerton's National Detective Agency, 152

Podruchny, Carolyn, 20, 24–25, 40, 61, 230, 254

Point Roberts, 153

Policing (of border). *See* Border(s): policing of

Population: of Canadian-U.S. immigrants, 28n40; proportion of Mexican heritage, in U.S., 7

Porfiriato, 51, 57n36, 231

Port Ludlow (Washington), 109

Port Madison, 109

Ports of entry, 18, 117, 128, 129–31, 133, 134, 179–80, 188, 265

Port Townsend (Washington), 91–95, 105, 106

Postmodernism, 6

Powdermaker, Hortense, 249

Powell, I. W., 106

Prairie du Chien (Wisconsin), 294

Pratt, Mary Louise, 247n24

Presidio (Texas), 186

Prince, E. R., 153

Production Code Administration (Hollywood), 268, 270–71

Progressive Era, 170, 175

Prohibition, 22, 173, 183, 185, 266. *See also* Alcohol smuggling

Property. *See* Land

Prostitution, 93, 104, 109

Protestants. *See* Missionaries

Provencher, J. A. N., 79

Provincial Fisheries Department (British Columbia), 143, 152

Pruett, R. L., 213, 214

*Public Enemy* (film), 268

Public Health Service (U.S.), 175. *See also* Diseases (transnational)

Pueblo Indians, 6

Wadewitz, Lissa, 18–19, 112n33, 118, 168

War of 1812, 10, 295

War of French Intervention, 50, 51

War of Reform (Mexico), 50

Washington, D.C.: as unable to police Canada-U.S. border, 143; as unable to police Texas-Mexico border, 34–35, 128–29, 132, 168, 188

Washington State, 19, 141–45, 147–52

Washington Territory, 91–96, 98, 99, 105, 107–9, 114n51

Waugh, William, 48

Weber, David, 53n1, 55n16, 282

Web of the Law, The (film), 264

Wendat Indians, 293

West (North American): Canadian border and, 5, 10–15; Hollywood films on, 251–59; imperial contests over, 282; Métis in Canadian, 59; Mexican border and, 18, 116–40; writers on, 279–80. See also Frontier; Old West; Pacific Northwest region

Westerns (films), 253

Westrump, Tomás, 50

Wheat, 284

Whiskey. See Alcohol

White, Bruce, 286

White, Richard, 5, 157n7, 286

Whites. See Europeans; White supremacy

White supremacy (in U.S.), 14, 20, 21, 23, 226–29, 232, 234, 238–39, 242, 260. See also Jim Crow laws; Racism

Whoop-Up Country (Sharp), 11–12, 16

Wilkinson, James, 34–35

Williams, Constant, 72–73

Wilson, Woodrow, 174–76, 262

Winnipeg (Manitoba, Canada). See Red River settlement

Wiswall, C. E., 131

Wolcott (steamer), 105

Wolf Willow (Stegner), 11

Women: American, as tourists, 240–42, 248n33, 262; in fur trade history, 18, 61, 100, 285–88, 297; Mexican, 182, 240

Wood Mountain, 59, 60, 63, 70, 73, 80

World's Fairs, 232

World War I. See First World War

World War II. See Second World War

Wrobel, David M., 251

Yanktonai Sioux, 68, 69, 74

Yanktons, 68

Yerba Buena. See Buenavista Ranch

York, Jacob, 147

Young, Elliott, 9, 52

Zacatecas (Mexico), 40, 45, 50

Zimmerman Telegram, 174, 262

Zorro films, 258

BENJAMIN H. JOHNSON is an associate professor of history and associate director of the Clements Center for Southwest Studies at Southern Methodist University. He is the author of *Revolution in Texas: How a Forgotten Rebellion and Its Bloody Suppression Turned Mexicans into Americans* (2003) and *Bordertown: The Odyssey of an American Place* (2008).

ANDREW R. GRAYBILL is an associate professor of history at the University of Nebraska, Lincoln, where he teaches courses on the United States, Canada, and the environment. He is the author of *Policing the Great Plains: Rangers, Mounties, and the North American Frontier, 1875–1910* (2007).

Library of Congress Cataloging-in-Publication Data
Bridging national borders in North America :
transnational and comparative histories / Benjamin H.
Johnson and Andrew R. Graybill, eds.
p. cm.—(American encounters/global interactions)
Includes bibliographical references and index.
ISBN 978-0-8223-4688-3 (cloth : alk. paper)
ISBN 978-0-8223-4699-9 (pbk. : alk. paper)
1. Mexican-American Border Region—History. 2.
Borderlands—United States—History. 3. Borderlands—
Canada—History. I. Johnson, Benjamin Heber. II.
Graybill, Andrew R., 1971– III. Series: American
encounters/global interactions.
E46.B75 2010
972'.1—dc22    2009041451